THE SKORZENY PAPERS

EVIDENCE FOR THE PLOT TO KILL JFK

by
MAJOR RALPH P. GANIS

foreword by
DICK RUSSELL

HOT BOOKS

Hot Books may be purchased in bulk at special discounts for sales promotion, corporate gifts, fund-raising, or educational purposes. Special editions can also be created to specifications. For details, contact the Special Sales Department, Skyhorse Publishing, 307 West 36th Street, 11th Floor, New York, NY 10018 or info@skyhorsepublishing.com.

Hot Books Press® and Skyhorse Publishing® are registered trademarks of Skyhorse Publishing, Inc.®, a Delaware corporation.

Visit our website at www.skyhorsepublishing.com.

10 9 8 7 6 5 4 3 2 1

Library of Congress Cataloging-in-Publication Data has been applied for.

Cover design by Brian Peterson
Cover photos courtesy of the author

Print ISBN: 978-1-5107-5564-2
Ebook ISBN: 978-1-5107-0842-6

Printed in the United States of America

FOR:

Rosa Lee Diggs Ganis, devoted mother
CWO4 Joseph F. Ganis, USAF Retired, World War II
Lance Corporal Ronald J. Ganis, USMC, Cuba 1962–1963
Specialist Four George R. Ganis, US Army, Vietnam, 1970

"The Warren Commission was not created to find the answer to the JFK murder but to deflect attention away from all intelligence and operational links to the assassination. Witnesses that should have been called were not, others acted as agents of deception. Superfluous and irrelevant data abounds in the documents, obtained by equally worthless witnesses and individuals called to testify. Mountains of documents were created to confuse, mislead, and divert attention away from the true conspiracy that was linked to a covert paramilitary network operating in Dallas and linked directly to Otto Skorzeny."

MAJOR RALPH P. GANIS, USAF, RESERVE RETIRED

CONTENTS

ACKNOWLEDGMENTS

To the brave circle of family and friends that supported me in the most remarkable ways during this monumental effort and to whom I am most indebted. They remained steadfast to the end and never wavered on their support for me or in the mission of delivering this important history to the American people.

To the men I interviewed that knew Otto Skorzeny, in particular my good friend, Colonel Jere Wittington, U.S. Army Retired; also, Attorney Robert Bieck, Jr., son of Lt. Colonel Robert Bieck; Lt. Colonel "Tad" Skladzien, USAF Retired; Commander Thomas W. Trout, USN, Retired, and several others who will remain unnamed.

Thank you also to Lt. Colonel Theodore C. Mataxis, Jr., U.S. Army, Retired; Sim Smiley, Mrs. Joan Forster, author Mary Ellen Reese, Dr. Gerhard Freund, publisher Roger Bender, Tom Polgar, Peter M. F. Sichel and others.

OVERVIEW TO THE 2020 PAPERBACK EDITION

"Mr. Director, only you can clear Otto Skorzeny of the guilt of being [an] agent in the Dallas operation with [the] passive complicity of Allen W. Dulles."

EXCERPT FROM A LETTER TO FBI DIRECTOR J. EDGAR HOOVER
BY FRENCHMAN PAUL GLUC, MARCH 1975

For many Americans—indeed the world at large—stories put forth describing the assassination of President John F. Kennedy are poorly explained, or not believable at all. In particular, the Lee Harvey Oswald 'Lone Gunman" storyline and Oswald's quick murder appear to have plunged the likely true events into chaos and unknowable obscurity. Until now, anyone attempting to explain this sordid event had the same poorly understood and incongruent "set of facts." Over the years, this static and stale evidence only produced repetitive confusion. It is not surprising that no one could satisfactorily explain what happened in Dallas. Now, in this book, new and startling facts, never before known or considered, are revealed. These revelations explain the assassination, why it happened, and who was involved—all within a new context. A new figure appears, Otto Skorzeny, a person unknown to most of the world, seemingly plucked from obscurity. This book describes how he would become a central figure in the tragic events of November 22, 1963. Read on, and learn who this person was, how his involvement with the assassination was discovered, and how he came to be the man who orchestrated Kennedy's murder. It is a riveting fact-based account, admittedly somewhat complicated and involved, but well worth the effort to understand. The road to Dallas begins in World War II.

The revelations in this book would never have been possible without the existence of the personal papers of former Nazi commando leader Otto Skorzeny acquired by the author in 2012. It was a daunting task to sift through and discover the key documents in the Skorzeny papers. At first, much of it seemed cryptic and obscure. But the clues were there and the pathways to the answer were ultimately revealed and are now disclosed in this book. After several years of research, the papers unveiled the following history:

At the end of World War II, Otto Skorzeny, the chief of Hitler's elite special forces, surrendered to American forces. Like many high ranking Nazis, Skorzeny was held as a VIP prisoner of war. In 1947, he was placed on trial by an Allied military tribunal. Since Skorzeny was not associated with concentration camps, he was tried on violating the Laws of War by issuing captured US uniforms to his men in order to deceive Allied forces during the Battle of the Bulge. Surprisingly, during his trial, several Allied officers actually came to Skorzeny's defense and admitting that the Allies had used the exact same trickery as Skorzeny during the course of the war. For this reason, Skorzeny was declared not guilty.

Immediately after his acquittal, Skorzeny was transferred to a low level denazification holding facility from which he then mysteriously escaped and vanished for nearly two years. Underground in Europe he would eventually surface in Madrid, Spain using the alias Rolf Steinbauer. This was in 1950 and from that point on Skorzeny remained in Spain and started a number of international businesses. The Skorzeny papers acquired by the author are the specific documents associated with these postwar businesses. A future section of this book gives a detailed explanation of these papers, but for now it should be made clear that they confirm Skorzeny led a shadow life. In fact, the businesses were a cover for unofficial secret activities carried out by Skorzeny and his network on behalf of Western intelligence agencies, NATO, and the newly established CIA. Skorzeny also created a school for specialized training of secret agents and special forces carried out at secret locations in Spain.

The overall purpose of Skorzeny's secret activites was to support the array of anti-communist operations then being conducted by the West throughout

Europe and Africa. The personnel trained at Skorzeny's camp were highly trained in unconventional operations, including assassination.

By 1960, President Eisenhower ordered the creation of a high level assassination program for the targeting of foreign heads of state. This program was called Executive Action and a center piece of the program was the utilization of the Skorzeny network. But instead of its intended purpose of targeting foreign threats, it would be diverted to carry out the most horrendous assassination in modern history.

On November 22, 1963, a Skorzeny assassination network was in place in Dallas, Texas. The particulars of the people involved and the events that transpired from this network's activities cannot be ignored or dismissed. The presence of this network is an impossible coincidence; it led to the killing of JFK. The events that led to this killing were triggered by a limited group of highly placed men in the American government. They were convinced that the West was in imminent danger and poised to suffer irreparable damage, and, for some of them, imminent exposure to personal disgrace beckoned. All of this sprang from reckless debauchery in the White House and beyond. With the situation likely breached by Soviet intelligence and ripe for exploitation, it became untenable for this group. They took action using Skorzeny's network since its operations were unique and conveniently obscure from any actual government.

The actual sniper, or team of snipers, in Dallas, was directed by a rogue former French commando, Captain Jean Rene Souetre. It was Souetre who would be dispatched to Dallas, an agent of the Skorzeny network. He would subsequently be secretly ushered out of the United States only one day after the JFK assignation, a fact verified by a declassified CIA document.

It is widely known that Lee Harvey Oswald was in the Texas school book depository on the day of the JFK assassination. But with the evidence from the Skorzeny papers, this simple fact becomes a major indicator of conspiracy. The depository was owned by D. Harold Byrd. Byrd's connection to the Skorzeny papers is explained in detail on pages 332-334 of this book. But, for conciseness here, let it be emphatically stated that Byrd's alibi, including his being out of the country on a hunting safari in Africa, is highly problematic since the hunting club he was with in Africa is the same one directly associated with Skorzeny's businesses and Skorzeny's key associates.

In regards to the Skorzeny papers, Lee Harvey Oswald was a dupe, apparently manipulated into the Skorzeny network as a ploy. Key people associated with Oswald in Dallas, such as George de Mohrenschildt, are linked directly to individuals associated with the Skorzeny network. Apparently, almost immediately after the assassination, Oswald deduced that he was in mortal jeopardy, that something was amiss, and he panicked. If Oswald had acted alone, he would have been left alone; there would have been no need to kill him. Jack Ruby's killing of Oswald was a desperate act to repair the botched operation.

Incredibly, Jack Ruby is also dramatically linked to the Skorzeny papers via a man named Thomas Eli Davis. Davis is documented to have been Ruby's business partner in illegal gun running activity. The connection of Ruby to the Otto Skorzeny network is provable through the arrival of Davis in Madrid, Spain only a few weeks before the assassination in Dallas to deal directly with Skorzeny's main business partner. We may never know what hold on Ruby existed that forced his action, but he expressed his high concern to his legal counsel over his relationship with Davis. Ruby's activities with Davis is consistent with Skorzeny's international arms network and associated activities.

The actual assassination of JFK was captured on the now famous Zapruder film acquired immediately after the shooting by Charles Douglas Jackson working for Time Life. Documents available in the Dwight David Eisenhower Presidential Library confirm Jackson was a CIA officer and a top psychological warfare officer of the US government. Jackson's affiliation with the CIA and his immediate response in securing the Zapruder film is incredible since the Skorzeny papers confirm he was a close associate of several members of Skorzeny's inner circle.

The Zapruder film eventually ended up being the subject of a television special with the famous news anchor Walter Cronkite. Cronkite worked for CBS, which had created a special documentary on the Kennedy assassination in 1975, called *The American Assassins*, which focused on Lee Harvey Oswald. In the film, which included correspondent Dan Rather, a detailed frame-by-frame analysis of the Zapruder film was conducted and evidence was examined that the CIA had a hand in the assassination. The film analysis showed Oswald was the only shooter and no conclusive evidence of outside influence by American intelligence was found. However, both findings are now in serious contention. What CBS did not know (or what they did not reveal) is the company that conducted the analysis on the Zapruder film was ITEK, a high-tech camera company that made spy equipment for the United States government and whose president, since at least February of 1962, was CIA officer Frank Lindsay. Declassified documents confirm Lindsay was directly involved in establishing the original assassination capability of Otto Skorzeny in 1949. The above facts indicate C. D. Jackson's acquisition of the Zapruder film approaches criminality.

The rise of Skorzeny, from postwar cooperator to one of the most secret, high-level clandestine foreign operators for American intelligence and NATO, is chronicled in this book. Otto Skorzeny was brilliant, effective, reliable, and deadly. But he wasn't chosen for his willingness to pull a trigger, rather, for his genius at planning and execution (both definitions apply). In the end, Allen Dulles, the very head of the Central Intelligence Agency that authorized the creation of Skorzeny's network and managed it after the war, served on the Warren Commission. This resulted in the ultimate fox-in-the-henhouse outcome and the greatest inside cover-up of congressional investigations in American history.

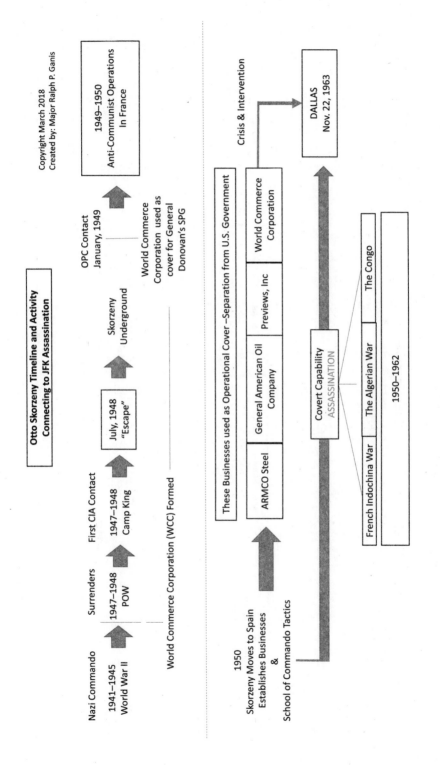

Otto Skorzeny Timeline and Activity Connecting to JFK Assassination

Copyright March 2018
Created by: Major Ralph P. Ganis

Nazi Commando
1941–1945
World War II

Surrenders
1947–1948
POW

First CIA Contact
1947–1948
Camp King

July, 1948
"Escape"

Skorzeny
Underground

OPC Contact
January, 1949

World Commerce
Corporation used as
cover for General
Donovan's SPG

1949–1950
Anti-Communist Operations
In France

World Commerce Corporation (WCC) Formed

1950
Skorzeny Moves to Spain
Establishes Businesses
&
School of Commando Tactics

These Businesses used as Operational Cover –Separation from U.S. Government

ARMCO Steel

General American Oil
Company

Previews, Inc

World Commerce
Corporation

Crisis & Intervention

DALLAS
Nov. 22, 1963

Covert Capability
ASSASSINATION

French Indochina War

The Algerian War

The Congo

1950–1962

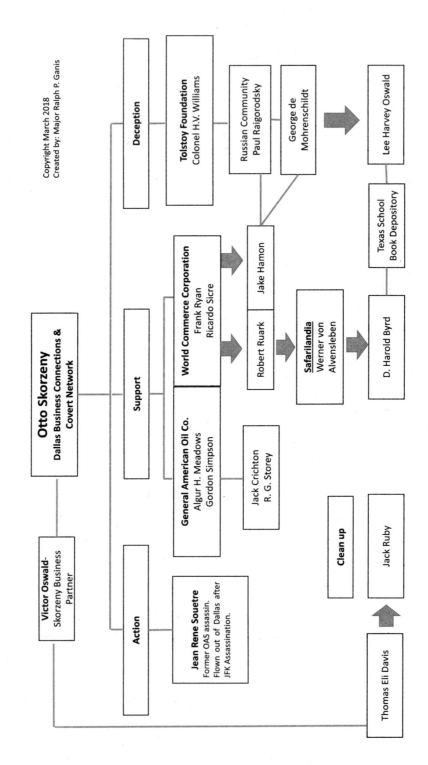

Copyright March 2018
Created by: Major Ralph P. Ganis

AUTHOR'S COMMENT ON SOURCES

My father, USAF Chief Warrant Officer Joseph F. Ganis, was a veteran of World War II and my greatest hero. As a young man, I would never tire of hearing about the campaigns he had been a part of in North Africa, Sicily, and Italy. In 1972, my freshman year of high school, I began collecting the series of illustrated histories on World War II by Ballantine Books. These small, reasonably priced books (only one dollar at the time), were a great source of knowledge to me. The extensive series covered a wide range of interesting topics, including the principle battles and biographies of various important personalities from the war. One book caught my attention—war leader book, no 11, titled, *Skorzeny*, authored by Charles Whiting.

The Ballantine book on Otto Skorzeny was my first introduction to a man who would capture my strong interest for many years. Ultimately, doing intense research on Skorzeny would consume several years of my life. In 1976, my attention was again directed toward Skorzeny by the release of the movie, *The Eagle Has Landed*, based on the bestselling novel of the same name by author Jack Higgins. This fictional account of a German plot to kidnap Winston Churchill from England, using German commandos disguised as Allied Polish paratroopers, was totally spellbinding for me at the time. To set the stage for the storyline, the movie opens with actual film footage relating to a daring German commando raid in September 1943, when then Captain Skorzeny, on orders from Adolf Hitler, rescued fascist dictator Benito Mussolini, who had been arrested by a pro—Allied Italian government. In the movie, the Skorzeny mission serves as the inspiration for the even greater objective of abducting Winston Churchill. *The Eagle Has Landed* became one of my all-time favorites and furthered my interest in Skorzeny and in special operations in general.

Not surprisingly, these early impressions influenced my own pursuit of a military career, and, as the years passed, I retained my interest in the story of Otto Skorzeny, and other famous commando leaders. In December 1994, during the fiftieth anniversary of the Battle of the Bulge, I happened to be stationed with the U.S. Army in Germany. With my intense interest in the Second World War, I naturally took the opportunity to visit the Ardennes forest where much of the action took place in that great battle. I took interest in the areas where Skorzeny's special Panzer Brigade 150, outfitted with American markings and special commandos dressed in American uniforms, began part of a great German deception plan to seize the initiative in the opening phase of the battle. Together with a friend, I retraced the exact route of the attacking German army and the points of heroic defense by the Americans.

As the years passed, I occasionally reflected on Otto Skorzeny, particularly when I served with the United States Special Operations Command, where the tactics and methods of famous commandos are a continuing subject of interest to military thinkers and historians.

In subsequent years, I had observed that, while much had been written about Skorzeny's exploits during World War II, very little was known about his postwar life. After being found not guilty by a war crimes tribunal, he reportedly escaped from an internment camp in 1948. Some accounts said his "escape" was assisted by U.S. intelligence. This curious beginning to his postwar life was compounded by quite contradictory information regarding his character. On one hand, there was a body of professional military men who expressed admiration for Skorzeny's soldierly qualities, his skill and daring, and his innovation and unconventional methods. On the flip side, there were those who suggested Skorzeny was involved with nefarious postwar organizations. Despite a considerable amount attention and fascination with Skorzeny, the enigma of his postwar life continued to be a contradictory mystery.

Then, in 2012, I became aware, rather by chance, that Otto Skorzeny's personal papers were to be auctioned in the United States by a reputable American auction house. Incredibly, the papers had come into the possession of a Spanish citizen in Madrid whose grandfather, a colonel in Francisco Franco's army and close friend of Skorzeny, had received the documents for safekeeping directly from Skorzeny's wife, Ilse. Skorzeny had moved to Madrid in 1950 and died there in July 1975. According to the oral history attached to the papers, before his death Skorzeny had charged his wife with the protection of his personal archive. As the story goes, much of the papers were burned over time, but a fragmentary grouping of documents (the ones used for the research in this book) survived. This archive ranges from 1947 to around the period of Skorzeny's death. They were originally secreted away by the Spanish colonel in a small trunk. The trunk was later passed to the colonel's son and eventually his grandson. There was a curious aura of fear attached to the papers, so it was the grandson, who first opened and began examining the documents. The papers presented several immediately challenges. Most of them are in German, comprised mostly of correspondence from Skorzeny to his wife Ilse concerning various business ventures they were engaged in after their arrival in Spain. There are very few letters of a strictly personal nature, although there are a multitude of references within the business letters concerning friends, acquaintances, and casual events. The papers do not read like a diary, but they do reveal Skorzeny's network of closest friends, his interest in Cold War geopolitical events, and his personal loyalties, which include covert relationships with the CIA and the American military.

The description of the collection by the auction house was quite remarkable, touting them as "the only surviving archives of Hitler's top commando." Overall, this seemed to me a great opportunity to shed light on the mysteries of Skorzeny's postwar life, to understand his personal relationships and businesses, and to perhaps confirm or disprove the existence of the ODESSA organization.

I was fortunate to win the bid on Skorzeny's papers. Perhaps to my advantage was the rising stigma in society of collecting Nazi-related material. But my growing fascination for Skorzeny over the years was always centered on his record as a military leader and the enigmas of his personal history. Overall, I was quite fortunate, for it is rare that a historian is privy to unexploited papers, especially of noted historical figures.

At the time, I was not fully aware of the history of the papers and how they came to survive; that came later. The archive would prove to be a tremendous challenge to reconcile, for what I thought I would discover, and what was revealed, was staggering. In the initial phase of reviewing the documents, my training and instincts as an intelligence professional were ignited by the content of the papers. The Skorzeny papers, from the first moment, were dumbfounding and perplexing. Within hours of receiving the material, I noticed evidence of intelligence and operational relationships between Skorzeny and U.S. officials.

To advance my research of the personal papers I purchased copies of all declassified documents from the National Archives of the United States government concerning Skorzeny. This included mostly information from U.S. military intelligence and the CIA, but also a small group of documents from the FBI and Department of State.

The declassified documents were quite voluminous with reports dating from World War II until the period of Skorzeny's death in 1975. Over the years, there had been some speculative writing that Skorzeny had a clandestine relationship with U.S. intelligence. This is also confirmed by the declassified documents but not to the extent of his personal papers. Skorzeny's personal paper reveal a clandestine relationship on a much, much deeper level than the government documents portrayed.

I was hoping that Skorzeny's personal papers could be reconciled against the declassified documents. In a few cases this proved to be possible, but overall the papers conflict with declassified reporting which is almost entirely related to counterintelligence and do not reveal any operational aspects of his life.

Within days of receiving Skorzeny's papers, I was surprised to discover that a retired U.S. Army colonel named Jere Wittington, who had known Skorzeny in the early 1950s was living in Florida. I contacted Colonel Wittington, who graciously invited me to his home and agreed to help me with my project. His assistance turned out to be invaluable. Wittington's firsthand account was a tremendous addition to revelations found in both the declassified CIA reports as well as in Skorzeny papers.

This pattern was repeated several times as I was able to make contact with other U.S. intelligence and Madrid embassy personnel who had known and worked with Skorzeny throughout the 1950s and 1960s. The conclusion was clear—what had appeared to the world to be an ever-diminishing World War II celebrity, had now been resurrected in the archive as a more and more important character in Cold War history.

Through the 1950s and 1960s, Skorzeny's special experience and skills in covert operations were increasingly utilized by the most secret agencies of multiple governments, including the United States. It's very clear the he enjoyed the confidence of highly-placed western intelligence officials eager to use his special skills in highly classified operations to combat the Communist threat in the Cold War. At an early point, it also became apparent, due to Skorzeny's business relationships that linked him intimately to Dallas that there was at least the potential for a link to the assassination of President John F. Kennedy. This line of research continued to expand dramatically, until I was convinced that either Skorzeny was directly involved in the Dallas affair or that those he was connected to were. I also believed the papers would act as a pathway to uncover the facts behind the event. The hypothesis was confirmed. I now present to the reader this body of evidence based on five years of research and exploitation of the Skorzeny papers.

FOREWORD
BY DICK RUSSELL

Among the hundreds of books published on the assassination of President Kennedy, conspiracy "whodunit" theories have ranged from the Cubans to the Mafia to the Illuminati. Very few have managed to connect the dots between American spy agencies, corporate enterprises, and clandestine global networks. Now we have *The Skorzeny Papers*, tying such a web of intrigue together in a surprising and unprecedented way.

Otto Skorzeny's is a familiar name to students of the Second World War. While in charge of Hitler's elite commando unit, among many other assassination and abduction missions, Skorzeny's daring raid rescued Mussolini as Italy was about to fall to the Allies. Not so well known is Skorzeny's postwar career during the Cold War against the Soviet Union, as a valued asset of numerous Western nations including the U.S.

Major Ralph P. Ganis, who acquired Skorzeny's personal papers at an auction in 2012, begins by examining how the roots of the CIA overlap with a number of agencies and big-business fronts having close links to the Nazi German hierarchy. These relationships, useful in the fight against communist aggression while expanding American global domination, would ultimately result in covert alliances aimed at overthrowing foreign leaders—and likely assassinating an American president.

Skorzeny's private network, painstakingly traced through Ganis's research, became a fulcrum for such operations. In these pages, the reader will discover many previously-unknown names—men such as businessman Victor Oswald and CIA official Al Ulmer—as well as organizations like the World Commerce Corporation and the Dallas-based General American Oil Company.

The reader will also learn of how obscure power players suddenly emerged with crucial roles in the effort to ensure Lee Harvey Oswald remained a "lone nut gunman." One of these was a Colonel Robert G. Storey, in 1963 a prominent Dallas attorney who along with his associate Leon Jaworski (of later Watergate fame) achieved liaison roles with the Warren Commission investigating Kennedy's murder. Indeed, Commission members Allen Dulles and John J. McCloy had been instrumental in originally establishing Otto Skorzeny's secret network.

In my book on the assassination, *The Man Who Knew Too Much*, I described connections between right-wing CIA/military operatives, Cuban exiles, and wealthy Texas oilmen. I also wrote about Jean Rene Souetre, involved in an assassination attempt against French President Charles de Gaulle shortly before being "deported" from Dallas by private plane on November 22, 1963. However, I was unaware until publication of *The Skorzeny Papers* about these various clandestine involvements with the ex-Nazi, extending prior to JFK's assassination into the era's conflicts in Vietnam, Algeria, and the Congo.

Author Ganis does not leap to conclusions. He cannot prove that Skorzeny and his brethren, including some in organized crime, conspired to kill the president. What Ganis does achieve is a chronological tracing of dark alliances that sheds fresh light on how long-suspicious CIA officials like William Harvey and James Angleton wove Otto Skorzeny into their tangled web, or vice versa. The evidence indicating that Skorzeny, from his base in Madrid, served as leader of the Agency's QJ/WIN assassination program is compelling. Equally intriguing is the role of the Tolstoy Foundation, a CIA front, in bringing Oswald under the wing of Dallas' White Russian community upon his return from the USSR in June 1962.

The devil is in the details. As with any great mystery—and the Kennedy assassination remains the most riveting of all—the reader is invited to "build the case," follow the chain as it emerges across many pages among Skorzeny and his henchmen. In the end, it is not a stretch to conclude that Ganis's work brings us closer than we've ever come to understanding the cabal who changed the course of American history on November 22, 1963.

PREFACE

Why was President John F. Kennedy killed and who carried it out? All of the investigations, commissions, and academic works have not answered these questions. This book integrates startling new information that does resolve the mystery. The pathway to the discovery involves the astounding revelation of a man most Americans have never heard of and whose life was previously only associated with sensational military operations of World War II. His name is Otto Skorzeny. He had been Hitler's chief of German special forces during the war.

Skorzeny's life after World War II has been an enigma since 1945, and conflicting stories abound. In some histories he is reported as a nefarious ex-Nazi, while other accounts suggest he was in some way involved in Western intelligence intrigues but give no details as to his involvement. Most of what is written about Skorzeny during the Cold War period has been pieced together from newspaper accounts and declassified U.S. government documents. The U.S. documents are predominately security files by counterintelligence that record Skorzeny's activities as reported by various sources. There are a few passing mentions that Skorzeny did assist the U.S. government with covert operations, but none were operational files. Overall, the available body of material, whether in the form of newspaper accounts or official documents, reveals an inaccurate history of Skorzeny.

Many authors have been transfixed on Skorzeny's association with Hitler and maintain Skorzeny was a die-hard Nazi who organized and maintained a worldwide neo-Nazi movement after the war. This is not accurate. Others blend Skorzeny's Nazi past with his poorly understood assistance to U.S. intelligence to suggest a Nazi faction within the U.S. government. This, too, is inaccurate.

The truth is found in the Skorzeny papers that show his postwar life was in no way a continuation of the Third Reich, nor a sensational U.S.–Nazi plot. This is simply a chapter in the history of the Cold War in which the survival of the West against Communism was the paramount motive. In fact, it will come as a startling pronouncement that this man Otto Skorzeny was a trusted asset of many Western countries, including the U.S. government, in the leveraging of all viable assets to ensure victory over Soviet aggression and prepare for a potential third world war.

In 2014, the German government admitted that in the immediate years after World War II, a secret emergency combat force, or "shadow army," had been formed, made up of former Third Reich soldiers prepared to defend Germany in the event of a Soviet invasion. It was revealed that Skorzeny was a part of this formation. In fact, all of the plans related to Skorzeny's involvement with the German contingency army are in the Skorzeny papers.

In 2012, Israeli historians revealed that Skorzeny had assisted their country with espionage directed against Egypt in the early 1960s. Then, in 2015, newspaper reporters added that Skorzeny had carried out assassinations for the state of Israel against individuals who were connected to weapons of mass destruction.

In regard to the use of Skorzeny by foreign governments and by the United States, it is important to note that he was an independent operator. In fact, the evidence gleaned from the Skorzeny papers indicates that his relationship with the United States government was unilateral and decisions by U.S. leadership involving his services in sensitive matters of national security did not include disclosure to foreign governments. Some operations may have been joint efforts. It is known, for example, that West Germany and the United States worked together on Skorzeny's missions to Egypt in 1953.

But assassination operations are distinctly different. Plausible deniability is the literal keystone to these operations; therefore, given the extreme need for secrecy, it is logical that any assistance Skorzeny gave to Western governments in regard to assassination was compartmented and known only to the government involved.

No one could have imagined that the contents of Skorzeny's personal papers were intimately associated with the people and organizations that had the motive and capability to carry out the assassination of President John F. Kennedy. It is widely known and well documented that government covert operations commonly require cover taking the form of commercial activities. The Skorzeny papers consist largely of business-related correspondence of commercial enterprises used for such cover. Specifically, the names, locations, organizations, and events in these papers correspond directly to the agents, places, organizations, and events associated with U.S. covert intelligence activities for the same period. This amazing relationship between Otto Skorzeny and Western intelligence services is nothing short of astounding. It arose from Skorzeny's extraordinary capabilities and his persona, which was a progressive extension of his wartime skills. His attributes were recognized and seized upon by the architects and leaders of Cold War secret operations and programs.

The Skorzeny papers reveal that these clandestine relationships developed over time, resulting in an escalation of his involvement and his importance in the implementation of secret operations. His activities were carefully guarded and maintained by individuals outside normal intelligence channels. His use originated from his extensive knowledge and contacts within former German intelligence networks from the war, which were absorbed and utilized by U.S. intelligence in the immediate postwar period. Skorzeny gained the confidence and admiration of certain powerful and influential U.S. military and intelligence leaders at the highest level.

Of special interest were Skorzeny's capabilities in covert operations, including the targeting of individuals. Assassination operations were carried out extensively during World War II by both the Allies and the Axis powers. When the war ended, the one-time allies, the United States and Soviet Russia, initiated a Cold War and instructed their intelligence agencies to begin extensive covert actions directed at each other. Assassination played an important role in this saga and included the elimination of enemy agents, military commanders, political leaders, and scientists involved in the development of weapons of mass destruction. Both countries developed special units to undertake the highest level of targeting in assassination known as Executive Action; in other words, those directed at foreign leadership.

Skorzeny was brought into these Cold War intrigues immediately upon his release from internment as a prisoner of war. Over time, he developed a postwar network that would eventually become a strategic assassination asset of the United States for implementing Executive Action. This assassination capability was known only to a select, highly secretive group. The author will present evidence that the operation that targeted President John F. Kennedy was the utilization of this capability. We will show that Kennedy's murder was neither an ad hoc event nor a conspiratorial arrangement with criminal enterprise, but the calculated implementation of a pre-existing government capability that was ordered into action.

The motive for the assassination of President John F. Kennedy is also revealed in this book. Ultimately, reliance upon Skorzeny by entities within the United States government would lead to his direct involvement in a perilous political situation, centered in the highest quarters of the government and one that poised the country for a catastrophic failure at the very height of the Cold War. The people who recognized and understood this threat and ordered the assassination are the same people associated with Skorzeny's earliest entry into postwar covert operations. Some of the people known or suspected to be connected with the Dallas event are also found in the Skorzeny papers and had been associated with Skorzeny for decades.

Perhaps one of the most incongruent revelations is the fact that two members of the Warren Commission, Allen Dulles and John J. McCloy, were instrumental in the establishment of Skorzeny as a covert asset and were fully aware of his secret network.

THE SKORZENY PAPERS

In 2012, the personal papers of Otto Skorzeny were made available in public auction in the United States. According to the story received by the auction house, his personal papers were passed to his wife, Ilse, in 1975, just prior to the death of the former German commando.

According to the story, Skorzeny told Ilse to "take care of these papers," for "my star will rise again."

The Skorzeny papers cover the timeframe of 1945–1975. As the analysis of the documents proceeded, it became apparent that Skorzeny was heavily involved with intelligence and covert operations of the United States and other foreign governments during the Cold War.

The Skorzeny papers are predominantly in German and were written after he had established a permanent home in Spain after World War II, in 1950. There are both typed and handwritten letters. Most of the letters are original carbon copies of typed correspondence with numerous handwritten annotations by Skorzeny in the margins. Almost all the correspondence is from Skorzeny to Ilse describing business opportunities, meetings with key individuals, status of negotiations and contracts, banking issues, financial arrangements, and business ventures, evaluations of potential partners and possible difficulties, and cost or profit estimations. There are several categories of businesses: banking matters, various financial opportunities, import–export, construction, steel manufacturing, raw materials (such as lumber), mining interests, surplus aircraft sales and parts, and a variety of other financial pursuits.

OPERATIONAL COVER—THE KEY

But the papers also confirm that Skorzeny's "Industrial Office" in Madrid was a cover for Skorzeny's private intelligence network, which was supplying information or clandestine operational support (to include assassination operations) to the Central Intelligence Agency and the U.S. military. This is very important. The legitimate businesses that Skorzeny operated permitted Skorzeny to act with complete separation from the United States government, they were essentially a cutout. When the author bought the business papers of Skorzeny he inadvertantly bought the "bridge" between Skorzeny and the United States government revealing the vital links described in this book. Without the papers, a link between the United States government and Skorzeny is highly problematic. With the papers, the clandestine networks are exposed. The business papers are a key that opens the door.

Skorzeny's businesses, particularly his import–export contacts in various European and African countries, were also connected to black market and underworld networks. Skorzeny would provide information to U.S. intelligence that was derived from his "agents," and he also served in various advisery roles for tasks ranging from paramilitary training to very sensitive covert action.

Skorzeny's valuable network also had major contacts within foreign intelligence, including the French, Spanish, Portuguese, Germans, Israelis, and numerous countries in Europe, Africa, and South America. Skorzeny always worked for "the good guys," and there is no evidence he helped the Soviet Union, East Bloc countries, or any country aligned against the United States or the West. This is not to say he helped military regimes or totalitarian governments. Simply stated, Skorzeny's network was an excellent intelligence and counterintelligence asset and it proved very useful. It also went undetected until Skorzeny's papers received a critical review by the author.

The Skorzeny archive is incomplete, so that only a general overview of the business relationships is possible, and some years are absent. Most of the Americans in the archive have some official intelligence background, as do many of the foreigners that Skorzeny dealt with. Most of the CIA officers identified in the papers never admitted to knowing Skorzeny.

This book is replete with terms of art that may or may not be generally familiar to the reader such as "clandestine" and "covert," which essentially mean secret. To assist the reader when ambiguities occur, the author has prepared a glossary of terms. There, the reader can find the specific definitions and explanations of such terminology.

Throughout this book, there will be mention of numerous personalities, as well as governments, quasi governments, private organizations, and groups. Many of these entities were found to have dual significance. Firstly, they revealed important relationships at the time they occurred, and, secondly, some of these entities later become connected to the events in Dallas relating to the assassination of President John F. Kennedy. For this reason, the initial chapters set the stage for the reader to understand the complex histories of individuals or organizations within the context of time, both when they occurred and brought forward to the events in Dallas.

Overall, the Skorzeny network is extremely complex, with multiple layers. Many of these layers have overlapping membership. Additionally, it is certain that any sensitive work was compartmentalized. Skorzeny was a brilliant operator who made few, if any, mistakes. His selection to lead the U.S. Executive Action program was based on his skills, trustworthiness, and ability to leverage his network while maintaining plausible deniability for the U.S. government.

In this book, the author has presented only a fraction of the associations found in the Skorzeny papers. The author encourages the reader to use the Glossary and Appendices (containing relational charts) to understand the complex relationships. Specifically, prioritized are the factual elements that lead to confirmation of the clandestine Skorzeny network, his relation to U.S. intelligence, and the network presence in Dallas at the time of the assassination of President Kennedy. Future historians are likely to expand on the research, and it seems certain other discoveries will be made of interest to the public. On that note, it is the author's intention to reposit the Skorzeny documents into a publically accessible venue, by sale or loan, as soon as feasible. He strongly believes that a failure to make public the actual documents concerning a discovery of this magnitude would dismiss the findings out of hand.

What follows is the true narrative of Otto Skorzeny on his dark road to Dallas as a "contract" adviser, arms dealer, front man, and confidant within the hidden recesses of U.S. (and other countries') intelligence and military activities. Revealed here for the first time are the incredible and undeniable connections to the people and actions that led to the assassination of President John F. Kennedy and the proof that JFK's murder was an international conspiracy involving the United States government and utilizing a clandestine network that had at its heart Otto Skorzeny.

THE LETTER

On March 24, 1975, an FBI analyst translating foreign mail surveyed a curious handwritten letter received at the bureau headquarters in Washington, D.C., that had arrived from France only a few days earlier addressed to the director. The translator summarized the document as "a long, rambling and somewhat incoherent letter" concerning, among other things, the assassination of President John F. Kennedy. The writer identified himself as Paul Gluc, explaining in the letter that he understood the FBI was investigating the assassination of Kennedy. He pointed out the tensions that existed between Kennedy and the CIA, and he identified those responsible for Dallas as the CIA agents "relieved of their duties" in the wake of the Bay of Pigs disaster.

But Gluc also included a very curious statement, which was more specific in nature and which, despite the hundreds of books written about the Kennedy assassination, appears in print for the first time here. Gluc wrote: "Mr. Director, only you can clear Otto Skorzeny of the guilt of being [an] agent in the Dallas operation with [the] passive complicity of Allen W. Dulles." He then ends the letter with, "I end here . . . with the hope of seeing the Dallas enigma solved."

The letter would eventually make its way into the archive of post–assassination correspondence received by the U.S. government. It is not known if the letter was ever seen by Clarence M. Kelly, then director of the FBI, nor do we know the fate of the mysterious writer Paul Gluc.

Why did this Frenchman associate the name of Otto Skorzeny with the assassination of President Kennedy?

At the time the Gluc letter was written, a government appointed body, the Church Committee, was conducting an investigation into CIA covert action and intelligence, including assassination attempts on foreign leaders. One of the members of the committee was Senator Gary Hart of Colorado, who was serving on a subcommittee looking into the assassination of President Kennedy. Of particular interest to Senator Hart was the identification of a CIA asset known by the code word (or cryptonym) QJ/WIN.

PROLOGUE

"Perhaps it was foolhardy to suppose that in real life we could undo what had been done, cancel our knowledge of evil, uninvent our weapons, stow away what remained in safe hiding place."

SIR WILLIAM STEPHENSON,

HEAD OF BRITISH SECURITY COORDINATION

It may seem incredible, but the foreshadowing of President John F. Kennedy's assassination was cast by adversaries and alliances born from the darkest days of post World War II. The origins of this story begin at the onset of the war. It was then, that England created an organization designed to carry out covert missions against Nazi Germany. The United States was soon to follow and also began to develop its own organization for covert war.

On the British side was the Special Operations Executive (SOE), on the American, the Office of Strategic Services (OSS). The men who created these organizations were highly intelligent, unconventional thinkers, with ice-cold decision making. The exploits of both organizations are legendary and much of what they did is still highly classified, including their missions to carry out abduction and assassination.

The actions carried out by the SOE and commandos had so impressed Adolf Hitler that he ordered the formation of his own special service to carry out similar missions for the Third Reich. The man chosen to lead this group was an unknown reserve SS captain named Otto Skorzeny. The Skorzeny commando group was highly successful and pulled off several of the most sensational operations in modern warfare. Skorzeny's most famous operation was the rescue of the Italian Dictator Benito Mussolini in September 1943, preventing the *Duce* from being turned over to the Allies. The Mussolini rescue is still studied in the halls of military academies to this day. Like his enemy counterparts, Skorzeny's commando group also conducted special missions involving abduction and assassination.

After Germany's defeat, the SOE and OSS were officially disbanded as part of a rapid postwar demobilization. The Allies also set about bringing to justice those in the Third Reich responsible for war crimes. As an SS officer, Skorzeny was in the immediate arrest category. During the final days of the war he could have easily escaped, slipping away to South American or some other destination. Instead, he surrendered himself to uncertain fate. He was then held for two years as a POW and ultimately charged with violations of the Laws of War. It was at this moment that an amazing and strange event occurred. Those present at Skorzeny's trial were suddenly shocked at the arrival of a distinguished party of his former adversaries—high ranking members of the SOE and OSS who came to the trial in his defense. This unlikely source of support was a major factor in the trial's outcome and Skorzeny was quickly found not guilty.

But this was only the beginning of the mysterious events surrounding the postwar career of Skorzeny. Immediately after his acquittal he was sent to a special camp for German POW VIPs where he stayed for several months. Ultimately, he was transferred to an internment facility where he was to await final disposition and release. Then, in July 1948, he suddenly escaped. This caused a sensation in the press and Skorzeny became the focus of an international manhunt—except there was no manhunt. Skorzeny had gone underground—his release actually orchestrated by the same SOE and OSS officers who had appeared earlier for his defense.

These men also held a secret, and that secret is revealed here for the first time in print. The Skorzeny papers confirmed the existence of a super secret postwar organization created by a legacy group of SOE and OSS operatives. This group, whose name is not known, had the official blessing of senior U.S. military and intelligence officials. The purpose of this secret paramilitary group was to conduct covert warfare against Communist expansion in Europe and to prepare for war against the Soviet Union. It was also used to liquidate double agents and others deemed a threat to the West. The group worked in concert with similar programs instituted by the American CIA and British MI6. It was, in essence, a separate parallel effort. As part of this private covert group, Skorzeny organized his own smaller group that was under his direct control. The entire enterprise operated under the cover of an international business corporation. This book will follow the saga of Skorzeny's inclusion in this secret network, the evolution of his covert actions within it, and the tragic legacy of its incarnation.

CHAPTER ONE
A WAR WITH NO RULES

"[Admiral] Darlan's murder, however criminal, relieved the Allies of their embarrassment at working with him."

WINSTON CHURCHILL,

THE HINGE OF FATE: THE SECOND WORLD WAR, VOL. 4

In May 1940, Great Britain was fighting for its national survival. Nazi Germany had defeated Belgium and France in a brilliant *blitzkrieg* outflanking the combined French and British armies. The entire campaign lasted a mere six weeks. Fortunately for English they did manage to evacuate 198,000 British soldiers from Dunkirk in rescue mission dubbed Operation Dynamo. A remnant of the French and Belgian armies was also evacuated.

England now stood alone and prepared to defend the homeland. Britain's military commanders knew the British Army would be too weak to stop a German invasion of the island. But, Prime Minister Winston Churchill was determined to carry on the fight, even if invaded. To do this, he authorized the creation of a special covert force—the Special Operations Executive or SOE. The SOE was controlled by the Ministry of Economic Warfare created to blockade Germany and destroy its economy. The SOE recruited from all branches of the military, the intelligence services, academia, industry, and the business world. During the early months after Dunkirk, the SOE assisted in the implementation a top-secret program for an underground army organization to be activated upon invasion. This "stay-behind" network was hidden within the

GHQ Auxiliary Defense Units and began training and establishing secret bases around the country.

Before any invasion could be carried out by the Germans, they had to secure air supremacy over the beach landing sites for their ground units. An air battle ensued over England, famously known as the Battle of Britain. In a feat of incredible tenacity and against all the odds, the Royal Air Force managed to inflict great damage to the German *Luftwaffe*. As a result, Hitler's air force came out of the battle too weak to provide air cover for the planned invasion codenamed Operation Sea Lion.

With the threat of invasion passed, Churchill immediately turned his attention to going on the offense as best he could and issued new orders to the SOE "to set Europe ablaze" using subversive warfare and covert action. Over the course of the next six years the SOE, along with units from the Commandos and Parachute Regiments, conducted espionage, sabotage, and reconnaissance across the occupied areas of Europe. These same forces paved the way for Allied landings at Normandy (D-Day), June 6, 1944.

The United States entered the war on December 7, 1941 when the Japanese conducted a surprise daylight attack against the U.S. military facilities at Pearl Harbor, Hawaii. After entering the war, the United States began the development of its own covert capability modelled on the British SOE. The idea for the American organization, eventually known as the Office of Strategic Services or OSS, actually originated from William Stephenson, the British intelligence liaison to the United States. Stephenson was the head of the British Security Coordination (BSC), an intelligence outfit tasked to speed America's entry into the war on the British side. Stephenson approached President Roosevelt with the concept of an American version of the SOE. The Americans had monitored with great interest the successes and efficiency of the British secret services, SOE and commandos. Roosevelt immediately supported the formation of such a group.

The man chosen to lead the American effort to establish a covert organization similar to the SOE was William J. "Wild Bill" Donovan, a highly decorated hero of the First World War. During that conflict Donovan held the rank of major and served as the 1st Battalion Commander, 165th Infantry Regiment, 42nd Infantry Division. His unit saw heavy action during which Donovan was always at the front. His valor awards included the Medal of Honor and every other medal for bravery in the American award system. Donovan came from an immigrant Irish family that settled in Buffalo, New York after a few years in Canada. He had once considered the Catholic priesthood but later became a lawyer. His education included St. Joseph's Collegiate Institute, Niagara University, and finally Columbia University of Law. While at Columbia he was a classmate of Franklin D. Roosevelt.

Prior to World War II Donovan had established a very successful law practice. He also served for a time as a U.S. Attorney for the Western District of New York and at the Department of Justice. During these years, Donovan established his credentials as an expert in international affairs, traveling extensively and meeting with world leaders. In 1940 and 1941, he was chosen as an informal emissary to Britain. The British were fond of him, particularly Winston Churchill who gave Donovan open access to classified information. Donovan was also close to Sir William Stephenson, a Canadian businessman, code named "Intrepid" who was Britain's top spy in North America.

Stephenson headed the British Security Control (BSC) a part of Britain's MI6. By all accounts, Stephenson was a brilliant man, highly successful in business and secret warfare. It has been suggested he was the inspiration for the James Bond character of fiction, but the reality is even far more sobering. Author Thomas Mahl, author of *Desperate Deception* comes the closest to capturing the essence of William Stephenson inner character in a documentary series, *Secrets of War: Espionage*, narrated by Charlton Heston. Mahl stated, "[Stephenson] was a tough, ruthless businessman . . . a very tough, hard individual, who once volunteered to kill Hitler with a high-powered hunting rifle, so this is a tough focused individual who will do whatever it takes to win." Stephenson turned the BSC into top-notch spy agency—and it was also deadly. Again, quoting Mahl, "In order to be an agent for Stephenson you had to be intelligent, ruthless and one of the recruiting things was—I can not tell you what sort of work you will be involved in but if you join us you not be afraid of forgery and you must not be afraid of murder." Stephenson's BSC operated out of several floors in the Rockefeller Building—and paid no rent.

Donovan's relationship with Stephenson became a matter of official government business on July 11, 1941, when Donovan was appointed by Roosevelt as the Coordinator of Information (COI) in an effort to develop a centralized national intelligence gathering capability. Donovan established the COI in a New York office building co-located with British MI6, appointing a New York lawyer named Allen Dulles as his office manager. Within the COI Donovan established several branches including a Secret Intelligence Branch (SI) and a Special Operations Branch (SO). SI was responsible for espionage, SO tasked with sabotage and liaison with foreign undergrounds. The SI and SO groups were affectionately known as the "cowboys" for the independent and sometimes rough nature of their work.

ENTER COLONEL ROBERT SOLBORG

In October 1941 Donovan selected Lt. Colonel Robert Solborg, a veteran army intelligence officer as his deputy for Special Operations. Solborg had received the recommendation of BSC chief William Stephenson's deputy, Dick Ellis. Colonel Solborg boosted a very colorful military career and had served as an undercover intelligence officer for both the Americans and British. An extremely learned man, it was said Solborg could speak eleven languages. He was born in Warsaw, Poland, on February 18, 1892, when that country was still part of the Russian Empire.

Solborg's father had been a Russian general and, as a young man, Solborg enlisted in the Russian cavalry, fighting in the First World War. After being wounded, he was sent to New York to work for the Russian military purchasing commission. He did not return to Russia, because of the outbreak of the Bolshevik Revolution. Afterward, Solberg was active in White Russian support groups, which he continued throughout his life. In fact, it was Solborg's White Russian contacts that had landed him the OSS position. British agent Dick Ellis's first wife was a Russian émigré who had met Solborg. Their wives became close friends and the friendship lead to Ellis recommending Solborg. As a foreshadowing, it was precisely the White Russian émigré groups associated with Solborg that will play a significant role in assisting Lee Harvey Oswald when he arrives in Dallas, Texas in the summer of 1962. These important connections will be expanded on later in the book.

During World War I Solborg served as a private in the 42nd Infantry Division with then Major Donovan. Solborg would end the war as a captain. After the war, Solborg became a special representative for the American Rolling Mill Company (ARMCO) selling Iron Sheets to foreign countries, including Russia. During this time, he spent many years in Paris, France and 1939 he was the company's managing director for Britain and France. At some point Solborg, as an American intelligence officer was selected as a liaison to British intelligence for whom he also conducted espionage missions. Using ARMCO as a cover, Solborg became a top intelligence agent, reporting on German war production, including a visit to Germany during the first year of World War II. In December 1940, U.S. Army intelligence sent him on secret missions throughout Portugal, Spain, and the Vichy French territories of North Africa. It was during his work for British intelligence he became close friends with Dick Ellis, later to become William Stephenson deputy at BSC. It can logically be assumed therefore that Solborg knew Stephenson prior to the entry of the United States into the war. Also, for several years before the war, Stephenson was closely connected to the Pressed Steel Company which provided metal to the British automotive industry and likely did business with ARMCO.

In the fall of 1941, Colonel Solborg departed for London on orders from General Donovan to tour SOE bases in England and Scotland. This was the first time an American officer had been allowed access to the SOE program and what Colonel Solborg saw really impressed him. He also received permission to be an active participant in the training, learning firsthand about the more lethal aspects of the business. He was even awarded "honorary" commando status, complete with a swagger stick and black beret.

When Solborg returned to the states he briefed Donovan on his ideas for subversion, sabotage, and guerrilla warfare. He told Donovan that operations should include the dissemination of black propaganda, the sabotage of enemy transportation, communications, and military installations, and the "fomenting, organizing, equipping, training, and leading of disaffected elements under enemy rule." Solborg also suggested that sabotage alone would not be sufficient but must be able to incite revolution starting with passive resistance and moving toward open violence. The basic concept was to establish an American force that could be inserted into Europe to assist, train and organize oppressed peoples to carry on secret warfare behind enemy lines.

Meanwhile, William Stephenson had established a highly classified secret agent training base in Canada known as Special Training School No. 103, (unofficially known as Camp X). The camp was established December 6, 1941 on the very eve of Pearl Harbor. There after it provided covert warfare training for American, British and Canadian operatives assigned to the COI (later OSS), SOE, and British secret service organizations. The Royal Canadian Mounted Police and FBI also trained at the facility. Camp X was shut down after the war. The site is the location today of Intrepid Park.

It is known that Colonel Solborg had difficultly working with Donovan and was critical of the way he managed the COI. In February 1942 Solborg was dispatched to Lisbon, to set up COI operations in neutral Portugal—a vital overseas station at the time. There he was to work closely with the American diplomat Robert Daniel Murphy who was part of the American diplomatic corps. Murphy was active in making clandestine contact with French and Arab underground movements in an attempt to sway them to the Allied cause.

Murphy, like William Donovan, hailed from an Irish Catholic family. A graduate of George Washington University, he started his career as a Postal Clerk but transferred to the Consular Service. Before the war he had various assignments in Europe including Bern, Zurich, Munich, Seville, and Paris. In Munich he had personally witnessed Adolf Hitler's attempt to seize control of the Bavarian government in 1923. Throughout the 1930s Murphy rose through the ranks of the State Department, and in 1940 was a senior diplomat at the American Embassy in Paris.

After France surrendered to Germany in June 1940, the French government was dissolved and a new puppet state was formed. The new government departed

Paris and established a capitol in the town of Vichy. The French leader of the Vichy state was Marshal Henri Philippe Petain, a World War I hero, who administered the southern part of France, while the northern part remained under German military occupation.

The U.S. Embassy also vacated Paris at this time and moved the American diplomatic mission to Vichy. In addition to Daniel Murphy, the embassy staff included, U.S. Army attaché Major Robert A. Schow and U.S. Navy attaché Commander Roscoe H. Hillenkoetter. After the war, Major Schow would rise to be a senior Army general and director of the CIA's Office of Special Operations (OSO), meanwhile, Hillenkoetter would attain the rank of admiral, and later serve as the first director of the Central Intelligence Agency.

From Vichy, Murphy set about leading U.S. covert diplomacy with various French underground movements, and although independent of Donovan's COI, worked very closely with Donovan's senior agents such as Colonel Solborg. Intelligence soon arrived from COI field officers that the Vichy-controlled areas of North Africa were not effectively under German control and ripe for exploitation. This gained the interest of the American government and Daniel Murphy was selected to explore options to advance the political and military situation in the North African region.

Two options for gaining control of the region soon emerged from this intelligence. One came from Donovan, the other from Colonel Solborg. Donovan's plan was a plot involving the removal of the pro–Vichy Arab Prime Minister, bypassing any direct manipulation of the French government. However, Murphy did not like Donovan's plan believing it potentially harmful to American–French relations and cancelled it. Instead he favored another plan being explored by Colonel Solborg. This plan revolved around Solborg's primary contact with the French underground, Jacques Lemaigre-Dubreuil, one of Solborg's prewar business contacts. Lemaigre was a wealthy businessman. He was also active in a plot to remove the French Vichy government in North Africa. Lemairge had developed, along with another Frenchman, Henri d'Astier de la Vigerie, a plan to incite a coup d'état in the French colonial army replacing the Vichy officials and establishing a pro–Allied provisional government.

LA CAGOULE—THE HOODED ONES

An important network in the secret scheming of Lemaigre was a group with far-reaching implications for Otto Skorzeny and others in this book. This was a prewar fascist-leaning organization called the Comite de Secret Action Révolutionnaire, or Secret Committee of Revolutionary Action, nicknamed *"La Cagoule,"* or "Hooded Ones." The origins of this dangerous secret organization lie in the divisions that existed within the French political system prior to World War II. Basically, *La Cagoule* was a secret Catholic brotherhood that was vehemently anti-Communist and had as a goal the return of the French monarchy.

The *Cagoule* directed violent action against Communists and operated from 1935–1937. It conducted ruthless assassinations and bombings to achieve its objectives. Eventually infiltrated by the French government, the organization was never fully rooted out, and an element existed within the French military. Its imprisoned members were released at the outbreak of the war to defend France. Lemairge network was heavily populated with *Cagoule* men making the secret enterprise very dangerous. It was these men with whom Colonel Solborg was negotiating.

In the development of the Lemaigre scheme, Solborg worked closely with COI operative, Colonel William A. Eddy, a highly decorated Marine who had been assigned to Donovan's COI in Tangier, Morocco. In the days and weeks that passed Colonel Eddy requested large sums of money, arms, and equipment for the French in preparation of the Lemaigre plan. Donovan however, was highly skeptical of these requests, as was the American military Joint Chiefs. In April, the Joint Chiefs of Staff decided not to back the Lemaigre plan. Instead, funding was designate for the buildup of guerrilla groups in anticipation of a North African invasion by the Allies. Disheartened by the negative response from Washington Colonel Eddy turned back to Donovan's original plan of supporting the Arabs, this time in Spanish Morocco.

Suddenly, there was a turn of events. At the end of May, Daniel Murphy was once again in communication with Lemaigre and reopened secret discussion pertaining to support for Lemaigre underground. Then new discussions developed involving the idea of installing General Henri Giraud, a military war hero, as the head of a temporary French government in North Africa. The champion of this new plan was Colonel Solborg who began high-level talks with various leaders to gain their support. Solborg traveled to London and met with General Charles de Gaulle, the leader of the French Army, who had escaped to England in June 1940 and designated the Free French Forces. Solborg was not impressed with General de Gaulle but reported to Donovan that de Gaulle was supportive of Giraud.

By June 1942, Solborg had undertaken a secret mission to North Africa to meet with Lemaigre who claimed to have General Giraud's support and a plan for the takeover of Vichy North Africa. Shortly after the meeting, Lemaigre departed for Vichy to confer secretly with Giraud, who was also a former member of the *Cagoule*.

Despite acting in concert with Daniel Murphy's encouragement to meet with Lemaigre, Solborg had not informed General Donovan of his trip to North Africa.

Meanwhile, on June 13, 1942, the OSS was authorized by President Franklin D. Roosevelt, selecting General Donovan as its first and only commander.

On June 15, a furious Donovan directed Solborg to stop all secret negotiations with the Lemaigre group and report immediately to Washington. Despite Colonel Solborg's pleas and assurances that no promises were made and that the plan was a viable option, Donovan was intransigent. In addition to insubordination, Donovan was concerned that any failure at this early stage in the formation of the OSS might endanger its existence. He subsequently relieved Solborg as Deputy for Special Operations, who then returned to Lisbon as military attaché, a post he would retain until the end of the war. Despite the reports of friction between Donovan and Solborg the entire affair could have been a ruse.

It was Colonel Solborg who set in motion the political intrigues between the Allies and the former *Cagoule* network of Frenchman. After Solborg's departure secret contact with the French resistance in North Africa was taken over by Robert D. Murphy and Colonel William A. Eddy. The next stage of events revolved around how the OSS could support an Allied invasion of North Africa which had been selected as the first large-scale combined effort against the Nazis in Europe. The plan which involved American, British, and other Commonwealth troops was set for November 1942. Lemaigre's underground meanwhile prepared for assisting the Allied landings, although the exact date remained a top secret.

THE DARLAN AFFAIR

The allies invaded North Africa on November 1942 at which time Lemaigre implemented his plans with Henri d'Astier leading a coup in the city of Algiers. During the coup the Resistance arrested the commander of Vichy forces Admiral François Darlan. The Allies had also secretly brought to North Africa General Henri Giraud in a coordinated attempt by Robert Murphy to secretly maneuver the general into position to take charge of French forces in North Africa. Although a respected general he was not recognized by the Vichy French forces opposing the Allied landings.

Unable to resolve the situation with Giraud, the Allies then negotiated with Admiral Darlan, who was the legitimate Vichy authority, thus ending French hostilities toward the Allies. A deal was then struck with Darlan remaining in control of the civilian government and General Giraud retained as military commander. After some intense negotiations Darlan ordered a Vichy-force ceasefire ending the short battle between the French forces opposing the Allied landings. Subsequently, Darlan signed an armistice with the Allies, incorporating the Vichy forces into the Free French military then under General de Gaulle. Darlan was not however trusted by the Free French.

Suddenly, on Christmas Eve, 1942, Darlan was assassinated by Fernand Bonnier de la Chapelle, a 20-year-old royalist, who had slipped out of France to North Africa after the German invasion in 1940. After the Allied invasion, Bonnier joined *Corps Franc d'Afrique*, a paramilitary security force, formed by Henri d'Astier. After d'Astier was appointed Deputy Secretary of the Interior he continued to maintain contact with the corps and met several times with Bonnier, who served as a courier, prior to the assassination of Darlan. The entire incident is recorded in history as the Darlan Affair.

The day after the assassination Bonnier was convicted in a trial that lasted less than an hour and sentenced to death, but the case was turned over to a military tribunal. Bonnier stated he had acted strictly for moral reasons. The military court rejected further inquiries into the facts as well as a number of pleas for mercy. Although the law required that Bonnier's case be heard by the French head of state, a high commissioner pronounced the sentence should to go forward. At this point, General Giraud, who was then head of military justice as commander-in-chief, ordered the execution to be carried out. Before Bonnier died he attempted to implicate Henri d'Astier but the confession was never revealed. The very day of the execution Giraud was elected to replace Darlan. Henri d'Astier had attempted an appeal for Bonnier but was told it was too late.

Darlan's sudden murder removed major political obstacles in the relationship between the Allies, the Free French Forces of de Gaulle, and the French Resistance movement. Was a conspiracy at play in the French admiral's murder? Could the Americans, British, Free French, or Lemaigre's underground network have carried out the assassination? Historians have examined this question in great detail with no clear answer, although the coincidental evidence suggests Henri d'Astier.

This book may provide information that will eventually be useful in resolving the mystery of the Darlan assassination. More research is needed. Perhaps the most relevant point at this juncture is the Darlan Affair could be considered a model in an assassination operation for establishing a fall guy or patsy. That being said, the reader may have already picked up on the similarities between the Darlan assassination and the JFK assassination involving Lee Harvey Oswald twenty-one years later. It is also telling that the men and organizations mentioned in this chapter will continue to be important characters throughout the history presented in this book.

CHAPTER TWO

THE FATE OF THE OSS

When you fall, my friend,
Another friend will emerge
From the shadows
To take your place

FROM SOE/OSS GREETING CARD

By early 1943 it was determined that the senior officer in the OSS should have military rank. Up to this point, Donovan, who held a commission as a colonel in the US Army Reserve, had served in a civilian capacity. Then, on April 2, 1943, he was promoted to brigadier general and returned to active duty. Unknown to General Donovan, or any other Allied officer at the time, only sixteen days after Donovan's promotion, the Germans conducted a promotion of their own—one that had far reaching implications for this history. On April 18, 1943, an obscure reserve SS officer by the name of Otto Skorzeny was advanced to *Hauptsturmführer* (Captain) and assumed command of a new German commando group. Despite the significant difference in their ranks, Captain Skorzeny was the German counterpart to General Donovan. In the last two years of the war both Donovan and Skorzeny would leave an indelible mark on the history of World War II. Unbeknownst to either man, they were headed for a rendezvous with destiny.

From 1943 to 1945 the various branches of the OSS conducted multiple activities and missions. At its height the organization employed almost 24,000 men and woman. A large part of the organization was involved in analyzing information from open sources such as newspapers to information obtained by espionage. In the meantime, the Special Intelligence and Special Operations branches performed acts of sabotage, waged a propaganda war, organized and coordinating anti–Nazi resistance groups in Europe, and provided military training and formed special teams for highly sensitive missions such as acquiring Nazi nuclear materials.

The OSS also worked very closely with the British SOE. Prior to the invasion of Europe special teams were formed under Operation Jedburgh to infiltrate, mainly by parachute, small four-man "Jedburgh" teams composed of British, American, French, Dutch, and Belgian SOE/OSS operatives. These were highly dangerous missions with orders to link up with local resistance groups and carry out guerrilla warfare. The Jedburgh missions paved the way for the large landing forces on D-Day, June 6, 1944.

Also formed at this same time was a joint SOE/OSS headquarters designed the Special Force Headquarters (SFHQ) to handle OSS and SOE management in the European Theater. The new headquarters formation did not change the functions of the two organization but directed their activities in an increased collaborative effort. Joint SOE/OSS units were then assigned to the various field armies.

ASSASSINATION OPERATIONS

Both the Allies and the Axis planned and executed assassination missions. That being said, it is very possible that the OSS, SOE, or both were involved in the Darlan Affair outlined above. The American OSS had learned about the darker arts of assassination from the British, who had their own capabilities housed within special sections of the SOE and Special Air Service (SAS). Section X of the SOE was specifically tasked with the assassination of German leaders. Operation Foxley was a plan to liquidate Adolf Hitler. The operation was not declassified until 1998. Other Third Reich personalities were also on SOE target lists including the main subject of this book, Otto Skorzeny. One of the most famous SOE assassination operations, conducted in May 1942, was codenamed Anthropoid. In the operation, two Czechs trained by the SOE were parachuted into their country where they successful carried out a grenade attack on Reinhard Heydrich, head of the Reich Main Security Office.

The Americans also formed special OSS units tasked with assassination. In one dramatic case, General Donovan issued an order to OSS Captain Aaron Bank to target Hitler. The OSS plan was codenamed Operation Iron Cross. Colonel Bank's special unit included a detachment of German Americans who were to be parachuted into Bavaria—their mission, kill or capture Hitler at his mountain headquarters near Berchtesgaden. The author interviewed a member of Colonel Bank's intelligence team, Tom Polgar, who later became a senior CIA officer. Ultimately, Operation Iron Cross was never carried out, coming too close to the end of the war when events were moving decidedly in the Allies favor.

THE FINAL MISSIONS OF THE OSS

In December 1944, with the end of the war in Europe in sight, the OSS received orders to begin securing documentation on Hitler's government and military organizations that would be required for a postwar prosecution into war crimes and Nazi atrocities. The OSS was already involved in various secret acquisition missions that included securing scientific personnel, research and development archives, advanced technology, military intelligence and a host of other pertinent materials.

In the fall of 1944, General Donovan submitted a secret memorandum to the White House (at President Roosevelt's request) outlining the creation of a postwar U.S. intelligence agency. The plan included a unified intelligence organization with representation from the Army, Navy, and State. Donovan's idea was supported by some influential military commanders within the government, including the General Omar Bradley. Donovan explained that a need for such an agency would be required to deal with the complexities of a postwar environment. The proposal specifically called for maintaining specialized OSS personnel and warned that they should not be dispersed.

Meanwhile, back in Washington, D.C., there were strong calls for the dissolution of the OSS as an unnecessary organization in time of peace. Actually, the

OSS had often been at odds with other intelligence branches during the entire period of the war. Army intelligence and J. Edgar Hoovers's FBI in particular disliked the OSS and Donovan.

Donovan was fully aware of the animosity towards him but continued the attempt to save the OSS. But his was to no avail. Unfortunately, (for Donovan) his proposal for a centralized intelligence organization became public, reportedly leaked by FBI Director Hoover. Touted in the press as an American Gestapo, the exposed plan caused great political turmoil resulting in the shelving of the entire matter. President Roosevelt, who held General Donovan in high esteem, then intervened and revived the proposal just one week before he died.

All of this was reversed again once Vice President Harry Truman assumed the Presidency. In the wake of President Roosevelt's death, a scathing report created by a group linked to Army G-2 (intelligence) and sent to the White House highlighting damaging information compiled from every agency that had ever lodged a complaint against the OSS. Truman would eventually act on this information and on his personal bias against Donovan. Truman had the opinion that the primary mission of the intelligence services was to provide him with daily updates on world events and not to be conducting covert action. To make matters worse, Donovan was highly vocal in his criticism of President Truman's view point on the OSS. Donovan also knew the writing was on the wall for his beloved OSS.

THE SUDDEN FORMATION OF THE BRITISH–AMERICAN–CANADIAN-CORPORATION (BACC)

British intelligence chief, Sir William Stephenson, shared the same deep concerns as General Donovan over the fate of the British secret services and SOE. Both men had not only created efficient intelligence and special operations services, but they also achieved the incredibly difficult task of creating organizations that worked well together. Both men were loath to relinquish the capability of their organizations as well as the special bonds of comradery and trust that had developed out of their combined efforts. In many ways the OSS and the SOE were one, and it was this effective coordination that emerged as a unique capability.

Unity of effort is one of the main principles of war—something Stephenson and Donovan understood well. When the war ended, the close bonds that had existed between the two organizations was seized upon by Donovan's critics as a security risk, highlighting the foreign intelligence connection to American intelligence. But Stephenson and Donovan remained undeterred and it was at this critical point in the history for their organizations that they moved expeditiously to save what they could.

Suddenly, in May 1945, Stephenson and a small circle of associates moved on the formation of a highly enigmatic private corporation called British–American–Canadian-Corporation, S.A. (BACC). The New York based company was formed with a Panamanian registry. It operated in New York in the same building that served as the headquarters for Stephenson's BSC. Nearly all of its corporate officers and almost all of its rank and file were former intelligence officers. Two of Stephenson top partners in the corporation were senior-level British intelligence officers Sir Charles Hambro and Colonel Rex L. Benson. In civilian life Benson was a merchant banker and put up most of the money for the new corporation. Hambro was also a powerful merchant banker and highly decorated World War I Veteran. At the beginning of World War II, he joined the Ministry of Economic Warfare to oversee several departments of the SOE including the French, Belgian, German and Dutch sections, also for five months beginning in November 1941, he was SOE deputy. He was involved in the earliest coordination with William Donovan over the start-up of an American organization for covert action.

Considering Stephenson and Donovan's extensive intelligence background the creation of BACC is most unusual indeed, especially when one considers the timing. But, the SOE had been part of the Ministry of Economic Warfare, a critical factor in the upcoming analysis. There is also every indication that General Donovan was directly involved in the formation of BACC as well. His OSS personnel represented a vital component of the overall salvage plan. Actually, from the start of BACC's formation, Donovan's law firm acted as the corporate legal advisery group. Newspapers covering the formation of BACC state that the company exported such things as adding machines, textiles, excavators, automobile equipment of all kinds, heavy machinery, tractors, chemicals, botanical drugs, waxes, gums, seeds, and fixed oils.

ANOTHER MYSTERIOUS FORMATION—
THE WORLD COMMERCE CORPORATION (WCC)

Following closely the formation of Stephenson's BACC was a separate company formed on August 13, 1945, called the World Commerce Corporation (WCC). The formation of WCC is directly linked to former OSS personnel. The president of WCC was Frank Ryan, an OSS officer who had been Chief of Special Intelligence for Spain and Portugal. During the war, Ryan had worked very closely with the previously described Colonel Robert Solborg, who managed the OSS station in Lisbon. Their close relationship will have major implications for our story down the line. Ryan, a textile exporter and business representative for J.S. Bache & Company, an investment company, had also provided a large portion of the American capitol for William Stephenson's BACC. This effectively ties the two corporations together.

Frank Ryan, was Francis "Frank" Timothy Ryan, born in Troy, New York in 1907. He remains a very mysterious character. Despite coming from a very wealthy family very little is actually known about him, or even how he entered service with the OSS. In the 1920s, Frank Ryan's father, John Jay Ryan, Sr. had founded a textile (cotton waste) business as John J. Ryan and Sons. The war found Frank in Washington, D.C., were he handled OSS operations for Spain and Portugal. In 1945, he returned to the family business which was operated by his older brother John Jay Ryan, Jr.

Frank had a reputation as a notorious playboy. His list of girlfriends after the war is impressive—model, Anita Colby, linked to actor Clark Gable; Mrs. Neal Vanderbilt, Jr.; actress Joan Fontaine; and actress Ann Miller. It was said of Ryan that he was seldom seen "with anything less than a beauty." His personal life aside, Ryan was personally selected by Donovan as the point man for the World Commerce Corporation.

The World Commerce corporate description also included a conglomerate of worldwide businesses, and like BACC functioned mostly as an import–export company. The background of WCC and how it came into existence was actually recorded years later by a female former OSS agent who was directly involved in its formation. The participant was Betty Lussier, a.k.a. Aline, Countess of Romanones. She served in the OSS in Spain from January 1944 to August 1945 and had worked directly with Frank Ryan during the war.

Her account of the WCC formation can be found in *The Secrets War: The Office of the Strategic Services of World War II*, edited by George C. Chalou. Lussier recounted her transition from the OSS to the WCC—"In August 1945, a cable came in from Washington ordering the immediate return of all OSS employees in Spain and the termination of all networks that had been working for us. That same week, I received a surprise. An OSS official from Washington visited and informed me that I was the only one of our SI group to be kept on for work in a *supersecret organization* inside Spain," (emphasis added). She continued, "I was told that this would depend on my being able to get my visa extended to permit me to remain in the country. A cable showing I had a serious job to reopen offices of the American firm of John J. Ryan and Sons, in Madrid." So secret was the new organization that the acting Ambassador Walter Butterworth made Lussier swear on a Bible not to reveal the organizations formation." Lussier said she had no problems taking the oath as she "believed" she "would be working for some other intelligence department of the U.S. government."

Shortly, thereafter Lussier opened an office in Madrid for John J. Ryan and Sons. Then, she was "abruptly ordered to leave for Paris." There she was to "work with a company called World Commerce, Inc." She further explained this move—"I took for granted that this was my new cover. I worked with Jack Okie there, who had been in the [OSS] Lisbon SI station. We did more or less the same work in Paris as in Madrid—opened offices, initiated business with French firms, and handled barter of products between Czechoslovakia and Sweden. Then suddenly, 6 months later I was asked to proceed to Zurich, where I opened bank accounts for World Commerce and established an office there for the same company."

In closing out her comments on World Commerce Lussier stated, "I had the impression that I would essentially be organizing networks for information on Soviet intelligence activities. I was scheduled to move to Prague to open offices there when I married. Only 40 years later did I learn that this company was not openly being used as a cover for U.S. intelligence, even though everybody I saw and worked with during the two years in that job had been an OSS agent in one country or another. The company's set-up seems to have been a precursor to the Iran-Contra situation, where sales from private companies were used to bolster pro-U.S. groups in a foreign country."

Lussier's husband was in fact Ricardo Sicre, another former OSS agent that had operated in Spain during the war. He was also vice president of World Commerce Corporation. Certainly, a man worthy of an independent study, Ricardo Sicre was a top agent of William Donovan and had conducted a number of sensitive black jobs for the general, including an operation to penetrate the Spanish Embassy in Washington in 1942. An extremely handsome man of Spanish descent, Sicre accomplished this mission by seducing unsuspecting secretaries, after which, he broke into the embassy at night, cracked the safe, photographed the contents, and exited with volumes of classified documents. Later, Sicre, placed under Frank Ryan, was transferred to the OSS station in Spain. There he used the alias Richard Stickler. Sicre would later set up a training school for spies who crossed into Vichy, France from Spain. It was during this period, that he met agent Lussier and, disregarding OSS policy, began a romance that eventually resulted in their marriage. Sicre ended the war as an Army captain and was awarded the Bronze Star for his dangerous exploits. He also became an American citizen.

Both Sicre and Lussier belonged to Special Counterintelligence (SCI) within X-2, the Counter Espionage Branch of OSS. SCI was the most highly classified section within the OSS since it was linked to the ULTRA program. ULTRA was the super-secret allied communications intercept program used against the Nazis. SCI had operational priority over both Secret Intelligence (SI) and Special Operations (SO). Its main purpose was to pass counterintelligence information between military units and to conduct a wide range of counterintelligence activity from deception to targeting of enemy networks.

PROJECT SAFEHAVEN

The timing and people involved in the events described above indicate William Stephenson and General Donovan had secretly transferred elements of their old organizations over to the private enterprises BACC and WCC even before the formal decision had been made to disband their official organizations. What then was the purpose behind the formation of BACC and WCC?

The answer is found in the wartime placement of the SOE under the umbrella of the Ministry of Economic Warfare that had the mission of blockading Germany and also securing Nazi assets. Here, the Skorzeny papers added an invaluable piece to the equation, since, as the reader will soon find out, the Skorzeny business papers are in fact, connected to World Commerce Corporation. Both OSS veterans, Frank Ryan and Ricardo Sicre, are found in the Skorzeny papers. Specific revelations from the Skorzeny papers will also confirm that BACC and WCC were born out of a highly classified project known as SAFEHAVEN.

The SAFEHAVEN effort actually began in May 1944, when the Allies had concerns that the Nazis could use hidden assets to reconstitute a Fourth Reich or escape justice. For this reason, U.S. and British intelligence units were formed to track down and block German assets in neutral and non-belligerent countries throughout Europe and the Americas. The Ministry of Economic Warfare created special committees to carry of SAFEHAVEN objectives. These groups were composed of both SOE and OSS personnel, hence the later use of both.

A major target of SAFEHAVEN was a vast German corporate entity known as Sociedad Financiera Industrial, or SOFINDUS. The corporation also served as cover for a vast Nazi intelligence network that extended into South America. The SOFINDUS network was controlled in Berlin from the same Reich security office that controlled Otto Skorzeny's commandos, although located in a different branch. Importantly, Skorzeny was fully aware of all operational aspects of SOFINDUS and its agent network. In the field, the SOFINDUS network was controlled out of Madrid, Spain, with tentacles in France, North Africa and South America. SAFEHAVEN was one of the primary reasons for the formation of BACC and WCC and the recall of SOE and OSS personnel to Spain.

There is a multitude of other collaborating evidence to support the conclusion that BACC and WCC were part of SAFEHAVEN, but for brevity, the author will cite only a few. For example, one of the senior corporate officers of BACC was George Huhle Merten who had been in charge of Operation George, an OSS investigation into enemy penetrations of South America. The target of Operation George would have been the SOFINDUS network. Also, another individual who worked with BACC, but was not a formal member, was Nelson Rockefeller, the wartime coordinator of inter-American affairs, the U.S. intelligence agency that intercepted Nazi activity in South America.

Finally, there was the public announcement in numerous U.S. Newspapers on September 25, 1945 that Nazi assets were being seized in Spain by the Allies. The article specifically mentions SOFINDUS. Since the date of the article matches the events described above it presents further evidence that SOFINDUS assets seizure and the formation of the World Commerce Corporation are linked. More details of the importance of SOFINDUS and its significance to Otto Skorzeny's personal archive, will be revealed in detail later in this book.

During the formation period of the WCC, General Donovan engaged in extensive world travel, including to the Far East, where he consulted with OSS officers in that theater. At the end of September, he departed for Germany. Ultimately, only a limited number of Donovan's former OSS operatives were recruited into the WCC, meanwhile other OSS personnel were slated to remained in government service.

THE FORMATION OF THE STRATEGIC SERVICES UNIT (SSU)

Happening simultaneously with the formation of World Commerce Corporation was an end to Donovan's seemingly futile struggle to save the OSS. Yielding to political pressure, but over the strong objections of Donovan, President

Truman signed Executive Order 9621 on September 20, 1945, terminating the OSS organization. Given the timing of the formation of WCC and President Truman's order for OSS disbandment, the events seem odd. Either there is truth to the accepted version of history that Donovan was at odds with Truman or perhaps there was a strategic deception at play. It is possible the friction between the two was a ruse to hide from the Soviets the fact that the United States had secretly shifted OSS capabilities under a commercial cover to recover Nazi assets. Either way, that is exactly what happened.

On September 26, 1945, Brigadier General John Magruder, Donovan's former Deputy Director for Intelligence and Assistant Secretary of War John J. McCloy reportedly circumvented President Truman's disbandment order and acted to save what they could of certain OSS branches. In this administrative action, OSS officers from the Special Operations branch and Special Intelligence branch were transferred to a new governmental organization, the Strategic Services Unit (SSU). General Magruder was then placed in charge of the SSU which was officially formed on October 1, 1945. Also under this revision, another branch of the OSS, the Research and Analysis Branch, was absorbed by the State Department's Interim Research and Intelligence Service.

DONOVAN LEAVES FOR GERMANY AND MEETS WITH OTTO SKORZENY

Immediately after the disbandment of the OSS, Donovan headed for Germany to close out OSS business, and with the creation of the World Commerce Corporation, to make back-channel arrangements for the recruitment of OSS personnel for the WCC. During this final tour as head of the OSS another event will transpire that can be added to the enigmatic history described above, especially in regard to the mysterious formation the WCC. This is also one with far reaching implications for the history presented in this book.

In early November 1945 General Donovan would interrogate SS Lt. Colonel Otto Skorzeny, wartime chief of Hitler's commandos, who was being held as a POW in Nuremberg. The event was mentioned by Skorzeny in his memoirs, *My Commando Operations*: "Donovan asked to see me during my time in Nuremburg Prison. The meeting was very cordial; there was neither victor nor vanquished, just two soldiers, both rather dare devilish and inventive, who had served their countries to the best of their ability." Skorzeny also claimed he did not know at the time who Donovan was and only found out later that he had met his "counterpart on the American side."

The meeting between Donovan and Skorzeny was held in a large briefing room at the Nuremberg detention facility. Also present were several senior staff officers who have never been identified. We do know the meeting lasted for some time. With the revelations cited above concerning the formation of the WCC and its role in Project SAFEHAVEN it is likely Donovan's meeting with Skorzeny was not a routine interrogation but rather a sounding out. He was there to see firsthand the man entrusted to carry out Germany's most secret missions and evaluate his inside knowledge of Nazi assets for possible inclusion in asset recovery operations.

In December, General Donovan announced his retirement. That same month the OSS was assigned the tasked to support the International War Crimes Tribunal under the leadership of Supreme Court Justice Robert Jackson. Justice Jackson had been selected by President Truman as chief counsel for the prosecution of Nazi war criminals. During his final days in Europe as OSS chief Donovan would clash with Justice Jackson over the procedures for handling high-ranking Nazi officials and the methods to be used to acquire testimony for the trials.

Meanwhile Back in Washington the Joint Chiefs of Staff were still in discussions about intelligence priorities and missions leading to a proposal for a new organization under the control of the State, War, and Navy departments, with each still retaining individual service intelligence branches. President Truman approved the proposal and subsequently on January, 22, 1946, the Central Intelligence Group or CIG was formed absorbing the only recently formed Strategic Services Unit (SSU). The CIG was the direct predecessor of the CIA.

THE MYSTERIOUS WAR DEPARTMENT DETACHMENT (WDD)

As time progressed in the immediate postwar period intelligence analysts noted that the threat of the anticipated Nazi underground turned out to be minimal, but a larger issue became apparent. This was the escalation of espionage by the Soviets and their allies, and the failure of the Soviet forces to demobilize their forces. This activity lead to mounting fears of a Soviet invasion of the West. It also changed the priorities of the OSS which was diverted from its initial post-war mission of an all-out hunt for Nazis to countering Soviet threats. This required finding agents who could operate undetected throughout Europe and had the type of background to carry out the dangerous work. Two immediate sources for this effort were former Nazi intelligence operatives, and recruits from the vast groups of refugees flooding into Western Europe. Some of these émigrés had also worked for the Nazis or, in some cases, the Soviets, but they were willing to change sides.

But there were problems, Army counterintelligence CIC also begun establishing its own clandestine networks with these same individuals. To make matters even more complicated, special intelligence units from Britain and France were also immersed in similar activity. In many cases, these secret networks were not aware of each other, and intense competition developed for control of assets.

Initially, coordination was very difficult, and activity was conducted in an ad hoc way or with no central planning. There were also local commanders running their own operations without any authorization. It took months to create positive working relationships and effective direction.

On the American side Allen Dulles, the senior OSS officer in Europe, later to become the iconic director of the CIA, set up a special unit designated the War Department Detachment (WDD), near Wiesbaden, to handle the removal or retention of agent networks and agents. The WDD was actually a cover name for the newly formed Strategic Services Unit (SSU). Dulles was specifically chosen because of his control of a number of extensive agent networks all over Europe. He was also a loyal friend to General Donovan leaving in place a conduit for Donovan to maintain excellent contacts within the SSU.

During the war, Dulles, from his station in Bern, Switzerland, had penetrated German intelligence to include important clandestine contacts inside the dreaded SS. It is even possible Dulles had been in contact with Skorzeny at the end of the war. This is however highly speculative and is still being researched by the author. As head of the WDD, Dulles retained management of his secret records to prevent exposure of former spies and double agents who had operated secretly for the Allies, and in some cases, were still being utilized as covert assets. The WDD also managed the disposition of former members of Nazi intelligence services and the Gestapo.

One of the initial priority requirements of the WDD was working with the International Military Tribunal in Nuremberg. The vast records compiled by the OSS on German intelligence and its operatives were considered vital for the Nuremberg Trial effort and it was Allen Dulles who handled these sensitive matters given his extensive knowledge of German clandestine networks. The mission of the tribunal was to prosecute prominent members of the Nazi party, including German military leaders, judges, and economists suspected of war crimes. Since the War Department Detachment controlled access to sensitive SS, SD, and Gestapo data, the interaction between members of the WDD and the Nuremberg staff included oversight of Otto Skorzeny's records and trial proceedings.

The senior officer at the heart of all document handling for the Nuremberg Trials was a USAF intelligence officer and OSS veteran, Colonel Robert G. Storey, who hailed from Dallas, Texas. Colonel Storey was also one of the very few officers in the entire U.S. military privy to ULTRA. Years later, Storey would play a very prominent role as an independent attorney working with the Warren Commission after the assassination of President John F. Kennedy. The National Archives website for records pertaining to the assassination states that Storey, had been "fully informed at all times as to the progress of the [Warren Commission] investigation."

Storey noted in his personal memoirs that Allen Dulles had provided invaluable assistance to his division during Nuremberg. When Dulles departed Europe to return to his law practice at the end of 1945 he would be replaced, on the orders of General Donovan, by OSS Attorney, James B. Donovan. The Attorney Donovan would in later years become a high-level CIA officer. During the Cold War it was James Donovan who was sent to East Germany to coordinate the exchange of U-2 pilot Gary Powers for the Soviet spy, Colonel Vilyam Fisher, a.k.a. "Rudolf Abel." The story was the basis for Steven Spielberg's movie *Bridge of Spies*, released in 2015.

Despite having returned to civilian life, Allan Dulles remained a high-level consultant to government officials involved in the transformation of intelligence organizations and the formation of official and unofficial organizations in support of new covert initiatives. As time progressed through the period of the Nuremburg Trials, the WDD would be involved with the recruitment and redirection of clandestine assets toward new intelligence priorities. Dulles had originally assigned former OSS operative Frank Wisner to manage the first agent activities of the WDD and to develop new spy networks. These new areas of interest included military, political, and security structures, as well as Germany's industrial, economy, and scientific elements. The program even extended into Germany's social, religious, cultural, and educational institutions. Knowledge of WDD activity was above top secret and known only to the highest levels of the U.S. government at the time.

Wisner divided his group into a Steering Division and a Production Division. The Steering Division was directed by Army Captain Harry Rositzke, who established liaison with other U.S. and friendly foreign intelligence organizations. He also established relationships with labor and church groups. These relationships allowed for the development of intelligence networks.

The Production Division was focused on agent recruiting and acted on the requirements generated from the Steering Division. Production Units, or "P Units," were formed across Western Europe and in the American Zone of Germany. An extremely sensitive area for the Production Division was the control of Allen Dulles's "Crown Jewels," or high-level secret agents Dulles had controlled during the war.

In 1946, when Frank Wisner left Germany for the United States, his successor was Crosby Lewis. Lewis had previously served as Chief of X-2 (Security Control Group) in Germany. Lewis was subsequently replaced by Gordon M. Stewart in March 1947. The Executive Officer for the WDD from 1946 until 1949 was Louis E. Kubler, a veteran of World War I. Before joining the military

Kubler had served eighteen years as a New Jersey State Policeman and had been called to testify as a fingerprint specialist during the famous Lindbergh kidnapping case in 1935.

THE BRITISH SOE IS DISBANDED

The British SOE would share a similar fate as its American OSS counterpart. Like General Donovan, senior British intelligence officers, such as Sir William Stephenson, proposed saving the organization after the war. The course of the British government in this regard is far murkier than the more documented disbandment of the American OSS. Winston Churchill, who had been the biggest advocate of the SOE, seriously considered keeping the organization realizing that the Soviet Union was rising as a major adversary to the West. But Churchill's loss in a general election in July 1945 removed the fate of the SOE from his able stewardship. As a matter of course, the new British prime minister, Clement Attlee held similar views as President Truman and ordered the SOE closed down. This occurred on January 15, 1946. William Stephenson's British Security Coordination (BSC) was to soon follow. Most of Stephenson agents returned to civilian life but he kept a small staff on until the middle of 1946. General Donovan too had quietly retired to civilian life having assumed his old law practice in New York in January 1946.

CHAPTER THREE
OTTO SKORZENY

"Otto Skorzeny worked differently. He was not a pre-war soldier, but a gifted amateur forced into the military by circumstances of the war."

CHARLES WHITING
SKORZENY: BALLANTINE'S ILLUSTRATED HISTORY, 1972

"I never learned to click my heels. I was never taken in by the conventions they call the 'military art.' But I have made a deep study of the soldier's mind. It is frequently too dense to go through. It is never too dense to be outflanked."

OTTO SKORZENY TO AUTHOR CHARLES FOLEY, 1955

"I did not plot to kill Eisenhower . . . naturally I should have done so if I had received the order. . . ."

OTTO SKORZENY QUOTED IN LONDON *DAILY EXPRESS*, APRIL 18, 1952

For a moment, we return once again to the interrogation of Otto Skorzeny. It was revealed previously that Colonel Rex Benson of the Secret Intelligence Service or MI6 was the lead British interrogator of Skorzeny. Benson was involved in the founding of the British–American–Canadian-Corporation (BACC). Perhaps, like many, Benson was impressed with the physical stature and characteristics of Skorzeny, who with a height of 6'4" possessed a dramatic face cut with a deep dueling scar on one side. He was also likely to have noticed

Skorzeny's calm demeanor and military bearing, which by all accounts was equally impressive.

So, who then was this man, Otto Skorzeny? Did he possess some knowledge or skills needed by Donovan and Stephenson for their hidden schemes? Were there backroom discussions about Skorzeny involving his inclusion in postwar covert planning? The answer to these questions will be delivered in the pages of this book. First, let us take a look at the remarkable early life and war record of this extraordinary yet controversial German commando.

SCARFACE

Otto Skorzeny was born in Vienna, Austria, on June 12, 1908. His father, Anton, was a successful civil engineer of the middle class. His older brother, Alfred, was also an engineer. Skorzeny's childhood years took place during the trying times of World War I, years of shortage and suffering that greatly affected young Otto. Skorzeny entered high school in 1919 and graduated in 1926, a normal length of time for the period. In school, Skorzeny excelled in mathematics and chemistry but struggled with English and French. Later in life, however, he would master the French language to the point of passing for a native speaker. His English was good but retained a German accent.

In 1926, at age 18, Skorzeny enrolled at the *Hochschule* (Technical University) in Vienna. Skorzeny credited three major influences during his college years. First were the older students who had experienced war; second, the high percentage of older teachers who were connected to the old imperial government; and third, and perhaps the most influential, the "*Schlagende Burschenshaft*," a dueling fraternity.

It was the *Burschenshaft* that was to have a major impact on Skorzeny's philosophy of life. From dueling, Skorzeny developed traits to which he would consistently adhere and later apply to military operations. Skorzeny wrote, "The original purpose of our fencing was to learn self-control. We were instructed to fight offensively and avoid being pushed into the defensive. Such training had a deeper meaning: A person who acts and thinks passively will seldom achieve success. Conversely, being active in all areas of life will bear positive results. The active person will achieve success more readily and have the greater influence than the passive one . . . I am grateful for this training, for I have often had to use it." After thirteen duels, Skorzeny received his famous nickname, "scarface." The saber cuts were his badge of honor and a constant reminder of his philosophy of war—"My knowledge of pain, learned with the saber, taught me not to be afraid and, just as in dueling when you must concentrate on your enemy's cheek, so, too, in war. You cannot waste time on feinting and sidestepping. You must decide on your target and go in."

Skorzeny mentioned in his autobiography that he originally joined the SS because they required a spotless police record and had developed a code of honor that appealed to him. By December 1938, Skorzeny had obtained the rank of *Hauptscharführer* (master sergeant), an SS rank of some authority usually associated with headquarters duties. He became active in events sponsored by the Nazi party; in particular, motorcar racing, a popular party activity. But the motorcar corps served a dual purpose, as a legitimate sport racing club to attract new members, and also as a cover for Nazi security activity, providing a rapid mobile force for party security and police augmentation. Additionally, Skorzeny was active in the German Gymnastic Association, another cover organization for Nazi party defense activity. The association with SS cover organizations even before the war proved to be fertile ground for the cultivation of knowledge that Skorzeny would later apply to covert operations.

As a senior SS leader, Skorzeny had a reputation for being cool under pressure. This got him noticed by Ernst Kaltenbrunner, head of the Austrian SS, and a friend of Skorzeny's through college dueling. Kaltenbrunner was destined to head the Reich Main Security Office (RSHA), the top Nazi organization for state security within the SS. Kaltenbrunner's selection to head the RSHA would be an important factor in the military career of Skorzeny.

On September 1, 1939, Hitler invaded Poland, plunging Europe into war. Skorzeny noted this in his memoirs, writing with dark humor, "The vacation was over." To meet his commitment for military service, Skorzeny volunteered first for the *Luftwaffe*. As a private pilot, and with his engineering background, he believed himself suited for that branch of service. His request, however, was turned down because of his height and age, thirty-one at the time. After initial training, Skorzeny was one of a handful of soldiers selected in December 1940 to be posted in the combat units of the *Waffen*-SS as an engineer officer-cadet.

By February 1940, Skorzeny had received orders to report to Berlin, where he was assigned to a reserve battalion of the elite *Waffen* SS, "*Leibstandarte*" Division. He was soon transferred to the 2nd SS *Das Reich* Division. Skorzeny's first action was the invasion of Holland in 1940. Later he saw action in Yugoslavia and in January 1942, he was promoted from sergeant to second lieutenant, or *Untersturmführer* in SS rank. In April, he single-handedly captured fifty-seven enemy soldiers, including three officers, without firing a shot, resulting in his first bravery award. Two months later, Skorzeny's division was ordered to take part in the invasion of Russia.

As a motor officer during the invasion, Skorzeny's job was to maintain the division's tanks and vehicles. His unit was in the thick of the fighting and he was often exposed to enemy fire.

After his promotion to *Obersturmführer,* or 1st lieutenant, Skorzeny became very ill with a chronic gallbladder condition. The illness was so debilitating that he had to be withdrawn from action and sent back to Germany for treatment. During his convalescence, he was posted to a vehicle repair depot in Berlin, where he contemplated his illness and Germany's military reverses, wondering if his military career was coming to an end.

In 1943, Germany had been at war for four years in a bitter contest that seemed to have no end. The situation was very serious for Germany and its allies, but Skorzeny, like many soldiers, still believed in his country and his leader, Adolf Hitler. He was convinced that Germany could turn the tide with speedy, resolute action. And Skorzeny longed for action. His current assignment as a standard regimental engineer was lackluster and undemanding. He wanted frontline action despite the dangers it entailed. Soon, fate would intervene. It is the nature of war that events can turn on a dime. In the spring of 1943, Skorzeny could hardly have realized that he was only months away from being catapulted to the very heights of military glory in an occupation far removed from the regimental motor pool.

THE RISE OF SKORZENY'S COMMANDO

Germany's first formation of special troops was small, consisting of specialized elements of highly trained saboteurs assigned to the *Abwehr,* or German intelligence service. These units saw action in the opening phases of the invasion of Poland. The members, dressed in civilian attire, would go in advance of German combat forces to destroy strategic targets and capture key bridges. As the war progressed, the unit was expanded from its original battalion size to a large division formation, but gradually moved away from its intended purpose of special missions.

In March 1943, a decision was made to expand special units using only politically reliable SS men. For the development of this force, the task fell to SS *Brigadeführer* Walter Schellenberg, head of the SD-*Ausland,* the foreign intelligence service of the SS. The reorganization would include training special agents in sabotage, espionage, paramilitary techniques, and, when called upon, performance of other high-risk missions in the same tradition of the *Brandenburgers,* an earlier special forces formation. Schellenberg created a new bureau—Section S (at first signifying "Schools" but later Sabotage). To lead this new outfit, SS headquarters began searching for a suitable commander—a politically reliable, technically proficient officer.

While stationed in Berlin, Skorzeny heard of these developments and the search for a commander to run the new unit. Inspired by the news, he moved quickly, and undertook research of Allied commando operations and the conduct of special covert warfare. He searched for every resource he could find on the topic, noting the tactics, techniques, and procedures of various Allied and Axis special forces. He took a particular interest in the causes of successes and failures, including a failed attempt by British commandos to capture General Erwin Rommel in North Africa. The more he learned, the more he envisioned a role for commando operations within the SS. Formulating his ideas on the subject, he submitted them through channels and let his interest in the subject be known.

His enthusiasm and knowledge got the attention of SS leadership and in the early part of April 1943, Skorzeny was summoned to headquarters for an interview with *Obergruppenführer* Hans Jüttner. Skorzeny also had secured a recommendation for the new position from his college dueling comrade Ernst Kaltenbrunner, head of the RSHA. He impressed Jüttner with his bearing and technical knowledge. Despite his low rank of Reserve SS *Obersturmführer* and his bouts with medical problems, Jüttner offered him the senior commando position with a promotion to SS *Hauptsturmführer* (Captain).

Skorzeny immediately accepted the position, recalling the moment he accepted the position by citing Nietzsche's famous advice: "Live dangerously!" On April 18, 1943, Skorzeny was promoted and assigned to command RSHA, Section VI-S. Skorzeny's unit would eventually be known as SS-*Jagdverband* or "Hunting Group." Skorzeny recruited personnel throughout the Reich's various military units. He wanted to acquire only those of the highest caliber and as such received special permission to recruit from all the services, not just the *Waffen* SS. Eventually, his commando group included army, navy, and air force personnel, which resulted in Skorzeny becoming the preeminent special forces commander of the Third Reich.

Besides having a foreign language requirement, the recruits had to demonstrate basic skills and knowledge of firearms, grenades, artillery, and the ability to operate automobiles, motorcycles, watercraft, and locomotives. They also had to be expert swimmers and able to parachute from aircraft. Many were capable of speaking foreign languages such as English, French, Italian, Russian, and Persian. An intense commando training regimen was instituted. Some individuals were selected for special agent training. All of Skorzeny's training was tough and included covert operations skills required for stay-behind missions in enemy territory.

Under normal command structures, the *Waffen* SS fell under the authority of the *Oberkommando der Wehrmacht* (Armed Forces High Command). However, Skorzeny's chain-of-command started with Walter Schellenberg, head of Section VI-S, then RSHA chief *Obergruppenführer* Kaltenbrunner, and finally, *Reichsführer* SS Heinrich Himmler. However, despite this command structure, Skorzeny would on several occasions take his orders directly from Hitler. At one point in the war, he carried written orders from Hitler directing all military and civilian authorities to obey his wishes, making him temporarily one of the most powerful men in the Third Reich.

For his unit command structure, Skorzeny appointed as his executive officer a friend and fellow Austrian named Karl Radl, a level-headed, intelligent man three years younger than Skorzeny. The two had known each other in the Austrian SS, and Radl was also a close friend of Skorzeny's wife, Emmi. Radl had studied law at the University of Berlin and possessed excellent staff officer qualities. Despite having originally volunteered for combat duty, Radl was attached to the SD (SS intelligence service). Radl accepted and accompanied Skorzeny, becoming an integral part of the daring missions that the unit would undertake during the war and as we shall see, remained by his side in the years afterward. There were other brave men and resourceful soldiers with Skorzeny who would accomplish or attempt great tasks with a fraction of the resources and support Allied commandos relied upon. Near the end of the war, Skorzeny would refer to these hearty fellows as his "beautiful men."

Hitler placed a great emphasis on the relationship between politics and war, and most of Skorzeny's missions had strategic political objectives. Some operations were successful, some were not, but there was never an end to Hitler's belief that missions tasked to Skorzeny could make a difference. From this point forward Skorzeny and his men would carry out some of the most daring commando actions of World War II. Skorzeny's most famous mission was a glider borne mountain top rescue of Benito Mussolini, on September 13, 1943. This mission, carried out on the direct orders of Adolf Hitler, was even praised by Germany's enemies for its daring. It was designated Operation Oak.

OPERATION OAK

The month of July 1943 was a major turning point in World War II and for Otto Skorzeny's career and notoriety. Things were not going well for Nazi Germany. On July 10, British and American forces invaded Italy, landing in the southern region of the island of Sicily. The Germans and Italian defenders put up stiff resistance but were eventually forced to retreat. The island was conquered by the Allies in just thirty-eight days, but the Germans managed to conduct a masterful evacuation of their forces to the mainland of Italy.

Across Italy, opposition to the fascist government under Mussolini was escalating, and there was a call from all quarters to end the country's involvement in the war. At a meeting of the Fascist Grand Council on July 24, a vote of no confidence was passed against Mussolini. The vote forced Mussolini, who had ruled the country for twenty-one years, to seek the support of King Emmanuel III. His appeal to the King for support was to no avail. The King instead backed the Council, appointing Marshal Badoglio head of the government.

The ousting of Mussolini was swift and orderly. After meeting with the King, Mussolini was arrested and placed under guard at an army barracks in Rome. For security reasons, he was soon transferred to the tiny island of Ponza, off the coast of Naples.

Hitler's alliance with Italy was now endangered and he demanded the immediate release of Mussolini. The new government, however, rejected Hitler's demand. It was then apparent to Hitler that Italy intended to betray its alliance with Germany and turn Mussolini over to the Allies. Hitler was now determined to rescue his friend and ally and restore the Fascist government to power. Due to the political tension in the state, conventional military options were limited. Nor did the Germans know where Mussolini was being held captive. Hitler decided on a commando operation to find and rescue the *Duce*. In order to select the right man for the high stakes mission, Hitler ordered his staff to bring to him the most qualified special operations combat officers in the Third Reich.

On July 26, 1943, Skorzeny was enjoying a drink at Hotel Eden in Berlin when the call came. He was immediately summoned to report to the *Führer*'s headquarters in Rastenburg. He arrived later that evening on a special plane dispatched to retrieve him. At the *Führer*'s headquarters, Skorzeny found several other officers of various services and backgrounds also awaiting the *Führer*'s summons. Skorzeny and the others were then ushered into a room where Hitler soon appeared to personally conduct the interviews. Despite being the lowest ranking officer amongst the group, Skorzeny impressed Hitler, especially since he, like Hitler, was Austrian. After speaking only briefly, Hitler dismissed the others and, turning to Skorzeny, announced he had selected him for the task of finding and rescuing Mussolini.

Hitler emphasized that the mission was top secret, stating only five individuals were to be informed of the true objective. Even the commander of German forces in Italy, Field Marshall Albert Kesselring, was not informed of the operation. Skorzeny was to receive his orders directly from *Reichsführer* SS Heinrich Himmler. After his initial briefings, Skorzeny called back to his unit, placing them on high alert status, ready to deploy at a moment's notice. When he returned, the entire unit was eager to volunteer for the yet-unknown secret mission, but he carefully selected fifty of his best men and departed immediately for Italy. For security reasons and to cover the operation, Skorzeny and his men donned German *Luftwaffe* paratrooper uniforms. For operational control, Skorzeny reported to General Kurt Student, who commanded Germany's airborne units in Italy. This command relationship gave Skorzeny access to logistics, transportation, intelligence, and force augmentation if needed.

Skorzeny established a base camp at an airbase near Rome and quickly set about gathering vital intelligence. This had to be done without revealing his mission, making the task of finding Mussolini extremely difficult. The latest intelligence indicated that Mussolini had been removed from Ponza Island and transferred to an Italian warship docked at the naval base in La Spezia. Assaulting a heavily armed ship with its confining quarters would have been extremely difficult. But information soon came in that Mussolini had been transferred to the tiny island of La Maddalena, near Sardinia.

Skorzeny conducted a preliminary reconnaissance of the site by boat and concluded the information was possibly correct. Next came an aerial mission on August 18 over the target. In the mission, Skorzeny flew in a bomber, taking photos of the location. But the bomber was spotted and attacked by Allied fighters, forcing the aircraft to ditch in the sea. Luckily, Skorzeny and the bomber crew were rescued by an Italian destroyer. In the crash, Skorzeny suffered three broken ribs; undaunted, however—he soldiered on.

When Skorzeny returned to Rome, a plan was devised to assault La Maddalena using fast boats, but a second reconnaissance indicated Mussolini had been moved yet again. The situation was now urgent, and time was of the essence. On September 3, the Allies made an amphibious landing on mainland Italy at Salerno, near Naples, attempting to gain a foothold. Soon thereafter, the Italian government surrendered. Hitler reacted quickly, ordering German units stationed in northern Italy to the south to reinforce those units engaged in fighting the American and British units and to stabilize the security situation within the Italian state.

While these new developments were taking place, Skorzeny received a radio intercept of an Italian police communication referring to the completion of certain security preparations at the Gran Sasso Hotel northeast of Rome. The hotel was located on the highest mountain in the Italian Apennines. Before the war, Gran Sasso was a popular ski resort. Importantly, from a military prospective, it was only accessible by cable car from the valley below.

After receiving the information, Skorzeny dispatched a paratroop medical officer under the guise of canvassing the site for a potential field hospital. After the officer was turned away by armed security, Skorzeny deduced that the intelligence might be accurate. On September 8, Skorzeny quickly flew an air reconnaissance mission over the target area, taking pictures with a plain handheld camera. When he returned, a combined attack plan was formulated by Skorzeny, with General Student and Major Harald Mors, a paratroop commander.

The photographs of the site revealed a small open area next to the hotel. Every assault option was considered, including an airborne operation and an assault from the base of the mountain. Neither option was feasible, as the target area was too small for an airborne drop and assaulting from the base would take too long. One option remained—an assault using gliders. This option would permit a rapid seizure of the hotel and could be supported with a secondary force seizing the lower cable car location. After the rescue, Mussolini could then descend the mountain by cable car and be flown to safety by an aircraft landing in the valley below.

The plan was formulated on carefully drawn maps created by Skorzeny. After a careful review, planners predicted an 80 percent casualty rate for men and gliders. It was a high-risk mission, and the odds seemed not to be in Skorzeny's favor. However, there were no other options. Time had run out and, most importantly, the *Führer* had ordered the mission. The mission, code named Operation Oak, was to proceed.

On September 11, 1943, Skorzeny and his men, along with elements of General Student's paratroopers, staged at an airfield only ten miles from Gran Sasso. The attack was set for 0700 hours the next day. There were twelve gliders assigned for the mission. The next day, the mission encountered several problems, including an attack by Allied bombers against the airfield, badly damaging the runway. This delayed the launch of the aircraft and gliders. The mission was finally underway at high noon.

There had been no time to arrange maps for the pilots, who arrived in Italy just before the raid, so they were instructed to just follow the lead aircraft, piloted by General Student's intelligence officer. In total, there were 108 men on the mission; 26 were Skorzeny's commandos and the rest were elite paratroopers from the paratroop demonstration battalion. Each glider carried nine combat soldiers. On board Skorzeny's glider was Italian General Ferdinando Soleti, a high-ranking Carabinieri whose presence with the assault force was hoped to create a momentary delay or even totally eliminate a response from the defending security force, numbering about 200 men.

Simultaneously with the air assault, a separate ground assault force under Major Hans Mors and thirty paratroops proceeded by road to seize the lower cable car objective, defend against reinforcements, and secure an area for Mussolini's rescue aircraft. Major Mors' force eliminated various roadblocks along the way.

As the air mission commenced, two planes were obstructed from take-off by bomb craters, including the only pilot who knew how to navigate to Gran Sasso. The new formation placed Skorzeny as the lead glider, but the tow pilot had no map. Skorzeny was able to talk with the pilot by means of cable communication. Thinking quickly, Skorzeny used his knife to cut a small window in the glider's bottom and then, recalling the earlier reconnaissance mission, navigated the lead aircraft to Gran Sasso.

At 1245 hours Major Mors' force reached the lower cable car location and quickly secured the facilities. High over the mountain, Skorzeny and the gliders were descending on the main objective. A new problem then revealed itself as gliders approached the ground. Skorzeny realized the landing area was strewn with boulders—but shouted for the glider pilot to crash land as close to the hotel as possible. With incredible nerve, the pilot skillfully landed the glider a mere twenty yards from the hotel.

Once on the ground, the assault forces jumped into action. Skorzeny ran forward, pushing General Soleti in front of him. Skorzeny saw Mussolini looking from a second-floor window. This was helpful, as Skorzeny now knew exactly where to go. He shouted to Mussolini to get inside to avoid being hit by possible gunfire and then continued to gain entrance to the hotel. The Italian guards were surprised by the presence of General Soleti, who shouted at them not to shoot. Skorzeny dashed upstairs, broke into Mussolini's room, and disarmed his two guards, just as two more of his men came in from the window after climbing the wall. Once Mussolini was secured, Skorzeny turned to the Italian dictator, saluted him, and declared in German, "*Duce*, the *Führer* has sent me . . . you are free."

Within a few minutes, all the Italian guards in the ski hotel and the upper cable car station were disarmed without a single shot being fired. Reinforcements were quickly sent up by cable car, led by Major Mors. The entire assault was over in just twelve minutes. As Skorzeny and his protective guard exited the building with Mussolini, they witnessed the crash of the final assaulting glider, caught in a thermal current, killing all on board. This unfortunate event resulted in the only German fatalities during Operation Oak.

The mission appeared to be nearly over, but a new problem arose. The rescue plane, a small two-seater Fieseler Storch short take-off and landing aircraft, damaged its undercarriage when landing at the base of the mountain. Skorzeny immediately called for a second rescue aircraft. The second plane was flown by Captain Heinrich Gerlach, General Student's personal pilot. Skorzeny radioed

Gerlach and ordered him to land next to the hotel. With great skill, Gerlach successfully landed the aircraft in the field strewn with boulders and assault gliders. The next challenge would be to get the aircraft off the mountain.

As paratroopers and their Italian prisoners began clearing a runway for the take-off, Skorzeny informed Gerlach that he would accompany Mussolini on the flight. Gerlach protested, citing the problems of the additional weight in the small plane. Skorzeny, however, insisted that he would go along. He would later explain this risky demand, saying that he was not willing to risk a situation in which, after a successful rescue, he would face Hitler only to report that Mussolini had crashed into the slopes of the Gran Sasso. He preferred to die too.

With Mussolini and Skorzeny crammed on board, Gerlach told the paratroopers to hold the small aircraft in place while he increased the engine's power to the maximum, and then signaled them to let go. The plane lurched forward, dropping off the edge and momentarily losing altitude, but Gerlach manage to level the aircraft off.

After a short flight, the plane landed at a German air base near Rome, where Mussolini and Skorzeny immediately transferred to a German bomber that flew them to Vienna. That same day, Mussolini was flown from Vienna directly to Hitler's headquarters at Rastenburg. Later that night, back in Vienna, Skorzeny was personally decorated with the Knight's Cross to the Iron Cross, Germany's most prestigious valor award, by a colonel dispatched under orders from Hitler. Entering Skorzeny's quarters, the colonel removed his own Knight's Cross from around his neck and placed the medal on Skorzeny. The *Führer* also placed a call to Skorzeny, congratulating him and promoting him to major.

Hitler warmly greeted Mussolini and persuaded the former dictator to demonstrate Axis solidarity by setting up a socialist government in northern Italy. The new government would give legitimacy for the German army to remain in Italy and the authority to raise new Italian forces to continue combat against the Allies.

After the Mussolini rescue, German propaganda minister Josef Goebbels masterfully promoted the success with an elaborate ceremony in Berlin decorating Skorzeny's men. The rescue event had been conveniently filmed, permitting extensive movie footage on state radio broadcasts. The author interviewed a man who heard the original broadcast proclaiming Skorzeny a hero of the Reich. Josef Goebbels proclaimed Skorzeny as "the most dangerous man in Europe." The enduring legend and notoriety of Skorzeny was born. Even Churchill acknowledged his bravery and bravado.

The object of war is to break the *will* of the enemy. Perhaps no other operation of World War II illustrated the unique contribution special forces can play, not only in tactics, but also in psychological warfare. The raid permitted the maintenance of a fascist government (albeit a weak one), and it delivered great success at a time when the German people were dealing with continual bad news from every front and a relentless reign of death from Allied bombing.

The raid was even respected by the Allies. Winston Churchill grudgingly admitted the daring of the raid in a speech before the British parliament. But the action at Gran Sasso continued to influence military thinking long after the fact.

In the fall of 2011, *Time* magazine released a special edition publication entitled *Special Ops: The Hidden World of America's Toughest Warriors.* This collector's edition was the result of the public's fascination with a spectacular Navy SEAL raid on Osama bin Laden's compound in Abbottabad, Pakistan, on May 1, 2011. The man who prepared the mission and ordered the Navy SEALs to attack the Bin Laden compound was Admiral William H. McRaven, commander of the United States Special Operations Command (USSOCOM). McRaven had started his career as a Navy SEAL and early on took an active interest in the study of unconventional warfare.

Through his studies, McRaven became well-acquainted with the exploits of Otto Skorzeny and his German commandos. In fact, McRaven focused specifically on Skorzeny's Gran Sasso mission and included an analysis of the raid in his book, *Spec Ops, Case Studies in Special Operations Warfare: Theory and Practice.* McRaven pointed out that Skorzeny's "plan to rescue Mussolini used the three elements of simplicity—limited objectives, good intelligence, and innovation— to reduce the frictions of war and improve the opportunity for success." The specific innovation was Skorzeny's inclusion of General Soleti to create hesitation among the Italian soldiers guarding Mussolini. The parallels between the Mussolini rescue and the bin Laden raid are striking, including the use of a doctor to recon the site. Obviously, Admiral McRaven learned from Otto Skorzeny.

ASSASSINATION AND ABDUCTION

Skorzeny's men could also be ruthless and, like their OSS and SOE counterparts on the Allied side, were called upon for abduction or "wet work"—assassination operations. For Hitler, the Mussolini rescue was proof that special operations forces could achieve strategic goals. The planning and execution of these types of missions were surrounded with great secrecy and, after the war, Skorzeny denied their existence. During the final two years of the conflict Hitler would issue orders directly to Skorzeny time and time again to conduct secret operations.

The *Führer* was no stranger to political assassination and used it effectively in the formative years of the Nazi party to eliminate political enemies. Perhaps the most famous of these was Operation Hummingbird, the SS liquidation of Ernst Röhm and other rival Nazi leaders of the SA or Brown Shirts. This operation had been secretly supported by the German military, who feared Röhm, as he had declared his SA troopers would replace the military as a new national armed force. The alliance between Hitler and the military was cemented with the removal of Röhm by Himmler's SS.

From the outset of World War II, Hitler saw the targeting of government leaders by abduction or assassination as a legitimate means of war. In 1940, after Germany had conquered France, planning began for the invasion of England, codenamed Operation Sea Lion. Part of the planning included an airborne mission to kidnap the Royal Family from Buckingham Palace in London.

Skorzeny's unit would be tasked with highly complex and dangerous missions, including the assassination of foreign leaders, elimination of battlefield commanders, and liquidation of anti–German resistance leaders in countries under Nazi rule. During the war, Hitler issued orders for the removal of Churchill, Roosevelt, Tito and Stalin, and perhaps others. What follows are the details of known assassination and abduction missions carried out by Skorzeny's Commando.

OPERATION LONG JUMP

In late November 1943, Hitler received intelligence that seemed to present an opportunity to execute an attack upon the highest level of Allied command and control. U.S. President Franklin Delano Roosevelt, British Prime Minister Winston Churchill, and Soviet Premier Joseph Stalin were scheduled to attend a leader's conference in Tehran, Iran, scheduled for late November 1943. Here, at one place and at the same time, would be a lucrative target.

Historians have debated the full extent of planning and execution of this mission. Officially dubbed Operation Long Jump, the plan entailed the dispatch of assassins to ambush the "Big Three" at the conference. Exactly who ordered the mission and who was responsible for carrying it out is not clear from the records. Skorzeny denied involvement after the war, but there is enough evidence to suggest he had some hand in the operation.

It is known that Russian intelligence on the assassination plot was passed to the Americans and British at the time. This may have been a Russian ruse, however, to get Roosevelt to stay in a bugged room at the Soviet Embassy. Russian accounts claim the mission was ultimately compromised by one of their sleeper agents posing as a German in the advanced element. In that account, the German transport carrying the assassins was intercepted by Russian fighters and shot down. It is not clear if this operation ever did, in fact, exist. Skorzeny always maintained his name was only used to add credibility to the story.

OPERATION KNIGHT'S LEAP

Another assassination target for Skorzeny's unit was Yugoslav partisan leader Marshal Josip Broz Tito. He was identified by Nazi intelligence as the principle Yugoslav resistance leader against the Germans. Earlier German attempts to capture or kill him had failed. Skorzeny and Arno Besekow set to task and developed a plan to abduct Tito at his headquarters, using inside agents. The task to locate Tito was carried out by several German intelligence organizations, including those supporting Skorzeny's commandos, who continued to operate independently from other German forces in the country. Skorzeny had collected enough intelligence to pinpoint Tito's headquarters and was prepared to work closely with other German forces. He soon devised a direct action raid that was to include an airborne (parachute and glider) assault on Tito's headquarters, with a subsequent linkup with the advancing German units. The plan was militarily sound, combining many of the elements so successful at Gran Sasso, including speed, shock, and surprise through air and ground assaults from all directions. This plan was not implemented, however, due to communication problems. Instead, a combined German army and SS paratrooper mission was launched that did not include Skorzeny's unit. The plan was called Operation RÖSSELSPRUNG (Knight's Leap), beginning in May 1944, which was eventually aborted due to heavy casualties and the inability to locate Tito.

OPERATION MICKY MOUSE

Skorzeny's unit was also receiving demands from Himmler to conduct special operations missions in Italy. Working with the SD office in Rome, several of Skorzeny's officers developed a plan to blow up General Mark Clark's U.S. Fifth Army headquarters by approaching the target by sea. Several problems were encountered in the run-up to the operation, including trouble finding British uniforms for the mission's assassins, and rough seas. Four missions were attempted, with the final one succeeding in getting underway. However, this last attempt, conducted on the evening of March 8, 1944, resulted in the team's boat being spotted, fired upon, and destroyed.

Despite setbacks, Skorzeny's unit's reputation remained intact and actually received expanded missions. His unit continued to train rigorously with new *Jagdverbande*, or Hunting Groups, set up on each army front for special operations. Skorzeny was given operational control of special units from the German *Luftwaffe* and navy. Chief among these was KG 200, the highly secret *Luftwaffe* unit that operated specialized and captured Allied aircraft. The secret unit had some of the best, most courageous pilots in the *Luftwaffe*, who flew harrowing missions behind enemy lines.

Working closely with Admiral Hellmuth Heye, Chief of the German Navy K-*Verbände*, or small battle groups, Skorzeny acquired a unit of midget submarines and manned detachable torpedoes. He also gained control of underwater demolition frogmen, who specialized in sabotage missions against enemy shipping.

The acquisition of KG 200 and the K-*Verbände* gave Skorzeny expanded planning capabilities for special operations combat missions. The human torpedoes were launched against the Allied landings at Anzio in Italy in 1944 but had little effect. They were also deployed during the invasion of Normandy on the coast of France but did not succeed in any measurable way. Skorzeny frogmen, however, did have success in France, targeting bridges. All of these responsibilities, commando operations actions, direction of air and naval assets, as well as the development of special weapons, are a testament to Skorzeny's leadership and technical abilities. These overwhelming duties, coupled with critical issues relating to logistics, maintenance, communications, distances of the areas of operation, and other major factors, led Skorzeny to delegate many of his operations to subordinates.

In September 1944, Skorzeny was again summoned by Hitler to carry out a seemingly impossible task, a military operation with high-stakes political objectives. Disaster was looming on the Eastern front as the Russians continued their relentless advance. Several key allies of the Nazis had fallen, including Finland, the Baltic States, and Romania. On the Western front, the Anglo-American armies had liberated France and were on the very border of Germany. The Third Reich was collapsing, and Hitler's only remaining ally was Hungary.

The Hungarians at that moment were fighting the Russians in the Carpathians, standing with a million German troops. Hitler had learned that Hungary's Regent, Admiral Miklós Horthy, was clandestinely negotiating his country's surrender to the advancing Soviets. Hungary's surrender would leave Hitler's southern flank exposed, thus cutting off a million of his soldiers in the Balkan peninsula. Hitler's intelligence was accurate, and Admiral Horthy was getting ready to open the western approaches to Budapest. Hitler ordered Skorzeny to find a way to end the negotiations and keep Hungary in the war. The code name was Operation Panzerfaust.

Skorzeny was authorized in writing by Hitler with supreme powers, including the forceful removal of Horthy if necessary. Skorzeny assessed the situation carefully, noting that the admiral was heavily influenced by his playboy son Miklos, Jr., who was a key figure in the negotiations with the Russians. Skorzeny then received intelligence that the younger Horthy was to have a secret conference with Soviet agents at an undisclosed location in Budapest. It was determined that an abduction operation removing Miklos, Jr. might be a leverage point to keep Admiral Horthy in the alliance.

The kidnapping was dubbed Operation Mickey Mouse, a pun on the target. Skorzeny's agents succeeded in storming the secret meeting location. The young Horthy was wrapped in a carpet, rushed to an airfield, and flown to Germany. Despite the kidnapping, Admiral Horthy refused to alter his course, announcing an armistice would immediately take place with the Russians. The SS commander in Budapest wanted to level Horthy's palace residence with a massive artillery bombardment. But Skorzeny determined to use guile and stealth, presenting an alternate plan to ensure political stability and not arouse the anger of the Hungarian people.

Horthy's palace was located on a high hill under heavy guard. On October 3, 1944, Skorzeny proceeded directly toward the palace, leading a convoy of German troops and four tanks. He casually approached the objective in a non-tactical formation, bluffing his way past the guard post. At the final moment, Skorzeny ordered his tanks forward and stormed the last barrier, heading straight for the palace. Overpowering the Hungarian force, Skorzeny seized the object and placed Horthy into custody.

Once again, Skorzeny had proven his superior methods of war. He would state in a postwar interview, "There are times when a million men can be saved by the removal of a single obstacle . . . so I had to remove one man to save a million." In another incredible commando action, Skorzeny, with a loss of fewer than twenty men, had maintained Germany's only remaining alliance.

After his success in Hungry, Skorzeny was again summoned by Hitler. The *Führer* congratulated him and advanced him to the rank of *Obersturmbannführer* (Lieutenant Colonel). This would be Skorzeny's last promotion of the war. At this meeting, Hitler informed Skorzeny of a planned offensive through the Belgian Ardennes forest in a great gamble to secure a decisive victory for Nazi Germany.

TARGET EISENHOWER

By the fall of 1944, Allied intelligence believed Skorzeny and his commandos were plotting to repeat their earlier success, this time capturing or killing Allied commanders and specifically General Eisenhower. On December 16, 1944, in a massive dawn attack, the Germans unleashed two panzer armies against a lightly held American sector of the Ardennes forest in Belgium and Luxembourg. This was the same ground on which the Germans had launched their successful surprise attack on France just four years earlier.

The attack in the Ardennes caught the Americans completely off guard. It was later remembered as the Battle of the Bulge. The Germans had chosen a sector of the front with green, inexperienced units that took the brunt of the onslaught. Initially, all was going well for the Germans, who began advancing west toward strategic objectives set by Hitler and the German high command. There had been "scuttlebutt," soldier's rumors, in the American ranks before the battle that the war would be over by Christmas. But the truth was far different. They were now confronted by a ferocious German counterattack that had been synchronized with bad weather to negate Allied air cover, something the common American infantryman depended on.

The German plan was daring in its conception but ill-conceived at a time when prudence dictated the need to prepare to defend the home front. Several German generals believed (correctly) that the Ardennes attack would waste Germany's last reserves. But the battle did result in a major Allied intelligence failure. Undetected, because of strict orders from Adolf Hitler for radio silence, the Germans had managed to secretly assemble nearly half a million men, over a thousand tanks, tank destroyers, and assault guns, and over 4,000 artillery pieces. The ensuing battle would result in more American casualties than any other battle of World War II, including an estimated 89,000 casualties, with at least 8,600 killed (a conservative estimate by some accounts). But there was little time to lay blame for the intelligence failure—only time to fight. And fight the Americans did on those snowy, cold December days in the winter of 1944. This was Hitler's last great gamble—and he gave Otto Skorzeny a lead part in its conception.

When the operation had originally been envisioned by Hitler, it was given the code name Operation "Watch on the Rhine," a defensive sounding name to hide the true intent of the plan. To history it became known as the Battle of the Bulge for the huge dent it made in the Allied lines. The main thrust of the attack was an assault through the Ardennes mountains to secure several key bridges over the river Meuse, thus paving the way for a vanguard of armored units to strike rapidly west. The ultimate objective was the vital port of Antwerp. If successful, the attack would deny the Allies the port and split the American and British forces in two, with the British in the north and the Americans in the south.

Hitler believed the deep penetration and disruption of the attack would create tension between the American and British leaders, thus buying time for the employment of new German jet fighters and other secret weapons waiting to be brought into action to halt the Anglo–American advance on Germany. With the Americans and British placed on the defensive, German forces in the east could then focus on blunting the advancing Soviet steamroller.

Despite the reservations of several German generals, Hitler would not be swayed, and the plan proceeded under great secrecy. To increase the element of surprise and add confusion on the battlefield, Hitler incorporated an elaborate deception to coincide with the main attack—this mission went to Otto Skorzeny.

Skorzeny had first heard about the Ardennes offensive at Hitler's headquarters, where he was being decorated for a successful special operation in Hungary that averted a major crisis on the Eastern Front. After awarding him the German Cross in Gold, Hitler took Skorzeny aside. Walking over to a huge war map and informed him of the planned Ardennes offensive. Skorzeny listened intently to the *Führer* knowing he was about to receive new orders. And then it came, "One of the most critical tasks of the offensive will be assigned to you and the units under your command . . . Your units will seize one or more of the bridges across the Meuse River, between Liège and Namur, in advance of our forces. They will execute this task while wearing British and American uniform . . . smaller units, disguised in American uniforms, will infiltrate enemy lines in order to issue false orders, disrupt communication, and spread confusion." Skorzeny was stunned by the order. His unit was currently involved in dozens of other complex operations. But before the commando chief could address his concerns, Hitler dismissed him, "I know you will do your best Skorzeny . . . but now comes the most important part. This matter is top secret!"

Although at that point Skorzeny commanded all of Germany's special forces, he was given command of a new unit designated Panzer Brigade 150. If successful, the attack would add greatly to the element of surprise for the general attack, creating massive confusion and allowing the advancing panzers to secure the vital bridgeheads. Skorzeny named his portion of the Ardennes offensive Operation "Grief" or Griffon, the mythical bird with the head and wings of an eagle on the body of a lion. Only three men on Skorzeny's staff were privy to the actual objectives given to him by Hitler.

According to Skorzeny, due to the high level of secrecy surrounding his new mission, and because of his reputation for extraordinary operations, a rumor soon developed that the actual goal of the operation was the assassination or abduction of Eisenhower. Skorzeny claims he became aware of the story early on but realized it would be impossible to stop. The rumor soon had legs and began to spread. Skorzeny would utilize the rumor to sow confusion within Allied ranks.

By happenstance, in the opening phase of the fighting, several of Skorzeny's soldiers were captured. During interrogations by American counterintelligence officers at the front, these men revealed that Skorzeny was their commander and claimed that their mission was to reach Paris and assassinate the Allied supreme commander. At that point, rumor become intelligence and promptly passed up the chain to Eisenhower's headquarters.

The news of an assassination mission was alarming enough, but attaching Skorzeny's name to it guaranteed panic within American intelligence circles. Eisenhower's chief intelligence officer, Colonel Gordon Sheen, became convinced of the threat and determined that major security precautions were in order. General Eisenhower was immediately confined to his office and a heavy guard was posted. The situation was serious. Eisenhower's military secretary, Kay Summersby, recorded the event in her diary for December 18, noting the general had received "the report of Skorzeny's assassins along with other heart-breaking news." She went on, "Security officers immediately turned headquarters compound into virtual fortress. Barbed wire appeared. Several tanks moved in. The normal guard doubled, tripled, quadrupled. The pass system became strict matter of life and death, instead of the old formality. The sound of a car exhaust was enough to halt work in every office, start a flurry of telephone calls to our office, to inquire if the Boss was alright."

As a senior adviser, Robert Murphy was present at the intelligence briefing concerning Skorzeny's alleged assassination mission. Murphy recorded the incident in his autobiography, "About this time it was discovered that the Germans were conducting an operation to assassinate members of the top Allied command in France, including Eisenhower, Bedell Smith, and others. The daring venture was being directed by Lieutenant Colonel Otto Skorzeny, the Nazi special operations chief. When Allied intelligence reported Skorzeny's men had 'parachuted' behind friendly lines in American and French uniforms there was considerable concern. Guards were doubled on all lodgings, and there was a lot of trigger-happy shooting with some unnecessary casualties, including four unfortunate French officers in a Jeep who did not stop at a sentry's orders and were killed."

Murphy then went on to describe the eventful evening at Bedell Smith's quarters in anticipation of Skorzeny's impending attack, "Nine guards were on duty. In the middle of the night we were awakened by a fusillade. With Smith leading in pajamas and equipped with a carbine, we deployed into the garden and began shooting right and left. The next morning a stray cat was found in the garden riddled with bullets."

But no attack on Eisenhower ever materialized, nor did Hitler's main assault through the Ardennes reach its objectives on time. Fighting pockets of courageous American G.I.'s unexpectedly held the line against the German advance. Hitler should have listened to his generals. His great gamble had failed.

Despite the failure, there still remained several more months of horrific fighting. Skorzeny and his commandos would continue to carry out daring missions during this last desperate chapter of the Third Reich. As to the validity of the Eisenhower assassination operation, there is no firm evidence to confirm whether there ever was a threat to Eisenhower from Skorzeny's commandos. It is true several of Skorzeny's men had been captured in U.S. uniforms in the Ardennes, but none were captured in France.

Skorzeny himself denied that an assassination plan ever existed, stating in a postwar interview, "It is not true that I tried to kill General Eisenhower. It is not true that I ever attempted to kidnap, maim, or in any way inconvenience America's favorite son." He added, "Naturally, I should have done so if I had received the order, but the order did not come." In the final analysis, it appears that Skorzeny was able to skillfully utilize psychological warfare to good effect, diverting U.S. forces toward a phantom attack. He would later describe the reaction that the deception had achieved: "It was as if a small rock had been thrown into the calm water of a pond, spreading concentric waves in all directions." Although Eisenhower and other Allied generals may not have been in Skorzeny's crosshairs, Skorzeny was not a stranger to the practice of assassinations.

In the death throes of the Third Reich, Skorzeny was again tasked with a long-odds mission. In February 1945, Skorzeny was urgently sent east and assigned command of an improvised force at a defensive bridgehead at Schwedt on the Oder river that was threatened by the advancing Russians. Skorzeny arrived at the site in a captured American Jeep left over from the Ardennes offensive. Using his *Jagdverbande* as a nucleus for a larger force, he quickly added to his ranks by commandeering retreating units and formations of elderly reserves. He also received personnel from the *Luftwaffe* units that had no planes and the Reich Labor Corps construction workers to build fortifications. Ultimately, Skorzeny was able to assemble nearly 10,000 fighting men, making him the equivalent of a division commander, a position normally afforded a major general. In early April, Skorzeny was ordered to Hitler's headquarters in Berlin for the last time. Despite failures, the actions of Skorzeny's men at the defense of the Oder bridgehead impressed the *Führer*, who awarded Skorzeny oak leaves to his Knights Cross.

THE INFAMOUS "PETER GROUP"

As part of the SD *Ausland*, Skorzeny directly controlled or supported a number of covert networks in countries occupied by the Germans. The networks were used to collect intelligence, counter enemy espionage activity, and facilitate special operations as needed. They were also designed with stay-behind forces to conduct direct attack or sabotage behind enemy lines in the event of the Allied invasion. A full examination of the various agents, operatives, and foreign political entities that these networks were associated with would require several books; for our study, a few concise paragraphs on several key aspects must suffice.

One covert group of operators from Skorzeny's command that merits particular attention is the notorious "Peter Group," or SS *Sonderkommando* Denmark. Despite the signing of a ten-year non-aggression pact with Denmark in 1939, Germany invaded the country on April 9, 1940. The Danish government quickly surrendered and became a protectorate of the Nazi government. This cooperative arrangement lasted until 1943. At that point, the Danish government refused further cooperation, scuttled its navy, and dispatched many of its officers to Sweden. Additionally, the Danish resistance, secretly supported by the British SOE, elevated its anti-German sabotage and targeted Danish collaborators.

The Germans mounted a counter-campaign and established the "*Schalburg Corps*," a counter-insurgency force manned by Danish volunteers. Various German intelligence and security organizations worked with the Corps, but eventually the situation became unmanageable. SS commanders in Denmark complained of a lack of manpower and experience to carry out the mission. For this reason, Skorzeny was called in to lend his expertise in helping to neutralize the resistance.

Skorzeny pulled together a six-man team and selected one of his top men, *Obersturmführer* Otto Schwerdt, to take charge of the group. The group was set up in Denmark towards the end of December 1943. Schwerdt assumed the alias "Peter Schäfer," from which the unit took its name.

Once the Peter Group arrived in Copenhagen, they set up liaison and planning with local German police and other intelligence units. The group was also augmented by Danish collaborators. The objective was to checkmate sabotage and carry out liquidations of the Danish resistance movement. A list of targets was developed that included journalists and writers. The Peter Group had an unparalleled history as a terror group. In the sixteen months the group was active, it conducted 102 killings and twenty-five attempted murders. It also used demolitions, setting off 157 blasts of property and businesses. In November 1944, Schwerdt was recalled by Skorzeny, and Horst Paul Issel was placed in command. Issel would remain at the head of the group until the end of the war. We have not heard the last of this notorious assassin in the pages of this book.

OPERATION *KARNEVAL* (CARNIVAL)

Another Nazi network that involved Skorzeny was the infamous "Werewolves" operation devised by Heinrich Himmler to wreak havoc on the Allied occupiers. The program, first developed in late 1944, was intended to be a resistance movement to operate behind the lines as the Allies advanced into Germany. *Obergruppenführer* Hans-Adolf Prützmann was placed in charge of the project, with Skorzeny in direct support.

Tactics of the Werewolves included sniping, assassination, arson, and other acts of sabotage. Efforts were made to pre-position supplies, arms, and ammo for the project, but much remained on paper. Skorzeny did not place great faith in the effort and had far more significant priorities on his plate, but he did provide limited support. In this regard, his unit conducted some training of Werewolf recruits and provided logistical support.

One Werewolf operation that does bear the mark of Skorzeny's hand was Operation *Karneval* (Carnival), which included the successful assassination of Franz Oppenoff, a Nazi official suspected of being a collaborator with the Allies in the city of Aachen in October 1944. Hitler took a personal interest in this case of Nazi treason and ordered the elimination of Oppenhoff. Werner Naumann, deputy to Reich Minister Joseph Goebbels, passed the liquidation order to *Obergruppenführer* Prützmann and Skorzeny.

The operation consisted of an assassination unit of four SS men and two members of the Hitler Youth. The team was dropped by parachute on March 20, 1945, from a captured U.S. B-17 bomber operated by KG 200, a top-secret *Luftwaffe* unit under the de facto control of Skorzeny, especially for SD intelligence operations. This is the unit Skorzeny utilized to drop foreign agents and special commando teams deep behind enemy lines.

The Oppenhoff assassination team was dropped into a forested area not far from the target area. Leaving an initial assembly point, they then moved toward the city with one member of the team, a female agent named Ilse Hirsch, becoming separated. She eventually linked up with the rest of the group.

Hirsch had used her contacts in the city to find Oppenhoff's location. Three members of the team proceeded to Oppenhoff's residence, posing as German pilots trying to get back to friendly lines. With Oppenhoff's guard down, the assassins shouted, "Heil Hitler!" as they shot him in the head. They made their getaway just in advance of a U.S. patrol. On their way out of the city, Hirsch stepped on a landmine, killing a member of the team and badly wounding herself in the leg. Following the war, they were tracked down, arrested, and tried. All were found guilty and received prison sentences of between one and four years. Hirsch and one other member of the team were set free.

Other Werewolf operations were carried out, but the one above had a sophistication that singles it out and indicates a higher degree of planning and execution. Overall, the Werewolf movement never gained momentum and accomplished little other than localized terror. In the waning hours of the Reich, Propaganda Minister Joseph Goebbels used the existence of the organization in an attempt to buttress the fading hopes of the Germany people—it had no effect.

"ORGANISATION TECHNIQUE"

During the war, Skorzeny, who was always astute to the political use of special forces, organized a group called "*Organisation Technique*" or (OT), to carry out "a number of independent operations aimed at provoking right wing resistance in France." The OT had the mission of creating "an alliance of anti-Communists." This effort was to exploit the close bonds of brotherhood that existed between former members of the *Cagoule*, regardless of who they sided with. In essence, the former *Cagoule* serving with Skorzeny's command were attempting to establish a dialogue with the former *Cagoule* serving in the French Resistance and French Army. These men were looking into the future of France and wanted to prevent a Communist takeover of their country after the war. They also believed it might provide a "conduit to the Americans," thus weakening the Allied partnership with Soviet Russia. Ultimately, this covert effort at the end of the war to rally former *Cagoule* into a common anti-Communist group lies at the heart of the French intelligence contact with Skorzeny.

After the successful Allied invasion of France in June 1944 and subsequent liberation of Paris in August, thousands of Vichy French forces bolted for Germany, where an émigré government was set up in southwestern Germany with an exile capital established at Sigmaringen. In October, the OT was created by Joseph Darnand, the former head of the Vichy *Milice* (French fascist paramilitary), consisting of 150–200 volunteers to be trained as agents and sent back into France to fight the Allied forces.

Command of the OT was given to Jean Degans, a former member of the *Cagoule* and former director of the Vichy police. OT liaison with the Germans came from Skorzeny's *Jagdverband*, and Jean Filliol, a former *Cagoule* who exercised "day-to-day" control of the group. Several OT sabotage and secret service camps were established in Germany with training and operational planning coming directly from Skorzeny's special forces.

After some hasty preparation, small teams of OT agents were parachuted into France to conduct operations and establish networks. These included secret contacts in Spain just across the border. Operationally, the OT did not have any significant accomplishments, but it was its networks that caught the attention of postwar Allied intelligence.

SKORZENY ORDERED TO THE REDOUBT

In April 1945, Hitler sent Skorzeny off to Bavaria on what was to be his last mission—the defense of Germany from the National Redoubt, also known as "the Alpine Fortress." Skorzeny bid the *Führer* farewell, believing his leader would soon follow to the south. But when Skorzeny arrived in Bavaria, there was no National Redoubt, and no army ready to make a last stand. The Alpine Fortress had been a deception. Undaunted, Skorzeny consulted with other senior German commanders in the area and then set about forming his last command, the "*Schutzkorps Alpenland,*" or SKA. Skorzeny intended to use this small unit (around 300 men) as a guerrilla force against the invading Russians moving in from the east. Then, on April 30 news came over the radio that Hitler had perished, fighting gallantly against the invading Soviets. In reality, Hitler had committed suicide, his body burned by a few faithful aides, adding to pathetic ashes of the Third Reich.

After Adolf Hitler's death, Skorzeny determined to fight on as long as Germany had armies in the field under legitimate orders. Hitler's successor was Grand Admiral Karl Döneitz who continued the struggle, mainly to allow German forces fighting the Russians time to retreat west and surrender to the Americans and British. When his stall tactics had expired, Doneitz issued the order for German forces across the continent to surrender. On May 8, 1945 all combat operations against the Allied forces ceased. No new troop movements were permitted. That same day, Skorzeny and his staff gathered in a small mountain cabin in Dachstein to discuss their options. Skorzeny wrote in his memoirs: "The responsibility for my soldiers, spread out in small groups in nearby valleys, weighted heavily upon me; they were still awaiting my final directive. Each of us pursued his own thoughts. Could we have done better? Had we really done everything possible? The German military would certainly be disgraced, but no one could ever accuse us of neglecting our duty." Skorzeny then contemplated escape to a neutral country and even suicide. Both were rejected: "I felt I had to stand with my comrades and continue to live among them. I had nothing to hide from my former enemies. I had done nothing wrong and thus had nothing to fear. I served my fatherland and done my duty as a soldier. For me a new day was dawning!"

Skorzeny and his men had arranged communication from his hide out with the help of two girls from the German Labor Service. From them they heard that the Americans had set up POW camps at Radstadt and Annaberg. The group did not surrender immediately and as Skorzeny put it "enjoyed a few more days of freedom." With no further orders, and not knowing whether the government still existed they decided to act on their own initiative.

As an SS officer, Skorzeny was in the immediate arrest category and given his notoriety Allied intelligence immediately went on the hunt to capture him. Wanted posters of Skorzeny were printed and dispatched to the field with his physical description and warnings concerning his background. The poster even had a picture of Skorzeny in American uniform and the declaration of "Assassin" in prominent wording. But in the end, Skorzeny decided to surrender honorably thus negating any dramatic ending that the wanted posters had eluded to.

Skorzeny had correctly assessed the Allies would be conducting a manhunt for him and sent one message out from his secret headquarters informing the Americans that he would soon venture out of hiding to surrender.

On May 20, 1945, Skorzeny together with his adjutant *Hauptsturmführer* Radl and an interpreter, wearing dress uniforms with side arms, went down into the valley to make contact with the Americans. They reported to the nearest American unit but were met by a disinterested U.S. Army sergeant who did not recognize the name or significance of Skorzeny. The sergeant did give them a Jeep and a driver to take them to Salzburg where they could surrender to the division headquarters. In Salzburg a U.S. Army major sent them on to yet another processing station. During the entire journey the party remained armed.

Finally, at one stop the casual treatment suddenly ended when the party was disarmed and covered by military police with machine guns. They were then driven back to Salzburg where their arms were bound behind their backs and brought before a room full of war correspondents, spectators, and heavily armed MPs. A female New York reporter who was present when the giant commando was brought in commented: "Skorzeny certainly looks the part . . . He is striking in a tough way; a huge powerful figure. The Beast of Belsen is something out of a nursery in comparison."

At this point a number of questions were asked of Skorzeny but he refused to answer while being manacled. The restraints were taken off and the first question came:

"Why did you try to murder General Eisenhower?" "I didn't," said Skorzeny who denied the allegation that he had lead an assassination party to kill the Supreme Allied Commander. He continued, "If I had ever been ordered to attack Allied G.H.Q., I should have made a plan to do so. If I had made a plan, I would have carried it out. And no one would have been left in doubt of what I was trying to do."

On May 21, 1945, Skorzeny and Radl, who were kept together, were sent to Augsburg. There, on the following day he was interrogated for six hours by Colonel Henry Gordon Sheen, Eisenhower's counterintelligence chief. Sheen attempted to get Skorzeny to admit that Hitler was alive and that the commando had escorted his *Führer* from Berlin. Skorzeny told Sheen he believed Hitler was dead and if he had taken him out he would still be by his side.

One week after Sheen's interrogation of Skorzeny, General Walter Bedell Smith, Supreme Headquarters Chief of Staff went before an assembled body of reporters in Paris and declared that there had never been a German plot to murder Eisenhower. (This despite it having been heavily reported during the Battle of the Bulge.)

Numerous interrogations now started. The Allies would question Skorzeny on all organizational and operational aspects of his commando. Much of these interrogations are declassified, none however, discuss assassination. Skorzeny was eventually transferred to Wiesbaden where his chief British interrogator was an intelligence officer who introduced himself as Colonel Fisher, this was actually the previously mentioned Colonel Rex Benson. From June 1945 to July 1947, Skorzeny was held in several different camps alternating back in forth from Nuremberg to Dachau. His final charges were not for War Crimes but to face violations of the Laws of War. The charge may strike the reader as odd but as events unfold the reasons will be made clear. Skorzeny's trial was set for September 1947.

CHAPTER FOUR

SECRET ARMIES

"In France the first stay-behind networks, successively called 'Compass Rose' ('Rose des Vents'), 'Mission 48,' and 'Rainbow' ('Arc-en-Ciel'), was set up in 1948."

EUROPE SINCE 1945: AN ENCYCLOPEDIA, VOL. I

"There was ultra-secret war planning established across Europe, stay behind and underground organizations, something along the same lines that existed in the final years of World War II."

RETIRED CIA OFFICER THOMAS POLGAR IN
AN INTERVIEW WITH MAJOR RALPH GANIS, 2015

"Shoot . . . we shouldn't try him. I think we ought to hire him."

COLONEL WILLIAM DENSON, 1947

W e left the conclusion of Chapter Two with the period 1945–1946 that saw the disbandment of the OSS and SOE and the formation of the British–American–Canadian-Corporation (BACC) and World Commerce Corporation (WCC). These corporations were formed to carry out clandestine operations within Project SAFEHAVEN. Then, in the fall of 1947, a new crisis emerged in France (and across Europe as a whole) that required the immediate commitment of British and American covert forces. As events further played out, British and American intelligence services would be severely strained. To alleviate the situation, a plan was devised by General

Donovan to restructure BACC under WCC and utilize the combined secret network of former SOE and OSS officers currently operating under the respective corporate structures. This new clandestine private paramilitary force would then be able to assist the official special forces in current operations. We will now examine the history of these events which will ultimately serve as the impetus for the inclusion of Otto Skorzeny in Cold War covert operations. These events will also have lasting implications far down the line for the Kennedy assassination.

PLAN BLEU

Immediately after the World War II, France was a country in extreme political turmoil. In October, 1945, the French people voted for a new constitution, creating the Fourth Republic. French military authorities in Austria and Germany were engaged in carrying out occupation duties along their British and American allies, each with zones of responsibility. In France, internal political conflicts between the right and left raked the country and had major implications for the inner workings of the French intelligence services.

In January 1946, General Charles de Gaulle resigned as president over heated disagreements with the French Assembly concerning his executive powers. He then retired to his country estate. In the meantime, the French Communist Party (PCF) was poised to take over the government. During the war, members of the PCF had held prominent positions in General de Gaulle's Free French Forces, including its intelligence services. The leadership of the PCF had originally planned to seize control by force but opted instead to infiltrate the centers of power and authority to achieve their ends. This included the police, military, secret services, and the government.

By garnering a great deal of public support, the PCF obtained high positions within the French government. Noting these disparaging developments, US Ambassador to France, Jefferson Caffery, warned Washington of a potential PCF takeover of the government. He also raised the concern of how communism would taint the French intelligence services writing to Washington, "by the time the French services began to reorient their activities toward the 'threat,' the rot of infiltration had spread to the very fabric of the state . . . "

Beginning 1946, American and British intelligence planners were tasked to neutralize the Communist threat in France which resulted in the creation of an operation code named Plan Bleu. The secret forces involved in Plan Bleu consisted of American and British operators with wartime experience in covert action. An exact date for the start of Plan Bleu is not known but the general date for its commencement is interesting. In January of 1946 the British SOE had been ordered to shut down. It must be assumed that the assets of the organization were transferred to another British intelligence service or perhaps to the British military. These then would represent the covert forces that the British included in Plan Bleu. It would be logical to assume that this joint unit headquarters and its subordinate units would be connected to the implementation of Plan Bleu. This is particularly true when considering the timing of the Plan Bleu activities. At the time of Plan Bleu activation, the OSS had been disbanded but its covert missions were picked up by the Strategic Services Unit (SSU).

According to research conducted by Daniele Ganser for his book, *NATO's Secret Armies: Operation Gladio and Terrorism in Western Europe,* Plan Bleu was fully underway by the early months of 1947 with covert cells established all across France. The Plan Bleu staff included highly experienced British SOE and SAS officers and equally experienced American special forces officers. Operations also included special units of the French secret service known as Direction Générale des Études et Recherches (DGER). This proved a great risk however as Communists had penetrated the organization. The DGER was eventually replaced with a military secret service called Service de Documentation Extérieure de Contre-Espionnage or SDECE. However, the British and Americans remained cautious.

On June 30, 1947, despite the best efforts of the Plan Bleu staff to maintain operational security, an unexpected roadblock emerged when the French Socialist minister of the interior, Édouard Depreux, intentionally revealed Plan Bleu to the French people. Depreux fully described the operation and even revealed the name of the plan. He also leveled an accusation (that was correct) that U.S. and British intelligence were working with French right-wing paramilitaries. He also claimed these forces were poised to carry out a coup d'état (a claim never substantiated). A national stir ensued with purported investigations uncovering caches of heavy weapons and plans. There were even suggestions that planning was underway to assassinate de Gaulle, in an attempt to incite public resentment. In the end, the scandal only served to fuel the political turmoil in the country.

A French investigation into the Plan Bleu affair was conducted by the director of SDECE, Henri Ribiére. He acknowledged the role of the intelligence services but insisted that arms caches found all over the country were staged to fight communists, not stage a coup. Despite the fact Plan Bleu had been exposed, the overall assessment from Washington and London was it had greatly diminished the strength of the PCF. Nor did the exposure of the plan alter American and British resolve to eliminate the Communist threat in France.

By 1947, rising concerns over Soviet intentions were mounting intensifying Western preparations for war. Intelligence was forecasting worst-case scenarios in which large portions of Europe would be overrun by Soviet forces or seized by internal treachery. Planning for these contingencies became a priority across the continent. New initiatives in the anti-Communist planning would now include the formation of secret armies, or stay-behind forces. One of those involved in these early stay-behind operations was William Colby, Director of the CIA from 1973–1976, who later recalled, "We sort of anticipated another world war . . . a world war that would be characterized by the occupation of Western Europe by Soviet forces, and, therefore, we were preparing to set up the base for a resistance movement that could exist during the war." Another first-hand participant, Thomas Polgar, who was interviewed by the author, referred to the effort as "ultra-secret war planning, established Europe-wide." Polgar also told the author that planning was made "following the pattern of organizations that existed in the final years of World War II" in Western Europe.

The month of August 1947, found General Donovan conferring with Defense Secretary Forrestal about the situation in France. Donovan had devised a plan to deal with the situation and re-engaged the missions that had been tabled by the exposure of Plan Bleu. Donovan suggested the formation of a private paramilitary group made up of former American, British, Canadian and French operatives and placing them under the cover of World Commerce Corporation. This plan submitted by General Donovan was approved in short order.

DONOVAN'S "SECRET PARAMILITARY GROUP"

The exact name of the covert group established by General Donovan and authorized by U.S. authorities in 1947 is not known. The author has therefore created a name and special acronym unique to this book for ease of presentation and understanding. Henceforth, the author shall use—"Secret Paramilitary Group" or "SPG" when discussing the hidden covert organization Donovan formed within the World Commerce Corporation (WCC).

The new anti-Communist operations of which the SPG would eventually be involved went under the code name *Rose des Vents* (Compass Rose). The name was specifically chosen as a direct reference to the card pattern found below a compass needle to which an azimuth is set to prevent a ship from drifting off course. It is also significant that the symbol chosen for the North Atlantic Treaty Organization (NATO) is the star shaped compass design.

For security reasons the Americans and British now relied on a separate *unofficial* French secret service called, *Service d'Ordre du RPF*, as their primary anti-Communist partner. The *Service d'Ordre* was created by General de Gaulle in the early part of 1947. It was hidden within an organization de Gaulle had formed called the *Rassemblement du Peuple Français* (Rally of the French People), or RPF. Not exactly a political party, the RPF was an assembly of like-minded political groups promoting a democratic vision for France. The inclusion of Communists was, of course, forbidden. Funding was secretly provided by wealthy French industrialist who were also the financial backers for funding Plan Bleu.

As an unofficial intelligence apparatus, *Service d'Ordre* operated completely independently of formal French intelligence and kept its activities secret from the government. No intelligence information was exchanged between the *Service d'Ordre* and other French Intelligence organizations. All *Service d'Ordre* members were carefully vetted for Western loyalty and they were the ONLY

French intelligence officers trusted by American and British intelligence. Most *Service d'Ordre* officers had served in the French Resistance or with the Free French Forces and after the war many continued active service within civilian and military intelligence organizations.

Service d'Ordre was based in France, but was also active in the French occupation zones located in Germany and Austria. Additionally, it had operatives in the American and British zones. The group was highly effective and had penetrated all levels of the French military and the French intelligence service SDECE, where it actively recruited intelligence officers at every rank to work for its purposes. Captains and colonels in the organization oversaw various clandestine field detachments. As a cover for its operations *Service d'Ordre* secret agents utilized press identity cards, including one from an agency called Kosmos.

ENTER GENERAL PIERRE DE BÉNOUVILLE

At the highest level, the *Service d'Ordre* was controlled by General de Gaulle's most trusted officers, including General Pierre de Bénouville, head of RPF Foreign Affairs and National Defense. General de Bénouville was born on August 8, 1914 in Amsterdam. As a young man he lived in Paris where he became very active in politics. He was a leader in *Camelots du Roi*, or King's Camelots, a far-right youth organization of the French royalist movement *Action Française*, in the early 1930s. *Action Française* was active, in the years before World War II, in an attempt to return the monarchy to France. The action arm of the movement, which conducted bombings and assassinations, was the dreaded *Cagoule*, first mentioned in Chapter One. In 1936, de Bénouville participated in the Spanish Civil War on the side of Franco with a close friend, Michel de Camaret, whose background will be covered later.

During World War II, de Bénouville joined the resistance rising high within its ranks. He worked closely with the British SOE and American OSS operatives in France. At age thirty, he was promoted to brigadier general by General de Gaulle and eventually serve as the senior liaison to OSS chief Allen Dulles. After the war, General de Bénouville remained a close personal friend of Dulles and, as our story will reveal, was also very close to Otto Skorzeny. Although this relationship is revealed here for the first time, their clandestine contact is confirmed by correspondence in the Skorzeny papers. As head of National Defense for de Gaulle's RPF, General de Bénouville would be instrumental in Plan Bleu and subsequent covert operations that will eventually involve Otto Skorzeny.

COLONEL ROBERT SOLBORG AND WING COMMANDER YEO-THOMAS

Two important leaders of the OSS and SOE that were in Paris at the time Donovan's plan to eliminate the Communist threat in France was activated were Colonel Robert Solborg, the former OSS Deputy for Special Operations and Wing Commander F. F. Edward Yeo-Thomas, former SOE operative. Solborg as highlighted before was a corporate representative of ARMCO steel. Commander Yeo-Thomas was a corporate officer of the Federation of British Industries. Both men would play pivotal roles in the pending use of Otto Skorzeny by Western intelligence.

Given his high level of experience in the formation of covert warfare units, Colonel Solborg was likely the operational commander of the SPG in Paris. Colonel Solborg had served as General William Donovan's chief of Special Operations during World War II and was the originator of the OSS "dirty tricks" department. Colonel Solborg arrived in Paris at the moment Compass Rose stay-behind projects were initiated.

Royal Air Force Commander Yeo-Thomas was one of SOE's top agents and was known during the war by the code name "White Rabbit." He had seen intense combat service in World War I, fighting for Poland against the invading Bolshevik forces. Yeo-Thomas' family had settled in France and he spoke perfect French. He was thirty-eight at the time of the outbreak of World War II. After the outbreak of hostilities between Germany and France, Yeo-Thomas volunteered for duty with the Royal Air Force (RAF) but was too old for flying duty, so he was eventually assigned to the SOE where his responsibilities included the coordination and direction of French Resistance groups. He was also highly instrumental in gaining air support and other logistical means for the French *maquis,* the French underground fighting force.

Although an unassuming man, Yeo-Thomas had the heart of a lion. His personal bravery and resilience is legendary. He even once had tea with an unsuspecting Nazi Gestapo chief, Klaus Barbie. In 1943, Yeo-Thomas parachuted into occupied France, linking up with his French contacts to attempt the rescue of a captured Resistance leader. The effort failed, and Yeo-Thomas was taken captive himself. He was brutally tortured by the Gestapo for weeks and then sent to Buchenwald concentration camp, where he soon escaped.

After the war, Yeo-Thomas returned to Paris where he returned to a prewar position at Molyneux, a Paris fashion house, and in 1950 took a position with the Federation of British Industries. His mere presence in Paris during Plan Bleu and Compass Rose must be taken as evidence of his participation in these operations, if merely as an informal adviser. Further research is needed, but it was at this time that the most intriguing activity by Commander Yeo-Thomas occurred, not in France but in Germany, that bears all the hallmarks of a secret operation linking both Compass Rose and Skorzeny.

SKORZENY'S TRIAL—SECRET COMMUNICATION

While Operation Compass Rose was playing out in France, Otto Skorzeny was preparing to go on trial. For over two years, he had formulated his defense and stood ready to stand against charges he had violated the rules of war during the Battle of the Bulge. On August 18, 1947, Otto Skorzeny and nine of his former officers were brought before the U.S. Military Tribunal in Dachau. It should be pointed out that Skorzeny was not associated with the notorious extermination camp run at Dachau during the war, however, the city had been selected for that reason as the location to conduct lower-level Nazi trials, including Otto Skorzeny's.

It was during Skorzeny's trial that evidence first appears of something deeper going on in the background, and that he was already in communication with people who were destined to play a role in covert activities. This revolves around an incident that came about clearly indicating Skorzeny had established a means of communicating with members of his old command on the outside. In one of the more dramatic moments of the trial, a witness for the prosecution was brought forth and stated under oath that Skorzeny had issued poison bullets to his command during the Battle of the Bulge in violation of the Laws of War. The information caused a great stir with the assembled audience. Immediately after the sensational charge the court recessed for the day.

Skorzeny promptly told his lawyer he thought that the man was mistaking types of ammunition used by his troops. Author Charles Foley describe what happened next in his book *Commando Extraordinary*, writing, "Skorzeny got to work to procure the evidence he needed" and "smuggled out a message" to his adjutant Karl Radl being held in a different camp. Radl then passed the message "to friends in the town" outside his camp. By breakfast the next day, a bullet was delivered to Skorzeny concealed in a piece of bread. Skorzeny gave the bullet to his lawyer, who in turn asked the prosecutions witness if the red ringed projectile was the same as the one he remembered. The witness acknowledged that it was the same as the one he saw during the war. Skorzeny's lawyer then announced to the court the ammunition was a waterproof bullet and not a poison one—the charge was immediately dropped.

The poison bullet story clearly illustrates the level of sophistication of Skorzeny's communication system to the outside world. It would seem nearly impossible that a specific type of ammunition could be acquired and dispatched clandestinely to Skorzeny inside a jail within sixteen hours from notification without a clandestine network in place. It is logical therefore to assume Skorzeny had contact with the former SS members standing by for orders to assist him. It is also likely, that some of these men were already secretly working for or in concert with Western intelligence services or the Donovan SPG.

THE "WHITE RABBIT" IS DISPATCHED TO SAVE OTTO SKORZENY

Skorzeny's trial lasted three weeks, and, in one of the most remarkable and unexpected events in the history of the Nuremberg Trials, a surprise witness appeared for Skorzeny's defense and, with just a few brief lines of testimony, destroyed the prosecution's case. The man who came to Skorzeny's rescue—Commander Yeo-Thomas! Despite his treatment at the hands of the Nazis during the war, Yeo-Thomas felt compelled to volunteer his testimony in defense of Skorzeny and had travelled from Paris to do it.

In a scene right out of a Hollywood war movie, Commander Yeo-Thomas was waiting in the courtroom for the arrival of Skorzeny, and as the former Nazi commando approached the dock, Yeo-Thomas with a dozen other American and British officers, rose from their seats in unison, stood at attention, and saluted. In retrospect, we now know Commander Yeo-Thomas's sign of respect was far more important than a salute between former enemies, but the first act in the saga of Skorzeny's postwar career. It is now evident, that working behind the scenes General Donovan and William Stephenson had arranged for a court-room rescue of their former enemy by arranging the surprise witness for the defense.

This is exactly how Donovan's plan played out when on the final day of Skorzeny's trial, September 9, 1947, Commander Yeo-Thomas himself testi-fied that he had worn German uniforms behind enemy lines, just as Skorzeny was accused of doing. This admission effectively shut down the case against Skorzeny. Additionally, Lieutenant Colonel Donald McClure, Skorzeny's defense council, made a powerful closing statement, "Honorable members of the court, if I had a combat unit under my command with me like these defendants, I would be proud of every one of them."

Within hours, the case against Skorzeny and his men was totally dismissed. The disappointed prosecutor, Colonel Abraham H. Rosenfeld, told the press, "I still think this Skorzeny is the most dangerous man in Europe," and as events will eventually play out, the colonel's assessment of Skorzeny could not have been more correct. Ironically, even before the start of Skorzeny's trial there was evi-dence of support for the former SS commando. In this case, the Chief Prosecutor for the United States for Nazi war crimes at Dachau, U.S. Army Lt. Colonel William Denson had received a formal request to prosecute Skorzeny. Denson, however, determined Skorzeny as a model soldier and quickly turned down the offer to prosecute Skorzeny remarking, "Shoot . . . we shouldn't try him. I think we ought to hire him."

A FORESHADOWING OF DALLAS

Immediately after Otto Skorzeny had been declared innocent an incident occurred that involved a character found in the post–JFK assassination investigations conducted by the FBI. The incident involved Judge Jesse C. Duvall who presided over Skorzeny's trial. After the proceedings, Skorzeny met with Judge Duvall and presented him with an ivory-embossed box and dagger and sheath. Duvall hailed from Fort Worth, near Dallas, Texas. During the war, Duvall held the rank of major in military intelligence and afterward was selected as one of the U.S. prosecutors for the Nuremberg Trials. Described as a modern-day Roy Bean and noted as an unorthodox judge, Duvall once threatened to invoke Muslim law (chopping off hands for stealing) to stop shoplifting. He was known for his off-color remarks to prostitutes.

Many years after Skorzeny's trial, Duvall gave an interview for a Dallas newspaper and mentioned the post-trial conversation he had with Skorzeny. He stated that Skorzeny told him at the time of the presentation, "these would buy me a house and lot sometime." The article went on to say Duvall treasured the gift and kept it in a safety deposit box for the rest of his life. Oddly, in the days following the JFK assassination, Duvall would be interviewed by the FBI for his association with George de Mohrenschildt, a principle character in the assassination.

Mohrenschildt had approached Judge Duvall in January 1963 to assist a young man named Lee Harvey Oswald with his dishonorable discharge from the United States Marines. The FBI inquiry also revealed Duvall was close to a man named Roy Pike, a former employee of Jack Ruby, who showed up at Judge Duvall's residence immediately after Ruby had shot Lee Harvey Oswald. These facts will be examined in more detail later in this book.

On September 14, 1947, in a final name changing event, the Central Intelligence Group (CIG), formed out of the Strategic Services Unit, was renamed the Central Intelligence Agency (CIA). Following shortly thereafter, on September 24, newspapers articles carried the public announcement by Frank Ryan stating World Commerce Corporation (WCC) had been "recapitalized" and would succeed the British-American-Canadian Corporation (BACC). This was

Donovan's plan effectively being put into action. To an all but unknowing public this seemingly routine corporate restructuring had effectively merged the secret covert assets of BACC and WCC under one roof. The combined American and British covert forces (SPG) were now in place awaiting orders. Soon thereafter, in November, General Donovan and World Commerce president Frank Ryan, would receive formal approval from General Lucius Clay, military governor of Germany and senior U.S. diplomat Robert D. Murphy, to use WCC as a cover for the establishment of a secret private paramilitary venture in support of Compass Rose. The stage was now set for Otto Skorzeny's phantom return.

CHAPTER FIVE

CAMP KING

"You did a jolly good job during the war! If you are ever looking for a place to stay I have a home in Paris . . . Escape!"

COMMANDER E. YEO-THOMAS,

WRITING TO OTTO SKORZENY, JUNE 1948

D espite being declared innocent, Skorzeny will not be released but will be held for unspecified reasons. His highly experienced former adjutant, Karl Radl will also be retained. Henceforth, the two would remain together. Soon, word arrived that they would be extradited to Denmark or Czechoslovakia to face charges there, however, nothing came of the rumors. Meanwhile, their holding conditions, which had been spartan during the trial period began to improve. Skorzeny remarked in his memoirs: "Everyone I meet makes me feel again that I am a soldier, even though I am still sharing the lot of a prisoner of war."

Soon a request arrived from American officials for Skorzeny and Radl to write a history of German special forces. Skorzeny recorded the event in his memoirs: "We had often heard about the activities of the American Historical Division in Neustadt on the Lahn [river], which was conducting research on the history of the war with assistance of German officers." Skorzeny and Radl accepted the offer but were surprised when they were not taken to Neustadt as expected but ushered out late one evening to Camp King in Oberursel, an urban town located northwest of Frankfurt. In retrospect, we now know that the request was a complete ruse and merely a cover to bring both men to Camp

King for a secret vetting process to prepare for their secret integration into the ongoing anti-Communist operations and creation of stay-behind networks under Compass Rose.

Camp King was a special internment base with a number of intelligence and operational staff. The camp had formerly been used by the German *Luftwaffe* as an interrogation facility, which the Americans took over at the end of the war. Located at the camp was the 7707th European Command Intelligence Center (ECIC). The mission of the ECIC was the exploitation of persons and documents for intelligence purposes. One of the most highly classified areas of operation was the interrogation of German scientists, intelligence officers, and other prisoners of war deemed of value to Western intelligence efforts, and many were recruited into U.S. intelligence and scientific programs. The Center also received intelligence reports from field agencies and Army Mobile interrogation units that maintained liaison teams at the camp. An operations branch handled the planning of clandestine operations resulting from information gathered and analyzed by the various intelligence sections.

The commanding officer at Camp King was Colonel Roy M. Thoroughman; his executive officer was Lt. Colonel John O. Taylor. Colonel Thoroughman, a veteran army officer from the First World War, oversaw the day-to-day functioning of the camp but was not necessarily involved with the projects going on there. He was primarily responsible for the administrative side of things, such as security, transportation, housing, and other areas of support.

The Camp King intelligence unit had nine sections, or desks, that focused on important intelligence-related areas, including economic and industrial information, political matters, scientific and technical data, counterintelligence, military studies, and special intelligence (information from espionage).

The intelligence chief was Captain Henry P. Schardt, who carried out his intelligence mission under the cover of the 7734th History Detachment, commanded by Colonel Harold E. Potter. So as not to draw attention to the real reason they were sent to Camp King, it was Potter's unit that Skorzeny and Radl were assigned to upon their arrival at Camp King. Captain Theodore C. Mataxis was assigned as their control officer at the historical detachment. The reader should keep both Captain Schardt and Captain Mataxis in memory as they will have important dealings with Skorzeny in the future.

The interrogations of Skorzeny at Camp King were personally conducted by Arnold M. Silver, a senior U.S. Army noncommissioned officer and chief of the counterintelligence section. Skorzeny had been thoroughly interrogated before his trial by various high-level U.S. intelligence officers but the interrogations at Camp King by Arnold Silver were of a different nature. Now Skorzeny was not a captured enemy combatant but a potential asset to U.S. intelligence.

Silver's recollection of his first encounter with Skorzeny is found in an article Silver wrote titled, "Questions, Questions, Questions: Memories of Oberursel," replete with humor—the type you often find between soldier adversaries—"On arriving in my interrogation room for the first time, he [Skorzeny] promptly warned me not to try to use any physical violence because he could overpower me in no time. He calmed down when I asked him in reply whether he could move faster than a bullet from a .45 calibre pistol." Obviously, the two men hit it off from the start, and Silver must have been very impressed with Skorzeny, stating he was "rightly acquitted," in his opinion. But it was Silver's comment on Skorzeny's motivations and character that are most illuminating—"He was not a Nazi, and in fact any ideology was alien to him. He was purely and simply a man of action and a patriotic German." These positive comments bring to light that Silver's actual relationship with Skorzeny was not to interrogate him for further prosecution but to evaluate Skorzeny and determine if he should be utilized by Western intelligence. An important factor in this equation is the creation of the Central Intelligence Agency (CIA) which occurred only nine days after Skorzeny's trial on September 18, 1947.

CODE NAMES "ABLE" AND "BAKER"

One of the initial indications that Skorzeny and Radl were brought to Camp King for special processing by U.S. intelligence was in the manner they were first received. For example, immediately after they had arrived, Colonel Potter arranged for the two to be set up in the Alaska House, a posh, multilevel Tudor-style building reserved for VIP prisoners. As the activities at Camp King were regarded "top secret," most prisoners were assigned code names. In his memoirs, Skorzeny wrote: "According to special security regulations we were assigned code names . . . Radl's name became 'Baker,' mine 'Able.'" Skorzeny also mentioned two other individuals as occupants in the Alaska House at the same time. These men were only identified as "X-Ray" and "Zebra," both, according to Skorzeny, "acquaintances of mine from Italy." These were likely former Italian officers who had worked with Skorzeny's special forces now selected to assist in CIA covert programs. Actually, the reason for secrecy and code words was well justified, as Camp King was the home of numerous highly classified projects— some which are still shrouded in secrecy.

According to Arnold Silver, the Camp King intelligence section "concentrated on questioning Germans who, by virtue of their wartime functions, had considerable knowledge of Soviet industries." It is known Camp King served as the main location for screening and processing of German scientists, in particular those with rocket or ballistics backgrounds. This project is widely known as Project Paperclip (originally Overcast), which brought such notable scientists as Wernher von Braun to the States.

As a senior Army counterintelligence officer at Camp King, Arnold Silver was aware of most, if not all, of the classified programs at the camp. He stated in "Questions, Questions, Questions" that he maintained close liaison with the Strategic Services Unit (SSU) in Frankfurt, which by the time of Skorzeny's arrival at Camp King, had morphed into the Central Intelligence Agency. Hence, Arnold was, during his tenure at Camp King, the conduit through which the CIA carried on its evaluation and communication with Skorzeny. Skorzeny at this point would not have understood the organizational aspects of those intelligence officials he was dealing with.

THE DOCUMENT DISPOSAL UNIT (DDU)

At some undeterminable point around 1948, and perhaps earlier, another unit appears in declassified documentation called, the Document Disposal Unit, or DDU. The documentary evidence is confusing, but it appears that the DDU was a sub-unit of the War Department Detachment (WDD) (read CIA) set up by Allen Dulles, or even perhaps a designation of WDD. Regardless, the DDU was a focal point for managing the disposition and control of networks involving former SS, SD, and Gestapo.

Also, the DDU apparently emerged from or had a relationship with the Document Research Unit (DRU). The DRU was originally a small group of OSS research analysts, who had analyzed aspects of the Nazi regime during the war. The DRU was activated in London on June 10, 1945 and initially headed by First Lieutenant Walter Rothschild, who despite the rank title, was not military. Many of the OSS and SOE staff were afforded notional military ranks as "cover" for intelligence work.

The DDU worked directly with the 7808th War Crimes Group and associated military legal teams of the Army's Judge Advocate Corps. This would have included all those involved in the trial of Skorzeny, including Judge Gordon Simpson, Judge J. C. Duvall, Colonel Telford Taylor, as well as, OSS Major Robert Bishop, who was personally responsible for assembling the documents used in Skorzeny's trial.

Since much of the documentation of interest to the DDU was also of interest to Allied attorneys in the War Crimes Group, the review and handling of these papers was extremely classified. It will be reiterated here that the Director of the Documentation Division and Executive Trial Counsel in Nuremberg was Dallas native Colonel Robert G. Storey.

In the field, the DDU worked very closely with Army counterintelligence. Many years after his tour of duty at Camp King, Arnold Silver stated he was responsible for recommending Skorzeny's "disposition." He also mentions that his higher headquarters was located in Frankfurt. In 1948, Frankfurt was the headquarters location for the Document Disposal Unit.

Interestingly, Silver had the same responsibility for the infamous Gestapo chief, Captain Klaus Barbie, the "Butcher of Lyon," who arrived nearly simultaneously at Camp King as Skorzeny, but under an entirely different set of circumstances. The word "disposition" used by Arnold in his article was thus a veiled reference to the control of Skorzeny by the DDU, a fate also shared by Klaus Barbie.

At the time of Skorzeny's stay at Camp King, the DDU was involved with a project to provide safe houses and operational aid facilities for all CIA activities in Germany. The project was called HARVARD. A declassified draft working paper on the history of the CIA reveals that a "Disposal Unit [DDU]," had two sections, one in Karlsruhe under Lt. Colonel Louis E. Kubler and another in Frankfurt under OSS Captain Lucien E. Conein. Kubler's office handled documents and identity cards, while the Frankfurt office under Conein handled housing, resettlement, and evacuations. Captain Conein was nicknamed "Black Luigi" due to his lethal reputation gained while fighting as an OSS operative with the French Resistance in World War II. Conein would later be a focus of many JFK researchers as a potential assassin or operative in the Dallas assassination. For this reason, we will look a little deeper into his background.

Conein was born in Paris, France, but sent to the United States when he was only five years old. Raised in Kansas City by a French aunt, he ran away at the outbreak of World War II and enlisted in the French Army. After France's defeat, he made his way back to the United States and was assigned to the OSS due to his language fluency and experience fighting the Germans. Conein was eventually transferred to the Pacific, where he conducted commando raids against the Japanese. After the war, he stayed on for the transitional period when the OSS was dissolved and reformed as the CIA. In 1954, Conein would be dispatched by the Agency to Vietnam as part of a military adviser team.

According to Kubler, Conein used two means to evacuate individuals from Germany deemed of value to the CIA. One was to South America or the United States using the International Relief Organization (IRO), since the asset could pose as either a refugee or a displaced person. The other method was through "black" channels.

THE RUN-UP TO SKORZENY'S "ESCAPE"

During his stay at Camp King there was a number of unusual visitors and activities associated with Skorzeny. On December 6, Skorzeny received a surprise visit from his former wife, Gretl. Their marriage had not lasted long, but during the war she worked at the Reich Main Security Office (RSHA) that oversaw

Skorzeny's unit. Nothing else is known about her background, but her visit to Skorzeny was a precursor to even greater intrigue at Camp King. Shortly after Gretl's visit, both Skorzeny and Radl received an unusual 14-day Christmas holiday pass to leave Camp King on their own and return, on their honor, in a timely fashion. The bizarre pass would allow Skorzeny to have freedom of movement. It is likely he took the opportunity to make contact with his former officers and soldiers. Some of these men were already working with U.S., British, or French intelligence.

Another odd occurrence during the holiday pass were trips to Wiesbaden, a city in central Western Germany, and Berchtesgaden, a small German town in the Bavarian Alps on the Austrian border. Hitler's wartime home, the Eagle's Nest retreat, was located just outside of Berchtesgaden. At Berchtesgaden, Army CIC agents were alerted to Skorzeny's and Radl's arrival. Field agents reported to headquarters asking for clarification on the status of the two visitors, especially Skorzeny. Specifically, they wanted to know if Skorzeny's presence in Berchtesgaden was authorized and if any action should be taken "in order to avoid unnecessary surveillance." Another interesting detail is that Skorzeny and Radl were "visiting with one Gerda Christian, former secretary of Hitler."

In fact, Gerda "Dara" Christian was one of Hitler's closest secretaries, having escaped from the *Führerbunker* in Berlin on May 1, 1945, with the breakout group lead by *SS Brigadeführer* Wilhelm Mohnke. Immediately after the war, Christian was wanted for testimony in the Nuremberg Trials, but, despite being held at the time by U.S. intelligence, she mysteriously vanished, going underground. She surfaced several years later in Düsseldorf, Germany, working at the Hotel Eden. Skorzeny's meeting with her remains a mystery to this day.

Skorzeny and Radl's first stop under the pass was in the town of Oberursel. In his memoirs, Skorzeny writes: "Everywhere I received a pleasant welcome from old friends and new acquaintances . . . It was the first opportunity since my captivity to experience life outside the barbed-wire fence. It was a winter of starvation, for the needs on the outside were greater than we had ever imagined. Our first visit was to Hanna Reitsch who lived in Oberursel." Hanna Reitsch was a famous German test pilot and a favorite of Adolf Hitler. She had made an incredibly daring flight into battle-torn Berlin with *Luftwaffe* General Ritter von Griem during the final days of the Third Reich in an effort to rescue Hitler, who refused to fly out of the capital.

While at Reitsch's house, another seemingly routine event occurred that again had unrecorded deeper implications. Skorzeny writes in his memoirs: *"I met a Roman Catholic priest. We had a long conversation and parted with mutual respect and understanding for each other,"* (emphasis added). There was an inference here to an agreement of some sort that may have dealt with Vatican intelligence operatives facilitating the movement of former Nazis through Europe at the behest of U.S. intelligence.

When their fourteen-day leave was over, Skorzeny and Radl, true to their word, returned to Camp King. The new year found events moving in a decidedly favorable direction for Otto Skorzeny with a full core press on contingency war planning being undertaken by Western intelligence. In February 1948, Skorzeny and Radl's work at the historical detachment came to an abrupt end. This was likely related to orders emanating from General Clay that all counterintelligence assets at Camp King were to be closed within 90 days. Arnold Silver recorded, "In early February 1948 we received the first signal that Oberursel's days as a center for detailed interrogation were numbered. General Clay issued a decree that Americans working for the Army or military government who had been citizens less than 10 years would have to leave the zone within ninety days. The grapevine had it that this decree was issued on the urging of the American Bishop Muench, then the religious affairs adviser on Clay's staff." Silver went on to describe Bishop Muench's personal aversion to CIC personnel, focusing on those who had fled Nazi Germany and become U.S. citizens. This decision greatly impacted counterintelligence in a negative way. Silver continued on the subject, "When the decree was issued, we had about 20 first-rate, experienced interrogators left in Oberursel, more than half of whom were affected by the decree. Attempts by G-2 in Frankfurt to obtain exceptions for some of these professionals were promptly rejected by Clay's headquarters in Berlin. General Clay having usurped a function of the Supreme Court, there was no allowance for appeals."

SKORZENY IS SUMMONED TO NUREMBURG (THE SCHACHT CONNECTION BEGINS)

The orders for the closure of Camp King seem to have also affected plans for the use of Skorzeny, for there now occurred a rapid set of events that appear related. Just at this moment, a curious incident erupted, centered on a claim that Skorzeny had rescued Hitler at the end of the war. Skorzeny referred to the individual who made the accusation as "a deranged former *Luftwaffe* soldier." This unsubstantiated story had been circulating in Europe for some time. A commission was quickly set up to investigate the matter and, in the meantime, Skorzeny was transferred from Camp King to Nuremberg to await the findings.

Skorzeny's stay in Nuremberg was short and the accusation against him was quickly dismissed. In fact, it was likely a fabrication—a cover story to justify bringing Skorzeny to Nuremberg to be briefed by senior-level officials and intelligence officers on his future.

This may have been the point Skorzeny was given instructions concerning his release and the green light for reconstituting elements from his old command. Skorzeny himself admitted that he was told to expect such contact and that he had received instructions to assemble men for covert operations. An interview conducted by the author with a former military attach who was familiar with Skorzeny's early history flatly stated, "he was released on purpose, to see what he could do for us."

Skorzeny also mentions in his memoirs that among those he had contact with during his short visit to Nuremburg were former Third Reich industrialists, leaders from the steel and chemical industries, economic experts, and highly skilled scientists. This is highly significant because these men will be intimately connected to Skorzeny's postwar business networks within a few years of this contact.

Skorzeny would later recall: "In the hours of conversation with these men I learned much which helped in my later life." Indeed, he did; one, in particular, Hjalmar Schacht, former Reichsbank President and Minister of Economics under Hitler, would become very close to Skorzeny in the postwar years. Schacht, who was universally acclaimed as a financial wizard with a brilliant mind, resigned his position in 1939 over disagreements with Hitler and Hermann Göering. Hjalmar Schacht was born on January 22, 1877. His father was a banker who had, as a young man, lived briefly in the United States from 1871–1876. Young Hjalmar followed in his father's profession, becoming a prominent banker." He was also an economist, a politician, and a founder of the German Democratic Party. During the years of the Weimer Republic, he served as Currency Commissioner and President of the Reichsbank.

Schacht was a man who had great conviction in his beliefs. He believed totally in the virtues of self-reliance. His postwar autobiography reveals his ideas on the root of liberty. He wrote, "Liberty is not synonymous with laziness. Freedom is not given away: it must be earned daily, in war by force of arms, in peace by the work of brain and hand. Whoever desires better housing, clothing and food must work for it. That is God's law . . . The idea of a welfare state as a kind of public benefactor under official leadership is an assumption leading directly to totalitarian communism, but which has nothing whatever in common with the sense of responsibility to the individual." These ideas, also shared by Otto Skorzeny, were the basis for their hatred of Communist doctrine.

Schacht never joined the Nazi party but was a supporter of Adolf Hitler. He served in Hitler's government as President of the Reichsbank from 1933–1939 and as Minister of Economics from August 1934–November 1937. Schacht's economic policies are credited with bringing Hitler to power, but he personally rejected much of the Nazi ideology. He also came into direct conflict with Nazi leaders like Hermann Göering. Schacht secretly supported the German resistance movement from 1934 on, and, although not fully a participant, he was vocal in his attitude. Schacht was dismissed as Finance Minister in 1943 and arrested after the failed attempt on Hitler's life in July 1944. He avoided execution but was arrested by Allied authorities when the war ended and faced charges at the Nuremberg Trials. He was subsequently acquitted by the tribunal, one of the few to achieve freedom.

While living in Nazi Germany during World War II, Schacht used his international connections to establish clandestine contact with the Americans and became a secret agent for Allen Dulles, then serving as OSS chief in

Switzerland. This is a very important fact considering Skorzeny's links to the CIA. It was Allen Dulles who had worked behind the scenes to facilitate Schacht's not guilty verdict at Nuremberg. Schacht will surface again in our story and play a high-profile role in postwar intrigues concerning Skorzeny, tying directly to Skorzeny's business dealings in steel, oil, and other industries.

After Nuremberg, Skorzeny and Radl were reunited at Camp King and then transferred to an internment camp in Darmstadt, Germany, to go through a program known as denazification. This was an administrative process to ensure that the individual in question did not retain Nazi ideologies. The move to Darmstadt would not be without risk. Prior to Skorzeny's departure from Camp King, Arnold Silver received a warning from intelligence concerning a Soviet plot to kidnap Skorzeny. Intelligence had already confirmed other plots, such as one targeting German intelligence officer Richard Kauder, alias Klatt. Kauder was also being held at Camp King for his protection and interrogation, along with two of his wartime associates.

Silver informed Skorzeny that a similar plot was brewing for him and this may have been one reason why Skorzeny and Radl were brought to Camp King. Under the kidnap plan, the Soviets intended to use Skorzeny's brother Alfred, who was in Soviet captivity, to lure Skorzeny into Berlin, where he would be captured. Once Skorzeny was taken captive, explained Silver, they "planned to use him as a rallying point for the youth of the Berlin zone." Silver added, "The Soviets intend to achieve by force in a special operation what they had been unable to do through persuasion." Here, Silver was referencing the Russian's first attempt to recruit Skorzeny during the earliest days of his imprisonment as a POW. At that time, Russian interrogators, visiting Skorzeny's internment facility, had offered him a lucrative job working for them, but he had flatly turned them down.

Skorzeny was fully aware of the dangers the Soviets represented. His brother's abduction had occurred on February 14, 1946, when Alfred was snatched off a busy street in Vienna by Soviet agents. Mistaking Alfred for Otto, they yanked him from the sidewalk and pushed him into a waiting automobile. Although the Soviets realized their mistake almost immediately, they brutally interrogated Alfred and placed him into solitary confinement. He was held in solitary for three years. When released from solitary, Alfred was a broken man and continued to be held until 1954. He never recovered from his ordeal.

Skorzeny found the conditions at Darmstadt to be better than other camps he had been held at, and wrote in his memoirs that civilian workers and guard personnel treated him with respect. He also mentioned that, to remain physically active, he and Radl volunteered for duty clearing rubble in the nearby city. Skorzeny's casual mention of this seemingly routine duty has far greater implications than meets the eye—as the reader will soon discover.

THE WHITE RABBIT SENDS A LETTER

"We sort of anticipated another world war . . . a world war that would be characterized by the occupation of Western Europe by Soviet forces and therefore, we were preparing to set up the base for a resistance movement that could exist during the war."

WILLIAM COLBY, DIRECTOR CIA 1973–1976

INTERVIEW OPERATION GLADIO BBC *TIMEWATCH*

"The greatest mistake I ever made."

STATE DEPARTMENT OFFICER GEORGE KENNAN REFLECTING

ON THE CREATION OF NSC DIRECTIVE 10/2

While Skorzeny and Radl ventured out of camp on work release other big developments were transpiring at a strategic level. By March 1948, General Clay, military governor of Germany had become firmly convinced of an imminent Soviet invasion of Western Europe and issued a warning that the United States and its allies "must prepare for the contingency of war." Others in the U.S. military and government concurred with General Clay, as did many of their Western counterparts. This accelerated stay-behind preparations and covert operations in general.

WESTERN UNION CLANDESTINE COMMITTEE (WUCC)

In Paris, on March 14, 1948, Western intelligence officials, meeting under a tight veil of secrecy, founded the Western Union Clandestine Committee

(WUCC). The WUCC evolved out of the earlier British and French collaboration on stay-behind networks for Plan Bleu. The reader will immediately note the highly confusing and unfortunate similarity (at least for this history) between the Western Union Clandestine Committee acronym WUCC and the World Commerce Corporation—WCC. Adding to the confusion both are intimately linked to the covert operations being carried out under Compass Rose.

The WUCC was the designated controlling body for the formation of Western stay-behind networks. Citing Daniele Ganser's book, *NATO's Secret Armies: Operation Gladio and Terrorism in Western Europe*, the mission of the WUCC was to carry out "peacetime preparations against an eventual Soviet invasion."

Events were now moved forward rapidly. On April 3, 1948, President Truman signed the Marshall Plan, granting $5 billion in aid to sixteen European countries. Directing the Marshall Plan was Richard M. Bissell, Jr., a Yale graduate and logistics expert who would later rise to be the Deputy Director of Plans at the CIA. Bissell's role also included a top-secret assignment to coordinate logistical and cover support to the CIA in the formation of covert networks to fight Communism in Europe. In this capacity, Bissell worked very closely with the CIA and the private SPG through hidden contacts in the World Commerce Corporation. Hidden within Marshall Plan was secret funding for covert operations which were transmitted through the Economic Cooperation Administration (ECA) to the CIA and other supporting elements of clandestine schemes.

At this point, three major players were involved in the formation of stay-behind networks all under the oversight of the WUCC. These were, the intelligence services of the various Western countries (such as the CIA and British MI6), the SPG network within World Commerce Corporation, and regular military advisers. Eventually, U.S. military and CIA support will be merged and formalized under the cover of the Military Assistance and Advisery Groups or MAAGs. MAAGs were assigned to Western European countries for the overt purpose of implementing foreign military aid but carried a secret mission supporting the creation of stay-behind networks. In April 1951, the WUCC would be retitled the "Clandestine Planning Committee," or CPC, and, in October of that year, MAAG became the secret cover for its operations. This is an extremely vital point to remember when analyzing Otto Skorzeny's heavy involvement with MAAG. In fact, it is so important that an entire section will be devoted to its description in Chapter Fourteen.

By May 1948, Donovan's SPG was fully operational, a fact confirmed by an unidentified CIA officer in confidential correspondence that month to FBI Agent Deloach, writing, "Various remnants of OSS personnel who had previously operated in and around Paris, France, were operating in that same locality on a private commercial basis under the leadership of their former director, William Donovan . . . [and] that Donovan had made a trip to Paris for the purpose of surveying and inspecting the activities of the group."

General Donovan is also confirmed to have been in Paris in that summer along with several other former OSS officers, most of whom would later join the CIA. These included Milton Katz and Frank Lindsay, both in Paris as counsel to the Marshall Plan. Also attached to the Marshall Plan, was Donovan's former OSS Far East operative, E. Howard Hunt, later of Watergate fame and a key character in the Skorzeny story. Author Mark Riebling rounded out the list of OSS legends in Paris was William J. Casey, a future Director of the CIA. Casey would later guide Colonel Oliver North in the formation of a "Panama-registered, private anticommunist network eerily akin to Donovan's" World Commerce Corporation.

BLOODSTONE

On June 10, 1948, a date just ahead of Skorzeny's escape, Operation Bloodstone, a major clandestine program involving anti-Communist operations using East European émigrés, essentially former Nazi collaborators, was approved by the State–Army–Navy–Air Force Coordinating Committee or SANACC. This official government body directed all U.S. covert activity. Selected to lead the Bloodstone project was the veteran OSS officer Frank Wisner, who had been very instrumental in the initial formation of postwar intelligence networks under Allen Dulles. Wisner fell under the State Department Policy Staff headed by foreign service officer George Kennan. Kennan was an expert on the Soviet Union and the guiding force behind the Bloodstone project. Within the Policy

Staff, Wisner headed the Office of Special Projects which implemented Bloodstone.

Two other important individuals active in the development of the Bloodstone project was diplomat Robert Murphy and a U.S. Army counterintelligence officer Colonel Boris Pash. The reader may have noted the recurring names in this story such as Robert Murphy. Colonel Pash will soon join the ranks of important characters in the continuing saga of Otto Skorzeny. The reader needs to hold the name of both men in close memory.

NSC DIRECTIVE 10/2

There is no revelation in this book more important for gaining the confirmation of Skorzeny's hidden role in postwar covert operations than a document issued by the National Security Council (NSC) on June 18, 1948. The timing of the document is also important as it was authorized only one month before Skorzeny "escaped" from a holding facility at Darmstadt.

This landmark directive laid the foundations of the modern national security state. It vastly increased secret operations and issued specific guidance for all types of clandestine activity, including, white and black propaganda, economic warfare, preventive direct action, including sabotage, assistance to underground resistance movements, guerrilla formations, and use of refugee groups, just to name a few. It also authorized violation of international law and deception in the interest of national security. It served as the baseline document for plausible and deniable planning and execution of covert operations.

The development of Directive 10/2 was a highly guarded secret and very few individuals in the government knew of its existence at the time. The principle architect of 10/2 was the previously mentioned George Kennan. He laid out top-secret paper dated February 24, 1948. The paper was used as the basis for drafting Directive 10/2. The full extent of the paper is a worthy of study but for the purpose of this book the author shall focus on three main areas in its contents—overt assistance, clandestine assistance, and counterforce.

Kennan identified overt assistance as the use of "trusted private citizens" and "public committees" to mobilize interest and support for selected émigré factions in the United States and Europe. Clandestine assistance was support to anti-Communist factions in countries outside the Soviet orbit, in areas where local communist might gain power. And finally, counterforce, described as "outright paramilitary actions." Kennan also articulated that in the general implementation of 10/2 the "general direction and financial support would come from the Government" and then "pass to a private American organization or organizations" meaning business enterprises. These would be "composed of private citizens" with "field offices in Europe and Asia." The use of private organizations and citizens is a clear reference to the World Commerce Corporation (WCC) and the SPG already in the field, having earlier been suggested by General Donovan to Defense Secretary Forrestal.

In regard to this history, it was the analysis and research conducted by this author of the Skorzeny papers that revealed Skorzeny's shocking connection to all of the components laid out by George Kennan and approved under NSC Directive 10/2. Going forward the author will use Directive 10/2 to reveal Otto Skorzeny's participation in these covert activities. Each objective, overt assistance, clandestine assistance and counterforce will be noted as they appear in the timeline. Ultimately, the reader will see that Skorzeny's postwar covert undertakings match verbatim the wording and instructions issued under Directive 10/2. Of critical note here within the Bloodstone project was the use of "a private American organization" to "dovetail with" Bloodstone. This is a clear reference to the World Commerce Corporation. The collaboration between Frank Wisner's OPC and Frank Ryan's WCC also aligns with the 10/2 instructions that the direction and financial support for the civilian group will come from the government. These facts also confirm that Skorzeny's future involvement with the CIA as it will pass through World Commerce will be indirect, with NO FORMAL CONTACT, making his use both plausible and deniable—another 10/2 imperative. As a final foreboding development—in July 1948, 10/2 was expanded with a new directive that included assassination and the rescue of Allied airmen just on the eve of Skorzeny's escape.

BLOODSTONE—THE IRO CONNECTION

A major part of the Bloodstone project was the use of the International Relief Organization or IRO as a cover for operations. Lt. Colonel Kubler (mentioned previously) had confirmed that the DDU was using the IRO as a means to secure scientists, engineers, informants, and intelligence operatives from the clutches of the Soviets. The underground system later dubbed "the rat line" was associated with these relief organizations. The Catholic side of the relief operation was headed by a Croatian priest, Father Krunoslav Dragonović, whose activities were secretly sanctioned by the Vatican. The American side was run by Dr. Morton W. Royse, an experienced OSS officer who headed the IRO. Royse was often in contact with other former OSS officials serving in the CIA. Father Dragonović could not work openly with U.S. intelligence officials, so his means of carrying out secret activities was facilitated by CIC and CIA operatives through the IRO.

One of the intelligence officers working with Father Dragonović was Major Robert Bishop, a Chicago lawyer who served in the OSS during the war. A highly significant fact concerning Major Bishop is he served immediately after the war as the legal officer assigned to compile Otto Skorzeny's SS records in preparation for trial. This means Bishop would have worked closely with the previously mentioned Judge J. C. Duvall who received a presentation gift from Skorzeny after the trial.

In 1947, Bishop accepted an assignment as an "independent operator," working for the CIA under Frank Wisner setting up intelligence networks in Romania. Wisner had been Bishop's superior during the war. In January 1948, Bishop moved again, this time to a position in Italy with the eligibility office of the International Relief Organization. In this capacity, Bishop would have worked very closely with Captain Conein who was arranging agent movements. Bishop would have also been privy to Skorzeny's secret records and with Skorzeny personally. Bishop later stated he did not believe Skorzeny was guilty of war crimes and let his superiors know it, he wrote in an official report that Skorzeny, "was the bravest man I ever met." The comment is odd. Was Bishop referring to Skorzeny's war record or perhaps something else?

Captain Paul E. Lyon of Army counterintelligence, who worked closely with the IRO, would later recall that Bishop was involved in constructing "a highly secret underground escape operation into a large-scale military force." Captain Lyon noted that it included "large numbers of underground troops, military supplies, sea evacuation, air evacuation and the like for clandestine warfare against the communist." Lyon's statement confirms the ties between Wisner's OPC operations and the IRO.

The CIA chief in Italy during this critical period was another former member of OSS, James Jesus Angleton. Angleton will eventually rise to be a legendary member of the CIA as its foremost counterintelligence officer. Both Frank Wisner and James Angleton will be a continual focus of research in this book and their early positions of authority in the CIA was a critical factor in the use of Otto Skorzeny by Western intelligence.

SKORZENY ESCAPES!

By the first of July all the final preparations (and authorizations) had been completed and Skorzeny was merely waiting for the signal from U.S intelligence to bolt from captivity. Skorzeny wrote in his memoirs that it was during the latter part of his internment that he received a letter, postmarked in Paris, from British SOE officer Commander Yeo-Thomas, the "White Rabbit," who had come to his defense during his trial. Here was the long-awaited signal from the Donovan 'SPG.' Commander Yeo-Thomas told Skorzeny in the letter, "You did a jolly good job during the war! If you are ever looking for a place to stay I have a home in Paris . . . Escape!" The timing of this letter is imperative and a clear cryptic reference by Skorzeny revealing the hidden forces behind his escape—Donovan's secret group.

With all the pieces now in place and with approval from American intelligence "to look the other way," Skorzeny made his "escape" on the night of July 25, 1948. Skorzeny himself gives the reason as simply having had enough of captivity, especially given the fact that he was found not guilty of any war crimes. He stated in his memoirs: "Three years and two months seemed to me to be enough. I warned the American colonel who was commander of the

Darmstadt camp that I had decided to get away. He didn't believe me. But two hours later . . . I installed myself—with some difficulty—in the trunk of his car. The German driver, who was going shopping for the camp commander, unwittingly drove me through all the checkpoints." Despite Skorzeny's account, it was Arnold Silver, in "Questions, Questions, Questions," who admits Skorzeny was released on official authority from Frankfurt (War Department Detachment, i.e. CIA).

As for Arnold Silver, at the end of June he would resign from the Army and return to the United States. Not surprisingly, by 1949, he had transferred to the CIA and was *promptly* "scheduled for operational assignment" and this is not the last time we will hear of Arnold Silver. Skorzeny meanwhile went underground to begin the development of his contacts and putting into place a personal undercover apparatus in anticipation of further contact by the SPG. In the final analysis, it was a joint clandestine group composed of former American, British and French secret agents at the heart of Skorzeny's release. Importantly, their actions had the full endorsement of senior military and high government officials, as well as selected members of various Western intelligence organizations. These personalities and forces will remain at the core of Skorzeny's covert history until the end of this story.

CHAPTER SEVEN

ALIAS ROLF STEINER-HART

"Otto was a fabulous-looking animal . . . he had everything you could want in a man, lots of charm, charisma, a good sense of humor."

ILSE VON FINCKENSTEIN, 1993 INTERVIEW
WITH AUTHOR MARTIN A. LEE

On the very day of Otto Skorzeny's escape from internment in July 1948, friends on the outside had arranged for a suitcase to be secreted at a nearby railway station. Some of these friends were in fact members of his old commando now working undercover for Western intelligence. Apparently, as part of the overall operation, a rescue of Skorzeny's wife Anna occurred simultaneously in Austria. This rescue was to safeguard her capture by the Soviets. Skorzeny had been briefed by Arnold Silver on Soviet plans to kidnap him prior to his release. The press covered the incident, but this is the first history to relate the significance and its link to Skorzeny's release. On July 31, the *News Herald* of Franklin, Pennsylvania, picked up the story and printed the headline, "Wife of Nazi Spy Missing from Home." The short article went on to describe the disappearance of Anna Skorzeny from her home in the U.S. zone in Austria—"three days ago." The date of the event coincides with Skorzeny's "escape," indicating that the two events were linked. No further details about her disposition were given or uncovered by further research.

Since the securing of Skorzeny's wife occurred in Austria, a critical point to introduce here is that CIA operations in that country during this period were controlled by Alfred C. Ulmer, the chief of station in Vienna. Ulmer was a former Naval intelligence officer who had served in General Donovan's OSS. Ulmer had arrived in Austria in 1946, and by 1947 he was in charge of all CIA operations in the country. A Princeton graduate, he would eventually rise to be a senior-level CIA officer. Ulmer's deputy, John H. Richardson, was a former Army CIC officer. Both men dedicated Cold War warriors. It is well documented that Ulmer conducted extensive covert operations in Austria. Ulmer also maintained excellent working relationships with U.S. Army counterintelligence, as well as the French and British. Ulmer, as the senior CIA officer in Austria, was certainly aware of the staged release of Otto Skorzeny. He will appear again later in this historical narrative dealing directly with covert activity connected to Skorzeny.

After his "escape," Skorzeny remained out of sight. He had immediately departed the train station at Darmstadt and afterward for the town of Berchtesgaden in Bavaria. There a safe house had been arranged. This was later confirmed by Skorzeny's third wife Ilse in an interview. Perhaps not by coincidence, the safe house was located in the same mountainous region where Skorzeny carried out his final orders in the service of the Third Reich.

An interesting document found in the Skorzeny archive was an identity booklet for this period that Skorzeny would have used at the time of his escape. This booklet contains a photograph of Skorzeny in civilian attire and identifies him as a "journalist" under the alias Rolf Steiner-Hart. Important here is that all press in Germany was controlled by U.S. intelligence through the Army's Information Control Division (ICD), set up by General Eisenhower's chief of psychological warfare, Brigadier General Robert A. McClure. The issuance of this particular identity booklet is a dead giveaway Skorzeny was assisted by Western intelligence with his escape.

ENTER COUNTESS ILSE VON FINCKENSTEIN

The safe house used to shelter Skorzeny was a mountain lodge rented by Countess Ilse von Finckenstein. From this point forward in Skorzeny's history she will be the key conduit through which Skorzeny will communicate with numerous contacts. As things sometimes happen, Skorzeny and Ilse became romantically involved during the initial period of his release. In a 1993 interview with author Martin A. Lee, Ilse admitted that she fell straight away for Skorzeny stating, "Otto was a fabulous-looking animal . . . he had everything you could want in a man, lots of charm, charisma, a good sense of humor." She also stated that Skorzeny was in contact with a U.S.–controlled intelligence entity known as Gehlen Organization.

Although not a subject of this narrative up to this point, the Gehlen Organization deserves more than a passing mention. In fact, the organization was an integral part of the backstory to Skorzeny's Cold War saga. The Gehlen Organization was named after General Reinhard Gehlen, Nazi Germany's former intelligence chief of the Foreign Armies East (FHO). Gehlen had been one of Hitler's foremost authorities on the Soviet military and its associated industries. By 1944, Gehlen had determined that Hitler's policies and failed military strategies would end in Germany's defeat. Hitler was unwilling to accept Gehlen's factual intelligence assessments and fired him. Gehlen had a keen understanding of the military situation. He predicted a postwar conflict between the West and the Soviet Union over the spoils of a conquered Germany and control of Europe, a conclusion he kept to himself.

In total secrecy, with the exception of a few trusted staff officers, Gehlen devised a plan to offer his services to the Americans after Germany's capitulation. Working in isolation, the small group began filming every document in Gehlen's intelligence division. These were then placed inside metal containers and buried in southern Germany. When the war ended, Gehlen promptly surrendered to the Americans and made contact with U.S. intelligence officers. Shortly thereafter, he presented his proposal to American leadership.

The Gehlen plan was brought to the attention of Brigadier General Edwin L. Sibert, the senior intelligence officer for the Twelfth Army Group. General Sibert, an astute officer who also shared Gehlen's view that the Russians were likely to become a foe, seized upon Gehlen's idea and formed a special intelligence operation to handle the matter and secure Gehlen's buried intelligence treasure.

Initially called Project X, then KEYSTONE, and finally RUSTY, the Gehlen project was one of the most closely guarded secrets in the postwar period.

Gehlen was clandestinely taken to the United States for closed meetings with U.S. intelligence at Fort Hunt outside Alexandria, Virginia. There, he impressed American leadership, and it was determined that his services and information should be exploited. In July 1946, the Gehlen group was formally set up at Camp King under Army control to begin assembling an organization of German intelligence experts. This has some bearing on Skorzeny's arrival at Camp King since Gehlen and his staff were, at that time, still located at the camp. Also, General Gehlen had worked closely with Skorzeny during the latter part of the war. This included a number of secret projects, including deep agent penetrations into Russia. The working relationship and knowledge of both men was of great interest to the Americans.

Two months after Skorzeny's arrival at Camp King, the Gehlen organization was transferred to Pullach, near Munich, in Bavaria. In 1949 Project RUSTY was passed from the control of Army intelligence to the CIA. In 1954, it became an entirely independent German intelligence service, the Bundesnachrichtendienst (Federal Intelligence Service), or BND, still in service today.

So, it was the Gehlen Organization that supported the secret release of Skorzeny in July 1948. This makes perfect sense since Gehlen German networks could have protected and facilitated Skorzeny's movements without direct American involvement. At the time of Skorzney's release the Gehlen Organization was still under U.S. Army intelligence control. One year later it will be formally transferred to the CIA. Instrumental in the transfer was Colonel James Critchfield, who was subsequently assigned as chief of the CIA in Munich. Colonel Critchfield had worked with Al Ulmer in Austria before being selected as a liaison officer to the Gehlen Organization, and thus was fully aware of all operations relating to Skorzeny.

Ilse had given information to author Lee that the Gehlen organization had dispatched one of their men to bring weapons to the safe house harboring Skorzeny. This was likely Captain Walter Girg, Skorzeny's former wartime intelligence officer. Girg had been one of Skorzeny's most trusted officers as well as a superior soldier and undercover operative. It is documented that Girg worked for both U.S. and French intelligence immediately after the war, including U.S. Army counterintelligence and the Gehlen Organization.

Ilse indicated Otto was told to be on guard, a likely reference to the Soviet kidnapping threat relayed to Skorzeny at Camp King by Arnold Silver prior to Skorzeny's release. Ilse recalled, "Otto was fearless. He had nerves of steel." From this secluded mountain hideout, Skorzeny would begin plotting his next moves and began making clandestine contact with his former unit members who were scattered all over the war-torn landscape of Germany.

Now we turn our attention to Ilse as she will be inseparable from Otto Skorzeny for the rest of this book. Skorzeny's female companion (later to be his wife) was born Ilse Lüthje, in Kiel, Germany, in 1919. Said to be a very attractive and highly intelligent woman, she was described by a later acquaintance to have held "a fairly high position in German intelligence," during the war. The same source said she spent considerable time in England before the outbreak of war, "in the interest of the [German] intelligence services."

During the early part of World War II, Ilse had married Adolf Finck von Finckenstein. It is generally understood that von Finckenstein was a wealthy man and had served as a German army officer. Although no children were born from this marriage, Finckenstein had a four-year-old daughter, Editha, from a previous marriage. Ilse would become very close to her stepdaughter during the short years they were together, and they remained close for life.

On January 30, 1945, in the latter part of World War II, Ilse and Adolf had developed marital problems, which resulted in a split. Ilse apparently then moved to Paris and took up with a man named Robert Laroy. Again, the circumstances behind these developments are almost completely unknown. We do know that Laroy (sometimes spelled Laroye) was a former SS officer who had served in the Belgian 28th SS Volunteer Grenadier Division Wallonian and with Skorzeny's commandos.

IMPORTANT FRENCH CONNECTIONS

It is known, by reason of later interviews, that certain French intelligence officers played a key role in the shadows of Skorzeny's escape. This was later confirmed by the officers directly involved in the operation, including Colonel Michel Garder. In reality, these officers, were actually part of the extralegal and secret organization *Service d'Ordre du RPF* (SO du RPF) embedded *within* French intelligence. This secrecy was reflected in a newspaper article during an interview with Colonel Michel Garder, who confirmed, "Of course, the [Skorzeny] operation was only half-covered by headquarters in Paris." Colonel Garder's use of the word "operation" confirms that the event was an organized clandestine event. As the reader will soon see, the highly secretive *Service d'Ordre du RPF* would continue to have a central role in the clandestine intrigues of Otto Skorzeny for nearly a decade after his release. Overall, the Skorzeny connection to *Service d'Ordre du RPF* is not unusual since it is documented that the organization actively recruited former SS men as operatives. One of these was a former SS *Hauptsturmführer* (captain) who used the cover name, Gerold Gordon. The author believes this was Skorzeny's former intelligence officer Walter Girg mentioned above.

The strong connections to *Service d'Ordre du RPF* has implications for Ilse as well, although they remain murky. Despite this lack of clarity, it would not be unreasonable, based on available evidence, to conclude Ilse had been a very important spy during the war. But her exact allegiances and associated activities are not known. At some point, however, Ilse developed *very* important French intelligence connections. This is confirmed in the Skorzeny papers. Her contacts included men in the very highest levels of French intelligence, but most specifically those within the *Service d'Ordre*. These included, the previously mentioned General Pierre de Bénouville, Colonel Gilbert Renault, Pierre Bertaux, and Roger Wybot. All were dedicated anti-Communists, and all were participants in postwar intelligence operations.

Let's look closer at these French connections. First, there is Colonel Renault, who used the alias Colonel Remy during the war. Renault was one of the most famous secret agents in the history of France and an important figure in the Resistance during World War II. Although a strong ally of de Gaulle, after the war Renault supported the rehabilitation of Marshal Pétain. This resulted in his repudiation by de Gaulle. A short time afterward, he resigned from the RPF and moved to Portugal in 1954.

Next there is Pierre Bertaux, he was Director of the *Sûreté Nationale* (national police equivalent to the American FBI). His organization controlled all the police forces in the municipalities of France. He was a highly experienced secret agent and a veteran leader of the French resistance. During the war, Bertaux organized the "Bertaux Group" in southern France to work with British SOE and American OSS operatives. Interestingly, Bertaux was also an authority on German culture and literature. He had a high regard for the German people, stemming from a family academic heritage in Germanic studies. His father and great-uncle were well-known French Germanists (scholars of Germany).

Finally, Ilse knew well Roger Wybot, a pivotal character in this book. Wybot was the head of the Directorate of Territorial Surveillance, or DST. His organization was responsible for foreign threats against France. Wybot used the alias Roger Warin. He has been compared to legendary CIA chief Allen Dulles and to the formidable FBI director J. Edgar Hoover. During World War II, Wybot was appointed to organize the French intelligence service French *Bureau Central de Renseignements et d'Action* (BCRA), and subsequently led its counterintelligence section. His ruthless methods and strict monitoring of the Free French and Resistance led to animosity toward him by other members of French intelligence. Because of this internal friction, he was subsequently reassigned to Italy. This assignment had later implications for this story since James Angleton was the senior U.S. intelligence officer in Italy at the close of the war. The two became very close friends.

Near the end of World War II, it was Wybot who was called upon to help organize the French postwar security organizations. He was ultimately selected to lead the DST. Since Roger Wybot and Pierre Bertaux were also members of the *Service d'Ordre*, they were among the top leadership of the anti-Communist networks hidden *within* French intelligence. A key point to remember about the *Service d'Ordre du RPF* was that it was also at the forefront in the establishment of anti-Communist stay-behind forces in Europe after the war and worked with American intelligence in developing these clandestine networks. This is the basic reason Otto Skorzeny had both French and American contacts that he was dealing with.

RADL ESCAPES

One month after Skorzeny's so-called escape, his faithful former adjutant Karl Radl also escaped. The fact that Radl's escape followed so closely on the heels of Skorzeny's has received no attention until this study. It is clearly a subsequent phase of the Skorzeny operation and it is also known that Radl worked for French intelligence in the postwar period. Meanwhile, information began coming in concerning sightings of Skorzeny and rumor mills began to stir about the formation of strange organizations.

The Berchtesgaden area where Skorzeny's safe house was located straddles the border region of Austria and Germany. It was in an area covered by two U.S. counterintelligence zones of control. The Austrian zone was controlled by the U.S. Army 430 CIC. The German zone, known as Region IV, was controlled by the 7970th CIC.

For example, Munich police reported to American intelligence that an individual brought in for false documentation had stated under questioning that he was a member of Skorzeny's *Jagdverein,* or "hunting society," adding it was "an anti-Communist organization." The report that Skorzeny was using the name *Jagdverein* (hunting society) as the cover for his activity is interesting due to the closeness of the name to his wartime commando unit, *Jagdverband* or hunting group. Another report concerned the formation of an organization called the "Skorzeny Group." These reports may have revealed Skorzeny's initial efforts to recruit individuals to work as undercover paramilitary advisers and agents.

Later, future researchers would pour over the CIC reporting on Skorzeny. Some determined that the reports alluded to Skorzeny's involvement with a mysterious organization known as ODESSA, reputedly an underground network set up to protect former Nazis. While not totally inaccurate, the reality is there were numerous underground networks. Some of these had sinister or criminal intent but others were networks established by Western intelligence or event Soviet intelligence. The author interviewed retired CIA officer Tom Polgar, who was in Germany at the time, about these postwar networks. Polgar stated that the ODESSA network, as it related to Skorzeny, was a total exaggeration. Polgar did not however volunteer any details about how he knew this or the extent of his knowledge of the Skorzeny operation.

Declassified documents from this period indicate that lower-level field agents of U.S. Army counterintelligence were likely totally unaware that Skorzeny's escape was orchestrated by Western intelligence. Thus, the reports generated by CIC are from individuals not in the know concerning Skorzeny's secret status. However, these reports did serve an important intelligence purpose. They served to monitor the situation and keep those in the know about Skorzeny appraised of critical information and a potential compromise to the operation. This counterintelligence methodology on Skorzeny will continue to be used over the entire course of his postwar clandestine career.

CHAPTER EIGHT
PB7

*"Who she was, I don't remember. I don't know whether I knew her name
then. She was in the group sitting around a table."*

FROM THE TESTIMONY OF COLONEL BORIS PASH,
SENATE SELECT COMMITTEE ON GOVERNMENT
INTELLIGENCE ACTIVITIES IN 1976

FRANK WISNER AND THE OFFICE OF POLICY COORDINATION (OPC)

In the midst of Skorzeny's efforts to reestablish contacts from his old command,
the National Security Council on August 19, 1948, confirmed the appointment
of Frank G. Wisner as director of the Office of Policy Coordination (OPC), the
division of the CIA responsible for covert action. Wisner officially took charge
on September 1, 1948 with the title, Assistant Director for Policy Coordination.
Although under the CIA administratively, the OPC took its direction from the
Department of State, an important distinction in these days when the new
anti-Communist strategies were being formulated by the United States government. As mentioned in the preceding chapter, OPC's missions were authorized
on June 18, 1948, in National Security Council Directive 10/2. This was the
key authorization for covert action put into place on the very eve of Skorzeny's
release, and in retrospect the two events are not coincidental.

With the creation of the OPC, the CIA, only one year old at this point, had
two main branches. In addition to the OPC a separate clandestine service operated as the Office of Special Operations or OSO. The OSO, unlike the OPC

was fully under CIA control. Eventually, in 1952, the OSO and OPC would be merged under one office, the Directorate of Plans. Until that point, Wisner had nearly no oversite from CIA leadership and embarked on highly secretive operations unknown to other sections of the agency. One of his early secret additions was Otto Skorzeny.

Described by veteran OSS officers as "brilliant," Wisner was specifically tasked with covert psychological and paramilitary operations. He graduated from the University of Virginia Law School in 1934. As mentioned in a previous chapter, Wisner served for a short time under Allen Dulles after the war setting up the first postwar cover networks in Germany but eventually left the OSS to take work with a law firm on Wall Street. Hungry for the type of covert action he saw during the war, in 1947 he joined the State Department as deputy assistant secretary for occupied areas. Here he was instumental in the formation of policy and planning for utilization of foreign intelligence assets. When the OPC was formed, Wisner was the logical choice to lead the organization.

Wisner established OPC representatives throughout Germany and Austria, including on the embassy staff of the Department of State, and within a year had a staff of 302 individuals with a budget well over $4 million—a considerable sum in 1949. Early OPC cover organizations included theInternational Refugee Organization (IRO) and the Economic Cooperation Administration or ECA. The ECA was an important U.S. government agency involved with labor issues in the European recovery programs which Wisner embedded with his officers. This is highly relevant because the Skorzeny papers indicate Skorzeny's early businesses were established using ECA contracts. The details of Skorzeny's involvement with the ECA and associated CIA activity will be covered in greater detail in Chapter Fourteen.

WISNER'S OPC

Author Tim Weiner, an authority on U.S. national security programs, noted in his history of the CIA, that although the public was aware of the CIA, they would not have known about Wisner's OPC. Not only were OPC operations secret, "the existence of the organization itself was also secret." Weiner also pointed out, that during OPC formative years the organization was, "the most secret thing in the U.S. Government after nuclear weapons" and OPC programs were actually part of the nuclear war planning. Wisner was specifically tasked to create stay-behind networks of foreign agents in the East Bloc countries to be used in the event of nuclear war. This included preparing forces and stock piling weapons. USAF General Curtis LeMay, Commander of the Strategic Air Command, also tasked OPC to set up escape routes for nuclear bomber pilots who would be shot down or as he knew would have to ditch east of the Iron Curtain because they would be out of fuel after delivery of their bombs.

These missions directly affect the CIA's interest in Otto Skorzeny since they demanded finding the right people with the skills, experience, and composure necessary for dangerous work. These missions also gave Wisner great authorities to leverage a wide range of government and non-government agencies. His power in the early years of the CIA was unprecedented. In this regard, he also turned to "black" assets such as the use of former Nazis, which he then placed into secret networks using the cover of the International Relief Organization (IRO) or a myriad of private business or foundations.

Wisner divided the OPC into two branches: one for *planning,* the other for *operations.* We will examine the Operations Branch first.

OPERATIONS BRANCH

Wisner's deputy, Frank Lindsay, headed the operational branches which carried out the missions directing foreign agents, a critical factor when considering Otto Skorzeny's use by OPC. Lindsay had been in Paris in June at the same time General Donovan was confirming with members of the Secret Paramilitary Group organizing for Compass Rose. This was on the eve of Otto Skorzeny's escape, which occurred in July.

Lindsay, whose full name was Franklin A. Lindsay, was the key planner for OPC covert intelligence and paramilitary operations. In his service as an OSS officer, Lindsay carried out dangerous behind-the-lines missions in Austria and in Yugoslavia, where he was assigned as head of the OSS liaison mission to Marshal Tito. Tito, it will be recalled, had been the subject of an attempted abduction (or assassination) by Otto Skorzeny during World War II under the code name Knight's Leap. Given his own background with Marshal Tito, the Skorzeny operation to abduct Tito must have been of great interest to Lindsay. In fact, Lindsay, as head of the operations branch of OPC was assigned abduction and assassination missions. This is, in the opinion of the author, the primary reason for OPC's interest in Skorzeny (a man with vast experience in both areas).

One of Frank Lindsay's main objectives was to leverage émigré populations for covert action. This effort zeroed in on Ukrainians and East Europeans who were escaping Soviet domination and as previously pointed out, many of these had fought for or collaborated with the Nazis. Otto Skorzeny had worked with these collaborators during the war and some were members of his commando. Vetting, organizing, and training these people into covert assets was assigned directly to Frank Lindsay. As the point man for the conduct of covert operations, Lindsay was also tasked to make sure official United States government involvement was not visible and was plausibly deniable.

PLANNING BRANCH

The other section of OPC is the Planning Branch. This branch drafted the operational plans that would then be sent over to Frank Lindsay's Operations Branch for execution. Understanding the Planning Branch makeup and its various missions is important since members of this branch will have direct contact with Skorzeny—as the reader will soon find out.

Here are the sections and missions for the OPC Planning Branch:

- PB1: Political warfare, including assistance to underground resistance movements and support of indigenous anti-Communist elements in threatened countries of the free world.
- PB2: Psychological warfare, including "black" and "gray" propaganda.
- PB3: Economic warfare.
- PB4: Evacuation, including the paramount responsibility for escape and evasion.

- PB5: Guerrilla and partisan-type warfare.
- PB6: Sabotage and counter-sabotage.
- PB7: Other covert operations (excluding espionage, counterespionage, and cover and deception for military operations).

SKORZENY'S MEETING WITH THE MYSTERIOUS "MR. MARTIN"

Information concerning Skorzeny's earliest contact with Wisner's OPC appears in a now declassified CIA document covering an interview conducted with Skorzeny at the U.S. Embassy in Spain in 1958. The interview had been requested by the Department of State which was processing a request by Skorzeny to visit the United States, as such, Skorzeny was asked to describe any contact with U.S. intelligence up to that point. Skorzeny gave a rather lengthy description of his activities, however, documents in the Skorzeny papers indicate Skorzeny *did not* necessarily give the interviewer, CIA officer Daniel E. Wright, who was under diplomatic cover, all of his contacts with U.S. intelligence from the preceding years. This indicates Skorzeny was likely dealing with compartmented or separate offices and thus he was simply obeying instructions not to reveal the activity. What Skorzeny did say points to a very significant meeting with U.S. intelligence shortly after his release that has all the hallmarks of an OPC operation. In the description, Skorzeny related how, shortly after his release in January 1949, he was secretly approached by a mysterious "Mr. Martin" who claimed to be from the U.S. State Department, although Skorzeny said he doubted that was his true position.

The author has narrowed the identification of "Mr. Martin" to David Martin, Director of the International Relief Organization (IRO), who was in Germany during this period and as mentioned above providing operational cover for Wisner's OPC. Skorzeny had preexisting IRO links at this time as well—the reader will recall Major Robert Bishop, one-time OSS officer under Frank Wisner who handled Skorzeny's records during the Nuremberg Trials and later assumed a senior position working as an undercover intelligence operative with the IRO in Italy.

The Martin meeting was likely the contact Skorzeny was told to expect before being released from Camp King. Skorzeny did not give the location of the meeting with "Mr. Martin" but would later recall that that it started at eight o'clock in the evening and went all through the night until 10 a.m. the next day. The focus was several key topics, and as we shall see, all of them were the exact covert missions assigned to Frank Wisner's planning branches at OPC. Martin explained his operations to Skorzeny, including the establishment of an underground system for the return of shot-down western pilots and the organizing of sabotage in the Soviet Bloc. Again, these accurately reflect Frank Wisner's OPC planning branches; for example, PB4 (Evacuation) and PB6 (Sabotage), as well as the documented assistance given to OPC by the IRO using its vast émigré networks.

Another area of discussion at the meeting was contingencies for a Soviet invasion of Germany; specifically, how to deny the Soviets from capturing vital German industries and how to evacuate scientists, engineers, and technical personnel. The fact that the evacuation of key personnel was a talking point of the discussions is critical. In fact, the Skorzeny papers contain correlating documents written after the Martin meeting specifically referring to plans Skorzeny termed as "rescue actions." Basically, these were specially trained commando units that Skorzeny had assembled from his wartime command and other contacts that could be sent in to denied areas to extract key personnel or rescue them if the Soviets had already seized them. The rescue capability developed by Skorzeny matches OPC missions precisely and leads us to another meeting that occurred at or very near this same time, and may have in fact been the same meeting.

COLONEL BORIS PASH AND PB7

Another meeting of great consequence to Skorzeny was one involving Colonel Boris T. Pash, an Army officer who had been detailed from the military to Wisner's OPC in the fall of 1948. Wisner assigned Pash, who had tremendous credentials in covert warfare, to lead PB7 where he handled war plans, front companies, and covert operations not tasked to the other planning branches.

Colonel Pash's assignment to PB7 was revealed for the first time during testimony before the Senate Select Committee on government intelligence activities in 1976. At that time, Pash had been called to testify because of comments made to the press by former CIA officer, E. Howard Hunt who claimed PB7 handled assassination. Hunt at the time was serving in a federal prison in Florida, jailed for his participation in the Watergate affair. In December 1975, Hunt told the *New York Times* that "The CIA had a small unit set up to arrange for the assassination of suspected double-agents and similar low-ranking officials." Hunt went on to claim that the man in charge of the assassination unit was none other than Colonel Boris T. Pash. Hunt's shocking revelation resulted in Colonel Pash being called to Washington to testify.

Pash denied under oath that his PB7 branch conducted assassination operations. The author believes this to be correct, but his full testimony gives evidence that his branch was associated with certain aspects of assassination and that he likely held a meeting with Otto Skorzeny where the discussion included these missions.

Specifically, Pash described to the committee a meeting that occurred around the time of his initial posting to PB7 in early 1949. Interestingly, the description of the meeting described by Colonel Pash matches in every manner the meeting described by Skorzeny with "Mr. Martin" which also occurred at this time. Pash recalled that at this meeting there was a discussion regarding a potential invasion of the West and what operations could be carried out to deny the Soviets key industries, such as blowing them up, and what actions could be taken to prevent the capture of certain "difficult to replace, highly technical individuals, whose skills had to be developed in years." On this last point, Pash remembered "a woman" sitting at the table who spoke up and said, "Why don't we murder them?" Pash claimed the bluntness of the woman's comment caught many at the meeting off guard; he also stated, "Who she was, I don't remember. I don't know whether I knew her name then. She was in the group sitting around a table."

It would be logical to conclude Pash was talking about Ilse Skorzeny, who, as we know, was working in concert with Otto in the execution of his secret activities for the West. Although Pash did not specifically mention the presence of Otto or Ilse Skorzeny, it is certainly non-coincidental when considering all the facts and the thesis grows stronger as more details about the meeting are revealed.

Naturally, the comment about murder caught the immediate attention of the Senate committee members, who pressed Pash for more information on his statement. When pressured, Pash reluctantly told the committee that assassination was mentioned during the meeting but maintained his group did not conduct assassination operations. As we shall see, Colonel Pash may have essentially answered correctly the functions of his office but skirted the truth by not revealing PB7 was connected to an outsourced assassination capability, such as one that could be set up by Otto Skorzeny.

Colonel Boris Pash was born Boris Theodore Pashkovsky in San Francisco, California, on June 20, 1900. His father, Theodore Pashkovsky was a Russian Orthodox Priest who had been sent to California in 1894 by the Church. In 1912, the family returned to Russia, and during the Russian Revolution they supported the White Russians against the Communist. During the struggle, Colonel Pash developed a great hatred for Communism, holding them directly responsible for the death of his mother who became ill and was cruelly denied medical treatment by Communist authorities.

In 1920, the family returned to the United States not wanting to leave under Communism. Pash married that same year and in 1923 attended Springfield College in Massachusetts, graduating with a degree in Physical Education. Also during this time, he changed his name to Pash, a common practice among many immigrant groups living in America at the time. Throughout the 1920s and 1930s, Pash continued his education, taught high school and eventually joined the United States Army Reserve. Given his background and education, he was given an officers commission and assigned to the intelligence branch. He also received certifications in counterintelligence from the FBI at a school set up for military officers.

Colonel Pash would become no stranger to sensitive covert operations and during World War II stacked up an illustrious war service record. His first assignment was preparing for a Japanese attack of the west coast of the United States. In this capacity, he dealt with the internment of Japanese Americans.

Pash also served in the early period of the war as an Army counterintelligence officer working on the highly classified Manhattan Project (U.S. Atomic Bomb project). Pash was tasked with investigating security breaches at the Manhattan Project's Berkeley Radiation Laboratory. As the program progressed, the director of the Manhattan Project, Army Major General Leslie R. Groves, created a section, to which Pash was assigned, to specifically target enemy scientists working on Germany's atomic program in the United States. Thomas Powers, author of *Heisenberg's War*, stated General Groves, "had an extraordinary resolution to win the war . . . It was not just to build a bomb, but to build it, to use it, and to prevent the Germans from building one. He was equally resolute about all three." In 1943, General Groves had received a green light from Gen. George V. Strong, the head of Army intelligence, to target German atomic scientists. In a letter to the Army Chief of Staff, General Strong wrote, "The killing of scientific personnel employed therein would be particularly advantageous." Although first focused on the German threat, an even greater danger turned out to be Soviet spies in the United States, not Nazi agents or atomic scientists. In particular, at the Berkeley Radiation Laboratory, Pash identified the greatest threat to the atomic program as Soviet agents attempting to steal classified research.

This threat would have demanded the removal and perhaps liquidation of Soviet agents, double agents, or anyone actually deemed a threat to the project if there were no other alternatives. A compromise of the Manhattan Project would have been catastrophic for the United States; hence, the safeguards were extraordinary. These agent assassination programs, by their very nature, required finding unique individuals with the character traits and abilities to successfully carry out these exceptionally ruthless but necessary liquidation missions. As a security officer assigned to the Manhattan Project, Pash would have monitored individuals who would have been exceptionally grave threats to national security. Later, in 1944, on the direct orders from General Groves, Pash also commanded the Alsos Mission, a joint intelligence group that searched for Germany's atomic scientists.

ABDUCTIONS AND ASSASSINATION

When responding to the Senate committee, Colonel Pash suggested assassination may in fact have been mentioned in the charter of PB7 a result of the influence of former OSS officers who had routinely carried out assassination missions during the war. Pash said he had "glanced over" the OPC charter language concerning assassination and therefore could not remember specifics regarding instructions or details. He emphatically stated PB7 was only involved in *planning* or, more specifically, exploring assassination options. He also stated, "There were a lot of entrepreneurs and adventurers," former OSS operatives with their "wild ideas and wild approaches." This is a veiled reference to the former OSS "cowboys" that were now working for Donovan's SPG under the operational cover of World Commerce Corporation. The *exact* group that had orchestrated the release of Skorzeny!

Another officer (not named) questioned by the Senate committee holding the title Director of Operations Planning or the individual in charge of supervising all seven OPC branches (i.e., Colonel Pash's boss), stated emphatically PB7 "was responsible for assassinations and kidnapping as well as other 'special operations,'" and he had "a clear recollection that the written charter of 'special operations' stated, 'PB7 will be responsible for assassinations, kidnapping, and such functions as from time to time may be given it . . . by higher authority.'" This same officer also stated that Frank Wisner "agreed that Pash should have jurisdiction over assassinations" and "kidnapping of personages behind the Iron Curtain," both those "not in sympathy with the regime" and those "whose interests were inimical to ours." In regard to assassination, the director clarified that "It was a matter of keeping up with the Joneses," pointing out that every other power conducted these operations.

THE KEYS—COVER AND DECEPTION

Pash stated that any involvement by his office in assassination would have had to originate from "people at the top." When asked to clarify who "people at the top" would be, he stated, Frank Wisner, the chief of OPC. Pash pointed out to the committee that his office was not an operational unit but a planning group.

Clarifying PB7's role, Pash stated that if he received instructions for an assassination operation, that his office would only involve the *conditions* for which the task was done—*who would be involved*. The timing, location and how the mission was to be carried out did not fall under his office. Pash stated it was Frank Lindsay, head of the OPC Operations Division, who took the general plan and then conducted detailed operational planning.

Colonel Pash's own explanation holds the key to his meeting with Skorzeny and Ilse. We refer back to the missions outlined for PB7—Colonel Pash handled—*cover* and *deception*! Since Pash's office supported Frank Lindsay's Operations Branch, PB7's direct role was providing the cover and deception necessary for Frank Lindsay's Operations Branch to plan and carry out assassination missions. With this information clearly defined, the inclusion of Otto and Ilse Skorzeny in exploratory meetings on assassination by Frank Wisner's OPC makes perfect sense. First, the secret objectives as outlined by National Directive 10/2 in June 1948, included assassination and abduction, matching precisely the talking points mentioned by Colonel Pash at the Skorzeny meeting. Secondly, as covered above, it was PB7 that was responsible for establishing cover (i.e. private or corporate structures) that would in turn, give Frank Lindsay's operations branch, both plausible and deniable aspects for his operational planning. The Pash meeting with Skorzeny can therefore be considered the starting point when OPC officials set up the cover details for Skorzeny, officially placing the network he was currently organizing under the World Commerce Corporation umbrella thus becoming a new clandestine entity within Donovan's 'SPG.'

When CIA official E. Howard Hunt had given information to the press that "The CIA had a small unit set up to arrange for the assassination of suspected double-agents and similar low-ranking foreign officials," it appears to confirm the early formation of a U.S. postwar assassination capability inherent to Frank Wisner's OPC. It is particularly interesting that E. Howard Hunt claimed the CIA unit was set up to "arrange" versus "carry out" assassinations. Therefore, assassination operations contemplated or planned by the OPC logically used surrogates—given the revelations above this would be Skorzeny's private network. Hunt had also been in Paris in 1948 assisting with the implementation of classified programs under the Marshall Plan and he may very well have known of OPC contact with Skorzeny.

Directives for the OPC demanded that covert operations be entirely untraceable. "We knew what we were doing," recalled CIA officer Harry Rositzke, a Soviet expert who had once worked with Wisner. Rositzke soberly added, "It was a visceral business of using any bastard as long as he was anti-Communist." Since taking over the OPC in the latter part of 1948, Frank Wisner had been a man on a mission. His OPC expanded rapidly, and he set about reestablishing the cloak-and-dagger operations of the old OSS and redirecting them at the heart of the new Soviet enemy.

Wisner was also fully aware of Soviet "wet affairs" carried out by the 13th Directorate, a KGB branch tasked with eliminating double agents and Western spies by assassination. Within the CIA, Wisner's OPC was directed to develop a similar U.S. capability. Colonel James Critchfield, a CIA liaison officer assigned to the super-secret Gehlen Organization, who was aware of Wisner's cloak-and-dagger operations, recalled, "Some of the people Frank brought in were terrible guys, but he didn't focus on it." Years later, CIA officer, Peter Sichel, a member of the Office of Special Operations, or OSO, would note with disapproval that, "OPC'ers had that missionary zeal in their eyes. We distrusted missionary zeal."

ASSASSINATION PROJECTS

The reader will note going forward that Skorzeny will be involved in nearly every mission category described for Wisner's OPC. However, for the purpose of clarity and focus, the author will continue to concentrate on specific activities involving Skorzeny with organizations or people with historical links to assassination.

One activity in particular can now be reassessed in light of this study. The writer refers back to a previously mentioned event recorded by Skorzeny in his memoirs. This was his participation in clearing rubble in a town outside Camp

King at the time of his interment and close to escape. This seemingly insignificant activity is actually linked to covert assassination operations. I will explain.

Clearing rubble in bombed out German cities was carried out by German citizens and émigrés (displaced peoples) formed in special workforce groups called Labor Service companies. The need for these groups was certainly legitimate, but their formation also created some very interesting dynamics in regard to covert operations. This arose from the fact that many of the people brought into the Labor Service companies were displaced immigrants fleeing the Soviet occupation of their countries. They had both fear and hatred of Communism and some had been Nazi collaborators or served in volunteer SS units fighting for Germany.

It was precisely these groups that were targeted for recruitment by Frank Wisner's OPC. It was under the guidance set forth under NSC 10/2 that Labor Service companies were secretly financed and used as a cover for paramilitary programs involving covert warfare. The secret formation was to serve as guerrilla units for a potential war with the Soviets. An excellent background on the use of Labor Companies and the reasons for their formation is described in the book, *Blowback: America's Recruitment of Nazis and Its Destructive Impact on Our Domestic and Foreign Policy*, by author Christopher Simpson. In *Blowback*, Simpson reveals the U.S. war planning involved in the use of Labor companies and their importance to much larger strategic nuclear war preparations.

U.S. intelligence was keenly aware that the Nazis had created similar work brigades of Ukrainians and foreign-born Germans for use during the invasions of Poland and the Baltic states. These Nazi Labor Service squads also served as hitmen, organized into special assassination units. During the war Skorzeny had established sabotage schools that trained Russian defectors, Ukrainians, Latvians, and others from the Baltic countries. During the latter part of World War II, Skorzeny was involved setting up stay-behind formations of the Ukrainian underground in a secret program designated Operation *Sonnenblume* (Sunflower). After the war, some of the foreigners associated with Skorzeny's schools ended up in the émigré camps and undoubtedly sought work in the Service Labor companies.

It is a matter of historical record that during World War II, the Allies were the undisputed masters of covert operations dealing with undergrounds. However, Skorzeny's knowledge of true stay-behind networks was actually more extensive given the Allies never actually had to deal with an advancing enemy into their territories. Skorzeny dedicated an entire chapter to his Russian and Ukrainian wartime contacts in his memoir. His personal knowledge of these émigré groups, their wartime covert activities, and especially his ability to reestablish contact with them, would have been of extreme interest to Frank Wisner and his planning staff. Skorzeny was likely pressed for his knowledge of these stay-behind groups by General Donovan and Colonel Benson during his initial interrogations as a POW. So, we can now determine that Skorzeny's knowledge of Nazi networks, secreting of assets and covert paramilitary operations as principle reasons Skorzeny and his adjutant Karl Radl were sent to Camp King in 1947. Since Skorzeny himself confirmed his connection to the Labor Service companies (i.e. clearing rubble) while at Camp King, it is not unreasonable to suspect his expertise was used in some capacity for the operations involving paramilitary auxiliaries. The timing of the meetings and activities described above involving Skorzeny can now be put into a broader context of documented assassination activity for this same period.

OPERATIONS HAGBERRY AND LITHIA

Documented evidence for official state sponsored assassination or paramilitary actions involving assassination are extremely rare. In many cases, these documents were uncovered as a result of official or unofficial investigations of assassination incidents. Two examples were cited in Christopher Simpson's *Blowback* that likely have implications for Skorzeny's covert history, although at this point they are parallel occurrences. None the less, the chances of some direct or indirect connection to the facts relayed in this chapter are very high.

The assassination operations in question were codenamed Hagberry and Lithia. It is known they targeted foreign agents who had penetrated U.S. and

British émigré espionage networks. Operation Hagberry was the liquidation of the Chikalov Ring that U.S. intelligence had identified as a Soviet intelligence net operating within the U.S. Zone. Operation Lithia was initiated in November 1947, and authorized the liquidation of the Kindermann Ring, a large Czechoslovakian espionage net also operating in the American zone. The mission of the operation was to terminate all suspected double agents within the Kindermann Ring. Records also indicated that the operation was directed by an unidentified joint U.S. and British command and control element as part of Operation Rusty. Operation Rusty was the codeword used for the Gehlen organization but may not be identical. At the time Operation Lithia went into effect, Otto Skorzeny and his adjutant Karl Radl were at Camp King being processed by U.S. intelligence. Both men were allowed a fourteen-day pass in December, during which they had a number of enigmatic meeting and from which they returned to the camp. Later, both men were given passes to "clear rubble" associating them with the Service Labor companies. These companies were under U.S. Army control and as covered above were the exact cover used for covert paramilitaries later linked assassination cases.

PROJECT OHIO

Christopher Simpson's research also revealed an even more violent project known as Operation Ohio. This assassination operation used "gangland-style" murders. The operators were a squad of "Ukrainian ex-Nazis" that carried out "at least twenty murders in the displaced persons camp at Mittenwald, south of Munich." Again, the targets were suspected double agents. The operational cover for Ohio was to attribute the murders to "factional violence among rival right-wing Ukrainian émigré groups." Of importance here is supporting evidence given by USAF Colonel L. Fletcher Prouty who was involved in the early formation of covert assets in Europe: "We kept personnel at several air bases around the world for these types of missions . . . some of these were the best commercial hit men you have ever heard of. [They were] mechanics, killers. They were Ukrainians, mainly, and Eastern Europeans, Greeks, and some Scotsmen. I don't know how the Scotsmen got there, but there they were. None of them were American citizens."

Evidence for Skorzeny's participation with the paramilitary formations being utilized to carry out assassinations is also revealed in a report from Colonel Aaron Bank's CIC Region IV from the period of Skorzeny's post-escape, and during the time of the operations described above. The nearly illegible declassified document, originated from an unidentified individual who came into Army CIC to report on information he had on Skorzeny. The source said he had gotten word that British intelligence was aware of the presence and clandestine activities of Skorzeny near Munich and had been joined by his former adjutant Karl Radl. Importantly, he stated the two were now working for U.S. intelligence "building a sabotage organization."

The use of the term sabotage is another vital clue in unraveling assassination. In fact, the historical precedent is quite clear. History has proven that the American OSS and British SOE had assassination programs during World War II. When we examine the men (and women) who trained, organized and carried out these types of operations we generally find they were formed *within* the designated sabotage unit of the parent organization. In the case of the OSS for example, sabotage fell under the Special Operations (SO) branch. These personnel received highly classified methods for destruction, subversion and the more lethal capabilities of spy work. Often the term sabotage is used as a blanket and more palatable way of saying the unit was conducting assassination.

There was an obvious reason in war for having an assassination unit, such as to disrupt the command and control networks of the enemy by eliminating important decision makers. Besides targeting the enemy leaders, assassination was also used to eliminate foreign agents, traitors, or individuals who might threaten exceptionally critical national security programs.

Skorzeny's experience and knowledge was not easily duplicated. Nor was his extensive network of former commandos. The Skorzeny papers confirm he was in contact with former officers of the infamous Peter Group, the SS assassination unit sent to Denmark 1944–1945. He could also tap those with the unique skills from the different nationalities that had served in Nazi units including Ukrainians and other eastern Europeans adept as secret agents and assassination.

When focused on Skorzeny's activities in the post-escape period we find therefore, ample evidence that Skorzeny meets the third objective set out by NSC Directive 10/2 dealing with counterforce. Counterforce as described by Kennan was "outright paramilitary actions: guerrilla units, sabotage, subversion . . ." in which "guidance and funds would pass to a private American organization or organization (business enterprise) composed of private citizens" with "field offices in Europe and Asia." This is the literal description for World Commerce Corporation and Donovan's SPG.

The official records for Boris Pash office (PB7) have never been released. But a reasonable historical reconstruction of evidence was established prior to the writing of this book by authors such as Simpson and through the efforts of other individuals investigating the facts. The research conducted by this author on Otto Skorzeny aligns with previous research to include the same personalities, organizations, and timeline. Ultimately, Skorzeny's personal papers and supporting documentation provided the solid evidence necessary to affirm Skorzeny was involved in training, organizing and conducting covert warfare for Western intelligence. Skorzeny's support was centered on sabotage, the traditional department for conducting assassination.

In his book *Blowback*, author Christopher Simpson rendered his academic opinion on the mysterious disappearance of PB7 records and concisely outlines the key elements in the rise of Cold War assassination capabilities. The author of this book quotes here a paragraph lifted from Simpson's conclusion in his section on assassination: "the early Bloodstone operations played a significant role in laying the groundwork for what one Senate investigator later called 'a procedure [within the CIA] which, although not spelled out in so many words, was generally understood and served as the basis to plan or otherwise contemplate political assassinations.'" This quote, is a more than fitting end to this chapter, and serves well in setting the stage for the final act found in this book.

CHAPTER NINE

DEADLY INTELLIGENCE

"We kill only for reasons of state."

MAURICE ROBERT,

FRENCH INTELLIGENCE SERVICE AGENT

"You can't even breathe about this—you can barely think about it."

SECRETARY OF DEFENSE JAMES V. FORRESTAL

TO MAJOR GENERAL LYMAN L. LEMNITZER, 1949

Almost immediately after the meeting with David Martin and Colonel Boris Pash, Skorzeny left Europe on a short clandestine trip to Argentina. Passage through Spain was arranged by the Spanish security service, *Dirección General de Seguridad* (DGS). This appears to confirm that members of Spanish intelligence were connected to the Secret Paramilitary Group through Frank Ryan's WCC that was operating out of Madrid.

We can only speculate as to the nature of Skorzeny business in Argentina, but it was likely to establish contact with former SS men and former Nazi émigrés he wanted to include in his organization or for some reason connected to Nazi assets. Declassified correspondence dated February 2, 1949, from an unidentified intelligence official at the 7712 European Command Intelligence School (ECIS), in Oberammergau, Germany, states that Skorzeny is "once more with us . . . [and] . . . his services were being put to some use." The same letter mentions he is not in Europe. Other correlating evidence from oral histories indicates Skorzeny's destination was Argentina. The letter confirms that U.S.

intelligence was aware of SPG activities as they related to Skorzeny. Skorzeny did not stay in South America very long and had returned to Europe in a matter of weeks. There is an unfortunate gap in documents for several months after this period. It can be reasonably assumed however, that after his return, Skorzeny's primary activity was expanding his covert network.

SKORZENY ARRIVES IN PARIS

The next significant event on the Skorzeny timeline occurred in May 1948, when he and Ilse met with two French intelligence officials, Pierre Bertaux, Director of the *Sûreté Nationale*, and Roger Wybot, head of the Directorate of Territorial Surveillance, or DST. Both men were part of Compass Rose, working alongside the CIA and the SPG to neutralize the Communist networks threatening the internal stability of France. This direct interaction from the highest levels of French intelligence with Skorzeny dramatically illustrates the level of secrecy surrounding Compass Rose.

Pierre Bertaux was also well acquainted with the senior leadership of U.S. intelligence agencies. In fact, Bertaux was a personal friend of James J. Angleton, a celebrated CIA officer and long-time chief of the Agency's counterintelligence office. But, at the time of Bertaux contact with Skorzeny, Angleton had just assumed responsibility for all foreign intelligence collection and foreign liaison. Thus, Angleton would have been in direct contact with Bertaux on intelligence matters, including the French coordination with Skorzeny.

Oddly, Pierre Bertaux and James Angleton even looked the same. This was pointed out by CIA agent James McCargar, who worked with Bertaux in Paris. McCargar observed, the "extraordinary physical resemblance . . . the same long, thin face, elegantly pointed chin, aquiline nose, sensuous but disciplined mouth, sunken cheeks, deep-set eyes illuminated by a kind of controlled fire, thick black hair surmounting an aristocratic forehead."

The reason for the meeting was to offer Skorzeny asylum in France in return for lending his expertise with anti-Communist operations. Here again, the subject matter and timing coincides with the agenda of the earlier meetings Skorzeny had with David Martin and Colonel Boris Pash. This was evidently a follow-on meeting to cement Skorzeny's role in Compass Rose, provide a safe house for him to operate and establish the cover he would use while moving about the country.

Skorzeny officially entered France on June 8, 1949, under the alias Rolf Hans Steiner-Hart, with a temporary resident card issued by the Prefecture of Seine and Oise (Paris district). The document is part of the Skorzeny papers. Initially, he and Ilse stayed at Pierre Bertaux's personal residence, but later were transferred to a secret location southwest of the capitol.

Prior to Skorzeny's arrival there were several significant developments regarding intelligence related organizational formations that would later affect Skorzeny. During this period, there were numerous unofficial committees and like-organizations formed under the guidelines set forth in NSC 10/2, that call for the formation of private entities for the express purpose of providing cover for official covert action programs. Several of these had relevance for Skorzeny, but for brevity the author will focus only on one, the American Committee on United Europe or ACUE, which maintains a course to the dramatic conclusion of this book.

ACUE was set up in April 1948, two months before Skorzeny's arrival in Paris. The basic purpose of ACUE was to counter the Communist threat in Europe by promoting European political integration. The structure of ACUE was designed by William Donovan and Allen Dulles. Dulles was not officially in the United States government at the time, but due to his extensive OSS background, was considered a high-level government adviser. In addition to helping Donovan with ACUE, Allen was also reviewing the internal structure and operations of the CIA. Dulles served as vice chairman of ACUE until he left to take a position as the CIA's Deputy Director for Plans at the personal request of then Director Walter Bedell Smith. Others involved in the creation of ACUE included Winston Churchill. The organization was funded by both the Rockefeller and Ford Foundations.

On the board of ACUE were an amazing and powerful group of intelligence officials and businessmen. These included General Walter Bedell Smith, CIA Director 1950–1953, Paul Hoffman of the Economic Cooperation

Administration, who replaced Dulles after the latter's departure for the CIA, and General Lucius D. Clay. Another board officer was journalist Thomas Braden, who had also served in the OSS. During the war Braden parachuted behind enemy lines and was considered a protégé to General Donovan. In 1950, Braden joined the CIA and took the reins of the International Organizations Division (IOD), a covert group that handled clandestine activities of global corporate entities. After Braden left the CIA he was replaced as head of the IOD by Ben Bradlee. Bradlee would in turn be replaced by deputy, Cord Meyer, Jr. All three of these men, Braden, Bradlee, and Meyer worked on the covert projects carried out by Frank Wisner at the time Skorzeny was being utilized as an asset within Donovan's 'SPG.'

Finally, we have ACUE board member Charles R. Hook, important to this history since he was chairman of Armco Steel Corporation (ARMCO) whose representative in Paris was Colonel Robert Solborg. Previous pages have covered the extensive intelligence background of Colonel Solborg, from his days as deputy to General Donovan in the OSS, to his postwar links to World Commerce Corporation and the formation of the Donovan 'SPG.' Colonel Solborg will also surface as a principle business associate of Otto Skorzeny in ARMCO related matters. It appears from available evidence, that at some point between his arrival in Paris in June 1949 and the early part of 1950, Skorzeny met and developed a close, clandestine relationship with Colonel Solborg.

The American Rolling Mill Company (ARMCO) was established in Middletown, Ohio, in 1910. The company had its beginnings in the American Steel Roofing Company, located in Cincinnati. ARMCO was a leader in producing rolled sheets of steel and was an innovator for new processes that improved efficiency.

ARMCO is one of the earliest Ohio companies to establish a shop committee, which allowed workers to organize. Shop committees were predecessors to unionization. The ARMCO shop committee was formed in 1904, making it not only one of the first companies in Ohio to take this step but also one of the first in the nation. Later, ARMCO changed its name to Armco Steel

Corporation but kept the old company acronym. The company exist today as AK Steel Corporation.

It is highly likely Charles R. Hook was aware of the clandestine use of Otto Skorzeny given the documented connections he had with people in the Skorzeny papers like Colonel Solborg and his board position on ACUE. Steel products from ARMCO are a major business activity in the Skorzeny papers and appear to have been a primary conduit for conducting his covert activity. That being said, it is fascinating to speculate if the corporate headquarters for ARMCO, Ohio, was the source for the codeword used for Operation Ohio covered earlier. Also, as previously stated, ARMCO representative Colonel Solborg would have been the logical choice to lead Donovan's SPG in Paris. Solborg also served as Chairman of the American Chamber of Commerce in Paris adding addition contact cover for his operations.

PAIX ET LIBERTÉ

We will now introduce an organization that was intimately linked to covert intelligence operations in Paris and created during Compass Rose. It was also linked to the CIA, French intelligence, Donovan's SPG and to Otto Skorzeny. This was *"Paix et Liberté,"* or Peace and Liberty, which first appeared in March 1949, in Paris, but later emerged in other countries of Europe.

Paix et Liberté was a private group, organized in France to combat Communism. In reality it was a highly classified covert operation conducted by the principle players engaged in Compass Rose. The encyclopedia *Europe Since 1945* described *Paix et Liberté* as a "parallel government-sponsored anti-Communist 'psychological warfare' agency."

Formed only one month before Pierre Bertaux and Roger Wybot made their approach to Skorzeny, *Paix et Liberté* was publicly dedicated to "countering Soviet propaganda initiatives," although "several branches carried out illicit covert 'action' operations against domestic opponents." The similarities between *Paix et Liberté* operations and the covert assignment tasked to Skorzeny by Roger Wybot and Pierre Bertaux are not coincidental. It was French Interior

Minister Jules Moch, another seasoned veteran of the French resistance, who first initiated the *Paix et Liberté*. Pierre Bertaux, as head of *Sûreté Nationale*, reported to Moch.

Minister Moch was a fiery anti-Communist. He served as Minister of the Interior from 1947 to 1950 and as Minister of Defense from 1950 to 1951. Pierre Bertaux served as Moch's chief of staff from 1946 to 1947, when Moch was Minister of Public Works and Transportation. In November and December 1948, Moch had used an iron fist to suppress violent Communist strikes. Moch's methods greatly impressed American authorities, and he was soon a key partner in the advancement of U.S. covert operations in the country. Moch had personally been involved in the creation of a clandestine "parallel" police unit and other covert organizations such as *Paix et Liberté*.

The man Moch selected to lead these paramilitary anti-Communist police forces was Jean Dides, a veteran police commissioner heavily engaged in the secret war in Western Europe against Communism. During World War II, he had directed internal security units, called "special brigades," in Vichy to hunt down internal enemies (mainly Communists). Dides believed that the French Communist Party (PCF) and other Communist political groups must be utterly destroyed. U.S. officials in France took note of Dides' efforts and cabled Washington, "To fight the danger of Communism, France has organized cells of restrained but efficient policemen . . ."

Dides frequently attended meetings of *Paix et Liberté*, since he worked closely with Pierre Bertaux and Roger Wybot. It is not known if he was aware of Skorzeny's presence in Paris. Dides himself had recruited for his ranks several former Nazi collaborators, including Charles Delarue; Marcel de Roover, the Belgian "black knight"; and Eberhard Taubert, an ex–Nazi court judge and leading former member of Josef Goebbels's Propaganda Ministry.

To lead *Paix et Liberté*, Moch selected Jean-Paul David, a young political leader active in French elite circles who brought together a broad coalition of anti-Communist parties. With a small staff of twelve, David pursued an aggressive information operation effort, arranging for the production of numerous provocative leaflets and flyers designed to highlight the French Communists as a Soviet fifth column in France. The group also conducted a weekly radio broadcast.

David directed the group's international committee that synchronized the activities of branches established in other countries, including Belgium, Great Britain, Greece, Italy, the Netherlands, Norway, Turkey, Vietnam, and West Germany. These are countries where stay-behind forces were being implemented by intelligence planners.

ENTER MAJOR GENERAL LYMAN L. LEMNITZER AND THE NATO LINK

At the time of events and activities described above there was also new European security agreements being drawn up to address the Soviet threat. Again, these developments would eventually impact Otto Skorzeny in a very significant way. On March 17, 1948, the Treaty of Brussels, a mutual defense pact between Belgium, the Netherlands, Luxembourg, France, and the United Kingdom was signed. This was the forerunner of the North Atlantic Treaty Organization. Concerns over the military strengths of these nations lead to further talks which included the Pentagon. The result was the NATO mutual defense alliance, a unified command of western countries, under American leadership. Headquartered in Paris, NATO was brought into existence on April 4, 1949 with the signing of its charter in Washington, DC.

Among the immediate challenges for the American planners was transforming NATO combat forces to be ready to deter the Soviet Union and their East Bloc allies. Unfortunately, at the time NATO was formed most members of the new alliance were in a very weak state of readiness. Additionally, economic recovery was a major priority in every nation leading to restrictions on monies for national defense.

Within these concerns were critical issues such as differences between the member states in equipment, logistics, training, tactics, command structures and a myriad of other issues that further complicated the integration and readiness. For this reason, a secret military assistance program was created by the Americans to bring their NATO partners "up to speed" as quickly as possible. The program also included both overt and covert arms programs. These were expanded to other areas of the world threatened by Soviet expansionism such as the Middle East and Africa. Assistance to these third world and developing countries was a matter of great security and secrecy, particularly in areas where a U.S. presence conflicted with internal politics.

The man confronted with the tremendous challenges of training and equipping U.S. allies and its proxies was the first U.S. Secretary of Defense, James V. Forrestal, who held the post through the initial critical years 1947–1949. Forrestal selected Major General Lyman L. Lemnitzer as the lead for American involvement with NATO. Secretary Forrestal issued orders to create a "mutual security organization involving the United States, the Western Union states, and others with reasons to fear Soviet aggression."

Forrestal was explicit in his instructions to Lemnitzer, "were going through with this alliance [but] it's no use of the United States government having an alliance with only weak allies, and all our allies are weak. I want you to begin thinking about putting together a military assistance program." Here Forrestal was talking about the overt assistance. But it was the hidden pieces of the program that the Defense Secretary knew carried the greatest danger. The stay-behind activity hidden within the military assistance program was highly classified and neither the U.S. nor its allies could ill afford to have these sensitive war plans compromised allowing the Soviets to develop countermeasures. It should be reiterated, that the stay-behinds were an integral part of nuclear war contingency planning. To emphasize this point we recall Defense Secretary Forrestal words of caution to Lemnitzer stating his role would be "super top secret. The secretary was adamant, 'You can't even breathe about this—you can barely think about it," General Lemnitzer would later remember (without reference to stay-behinds) that he could not remember an issue, (with the possible exception of the Manhattan Project)—"that was shrouded in so much secrecy." This paragraph also underscores the level of caution that would have existed among those with knowledge of Otto Skorzeny's involvement in stay-behind programs.

STAY-BEHIND NETWORKS—THE *PAIX ET LIBERTÉ* CONNECTION

It was this military assistance program associated with NATO that Skorzeny would eventually become deeply enmeshed. On October 3, 1949, Roger Wybot and Pierre Bertaux made a trip to Washington to meet with CIA Director Walter Bedell Smith. The meeting was likely to discuss details of ongoing anti-Communist projects in France, to include the use of *Paix et Liberté*. Logically, discussion points at the meeting should also have included Otto and Ilse, who at that very moment were working with Wybot and Bertaux in an operation involving the CIA. It is even feasible they were the main reason for the meeting.

The CIA director's log indicates that among those present was the head of CIA Staff C (counterintelligence), William K. Harvey. This is particularly noteworthy as Harvey will later, in 1958, be assigned as the CIA point man tasked to develop the Agency's executive action program for assassinating foreign leaders under the code word QJ/WIN. The QJ/WIN program will be covered in great detail later. In 1951, Harvey would move from Staff C to assume leadership in Berlin, taking over CIA operations in this hotbed of the Cold War. Harvey's operation would become known as the Berlin Operations Base, or BOB.

Other CIA officials at the director's meeting were Park W. Armstrong, from the State Department; Brigadier General E. Moore, Acting Director of USAF intelligence; D. Milton Ladd, of the FBI; Colonel Robert A. Schow, from the CIA's Office of Special Operations; R. Kingsley; and R. A. Richard, personal assistant to the director, as well as two individuals whose names are redacted.

During the early stages of World War II, Colonel Schow had served as military attaché in Paris under Robert D. Murphy assisting in the coordination of French resistance activities with Colonel Robert Solborg. Schow would continue to advance in the intelligence community and military ranks. When Skorzeny arrived in Paris in 1949, Schow was a staff officer on the Joint Chiefs of Staff having come directly from duty in Paris. His career intelligence positions would indicate he was one of the senior American officials "in the know" about Otto Skorzeny.

Shortly after the meeting of Wybot and Bertaux with Director Smith, a private American support group, the American Friends of *Paix et Liberté*, appeared on the scene to support Jean-Paul David's efforts from the United States. Research conducted by historian Daniele Ganser revealed that *Paix et Liberté* was "a large CIA front organization" heavily financed by the Agency. The Agency also funded satellite organization in other European countries. It is known that the CIA branch of *Paix et Liberté* in Italy went under the name *Pace e Libertá* and had its headquarters in Milan.

Paix et Liberté operations may also have included assassination as described in *Europe Since 1945: An Encyclopedia*: "Several leading Peace and Liberty activists were directly implicated in anti-constitutional political activity, including serious acts of violence and anti-government coup plots." A former member of the Belgian *Paix et Liberté* organization "confessed on his deathbed" that the group had carried out the 1950 assassination of Julien Lahaut, head of the Communist Party of Belgium.

ENTER CLIFFORD FORSTER

The American Friends of *Paix et Liberté* was based out of New York and run by Clifford Forster, a senior staff council attorney of the American Civil Liberties Union. Forster was born in New York City in 1913. His father Karl Von Forster, was born in Vienna, Austria but later moved to France opening a luxury linen company named Leron, Inc. in Paris. After a few years the family moved to the United States and opened an upscale business in Manhattan. In Clifford Forster we will find yet another French connection to Skorzeny as well as a direct family connection. The author will explain.

Forster was a law graduate of Yale, class of 1935. From 1940 to 1954 he worked as a staff and special counsel for the American Civil Liberties Union (ACLU). He apparently also worked as an intelligence operative although no official records exist. After the war he would be decorated with the Jeanne D'Arc medal, given to those who helped the Resistance during the war. The medal was personally presented to Forster by General Pierre de Bénouville, the former French Resistance contact to Allen Dulles. Forster and de Bénouville were lifelong friends. Due to his family's linen business, it is logical to assume that Clifford Forster was close to people and businesses in Paris and throughout France.

Additionally, we find that Clifford Forster had a pre-existing connection to Skorzeny. Forster's family was from Austria and lived in the same neighborhood as the Skorzenys' in Vienna. It is likely, that Forster's work with French intelligence and his family acquaintance with Skorzeny was why he was selected as a secret contact to Skorzeny. Although there is no direct record of Clifford Forster being in the CIA, there is ample evidence he was involved in numerous intelligence front groups linked to the Agency. This was at the time he was also in direct contact with Skorzeny.

There are other curious connections to Clifford Forster that should be highlighted. First, directly after the war, Forster was the lead staff officer for the head of the ACLU under Roger Nash Baldwin. Baldwin had hired a former U.S. Navy intelligence officer named Ben Bradlee as a clerk in his office. Bradlee later became a famous journalist and connected to the famous challenge to the federal government over the right to publish the Pentagon Papers, documents detailing the history of the United States deep role in Indochina.

Bradlee only worked for the ACLU a few months but for that short period worked side by side with Clifford Forster who ran the office. This connection opens an amazing web of intrigue and historical speculation. For example, Bradlee was a childhood friend of Richard Helms, a veteran OSS officer and later CIA Director under Richard Nixon. Bradlee also worked in Paris with Richard Ober, a veteran CIA officer at the time Skorzeny was underground in the city. Ober had served in the OSS during the war as liaison with the anti-Fascist undergrounds in occupied Europe.

Given the intelligence background of both Bradlee and Ober their presence in Paris should be considered a part of Operation Compass Rose, especially since Ober transitioned directly from the OSS to the CIA. In later years, Ober was assigned to the special operations branch of the CIA that conducted wiretaps, break-ins, and burglaries as directed by CIA chiefs. Historians have also identified Ober as the famous "Deep Throat" operative in the

Watergate scandal. After 1954, Ober was assigned as deputy to CIA officer James Angleton, when the latter took over as head of the Agencies counterintelligence office.

Returning again to Ben Bradlee, his life takes on the essence of a classic spy novel. Bradlee's wife, Tony Pinchot, Vassar class of 1944, was the sister of Mary Pinchot Meyer, Vassar class of 1942. Both Pinchot girls were close friends with James Angleton's wife, Cicely d'Autremont, also Vasser class of 1942. Mary Pinchot Meyer was married to Cord Meyer, Jr. a highly decorated World War II Marine who was invited to join the CIA by Allen Dulles after the war. Meyer was assigned to Frank Wisner's Office of Policy Coordination, which as we have already seen was controlling body for organizations acting as the operational cover for Otto Skorzeny. In 1950, Meyer was appointed the deputy of the International Organizations Division (IOD) under Tom Braden, a highly experienced veteran of the British SOE and American OSS. The IOD was the CIA group that handled the cover organizations associated with Otto Skorzeny throughout the 1950s and into the 1960s.

A DARK FORESHADOWING

Cord Meyer's wife, Mary Pinchot, had met then Marine Lieutenant Meyer in 1944. Meyer had lost his left eye in a horrific battle against the Japanese in Guam. At the close of the war, they married, and, over the years, had several children. Mary was a popular woman in CIA social circles and she was especially close to James Angleton and his wife Cicely. In 1954, the Meyers were the neighbors of then Senator John F. Kennedy and his wife Jackie. The Kennedy's had bought a house next door. Over the course of time, the Meyer's marriage came under tremendous stress because of Cord's work at the CIA and the loss of a child by an unfortunate accident. In 1958, Mary filed for divorce and left Cord.

Then, at some point early in the Kennedy presidency, Mary began a romantic relationship with the president. In October, 1963, only one month before his assassination, Kennedy wrote a passionate letter to Mary entreating her to join him for a secret rendezvous. The letter, written on White House stationery, was never sent but secretly retained by Kennedy's secretary, Evelyn Lincoln. The letter sold at auction in June, 2016 for just under $89,000.

After the death of Kennedy, Mary expressed grave concerns for her life. Then, on October 12, 1964, after finishing a painting, she went for a casual daily walk along the Chesapeake and Ohio Canal. Later that day, she was found murdered—the case remains unsolved. Shortly before her death, Mary had confirmed her relationship with President Kennedy with a correspondent from the *Washington Post*. According to the reporter, Meyer and Kennedy met approximately thirty times in a period from January 1962, until the time of the assassination in November 1963.

Ben Bradlee stated in a 1995 memoir that he had received a phone call on the night of Mary's murder from a friend of hers who knew of the existence of a private diary. This sparked a bizarre chain of events to retrieve the diary since it purportedly had details of her affair with the President. According to Bradlee, a search commenced that day at Mary's studio. Bradlee claims that when he and his wife arrived with tools to gain entry they found James Angleton already in the process of breaking in. Bradlee and his wife viewed the contents of the diary, which confirmed the extramarital affair, but they felt it not in the public's interest to release the information. Angleton took possession of the diary and at some point, destroyed the document. But there is more to come later in this book about Mary Meyer's murder and an important connection between Otto Skorzeny and a powerful Washington lawyer who received information concerning Mary's death in advance of her murder.

ENTER ISSAC DON LEVINE

Now we return to the examination into *Paix et Liberté* and a further significant link to Clifford Forster. A 1951 list of board members for the American Friends of *Paix et Liberté* reveals a Russian–born American journalist with strong anti-Communist sentiments named Isaac Don Levine. Although the board contains many interesting names, the author singled out Levine as he played a significant role in 1964 as a suspected CIA operative involved in the manipulation of Lee Harvey Oswald's wife Marina.

Issac Don Levine came to the United States in 1911 and worked for the *Kansas City Star* and the *New York Tribune*. After World War II, he was the editor of the anti-Communist monthly *Plain Talk*. In 1948, he was a central figure in the case of Alger Hiss, a U.S. official who was accused by magazine editor Whittaker Chambers of having been a Communist Party courier working within the government. A lawyer in the case was Clifford Forster. It was Levine who first brought Chambers's accusations against Hiss to the attention of Assistant Secretary of State Adolf A. Berle, Jr. The case became a national drama, ultimately ending in the conviction and incarceration of Hiss.

Given his extensive Russian connections Levine was hired by Frank Wisner in 1951 to develop a secret program to exploit Russian and Ukrainian émigré populations that had poured into Germany and other parts of Western Europe. The author has already established that Skorzeny was also part of this secret program. With heavy CIA funding, Levine set up the American Committee for the Liberation of the Peoples of Russia, which was part of an OPC project under the code name QKACTIVE.

Levine arrived in Munich, Germany, to oversee the committee's activities, which included organizing displaced Russians and Ukrainians in a cohesive propaganda effort, using both overt and covert means directed against the Soviet Union. The program was not altogether successful, particularly due to Levine's personal style of leadership, which alienated many of the Russians and Ukrainians. Nevertheless, an associated radio broadcast, *Radio Liberty*, did have some measure of success.

Levine arrived in Dallas almost immediately after the assassination of President Kennedy and met with Lee Harvey Oswald's wife Marina to get exclusive access to her story. This contact resulted in Levine being brought before a secret session of the Warren Commission in January 1964. It was Warren Commission member Allen Dulles, former CIA director who arranged for Levine to come in. Levine told the Warren Commission members he was helping Marina write her story for *Life* magazine and that she claimed to have had contact with Russian intelligence. Subsequently, Marina's story was never published. The facts in all of this are incredibly murky and raise many questions, but once again we find that a trail to Dallas can be found by examining the covert relationships of those found in the Skorzeny papers.

SEMIC—"MADAM BOUVARD HERE"

On September 13, 1949, Roger Wybot visited the CIA and met with Director Walter Bedell Smith. He advised the Director Smith that he had been assigned by the military leadership of NATO to develop a peacetime counterespionage organization. He told the director his concept called for an organization similar to the International Criminal Police Commission, commonly known as INTERPOL. The name of the NATO counterespionage unit proposed by Wybot is not known. It may be given the timing Otto Skorzeny was also an adviser to this effort.

Wybot did use his own cover organization for Skorzeny that may be linked to the counterespionage unit that he briefed to Director Smith. This was the Society for the Study of Industrial and Commercial Markets, or SEMIC. This group served as a private detective agency for Wybot, with Skorzeny apparently as its head or, at a minimum, a key operative within it. Some details about the black operations (dirty tricks) of Wybot's SEMIC were revealed by a disgruntled former deputy, who came forward in 1951 with allegations that Wybot had been involved in a major jewel heist in Cannes, France, in 1949. That robbery, known as the Begum Aga Khan jewel heist, raked in over half a million dollars in jewels and was carried out by four unidentified gunmen. The former deputy, whose name was Georges Valentine, accused Wybot of being in league with the hold-up gang. He claimed Wybot, who was in charge of the robbery investigation, had stonewalled the case and dismissed Valentine for incompetence. He also claimed that he feared for his life, but defiantly said, "If that is how it is the muck will be stirred up and it will not smell good." Valentine also made a comment concerning the DST organization, stating that Wybot had "formed a joint gang of police and underworld elements." It is also known that Wybot's operations were coordinated closely with the secret service of the *Service d'Ordre*, which "made use of Corsican gangsters," and directed at political targets. All of this fit squarely into the facts uncovered in this research concerning the structure and members of the Skorzeny network.

Wybot survived Valentine's accusations and continued as head of the DST for seven more years. Direct proof of Skorzeny's involvement with SEMIC is found in a letter between Pierre Bertaux and Skorzeny (in the Skorzeny papers) from 1951, in which they are "getting their stories straight" about what transpired with Wybot. The letter mentions SEMIC as the organization Skorzeny was working with. Skorzeny also states the need to protect the identity of his partner Ilse, who was apparently working as an agent for the SEMIC network. The letter even provides the code line for identifying SEMIC members— "Madam Bouvard here." The bottom line—Skorzeny was in deep with Wybot's covert operations.

Wybot was a controversial intelligence director and the public was alerted to his questionable methods that ultimately resulted in the termination of *Paix et Liberté*. This occurred in 1954 when he became the center of national attention in France over a political operation designed to discredit Interior Minister Francois Mitterrand and bring down the government of Pierre Mendès France. Called the Affair of the Leakages, the scandal resulted in the disbandment of *Paix et Liberté*, when information came out exposing American intelligence involvement in French politics. There will be more details on Roger Wybot's covert relationship with Skorzeny in Chapter Sixteen covering the war in Algeria (1954–1962) and Skorzeny's role in assassination operations for that conflict.

CAPTAIN MICHEL DE CAMARET AND GENERAL PIERRE DE BÉNOUVILLE

Two highly important intelligence and covert operations contacts that developed in the early period of Compass Rose for Skorzeny was General Pierre de Bénouville, Allen Dulles's key contact to the French Resistance during the war and former SAS captain, Michel de Camaret. Correspondence from both men in the Skorzeny papers indicates a very close friendship to Otto and Ilse. Both men's fates were tied together, and they even share the same burial crypt. Both were truly exceptional combat soldiers and men who had a great deal of passion for the ideological causes they believed in. A short biography of General de Bénouville was presented in a previous section.

Michel de Camaret was born on January 18, 1915, in the Isère area of France, in his formative years he was politically aligned with very conservative Catholic monarchist organizations. While active in the *Camelots de Roi*, Camaret became friends with the future General Pierre de Bénouville. Around 1936, de Bénouville and de Camaret enlisted together in the Requetés, a group of Carlist (Spanish monarchists), fighting in the Spanish Civil War. The outcome of that struggle saw the eventual victory of Francisco Franco. After de Camaret returned to France, and with war clouds looming, he entered military service, being assigned duty in the cavalry. In April 1940, he was a lieutenant in the 12th Motorized Cavalry, and, as a tank platoon leader, would see combat against the Germans during their invasion of France. The French Army capitulated on June 18. In late July, Camaret joined the Free French Forces and September was working together with his close friend, Pierre de Bénouville. By this time, de Bénouville had become a leader in a French underground movement, known as Combat.

Combat operated in the non-occupied sector of France. In 1941, de Bénouville and de Camaret fled Vichy for French Algeria, where they joined the Free French Forces. At this point, Pierre de Bénouville returned to France and became a major French underground leader, and eventually the main French Resistance contact to the OSS chief in Switzerland, Allen Dulles. After arriving in England, de Camaret was promoted to lieutenant and assigned to a French Air Force infantry parachute unit. In the infantry air unit, he would serve with Captain François Coulet, the French Air Force officer who would later found the French Air Force Commandos.

The Infantry air units underwent extensive training with the elite British Special Air Service, or SAS. In 1944, de Lieutenant Camaret's unit was one of several French commando units assigned the British SAS Brigade. After World War II, Michel de Camaret left the service to pursue a diplomatic career and, in 1945, found himself posted as the Second Secretary in the British Embassy in Rio de Janeiro, Brazil. Only two years later, he was back in uniform, having rejoined the military and volunteering for duty in Indochina. With a promotion to Captain, de Camaret was sent to Indochina to serve in a Colonial airborne unit, the *Demi-Brigade Parachutiste* SAS. Upon completing this assignment

Captain de Camaret made his way back to France and in some manner not yet known became part of the French paramilitary contingent to Compass Rose. In this latter capacity he worked directly with Skorzeny on covert matters including advising members of elite French units specifically set up for Compass Rose operations.

11TH SHOCK

The foremost unit involved with Compass Rose was the 11th Shock Battalion, composed of special operations soldiers and commanded by Colonel Yves Godard. The unit was assigned to the SDECE Action Service. The history of the 11th Shock Battalion is fascinating and has relevance to Skorzeny's history as he would be an adviser to the group during Compass Rose and for the war in French Indochina and later, Algeria. This history of the 11th Shock began when a special unit had been created to conduct covert warfare called "Service 29," later called Action Service, within the French SDECE. The Action Service was, in essence, a "dirty tricks" department. Colonel Jacques Morlane was the first head of the Action Service. At the beginning of 1947, Morlane arranged for soldiers of the 11th Shock parachute regiment, specialists in unconventional warfare, to be assigned directly to Action Service. The 11th Shock was formed in September 1946, from a nucleus of former French SAS commandos and other special forces soldiers. Initially, only a battalion size unit, it would later be expanded to be a regiment. The motto of the 11th Shock clearly indicated its roots—"Who Dares Wins," the same as the British SAS.

Colonel Morlane only accepted the most qualified candidates for the 11th Shock, carefully reviewing the dossiers of every former French special forces soldier or covert operator selected for the unit. Its ranks also contained a number of reserve officers, including Jacques Foccart of the *Service d'Ordre*. The first commander of the 11th Shock was Captain Edgar Mautaint. He assumed command of the unit at Mont-Louis, a border town in the Pyrenean Mountain region between France and Spain. During World War II, Mautaint had served with the Jedburgh, special commando teams composed from the British Special

Operations Executive (SOE), the American Office of Strategic Services (OSS), and the French *Bureau Central de Renseignements et d'Action* (BCRA).

As the organization of the 11th Shock continued to develop, a new officer, Captain Paul Aussaresses, was given command of the unit, in July 1947. Aussaressess, like Mautaint, had an extensive Jedburgh background working behind enemy lines in World War II. Aussaressess commanded the 11th Shock from 1947–1948. Aussaressess, later wrote about the 11th Shock, stated the unit's mission was to "perform what was then called 'psychological warfare,' " and that his men trained for clandestine operations "that could range from building demolition to sabotage or elimination of enemies." Here Aussaressess means assassination. The unit's second commander, Yves Godard was a former French parachute commander who fought in World War II. Godard was in Austria at the end of the war when French intelligence was setting up covert intelligence networks using former SS men, including Skorzeny's commandos.

Historian David Talbot relates in his book, *The Devil's Chessboard,* that the 11th Shock conducted targeted assassination wherever their orders dictated, including inside France. Philippe Thyraud de Vosjoli, a French intelligence officer assigned to the SDECE and liaison to the CIA, stated that in this period, "Liquidations [were] an almost daily routine." Former SDECE agents Roger Faligot and Pascal Krop summed up working inside these organizations— "This job is not for choirboys . . . It's a hoodlum's trade carried out by honest men. We kill only for reasons of State."

CHAPTER TEN
SPAIN

"The Wolf shall also dwell with the Lamb."

PROPHET ISAIAH 11:6

F or nearly seventeen months, Skorzeny managed to avoid detection by Communist agents as well as from public attention while operating in France. All of that would change in February 1950, when reporters from the Communist newspaper *L'Humanité* spotted him "strolling with a girl down the Champs-Élysées" in Paris. The reporters also took a picture of him. The spotting of Skorzeny was covered widely by the press, both in Europe and in the United States. At this point, Skorzeny was still considered a fugitive from German internment, so his presence in France was highly controversial, especially given the tense political atmosphere discussed in the last chapter.

After being seen, Skorzeny immediately took flight out of Paris. Within hours police raided his boarding house and confiscated his personal effects. They also found a working copy of his memoirs. It is highly unlikely that the local police were privy to the fact that Skorzeny was operating in France under the secret orders of French Intelligence chiefs Roger Wybot and Pierre Bertaux, who could ill afford to reveal their clandestine relationship with him. The French newspapers, reported the French Interior Ministry, had nothing to say about Skorzeny "except that he was not on any war criminals list"—and interesting comment since both intelligence services protecting him fell under the ministry.

Skorzeny's quick reaction to being detected clearly indicates that he knew he could not become the subject of public scrutiny. His arrest would have endangered the intelligence operations he was involved in and could have exposed his collusion with the French and the Americans, causing a government scandal. In fact, he left in such great haste that he did not even take time to collect his personal papers. Follow-up reporting by the press revealed Skorzeny's alias as "Rolf Steiner" and said he was "working for American newspapers." It was also reported that he was tailing Communist operatives—a claim that was likely correct.

By the end of March 1950, Skorzeny's seized memoirs were published in the French conservative newspaper *Le Figaro*. The appearance of his memoirs incited massive riots in Paris, some of the largest since the end of World War II. Papers reported that the protests were led by "infuriated left-wing veterans."

Despite outward appearances and sensational press reporting, Skorzeny was not on the run, but was passed secretly into Germany, where he was harbored by a special underground network managed by Western intelligence. This time period was a very intense point in the Cold War. The United States was engaged in a major regional conflict in Korea, France was involved in a war to hold on to her colonies in Indochina, and internal Communist threats abounded across Europe. Soviet backing of North Korea also heightened concerns of a war in Europe. Since NATO was still in its formative stages and not ready for a major confrontation, new contingency war planning was initiated in great secrecy— planning that included Skorzeny. Soon, Skorzeny was once again on the move, this time to Spain. On September 16, 1950, Skorzeny crossed over the border under the alias Rolf Steinbauer. He was accompanied by Ilse, who had apparently left her boyfriend Robert Laroy to remain with Skorzeny. Spain would be Skorzeny's final move and base for his operations until his death in 1975.

When Skorzeny arrived in Spain it was at a very intense point in the Cold War. The United States was engaged in a major regional conflict in Korea, France was involved in a war to hold on to her colonies in Indochina, and internal Communist threats abounded across Europe. NATO was making top-secret preparations for conventional or nuclear war with the Russians, all the while carrying out a secret war with them in the shadows.

The Skorzeny papers indicate that Skorzeny's business network would emerge in full force nearly simultaneously with his arrival in Madrid. This would include the World Commerce Corporation (WCC) run by former OSS operatives Frank Ryan and Ricardo Sicre. Both men are found in the Skorzeny papers on documents concerning businesses for this period. These documents also tell us that two important businessmen in the Skorzeny network were Victor Oswald and Johannes Bernhardt. Both men were pivotal in the secret history of Project SAFEHAVEN and the former SS intelligence network SOFINDUS described in Chapter Two of this book. We now return to look at these connections as they reveal more details of Skorzeny's clandestine operations with hints of assassination as well.

SAFEHAVEN AND THE SOFINDUS NETWORK

Beginning in May 1944, Operation SAFEHAVEN was initiated by the Allies. Fearing that the Germans could use hidden assets to reconstitute into a Fourth Reich, the SAFEHAVEN mission was to track down and block German assets in neutral and non-belligerent countries throughout Europe and the Americas. With its vast operations in Spain, France, and South America, SOFINDUS was obviously a major target of the SAFEHAVEN operation.

However, several months before the end of the war Johannes Bernhardt had secretly contacted British Intelligence in an attempt to strike a deal with the Allies to turn over the SOFINDUS network. The Spanish government, which had investments in the company and had worked closely with German Intelligence, was also involved in this secret arrangement.

As a result of these clandestine negotiations, SOFINDUS assets were eventually taken over by the Allied Control Commission (ACC) as soon as the war ended. This was a joint operation in which an American corporate president was placed in charge of SOFINDUS assets, with a British vice-president. Also involved in the transfer of assets was the Spanish government, which negotiated control in Spanish industry tied to SOFINDUS. Under the agreement, the former SOFINDUS network was rolled up into a government-controlled organization called *Instituto Nacional de Industria* (National Institute of Industry) or INI, under Juan Antonio Suanzes.

The acquisition was announced publicly but details were not given, and the takeover of SOFINDUS was conducted in great secrecy. In one clever move, U.S. and British Intelligence had acquired the entire former SS intelligence network embedded in SOFINDUS. Subsequently, SOFINDUS companies were revamped and incorporated into the World Commerce Corporation (WCC) formed by General William Donovan and operated by Frank Ryan and Ricardo Sicre. For his cooperation with the Allies, Johannes Bernhardt received Spanish citizenship in 1946. Additionally, the Skorzeny papers provide evidence that Bernhardt was kept in an adviser role and subsequently partnered with Skorzeny upon the latter's arrival in Madrid in 1950.

Shortly after his arrival in Spain, Skorzeny established a private engineering office in Madrid and immediately formed a business partnership with Johannes Bernhardt, a former high-ranking Nazi SS intelligence officer who served in Spain during the war and remained there afterward. Prior to World War II, Bernhardt was an important corporate leader and a key figure in German espionage. He offered his services and vast business networks to German intelligence to further the cause of Nazi Germany. This offer was accepted, and a sophisticated espionage network grew out of Bernhardt's businesses.

WORLD COMMERCE CORPORATION TAKES OVER THE SOFINDUS NETWORK

Johannes Bernhardt was born in 1897 in East Prussia and served in World War I, afterward becoming a successful businessman. By 1930, he had established a residence in Spanish Morocco, where he became involved in mining and other lucrative enterprises. Through his contacts, he became personally acquainted with Franco, which led to his friendship and support of Franco's Nationalists. At the outbreak of the Spanish Civil War, Bernhardt, who was already a Nazi agent, offered his services to Franco, through whom it was arranged for Bernhardt to manage the exchange of Spanish products for German war supplies. It was Bernhardt who delivered the letter from Franco to Hitler that led to Germany's support of Franco's army in the Spanish Civil War. This support, much of which was clandestine, was carried out by two holding companies: ROWAK in Berlin and HISMA in Tétouan, Morocco.

In 1938, ROWAK and HISMA were replaced by SOFINDUS, with Bernhardt assuming the directorship of the company. Bernhardt also placed SOFINDUS at the disposal of Nazi intelligence services and was eventually given an administrative rank of general in the *Allgemeine* SS. The *Allgemeine* SS was composed of SS Departments not associated with combat units, which were called the *Waffen* SS (Skorzeny was in the *Waffen* SS).

Bernhardt's SOFINDUS intelligence network was managed out of the Reich Main Security Office (RSHA) Section VI, or Foreign Intelligence Service, also known as Ausland-SD. This is the same department that handled Skorzeny's commando unit, which fell under RSHA Section VI-S. Therefore, Skorzeny was very familiar with the SOFINDUS intelligence network and would have used it for his covert operations. The SOFINDUS network supported the secret activities of all major Nazi intelligence services.

Bernhardt was also given large sums of money to invest SOFINDUS assets in Spain, to produce capital for the Third Reich. On the Spanish side, SOFINDUS was integrated into Spanish industry through INI, created in October 1941. The head of INI was Juan Antonio Suanzes, a Spanish naval officer and member of the National Defense Council. Suanzes worked closely with Johannes Bernhardt and was certainly involved in espionage activities for the Germans. In July 1945, Suanzes was appointed Minister of Industry and Commerce but retained his position as president of INI.

In 1951, the INI's responsibilities were split, with Joaquín Planells Riera taking over industry and Manuel Arburúa de la Miyar assuming the lead for commerce. However, Juan Antonio Suanzes remained as president until 1963. In addition to directing the INI, Suanzes maintained his status as a Spanish military officer and in 1950 was appointed brigadier general.

The SOFINDUS business networks were expansive. In addition to operations in Spain and Morocco, Johannes Bernhardt also oversaw operations in South America (particularly Argentina) and France. One of the most important roles of SOFINDUS was the delivery of vital mineral resources from Spain,

Morocco, and Portugal to the Third Reich. Foremost in this operation was wolframite (tungsten), a mineral that was vital in the production of armor-piercing ammunition. The SOFINDUS delivery of wolframite had to be protected by Germany at all costs. The war could not be fought without this critical mineral.

Through the SOFINDUS network, Nazi intelligence services carried out espionage, sabotage, and even assassinations. SOFINDUS assassination operations are referenced in declassified documentation involving SS Lt. Colonel Walter Mosig. Like Johannes Bernhardt, Mosig began his career as a German businessman, working as a salesman for various firms operating in Spain in the early 1930s. Then, in 1934, he began a career as a criminal police officer, eventually ending up in the Gestapo. Given his background and familiarity with Spain, in 1936 Mosig was assigned by German Intelligence to collaborate with Franco's intelligence services. In 1938, he became ill and returned to Germany. Afterward, he was assigned to various criminal police departments in Germany until February 1942, when he was assigned to Section VI-B-4 of the RSHA as a foreign intelligence operative in Spain working undercover in SOFINDUS.

Mosig was given the rank of *Sturmbannführer* (Major) in the *Sicherheitsdienst* (SD), the foreign intelligence arm of the Nazi party. Once assigned to SOFINDUS, he answered to Bernhardt. As a key operative in the SOFINDUS network, Mosig was tasked with gathering political intelligence, but his primary purpose was to prevent organized sabotage against SOFINDUS assets.

After the war Mosig was in the automatic arrest category so he remained in Spain to avoid arrest. His declassified biography from the British National Archives states he left SOFINDUS in September 1945, the company having been "taken over by the Allies."

It also appears he continued to direct assassination operations even though the war was over. On November 5, 1945, many months after the war had ended, U.S. Attaché D. P. Medalie reported that a reliable source had stated that Mosig's job was "keeping an eye on the German colony and liquidating 'traitors.'" The same report stated that he was "known by the British to be very dangerous."

From May through August 1945, Mosig became a collaborator with the Spanish General Staff when he was offered a position with British Intelligence. For unexplained reasons, he turned the offer down.

Then, in August 1946, he was arrested and turned over to U.S. authorities. In February 1947, he was interrogated at Camp King by Arnold Silver, the same intelligence officer handling Otto Skorzeny and the one who arranged his escape. Like Skorzeny, Mosig also escaped, although several months earlier. This occurred during a prisoner transfer in October 1947. Only days later he had made his way to Madrid, indicating he had assistance with the escape and the move. Mosig remained in Spain for another year, immigrating to Córdoba, Argentina, in 1948, where he continued as an agent for the Americans reorganizing the SOFINDUS network.

ENTER VICTOR OSWALD

Skorzeny's business relationship with Johannes Bernhardt also included a former American OSS and British SOE intelligence operative named Victor Oswald. The reader should pay special notice of the name Victor Oswald as he will have very important connections to the events that unfold during the Kennedy assassination that will also involve Otto Skorzeny. Oswald is a highly mysterious character and not much is known about him. He is a major figure in the Skorzeny papers as both a key business partner and special confidant. It is known he was involved at the end of the war with SOFINDUS asset transfers.

Born into an apparently affluent family in Lucerne, Switzerland, in 1909, his exact arrival in Spain is hard to pinpoint, but he was later described as a successful dealer in arms and surplus aircraft parts. In both of these ventures, Otto Skorzeny was his business partner throughout the 1950s and into the early 1960s. At some point in the 1950s, Victor Oswald also became the representative of the Chase National Bank in Spain. This meant he worked for John J. McCloy, the High Commissioner of Germany, who was also a senior Chase National Bank executive.

Skorzeny's association with Victor Oswald also involved a man named Frank Gallati, an American who was formerly with the Allied Control Commission in

Spain. This would give evidence that the Allied Control Commission had a secret function after the war in setting up intelligence networks. Gallati eventually became a manager for the Otto Wolff Company of Düsseldorf, a major steel producer. Skorzeny was appointed as the Otto Wolff representative in Africa in 1952, giving him an excellent cover for covert missions into that region. Again, the steel industry is the common denominator for Skorzeny secret network within the Donovan 'SPG.'

ENTER UNCLE HJALMAR

On the financial side of the house, Skorzeny's business networks described above include Dr. Hjalmar Schacht, a leading figure of the Third Reich and Hitler's prewar economics minister. Major Bob Bieck, one of the air attachés at the Madrid Embassy close to Otto and Ilse, later recorded in his unpublished memoirs that he found Ilse's comment that Hjalmar Schacht was her uncle very curious—and he was right. The reader will recall, Skorzeny had met with Schacht in a trip to Nuremberg when Skorzeny was being held at Camp King. This was when the CIA was arranging the details of Skorzeny's release.

Actually, Schacht was not at all related to Ilse, but alleged to be a close friend of her family in Germany and hence given an honorific title of "uncle." Given the intelligence connections to Skorzeny and Ilse it is more likely the entire relationship is contrived for operational reasons. It is also possible that Ilse worked for or with Hjalmar Schacht during the war. This raises some very important questions concerning her participation in wartime espionage, as a short biography of Schacht will reveal.

His final release occurred in September 1948, only two months after Skorzeny's "escape." Schacht remained in Germany but then began to travel around the world as a financial consultant to developing countries, most of which were of high interest to the CIA, such as Indonesia, Chile, and the Bahamas. Careful analysis of the Skorzeny papers indicates Schacht was in a covered status for intelligence gathering on foreign governments and their leaders.

In 1952, Schacht entered into a complex and significant financial relationship with Skorzeny and his business associates in Madrid, but exactly who organized this partnership is not known. Schacht became head of a banking house in Düsseldorf and was a major financial backer of Skorzeny's many business ventures. It should be noted that Madrid CIA station chief Al Ulmer had a follow-on assignment as Chief of the Far East Division under Frank Wisner, then Deputy Director for Plans (the new name for the OPC after 1952).

Schacht began financial backing of Skorzeny on cue with Skorzeny's entry into business with Johannes Bernhardt, the former head of SOFINDUS, and Victor Oswald, the former American OSS/British SOE operative. This confirms Schacht was running finances for the business networks that were serving as cover for Skorzeny to carry out CIA covert operations. The Schacht–Skorzeny financial network would remain active until well into the 1960s.

CHAPTER ELEVEN

RESCUE COLONEL PEIPER!

"[President] Eisenhower was fascinated by covert action . . . he turned the CIA into a private Presidential army."

HISTORIAN ARTHUR SCHLESINGER, JR.

Although Skorzeny had been very active in helping Western intelligence from the earliest days of his release, there remained a major point of contention between Skorzeny and the West that threatened to bring his cooperation to an end. The conflict revolved around the continued incarceration and potential execution of SS Colonel Jochen Peiper, an infamous tank commander from World War II.

Peiper had seen combat on both the Eastern and Western Fronts and, like Skorzeny, was awarded the Knight's Cross of the Iron Cross for gallantry. He later received two higher levels of the medal Oak Leaves and Swords.

During the Battle of the Bulge, Peiper commanded the tank unit designated as the spearhead for the entire attack. His unit fought desperately, passing through the town of Malmedy, the site where unarmed U.S. soldiers who had surrendered to the Germans were slaughtered.

After the war, Peiper was arrested as a top SS officer and placed on trial for the Malmedy massacre. Peiper denied the accusation but accepted responsibility for his men's actions on the battlefield, which he claimed had been honorable. Supporting his claim was Lieutenant Colonel Hal McCown, who fought against Peiper during the battle and was captured by him. He testified that Colonel Pieper had conducted himself as a professional soldier.

The prosecution could not deliver conclusive evidence that Peiper had ordered his men to kill the unarmed U.S. soldiers, but he was found guilty nonetheless. Peiper and forty-two others were sentenced to death by hanging on July 16, 1946. The sentences were controversial, and official complaints of unjust trial procedures resulted in most of the sentences being changed to life imprisonment, although twelve of them remained in effect.

Subsequently, a U.S. Army attorney, Lt. Col. Willis M. Everett, made claims that the proceedings had amounted to a mock trial and cited several illegal procedures. Everett appealed his findings to the U.S. Supreme Court. As a result, Kenneth Royall, Secretary of the Army, established a commission to investigate the trial. Selected to head the commission was Judge Gordon A. Simpson of Dallas, Texas. Simpson had served as a lawyer during the war and was considered an expert on war crime trials.

The Simpson Commission, as it became known, arrived in Europe on July 30, 1948, two days after Skorzeny's escape from Camp King. Simpson's final report, which came out in September 1948, was critical of the trial proceedings and recommended that the twelve remaining death sentences be commuted to life imprisonment. General Lucius Clay then commuted six more death sentences to life imprisonment but refused to commute six others, including Peiper's, although the remaining sentences were delayed. In the states, the U.S. Senate also conducted a separate investigation of its own, propelling Joseph McCarthy into public limelight and launching his infamous career.

The progression of events was watched closely by Skorzeny and other former German officers. For Skorzeny, the matter was one of honor. Skorzeny knew Peiper from the war, and his men had fought side by side with Colonel Peiper during the Battle of the Bulge. Skorzeny, too, had been accused briefly for the Malmedy massacre, but the charges were dropped for lack of evidence.

Skorzeny also met with former Wehrmacht General Heinz Guderian, and together they actively campaigned to get Peiper released. In 1951, Guderian wrote to one of his former officers about an appeal he had sent to John J. McCloy, the High Commissioner of Germany: "At the moment I'm negotiating with General Handy [Heidelberg] because [he] wants to hang the unfortunate

Peiper. McCloy is powerless, because the Malmedy trial is being handled by EUCOM, and is not subordinate to McCloy. As a result, I have decided to cable President Truman and ask him if he is familiar with this idiocy."

The Peiper issue was one of deadly resolve for Skorzeny, and he used the news media to broadcast a warning to his clandestine partners in the CIA. On July 11, 1951, a CIA internal memo concerning a news report on Skorzeny coming out of Argentina was sent by the Chief of the Contact Division, whose identity was redacted, to a Mr. Chauncey Stillman, located at Room 1610, Building L. That building was the office headquarters for William K. Harvey head of Staff C. Located in Washington, D.C., at the old CIA complex temporarily housed in run-down government buildings near the Capitol Reflecting Pool, it is none the less remembered fondly by those who roamed its "dank halls."

The Contact Division chief started the memo by stating that his division had "acquired certain information which may be of interest to your office, obliquely, at least." Here, the writer verifies he knows that the information on Skorzeny would be of interest to Harvey's staff or at least somehow associated with it. As we know, that was exactly the case at the time—Skorzeny was working *with* OPC through various cut outs such as the Gehlen organization, the World Commerce Corporation, and French Intelligence, amongst others. Harvey, as head of counterintelligence would have been monitoring reporting for OPC operations.

The second and third paragraphs contain information that Skorzeny had given to the Argentine press, "some rather disturbing opinions." The report went on to say that Skorzeny had delivered a warning to the Western Allies that if Colonel Peiper was executed, "We will never lift a finger again nor open our lips . . . If Peiper dies, the Americans can be certain that we will not collaborate for an instant more."

Stillman's full name was Chauncey Devereux Stillman, an heir to a banking fortune. He was born in 1907 in New York and died in 1989. During World War II he served as a U.S. Navy air intelligence officer on the U.S.S. *Enterprise* in Air Group 20. After the war, he served as a staff officer for the National Security Council and in the CIA. Virtually nothing is known of his CIA service; however, a newspaper article dated January 1952 said, "He had been in the CIA."

To Harvey this may have been old news since Peiper's death warrant had been commuted to a life sentence on January 30, 1951, but the issue of Peiper was not taken lightly and the fact that Peiper still languished in prison was enough for Skorzeny. If details are correct, Skorzeny was even involved in attempting to rescue Peiper from the Landsberg prison where he was being held. The rescue was written about by historian Danny S. Parker, who penned an authoritative biography on Peiper. As the story goes, in late September 1951, Peiper's wife arranged to see her husband, and during the visit she passed him information on Skorzeny's plan.

It was well known that the Polish guards watching Peiper liked to drink. The plan was to drug the guards with a chemical that would make them sleep for hours. The plotters had a contact in the Landsberg hospital where Peiper was being held for medical treatment on the first floor. With the guards incapacitated, the inside contact would whisk Pieper out a window into a waiting vehicle to make a getaway. Peiper was then to be taken to the Swiss border, where he would be turned over to Skorzeny—from there to vanish forever within Skorzeny's network.

The plan was conveyed to Peiper by his wife during the hospital visit but Peiper objected, stating he would not leave "as long as one man in my command is still in prison." This ended the rescue operation.

Within months of receiving the memo concerning Skorzeny's threat to end assistance to the West, a series of events began to occur that would be difficult to comprehend without knowledge of Skorzeny's deep involvement with the CIA and U.S. military in the 1950s. Importantly, Jochen Peiper's status, while not resolved, began to ease and by 1954, he would be set free. It also was during the two-year period, from 1952 to 1954, when Skorzeny would establish a new curious business connection would that extended to Dallas, Texas.

THE CONFLUENCE OF DALLAS

Why did President Kennedy die in Dallas, Texas?—The Skorzeny business papers hold the answer, and it all started in 1952, eleven years before any of those involved with Skorzeny knew that their actions would set the stage for the final act in President Kennedy's life.

On September 10, 1952, the *Dallas Morning News* announced that the Spanish government had granted permits for several Dallas oilmen to begin oil exploration in their county. The permits were granted under the authority of the National Institute of Industry, or INI, headed by Juan Antonio Suanzes who handled the Spanish governments coordination with SOFINDUS during World War II.

Oddly, Spain had done very little to explore potential oil reserves and geologically speaking, the country was not considered a viable area for oil discovery. The timing of the enterprise is also interesting, since the U.S. military was just beginning negotiations with Spain to build bases across the country and in Spanish Morocco for NATO defense.

A large, private oil operation could serve as an excellent cover, in fact this exact cover was used by the OSS in Spain during World War II. It would allow for heavy equipment to be brought in for the construction of underground facilities and tunnels. This type of large-scale industrial cover would not be without precedent. For example, in 1974, the CIA sent a large geological survey ship called the *Hughes Glomar Explorer* to the Pacific Ocean under the guise of private industry. There, the ship was reported to be exploring the seabed for minerals, but in reality, it was on a mission to recover a sunken Soviet nuclear submarine.

Otto Skorzeny was also directly involved in the Spanish oil venture. This is established in the Skorzeny papers that confirm Hjalmar Schacht was handling financial aspects of the venture and was on hand to greet the visiting Dallas oil executives when they arrived. This was toward the end of September 1952. It is not known who coordinated Schacht's involvement on the American side. The idea for drilling in Spain was an initiative of DeGolyer & MacNaughton, a famous Dallas geological firm. Earlier, in the summer of 1952, several Dallas businessmen formed a syndicate to go to Madrid and begin operations.

Other members of the syndicate included John H. Murrell, William D. Felder, Jr., C. Andrade III, Oil Corporation, Howard Corporation, E. E. Fogelson, and Texas Instruments. Other companies involved were Geophysical Services, Inc. of Dallas and Delta Drilling of Tyler, Texas. Delta Drilling, run by Joe Zeppa, was slated to do the actual drilling in Spain.

As Skorzeny's financial banking partner, Schacht not only informed Skorzeny of the Dallas oil executives' visit but invited him to attend the very first meeting. This is confirmed by correspondence with Ilse for the last week of September 1952. He also attended a dinner afterward with the Dallas oil executives that included Algur H. Meadows and Judge Gordon Simpson, the president and vice president of General American Oil Company. Judge Simpson, it will be recalled, was the former head of the Simpson Commission that investigated Colonel Peiper's trial proceedings! One must wonder if this could possibly be a coincidence. At the time, Colonel Peiper was still being held in the Landsberg military prison. Judge Simpson's contact with Skorzeny is also highly significant for other reasons, including the fact that there were several others involved in the oil venture who had also served at the Nuremberg Trials and had interacted closely with the CIA's War Department Detachment, the unit involved in Skorzeny's release in 1948.

COLONEL JACK CRICHTON

A third man who was deeply involved with the Meadows oil deal was Colonel Jack Crichton, vice president and director of DeGolyer & MacNaughton. Crichton too was a veteran OSS officer from the European Theater during World War II. Crichton remained in the U.S. Army Reserve after the war and by 1956 had organized a U.S. Army Intelligence unit in Dallas—the 488th Military Intelligence Detachment. The 488th was tasked with strategic analysis but by virtue Colonel Crichton's ties to Skorzeny through the Spanish oil venture it opens up the possibility that Colonel Crichton's unit was somehow connected to the Skorzeny network. Certainly, Crichton had a communications channel to Skorzeny via the General American Oil Company.

Skorzeny's meeting with the Meadows oil group in the fall of 1952 would result in a long partnership between him and the American General Oil Company that stretched from 1952 until at least 1963. Clearly, the Texas oil connections to Skorzeny mentioned above are extremely important given the profile of its participants and the fact that Skorzeny was connected to CIA cover organizations. Add to this the earlier facts of Skorzeny's business connections to Johannes Bernhardt, Victor Oswald, and others involved with SOFINDUS and the World Commerce Corporation and the evidence becomes overwhelming. What has emerged is a clandestine network dedicated to covert action, including assassination. The timing of the oil venture is also of importance. General Eisenhower retired from military service in May 1952. This was just before the oil venture. Eisenhower's previous post had been Supreme Commander of NATO and as such would have approved all major covert operations in Europe. The NATO officer in charge of top-secret logistical matters at the time was a Dallas native Paul Raigorodsky who was selected as the Special Representative to Europe (SRE) for oil production. In future years, Raigorodsky will be closely associated with the saga of Lee Harvey Oswald after the JFK assassination. Raigorodsky was handpicked for the NATO position by another Dallas oilman Fred L. Anderson who had held high-level strategic oil positions within the U.S. government. The bottom line is, General Eisenhower was likely aware of the inclusion of Otto Skorzeny Spain oil project. Eisenhower was elected to the presidency in 1952 and assumed the office in January 1953. He immediately stepped up covert action and according to historian, Arthur Schlesinger, Jr. turned "the CIA into a private Presidental army."

CHAPTER TWELVE
THE ATTACHÉS

"Stay away from that S.O.B., that's Air Force business."
CAPTAIN "SPIKE" CLAUSNER, MADRID, 1961

O ne of Skorzeny's first contacts upon his arrival in Spain in late 1950 was an innkeeper from Dublin, Ireland, named Philip Mooney. It is not known if Mooney was an intelligence operative or part of Donovan's Secret Paramilitary Group, but Skorzeny remained in contact with him for years afterward. Mooney subsequently introduced Skorzeny to another Irishman, William Hynes. Like Skorzeny, Hynes was an engineer. During World War II, Skorzeny had two Irishmen in his command, James Brady and Frank Stringer. Both men survived the war, then "all but disappeared from history in 1951." The author was unable to make a connection between Skorzeny's Irish friends in Madrid from 1951 and either Brady or Stringer.

Later, the Irish engineer Hynes would introduce Skorzeny to an American, Edgar H. Smith, of Bristol, Pennsylvania. Smith was also an engineer who had evidently met Hynes in Madrid social circles. Skorzeny then introduced Edgar Smith to Ilse, whom Smith would later recall as intelligent, charming, and attractive. Smith had been told by Ilse that she lived in England "for a number of years" before the war. For this reason, he suspected Ilse may have worked for German Intelligence prior to the conflict. In this regard, he noted her superior intellect and the fact that Otto had some inside joke with her concerning her membership in the "Hitler Youth Movement."

Smith soon introduced Skorzeny, as Rolf Steinbauer, to a young American Army officer named Captain Jere Wittington. This seemingly simple introduction in the fall of 1950 would actually be the beginning of a long-standing CIA contact cover program with Skorzeny using the military attaches at the American Embassy in Madrid. The system would remain in place until Skorzeny's death in 1975.

Captain Wittington had just completed a tour with the U.S. 11th Airborne Division in Japan before arriving in Madrid for a ten-month tour of duty. His assignment to Spain was actually a prerequisite for follow-on duty to the language department at West Point. Wittington was accompanied by his wife Peggy and two-year-old daughter Anne. When the family arrived in Madrid, there was as yet no U.S. Embassy in Madrid, only a Consulate. The author had the privilege of becoming friends with Captain Wittington in 2012 when he was a retired Colonel living in Florida. For over two years the author gained incredible insight into Skorzeny's earliest period in Spain and his involvement in CIA operations from the colonel.

When Captain Wittington arrived in Spain, which nearly coincided with Skorzeny's own arrival, Europe was in economic recovery from the war. Like most Americans in Madrid, the Wittington family had to live in the city, so they immediately set about finding housing and soon located a small apartment. Food and other commodities were scarce, but the Americans fared better than the locals. Wittington would later recall he got the apartment and a housekeeper, who also did duties as a nursemaid, for seven dollars a month. The "commissary" at the U.S. Consulate was very limited, so most supplies came from local vendors.

Captain Wittington's specific mission was to gain expertise in the Spanish language, but for administrative purposes he reported directly to the senior Army attaché at the Consulate. At the time, there was only a very small contingent of U.S military personnel, mostly attachés, and no permanent U.S. bases in the area.

When Smith introduced Otto and Ilse Skorzeny to Wittington during an evening dinner party, he introduced them of course as "Rolf and Ilse Steinbauer."

Otto and Jere were both fond of scotch and the ladies seemed to have many mutual interests as well. Wittington was under the impression when they first met that Ilse was Skorzeny's wife, but then realized she was his girlfriend. Ilse and Skorzeny would eventually marry in 1954 after her divorce from Count von Finckenstein was final.

The initial meeting between the Wittingtons and "Rolf and Ilse" was soon followed by another evening "get together." After a week, an unusual event occurred. While visiting at the Wittingtons' apartment, Ilse asked Peggy, "Does the American Embassy object to you knowing us?" The question caused Peggy Wittington to pause, and she seemed confused. She then told Ilse she did not understand the question. "Well, it's about Rolf," said Ilse, "He is actually Otto Skorzeny, a hero of Germany, and during the war he was Hitler's commander of special troops." Peggy was caught totally by surprise and said, "No . . . *we did not know!*" Nor had anyone else hinted at Rolf's true identity. Ilse, too, was shocked that they did not know, for it was something of an open secret in the city that "Rolf Steinbauer" was actually Otto Skorzeny.

Of course, this new information became the immediate subject of conversation when Jere returned home later that evening from work. Jere, too, was surprised. Indeed, he had heard of the great German commando Otto Skorzeny, but he had not made the connection. Skorzeny had told him that he had been a German soldier during the war and that he had seen hard fighting on the Eastern front, but that was the extent of their discussions.

Madrid, just like Paris, was a hotbed of foreign espionage, the same as it had been during the war. Soviet agents were a real threat and some of the Russian spies were former German soldiers who had been recruited after the war by the KGB. Obviously, Wittington knew that his contact with Skorzeny was something he would have to report, and he even wondered if he might be in trouble over the friendship.

Wittington went to the Consulate the day after he found out about Skorzeny's real identity. There, he asked to speak to the senior military attaché, Colonel William E. Shipp. As Wittington suspected, the colonel was quite interested in this new development. "Skorzeny!" the colonel exclaimed, "The SS commando!"

Wittington acknowledged he had befriended the Nazi hero and then proceeded to ask if he should continue seeing him. "Hell, no!" said the colonel, "End the friendship at once, and stay clear of him . . . and that's an order." Although Wittington was relieved he was not in any trouble, he was nonetheless a little upset that he would have to tell Peggy the news about ending her friendship with Ilse, especially since the ladies had hit it off so well.

But things quickly changed. Immediately after Wittington left, the colonel went directly to the CIA's office in the Consulate to deliver the news there. The CIA chief of station was Al Ulmer, the former station chief in Austria when Skorzeny had been released by U.S. Intelligence. Hence, Ulmer was fully aware of Wisner's OPC contact with Skorzeny and his role in the SPG within World Commerce Corporation. It is not known if Colonel Shipp knew of these secret connections. Ulmer asked Colonel Shipp about Wittington. Specifically, he asked what kind of officer he was. Shipp replied that Wittington was "a very sharp captain." With this information, Ulmer contacted Washington. It was quickly determined that it could be more advantageous to have Wittington continue contact with the "Steinbauers" as an effective intelligence channel to Skorzeny directly from the Embassy—thus the "Madrid Op," as it was known, was born.

The next morning Captain Wittington was ordered to the Consulate. Colonel Shipp was waiting, "Captain, the CIA wants to talk with you." The colonel then took Wittington to see Al Ulmer, who introduced himself and explained the situation. Ulmer did not reveal existing CIA links to Skorzeny to Wittington. Instead, he congratulated Wittington on finding the infamous commando and added, "We've been looking for him!" He then told the young captain that CIA headquarters wanted "to keep tabs" on Skorzeny and for that reason they wanted Wittington to keep the friendship going. He told Wittington the CIA operation involving contact with Skorzeny was secret and not to be revealed to anyone. Ulmer then gave him instructions to report his conversations and activities on a regular basis. Wittington was excited to accept the intelligence mission, which was especially unusual for an infantry officer. Wittington stated years later, "From that moment on, Skorzeny was my special business."

Wittington would also recall that even though he was "ordered" to be Skorzeny's friend, he never felt like he was spying on him. In fact, the two became quite close, as did the ladies. Immediately after receiving his assignment, Jere informed "Rolf" that he had told his chain of command about their friendship, of course without mentioning the discussions with the CIA. He explained that there were no issues and the couples would continue to meet frequently, especially in the evenings after work. As Skorzeny was fond of cigarettes and scotch, these items were amply supplied to Wittington by the CIA to help foster the "friendship." Wittington later confided to the author that these gifts may have contained secret communications from the CIA to Skorzeny.

In describing Skorzeny, Wittington would recall that he always "dressed a little more formally than others . . . even when coming over in the evenings." One thing in particular that Wittington noticed immediately was the small size of Skorzeny's apartment. He also noticed that he did not appear affluent but neither did he seem needy. In describing the man, Wittington said he "looked important," and "His appearance helped him . . . he was very interesting to be around." Many years later, reflecting as a retired infantry Colonel, Wittington said he relayed to his superiors at the time that he thought Skorzeny would make a superb military adviser to the United States and was of the opinion he should be used in that manner.

Overall, the days in Spain as Otto Skorzeny's friend were memorable for Wittington. Skorzeny, too, became close to the young Army captain. Ilse mentioned in a letter to her sister that Jere and Peggy Wittington had become their close friends. During evening chats over scotch, Skorzeny would recount his famous raids, including the commando mission to rescue Hitler's ally Benito Mussolini. Wittington recalled years later, "I got the feeling when he spoke to me that he was educating a young officer." He added that Skorzeny was "straightforward . . . more so than other people," and although he never apologized for fighting the Americans, Wittington did not believe Skorzeny to be a Nazi, but a highly patriotic German soldier. In fact, his only hatred was for Communists; Wittington recalled, "He laid it on the Russians alright."

In one of the lighter episodes of their friendship Wittington relied an interesting story to the author—I call it, The Great Christmas Tree Raid:

The Christmas holiday in 1950 found Otto and Ilse at the Wittington apartment for an evening cocktail. Soon the discussion turned to preparations for Christmas. Jere pondered out loud about the possibilities of finding a Christmas tree for the apartment and suggested he might go out and look for one. Otto and Ilse said that they, too, were interested in getting one. A little while later, Jere received a call from Skorzeny, for whom everything was a mission, "Jere! I have good intelligence on where to get some trees." Skorzeny then suggested they use the Wittington's 1947 wood-paneled Ford station wagon, the only one in Madrid. He also mentioned that he had a friend who could go along with them and help.

When Wittington arrived at the apartment, Skorzeny came out with a friend whom Jere did not recognize. The stranger was actually Hitler's former Ambassador to Argentina, but that would only be revealed later. Some quick introductions were made and Skorzeny explained his plan. Of course, the expedition was not without some risk, as the trees would have to be acquired from a Spanish national preserve outside the city. They did wonder how much trouble they might get in if caught, but with Skorzeny leading the raid, what could go wrong? They loaded up and set out. Wittington recalled, "We had a pretty good drive . . . at least thirty miles."

The route took them into a forested mountain area. After surveying several potential sites, some too far off the road, they finally found suitable trees close enough for a quick extraction. With Otto in the lead, the three men made a dash in for their prizes. Otto had brought along a hatchet, and the former commando made quick work of the trees after each man had made his selection. So far, so good . . . the party had not been noticed. The men quickly stuffed the three trees, each at least six feet in length, into the back of the station wagon and set off for home. Of course, the return was the trickier part. Hoping the trees would not draw the attention of the Spanish police, they made their way cautiously back to the city. A few moments of anxiety arose as the station wagon passed the watchful eyes of a police checkpoint, but there were no problems and soon they were rolling in . . . Mission Success!

On the return, Wittington was informed by Skorzeny that the other man with them was the former Nazi Ambassador to Argentina. For Wittington, it was a very memorable day. Skorzeny, too, was beaming, having added another notch in his belt. It is remarkable to think that only eight years after rescuing Mussolini off the mountain at Gran Sasso, Otto Skorzeny, riding in a Ford station wagon with Texas license plates, would lead a U.S. Army Captain and the former Third Reich Ambassador to Argentina into a forest outside Madrid to conduct a Christmas tree raid. The historical irony was never lost on Captain Wittington, who fondly remembered the event into his old age.

CAPTAIN WITTINGTON'S OBSERVATIONS AND REPORTS

Wittington made regular visits to report on Skorzeny, as instructed by the CIA, and to pick up Skorzeny's cigarettes and scotch. What the CIA wanted to know from Wittington's reporting was whether any of their operations had been compromised. Over the course of their many conversations, it became apparent to Wittington that Skorzeny sincerely believed a showdown with the Soviets was coming soon. Skorzeny had told Wittington about his plan to counter this Soviet threat although, like his discussion with the engineer Edgar Smith, not in any great detail. Skorzeny also mentioned to Wittington that he had told the French about his plan and was working with senior Germans who supported it. All of this was a deflection. Wittington passed the information on Skorzeny's plan directly to Al Ulmer. Wittington knew that Skorzeny maintained a small industrial engineering office in downtown Madrid and frequently traveled from Madrid to Germany to meet business contacts. As Ilse would often accompany him on these trips, Wittington also reported that he believed Skorzeny's engineering business was a cover for activities dealing with his plan. This would have been evidence the ruse was working.

Wittington was unable to determine if the Spanish were aware of Skorzeny's plan or find out the full extent of Skorzeny's Spanish government contacts. He did know that Skorzeny was friends with the head of the police in Madrid and was very close to the influential restaurant owner Horcher. Like Skorzeny, Otto Horcher was born in Vienna. During World War II, he ran a very popular restaurant in Berlin that was frequented by the Nazi elite, including Himmler and Göering. Unknown to the guests, the restaurant "was planted with secret microphones to capture the conversations of foreign visitors." In 1943, Horcher moved his business to Madrid with the help of Walter Schellenberg, former SS Chief in the RSHA and Skorzeny's immediate supervisor. After the war, the restaurant continued to be a popular meeting place for former Nazis and has been cited in several history books as a major center in the Nazi escape networks to Argentina. After Skorzeny arrived in Madrid, he became a frequent visitor to the establishment and had his own room for entertaining his business clients.

Wittington observed that Skorzeny did not entertain much but had many visitors come to see him. Importantly, Wittington reported there were no indications that Skorzeny was a member of any organized intelligence group, but he was definitely in contact with a group of former German Army officers. The fact that Wittington did not pick up on intelligence activity by Skorzeny means Skorzeny's security methods were working. Getting such feedback is exactly why the CIA wanted Wittington to maintain the friendship. On the American side, Wittington would later recall that by the spring of 1951 he was "up to date on everything going on," insinuating he may have eventually been privy to other clandestine actions involving Skorzeny.

In June 1951, Captain Wittington's tour in Spain was coming to an end. A few weeks out, the CIA arranged for his role as a contact to Skorzeny to be taken over by a USAF attaché, Major Robert B. Bieck. Also at this time, there was a rotation of CIA station chiefs. Al Ulmer was replaced by Alfonso Rodriguez. To assist Rodriguez, Edward Barber, a former Army general and OSS officer, joined the CIA staff in Madrid. Major Bieck was called in and briefed by the new CIA personnel on his duties with Skorzeny, including continuing the friendship with him started by Captain Wittington. It was at this time that USAF Intelligence at the Pentagon was also informed by the CIA of the secret operation involving Skorzeny and the utilization of one of their officers, Major Bieck. Actually, from this point forward, the CIA cover program on Skorzeny would remain under USAF cover. Perhaps a significant point is Frank Wisner's OPC, which had been in contact prior to Skorzeny's arrival in Spain was also under Air Force cover.

The actual "hand off" between Wittington and Bieck began in March 1951, when Wittington invited Bieck and his wife Mary Jean over to his apartment one evening to meet "Rolf" and Ilse. Things went as planned and the new couple were soon seeing the "Steinbauers" on a regular basis.

Captain Wittington departed Spain in June 1951, but that would not be the last time he saw Skorzeny. He would briefly renew his friendship with him in 1956, when he returned to Europe with Peggy for an assignment as a general's aide in Germany. While there, he phoned Otto in Spain and arranged for the couples to reunite at a German hotel. Otto and Ilse made the trip over and the four had a wonderful evening dinner together. Jere recalled that while they were all sitting on a couch, Skorzeny "patted Peggy on the leg" and laughed about it. As far as business is concerned, Skorzeny informed Wittington that he was "trying hard to get work" but without much success, and that he was currently, "working on an airstrip."

Sixty years later, Wittington reflected on his friendship with Skorzeny, saying, "He should be remembered for what he was—an excellent soldier, a worthy enemy, and in my case, a good friend." That same sentiment would be echoed by Wittington's replacement, Major Bieck. But for Bieck, the "Madrid Op" was to take on even greater importance. The "friendship" contact system set up by the CIA between USAF attachés and Skorzeny does reveal much of Skorzeny's character and that of Ilse, too. Extensive interviews conducted by the author included several of these attachés and other staff personnel assigned to the American Embassy during the many years of CIA involvement with Skorzeny.

Major Bieck, the first Air Force officer in this chain, was replaced by USAF Captain Thaddeus S. ("Tad") Skladzien in November 1956, and over the next three years Skladzien would handle contact to Skorzeny. Like Captain Wittington and Major Bieck, he developed a close personal friendship with Skorzeny.

Skladzien had graduated from West Point in 1946, in the same class as Captain Wittington. He would eventually retire from the USAF as a full colonel. In the Korean War, he had flown 100 combat missions in F-86 jet fighters. Skladzien's girlfriend (and future wife) Sarita was the daughter of the U.S. Ambassador to Panama, and she became close to Ilse. Colonel Skladzien would later recall that Sarita would take trips with Ilse to Germany, which was always something of an adventure, since Ilse "was always driving like a mad Indian . . . full-bore at ninety miles per hour." The Colonel also recalled, "She was a little firecracker" and "very sharp on the business side."

Around the time Skladzien took over from Major Bieck, Skorzeny had dropped his Rolf Steinbauer alias and was using his real name. Skladzien thought fondly of Skorzeny stating, "He was a friend of mine . . . an intelligent man and friendly to the United States." When the author asked Skladzien in an interview if Skorzeny had any CIA dealings, he simply replied, "Yeah, I sort of thought he had his nose into something." He also added that Skorzeny was involved in some type of training relating to foreign personnel, but it had "started before [they] had actually met."

At the end of his tour, Skladzien did a hand-off to Major Mario DiSilvestro, who arrived in September 1959. Major DiSilvestro's relationship with Skorzeny came during the critical years when Skorzeny would be brought into very sensitive CIA programs. Unfortunately, DiSilvestro passed away before this book began, so an interview was not conducted. However, a U.S. Naval officer assigned to the Embassy during this same period was contacted and interviewed. This was Lieutenant Thomas W. Trout, who arrived in Spain in August 1959. Trout had contact with Skorzeny and also remembered Major DiSilvestro. "Oh yes," Trout recalled, "I knew him [Skorzeny] . . . we met at a cocktail party . . . my wife was German and was very friendly with Skorzeny's wife."

Trout was extremely impressed with Skorzeny, recalling, "He was very military—very proper in appearance—we all liked him." When asked if Skorzeny helped the United States in any way, Trout clearly remembered, "He was a source of intelligence we got—I don't know if it was formal or informal—at briefings air attachés would state, 'I got this from Skorzeny himself'—he was very much at ease with our attachés—he wasn't into politics or Nazism—he wasn't on board with Nazis at all—he was strictly military."

Another Embassy attaché confirmed the USAF cover. Navy Lieutenant Lamar W. Tuzo, assigned to Madrid in August 1961, said he never actually met Skorzeny but recalled seeing him at the American Embassy. He was also aware that certain attachés at the Embassy had contact with him. In fact, Tuzo was specifically told by his superior officer Captain "Spike" Clausner not to have any contact with the former German commando and given a direct order to "Stay away from that S.O.B., that's Air Force business."

FROM MUSSOLINI TO THE MOON

It was during the attaché transition period between Captain Wittington and Major Bieck in June 1951, that the Chief of USAF Intelligence, Major General Charles P. Cabell, arrived in Madrid. Cabell was from an old Texas family. His brother Earle Cabell became the mayor of Dallas in 1961 and gained notoriety in that position after President Kennedy was shot in 1963.

Major General Cabell had arrived in Madrid under secret orders to discuss with Al Rodriguez, the new CIA Chief of Station, the use of Major Bieck in an approach to Skorzeny for assistance in locating former Nazi scientists deemed vital to U.S. rocket and missile development. It can be reasonably assumed that the Secretary of the Air Force, Thomas K. Finletter, authorized General Cabell use of Otto Skorzeny by the USAF. The authorizations of these two men concerning the early clandestine use of Otto Skorzeny is a very important factor in later events concerning Skorzeny's involvement in covert missions for the U.S. government and in particular, Skorzeny's network connections to the Dallas assassination of JFK.

Skorzeny's assistance to the CIA and USAF in finding German scientist was actually part of a program widely known today as Project Paperclip. It was originally started under the code name Overcast immediately after the war to safeguard scientific and military technology experts and prevent their acquisition by the Soviet Union. The early Overcast missions were carried out by the OSS and other special military teams. Later, a special government organization was eventually set up to administer the project, called the Joint Intelligence Objectives Agency (JIOA).

As the senior USAF Intelligence officer, Major General Cabell was a key official within the JIOA. Over the course of many years the JIOA recruited several thousand former Nazi scientists and secretly brought them to the United States to work on top-secret research in various scientific fields. The most famous personality associated with the Paperclip project was Hitler's former chief rocket scientist, Wernher von Braun. An interesting fact is that von Braun had held the rank of major in the SS. After the war, he was brought to the United States, where he was placed in charge of U.S. missile development. Ultimately, he would lead the U.S. space program, which put the *Apollo* spacecraft on the moon. Much has been written about Project Paperclip, but revealed here for the first time is the fact that Skorzeny assisted in the program.

The CIA knew that Skorzeny had very valuable contacts in the former Nazi underground networks that might be particularly useful in finding two key ballistics specialists, Dr. Gunther Voss and Dr. Heinrich Klein. Immediately after Major General Cabell's departure, Major Bieck was called to the CIA office, where Al Rodriguez and Ed Barber tasked him to approach Skorzeny to see if he would be willing to find Voss and Klein.

Within days, Bieck carried out his instructions. His approach to Skorzeny was made in an informal but confidential manner one evening while he and his wife Mary Jean were over at Skorzeny's apartment for cocktails. Taking "Rolf" out to the balcony, he explained the situation and asked if Skorzeny could locate the two German ballistics experts for the U.S. Missile program under Wernher von Braun at Fort Bliss, Texas. Bieck was instructed to tell Skorzeny the request was coming from the USAF.

Skorzeny agreed to find the men. In the meantime, Skorzeny and Ilse decided to meet with Bieck and his wife in Bavaria while on vacation. By chance, Skorzeny had mentioned to Bieck that he and Ilse were going to that area and would be staying at Tegernsee, a beautiful lake south of Munich.

A few days later the two couples met at a huge *Gasthaus* where Skorzeny and Ilse were staying. Bieck and Mary Jean entered the restaurant, where they found

Skorzeny "holding court." Major Bieck recalled what happened next. Soon, "Various men would approach the table . . . advance to within a few feet . . . stand at rigid attention, arms down, hands pressed to their thighs, and exclaim, *"Herr Oberst, Ich bin,"* (Colonel sir, I am so and so). After identifying himself, each man gave his rank and where he had served with Skorzeny. At least twenty-five men, mostly former SS, came up in this manner.

But was Skorzeny really on "vacation" in this region of Bavaria? The timing and location suggest not. Ongoing at that very moment and in that very area of the Alps were the highly classified war preparations mentioned earlier being carried out by Frank Wisner's OPC. Under the code names Pilgrim-Baker and Pilgrim-Dog, the French and the Americans were working to create an Austrian guerrilla force to defend the "alpine fortress" from a Soviet move from the east into that area. The operation involved the secret stockpiling of weapons and preparation of guerrilla cadres. It is likely that Skorzeny was in the area recruiting and training officers for these missions and advising the OPC.

By the time they returned to Spain, Skorzeny had located Voss and Klein. Skorzeny visited the scientists and explained the situation. They immediately agreed to help the Americans. Shortly after this point Major Bieck, working through his CIA contacts, arranged for the two men and their families to be secretly flown to the United States. Amazingly, by finding scientists for Werner von Braun, Otto Skorzeny, the man who rescued Benito Mussolini for Hitler, played a small but not insignificant role in getting the United States to the moon.

CHAPTER THIRTEEN

BOB VISITS SKORZENY

"The Agency that is collecting intelligence should not get involved in dirty games . . . We got all sorts of rightist groups in Germany to set up resistance groups in case the Russians attacked, et cetera. It never works when you become the client and the provider of intelligence at the same time. Your intelligence gets slanted."

VETERAN CIA OFFICER PETER SICHEL

COMMENTING ON COLD WAR OPERATIONS

"No one controlled Jim. There were no superiors who insisted that he do things properly. He built an empire out of CI, and they allowed him to do it. In a way, that empire is a tribute to Jim's genius—or, as some might say, his misguided genius. Jim was brilliant man with a number of flaws, including a marked tendency toward the Machiavellian. Yet no one dared to say no to him."

VETERAN CIA OFFICER ED KNOWLES COMMENTING ON THE

CHIEF OF CIA COUNTERINTELLIGENCE, JAMES J. ANGLETON

William King Harvey was born in Danville, Indiana, in 1915. He was the son of a lawyer and followed in his father's footsteps, graduating from Indiana University Law School. He practiced law for a time and then, in 1940, he joined the Federal Bureau of Investigation. After a disagreement with J. Edgar Hoover over a reassignment, he left the Bureau and joined the newly created CIA.

Tom Polgar, a retired CIA officer who worked with Harvey in Germany and who was interviewed extensively by the author, recalled Harvey, and with a slight smile, remembered, "he was quite a character, a controversial man, but very intelligent." Harvey was called "the Pear" by colleagues, because of his odd-shaped body. He had bulging eyes and a "frog-like voice." Despite these attributes, Harvey was an extremely competent intelligence officer, known for his street smarts and unconventional approach to clandestine operations.

With Harvey's investigative background he was assigned in 1947 to Staff C, which handled counterintelligence and counterespionage. His immediate boss was James Angleton, who had left Italy to take over as Assistant Director of Special Operations (ADSO). A few years later, in 1954, Angleton would be appointed Counterintelligence Chief.

Mentioned previously was the fact that in the fall of 1949, Harvey had been present at a CIA Director's meeting in Washington that included Roger Wybot and Pierre Bertaux the French intelligence chiefs who were harboring Otto and Ilse in Paris during Operation Compass Rose. At that point, Skorzeny was integrated into the World Commerce Corporation network under the direction of Frank Wisner's OPC. The bottom line is that these later legends of the CIA—Harvey, Angleton, and Wisner—were all aware of the CIA operational use of Skorzeny in the months after his escape and possibly before. It should also be pointed out the Lucien Conein, the CIA operations officer who handled "black channels" for Germany, had been promoted to Major and was working alongside Harvey and Wisner during this early period as well, as were a number of other CIA officers of note.

In 1952, Harvey was transferred from Staff C to take charge of the OPC's Berlin Operations Base, commonly known as BOB. This effectively put Harvey under Frank Wisner. BOB was headquartered at Tempelhof Airport under the cover of a civilian firm contracted to the U.S. Air Force. While stationed in Berlin, Harvey utilized "a string of prostitutes" as agents, indicating that he was not averse to using criminal elements and illegal activities for his operations. These "creative" methods had earlier been established by OSS operatives in World War II as an effective means to achieve operational ends. One CIA officer noted, "He was disciplined and superb at making ops. He thought out every detail." Harvey was a perfect fit for the Cold War spy world. It is said he trusted no one and carried two guns on his body at all times. His office, too, was ready for war, with thermite destruction grenades on top of every safe. He was once introduced to President John F. Kennedy as "America's James Bond."

In 1953, Harvey was given the lead for Operation Gold, the construction of a nearly 1,500-foot tunnel running into East Germany where subterranean telephone lines were tapped to record Soviet communications. The project became known as the Berlin Tunnel but was only operational a short time. It was terminated in 1956 when it was compromised by a British MI6 double agent.

DTLINEN

Despite the failure of the Berlin Tunnel, Harvey had numerous other OPC projects he was responsible for, and two in particular evidence Otto Skorzeny's involvement. The projects began around 1950 under the code words EARTHWARE, then GRAVEYARD, and finally DTLINEN. Their purpose was covert propaganda, harassment, and sabotage activity involving both covert and overt operations. DTLINEN was a psychological warfare sub-project of QKDEMON, which continued until 1960.

To execute the missions, the CIA was using a West Germany political action group called the Fighting League against Inhumanity (*Kampfgruppe gegen Unmenschlichkeit*), or KgU. The group was headed by Rainer Hildebrandt, a surviving member of the network that carried out the attempted assassination of Hitler on July 20, 1944. Hildebrandt was imprisoned by the Nazis for his connections to German resistance but managed to survive the war. He was a staunch anti-Communist, and with help from the U.S. Army CIC, he founded the KgU in October 1948. It seems likely that Otto Skorzeny was contacted through secret channels to assist in the effort just after its formation. It is also possible that he was an original paramilitary adviser to the project. The KgU organization received its entire financial support from the CIA.

The formation of the KgU was announced publicly by its German founders, who resolutely declared its objectives as "to rally opinion against political oppression in the Soviet Zone [of Berlin]." A primary goal of its organizers was "to discover the fate of those who had disappeared into Soviet concentration camps." In reality, the KgU was in close communication with Western intelligence from its conception. The organization was assessed by individuals in the Army CIC, who saw the organization as an excellent vehicle for counterespionage, intelligence gathering, psychological warfare, and other covert activities.

The original group formation was coordinated by CIC agent Severin Wallach, who was described as a "brilliant and solitary man" and who was "convinced of the Soviet threat." It is also said he kept his working projects "close to his chest." At some point, the CIA's Office of Special Operations, or OSO, became interested in the project and coordinated with Wallach and the CIC. In January 1951, Lieutenant General Lucian K. Truscott was ordered to Germany as the senior CIA chief of mission and took over direct supervision of OPC and OSO operations.

A declassified CIA memorandum of March 30, 1951, reports that Skorzeny was in Berlin, involved with "preparations for the establishment of sabotage and resistance groups, presumably with the KgU and with a certain American Colonel Thompson (?) or Stimpson (?)." The same memo says Skorzeny has "settled down officially in Madrid and opened an engineering office." It goes on to say, "This is obviously a cover."

The information in the memo came from a source being utilized by the Gehlen organization. While it is true that Gehlen knew of Skorzeny's use by the CIA, only a handful of others on his staff also knew. The authenticity of the report is confirmed, however, by two pieces of evidence. First, the name "Colonel Thompson" was an alias used by CIC agent Severin Wallach. Later, Wallach would transfer to the CIA. Secondly, the author interviewed CIA officer Tom Polgar, who was the project manager for DTLINEN. When shown the declassified document revealing Skorzeny's connection to the KgU, Polgar stated, "It cannot be ruled out that a lower level U.S. official was in contact with Skorzeny." He added, "You have to read between the lines." The author took the answer to be in the affirmative, and the "lower level official," Severin Wallach.

In December 1952, William Harvey arrived in Berlin and took over management of OPC operations, including direction of the KgU and another group called the Investigative Committee of Free Jurists (*Untersuchungsausschuss Freiheitlicher Juristen*), or UFJ. The KgU and the UFJ were Harvey's primary psychological warfare initiatives.

By 1952, Colonel Robert G. Storey of Dallas, Texas, a former USAF intelligence officer who had served with General Charles Cabell during the war, arrived in Europe to assist with OPC Free Jurist efforts. It had previously been mentioned, but desires a second highlight, Storey was a key attorney supporting the Warren Commission in the wake of the Kennedy assassination. General Cabell would become the deputy CIA director under Allen Dulles in April 1953. Cabell, was intimately familiar with the CIA's use of Skorzeny prior to Colonel Storey's arrival in Berlin. General Cabell's brother Earle, would become mayor of Dallas, Texas in 1961 and serve until 1964.

In Dallas, Colonel Storey was president of the Republic National Bank and head of the American Bar Association. He had a number of other important positions including Director of the State Bar of Texas and Chairman of the Board of the Southwestern Legal Foundation. From 1949 to 1959, Storey served as the Dean of the Southern Methodist University School of Law.

With his vast legal experience and knowledge of secret networks in Germany, he was assigned a leading role in directing Free Jurist operations. In September 1952, Colonel Storey attended a widely publicized meeting of the Congress of Free Jurists (CFJ) in Berlin. This was of course the cover for the UFJ. Newspapers reported Colonel Storey attended in his *official* capacity as a senior-level military lawyer.

The CFJ evolved into a very effective organization against Communist tyranny. Of great interest to the Western intelligence community was the detailed information the Free Jurists had compiled on thousands of Soviet and East German officials. This valuable data was deemed critical for counterintelligence and espionage operations. Equally important was the access that the CFJ gave Western intelligence to denied areas within private, commercial, and government areas of Communist control. This information was then exploited under covert programs implemented by the KgU and the UFJ.

There, under a tight veil of secrecy, Colonel Storey assisted senior level psychological warfare planners in developing operations aimed directly at Communism. These operations had many facets, including a defector pro- gram. Other parts involved the development of resistance movements inside Communist-controlled areas with the capability to conduct attacks behind Red Army lines in the event of war. Harvey assigned paramilitary experts from BOB to the staff of UFJ, which likely involved Otto Skorzeny, since he was already being utilized in KgU operations.

The OPC's use of the KgU and the UFJ involving Skorzeny and Colonel Robert G. Storey may be the point where these two men established a working relationship supporting CIA covert action. It may also have occurred much earlier when Colonel Storey as head of the Nuremberg Trials documents divi- sion worked closely with the War Department Detachment described in an earlier chapter.

Another hint appears in an earlier declassified document from June 1951 concerning information from "a Non-US-Government intelligence network which has been operating for years" reported Skorzeny was "in contact with US citizens interested in the formation of resistance groups in Germany." The gen- eral statement does match Skorzeny's documented support to Harvey's Berlin base operations and participation of Colonel Storey.

Harvey, or a senior officer from BOB, had in fact been meeting personally with Skorzeny in Madrid as evidenced by a dramatic piece of correspondence to Ilse. On March 4, 1953, Skorzeny wrote to her in a poorly veiled manner of writing (which is an exception within the papers) that he had a visit from "BOB" (capitalized). He then went on to explain a number of intelligence-related activ- ities, which we now know from declassified documents were connected to CIA operations. Skorzeny mentions that he showed BOB a letter he had received from Gamal Nasser, the president of Egypt, and also discussed with BOB "var- ious other news from the Middle East." This is a critical admission, for at that very moment in 1953, Skorzeny was working a CIA-related mission directly involving Egypt.

SKORZENY'S SECRET MISSION TO EGYPT

In 1951, CIA Director Allen Dulles dispatched CIA officer Kermit "Kim" Roosevelt, Jr. a leading Middle East expert, to the country to take over covert operations in the region. Kermit was the grandson of President Theodore Roosevelt and had previously carried out successful clandestine missions in Syria and Iran. Assisting Kermit was Miles Copeland, Jr. who had coordinated intelligence matters relating to Skorzeny in the period immediately after his release in 1948.

After arriving in Egypt and assessing the situation, Roosevelt undertook secret negotiations with a receptive young Egyptian colonel named Gamal Abdel Nasser. Within a year, Nasser had assumed power and the CIA considered him an ally in preventing Russia from gaining a foothold in the region. In addition to providing massive financial aid, the CIA developed a plan to assist Nasser in modernizing his military and organizing state security forces.

To facilitate the building of military and security structures for Egypt, Dulles turned to the chief of West German Intelligence, Reinhard Gehlen, whose highly classified intelligence organization was still under CIA control. Gehlen may have known that Colonel Nasser had actually worked as a young officer with German intelligence networks run by Skorzeny. Gehlen himself had worked with Skorzeny during the war and knew he was extremely capable and well connected in the secret army underground being run by Special Connections.

This led to Gehlen's apparent recommendation in early 1952 to locate military experts for President Nasser of Egypt. This mission was confirmed by Miles Copeland, Jr. who wrote about Skorzeny's involvement in the project for his book *The Game of Nations*, published in 1969. Copeland made it a point to inform the reader, "Skorzeny has long ago been cleared of any war crimes." Also of note is the fact that Copeland had received his initial appointment to intelligence through an introduction to General William Donovan of the OSS by

Alabama Representative John Sparkman. Interestingly, it was through the efforts of Senator Sparkman that the secret missile development program under Wernher von Braun was moved from Fort Bliss, Texas, to Redstone Arsenal in Huntsville in 1949. Thus, it appears Copeland may have also had a hidden hand in Skorzeny's assistance to Operation Paperclip.

The CIA likely knew from classified sources that President Nasser had worked with Skorzeny during World War II, and that the two were acquainted from that time. Nasser had a great respect for Skorzeny. This made him a logical choice to send to Egypt. Not by coincidence, in 1953, Miles Copeland, Jr. was on non-official cover for the CIA, working for the consulting firm Booz Allen Hamilton in Cairo, where he was one of Nasser's closest Western advisers. Nasser was looking for military advisers to bring discipline to his military and also needed technical expertise to modernize his forces. Copeland wrote, "He [Skorzeny] was approached in a routine manner, then at a higher level, then through a personal visit from a certain well known Major General of the American Army, and finally through his father-in-law, Dr. Hjalmar Schacht, Hitler's former Minister of Finance."

Of course, Schacht was not Skorzeny's father-in-law, as previously covered. The "certain well known Major General of the American Army" was in fact Charles Willoughby, General MacArthur's former intelligence chief, who had just retired from service. Newspapers in the United States actually recorded General Willoughby's mysterious arrival in Spain. The *Oregonian* in Portland, Oregon, for example, covered the visit with the headline, "Mac's Aide in Spain," but the paper gave no clue as to why the general was there, relaying, "The exact purpose of the retired general's visit was not learned but he will confer with Spanish military men." The use of such a high-ranking military intelligence officer is indicative of the senior-level interface that would be carried out between the CIA and Skorzeny from 1952 onward. As related also in other chapters, Skorzeny's CIA intermediaries, were, for the most part, senior U.S. executive-level contacts and thus highly sensitive.

It has been suggested in other histories that, while in Egypt, Skorzeny conducted training of Nasser's forces and he may have, but it appears that was not his primary purpose. Skorzeny stayed in Cairo for several months. Eventually, through his network contacts, he managed to recruit about a hundred German scientists and engineers for the project. Copeland later wrote that Skorzeny "had done the best he could under the circumstances" and remained on good terms "with the American friends who were instrumental in getting him to Egypt."

THE MAN BEHIND THE CURTAIN—JAMES J. ANGLETON

Security is a major consideration in the development and implementation of covert operations. Monitoring Skorzeny's activities while he carried out covert missions in support of the Agency would have been a vital component of counterintelligence. The oversight of CIA operations outside the Agency was handled by the Counterintelligence Staff or CIS. This office had been aware of the agency's use of Skorzeny since 1948 when the CIS was under William K. Harvey.

The ultimate purpose of CIS reports on Skorzeny was to give the agency a "heads up" on any potential compromise of covert operations. This CIS oversight reveals a much deeper level of security on Skorzeny than declassified records on him appear to indicate. Angleton's staff worked closely with the Covert Action Staff (CAS) and Special Operations (SO) to mitigate potential security problems. The oversight included evidence of foreign agent penetration or even unwanted public scrutiny.

In 1954, General James Doolittle was asked by President Eisenhower to form a commission to review CIA covert operations and intelligence capabilities. The Doolittle Commission determined that the Russian KGB was besting the CIA and recommended ideas to increase its proficiency and produce a "more ruthless" approach. Doolittle advised, "the intensification of the CIA's counterintelligence efforts to prevent or detect and eliminate penetrations of CIA." Soon thereafter, CIA Director Allen Dulles expanded the Counterintelligence Staff (CIS) and selected James Angleton, one of his most trusted lieutenants, as its chief.

From the history presented herein, we know Angleton had direct knowledge concerning Skorzeny as a CIA asset since the formation of the CIA. In the early years before becoming counterintelligence chief, Angleton was the chief of Staff A, the foreign intelligence operations office.

In 1951, Angleton assumed exclusive control of the "Israel Desk" and kept it under his personal authority "for the next twenty years." At some point in 1962, he was made aware of an Israeli intelligence plan to use Skorzeny in a clandestine operation designed to shut down Egypt's rocket program, which was threatening their nation. Intelligence reporting also indicated the Egyptians might have developed radiological warheads for their missiles.

Since Skorzeny was familiar with the Egyptian scientist program, which he helped set up in 1953, he was seen as an ideal candidate and would not be suspected as working for the Israelis. This unconventional approach was the brainchild of Isser Harel, a close confidant of Angleton and head of the Mossad, who dubbed the plan Operation Damocles.

Harel's plan specifically targeted German scientists and technicians at a secret site known as Factory 333. To recruit Skorzeny, Harel dispatched to Spain their best Mossad agent, Rafi Eitan, who along with another secret agent arrived in Madrid under the guise of NATO representatives. They met with Skorzeny and explained the situation. Skorzeny immediately agreed to help and, to the shock of the Israelis, did not want payment for his services. He requested only that the Israelis arrange for the publishing of his memoirs in Israel. The original draft copy of the Israeli-published Skorzeny memoirs is in the Skorzeny papers.

Skorzeny made all the necessary arrangements, departing for only a few days to Egypt to activate his network, and did not go to Israel during any aspect of the operation. For the simple publishing bargain, Israel received the intelligence they needed to shut down the Egyptian program, yet despite the success of Damocles, in March 1963 Israeli Prime Minister David Ben-Gurion terminated the program, since it had included intimidation, abduction, and assassination. Ben-Gurion also demanded the resignation of Isser Harel. There is more to this story that should and will be elaborated on at a future time.

CIS chief James Angleton was not only close to his boss, Allen Dulles, but also to Richard Helms, another legendary officer and future CIA director. It was said of Angleton that his hallmark was the formation of "secret units within secret units." Shortly after taking over the CIS, Angleton created a section to investigate Soviet penetrations into the CIA called the Special Investigation Group, or SIG. The unit was "so secret that many members of the Counterintelligence Staff didn't even know it existed." The unit's deputy chief was Newton "Scotty" Miler, Angleton's most trusted subordinate. Miler's name is on the distribution list of several declassified CIA documents pertaining to Otto Skorzeny.

Other members of CI/SIG included Raymond and Jane Roman. They were also aware of Skorzeny. Angleton's "gatekeeper" was his loyal secretary, Bertha Dasenburg. She was of German descent and had served in the Red Cross in Italy during World War II. She joined Angleton's CIA in 1952 and had the power to grant or deny access to her boss.

Investigating potential Soviet penetration was known to be an obsession with Angleton. Former CIA general counsel Lawrence Houston recalled that, "Jim's staff spent far too much time reviewing old historical cases which had little relevance to current affairs. They would go over and over old cases like the "The Trust" and *Rote Kapelle*. They spent weeks and months on it. And Angleton actively encouraged this work. To me it seemed a waste of time." The *Rote Kapelle*, or "Red Orchestra," was the German codename for an immense Soviet espionage operation during World War II. It was believed to have continued operations after the conflict. Houston's observation about the CIS focus on Red Orchestra brings us to another highly significant finding in the Skorzeny papers that also matches declassified CIA reporting. On August 25, 1955, the FBI office in Madrid became aware of the fact that USAF attaché Major Bob Bieck was informed by Skorzeny that he could provide previously unknown decodes of Red Orchestra traffic. This caught the attention of the FBI who immediately wanted to know the validity of the information and requested any new data that the CIA might have on the Communist organization. The outcome of the FBI inquiry is not known, but the highly detailed decodes are in the Skorzeny Papers!

In the end, Skorzeny emerges as a clear asset of Angleton's Counterintelligence Staff, shared with the equally secretive offices of Frank Wisner and

William K. Harvey. These men had close personal relationships and contact with Skorzeny seems to have been restricted to this very tight inner circle of CIA executive officers and selected staff. Use of Skorzeny appears to have been entirely unknown to the rank and file of the CIA. Under normal lines of authority, Angleton would have reported to the Deputy Director for Plans, then to the Director, but it has been reported that Angleton "was unhindered by the normal chain of command." His authority was such that he developed an "unshakable power base within the CIA." With Angleton at the helm, the CIS would become undeniably the most powerful office within the CIA.

CHAPTER FOURTEEN
"SKORZENY'S SCHOOL OF COMMANDO TACTICS"

The relationship between Skorzeny and French intelligence, which began in earnest in 1949, was centered on anti-Communist operations and the preparation of stay-behind forces. This was part of Donovan's Secret Paramilitary Group in support of Compass Rose. At some undeterminable point, but approximately 1951, the Donovan SPG was either disbanded or reorganized. At this point, Skorzeny's group seems to have been established as trainers and advisers. Another important development was his small commando group was rolled up under the a highly classified body called the Clandestine Planning Committee (CPC). The CPC was placed under the U.S. Military Assistance Advisery Groups, or MAAGs for operational cover.

The overt mission of MAAG was to assist foreign nations with training on weapons and equipment provided by the U.S. government, but a host of classified missions were also carried out, including unconventional warfare training for stay-behind networks. This mission went to Skorzeny's men who acted as key instructors of personnel being trained for covert units or special clandestine assignments. This training, was very reminiscent of the wartime SOE and OSS Camp X and included assassination.

Specifically, MAAG interacted with Skorzeny at the paramilitary commando training camps set up in Spain and other locations. A retired U.S. Army Special Forces officer, Lt. Colonel Anthony Herbert, who attended several of these training camps in 1960, referred to them collectively as "Skorzeny's School of Commando Tactics." Skorzeny's connection to MAAG is a vital component in his clandestine relationship to the United States. Authorization for MAAG to interact with Skorzeny came from the highest levels of the U.S. government. Other countries also knew of these camps including France, Great Britain, and of course Spain. Skorzeny would continue tobe associated with MAAG well into the early 1970s. Therefore, to understand how this arrangement occurred, we must take a closer look at the development of MAAG in Spain and the people connected to its early history.

MAAG, THE CIA, AND SKORZENY

The first overtures by the United States to normalize relations with Spain after World War II came from U.S. military commanders who understood Spain's strategic importance to Western defense. Geographically, Spain is vital to the military considerations of the European continent and North Africa. The two major motivations for Spain to seek close relations with the United States was defense against Communism and, perhaps most importantly, the country's struggling economy. Politically, tension ran high between certain elements within the U.S. government due to Spain's neutral stance during the war and Nazi sympathies. Francisco Franco, the country's leader, was a fascist and had warm relations early on with Hitler and Mussolini. Franco had permitted economic trade and diplomatic exchange with the Axis. Additionally, several thousand Spaniards had volunteered for duty in the "Blue Division," a Spanish army unit that fought for Germany on the Russian front.

Inroads into improving U.S.—Spain relations began in 1951, pushed along by U.S. military officers, who encouraged closer diplomacy and negotiations between the two countries. The basic premise of the emerging partnership was economic development for Spain in return for military concessions, such as U.S. basing rights. A seemingly reluctant President Truman consented to these negotiations, stating, "I don't like Franco and I never will, but I won't let my personal feelings override the convictions of you military men."

Later, with the election of President Dwight Eisenhower, more urgency came to the process. As a military thinker, Eisenhower did not need convincing of the logic of a strong U.S. relationship with Spain, particularly in regard to military imperatives. Enticed by U.S. financial aid and eager to show their resolve against

Communism, the Spanish government became full partners in the effort to establish their country as a Western ally. This greatly boosted Spain's prestige on the world power stage and was the first steps on the road to full membership in NATO.

Spain was not the only European country to receive such aid but, for the purpose of this study, certainly the most important. The aid to Spain was part of a military program born in World War II and was expanded immensely under President Harry Truman in the early 1950s. This was the Military Assistance and Advisery Groups, or MAAGs, mentioned at the beginning of this chapter. MAAGs existed in all the major NATO countries of Europe and several countries in Africa, South America, and the Far East. One of the more important MAAGs was in Indochina, where a small group of U.S. military men was assisting the French to hold Vietnam against the communist leader, Ho Chi Minh.

MAAG's main role was to provide technical assistance on arms sales, maintenance programs, and military training, such as tactics, combat techniques and other military procedures. The overall goal of MAAG was to enhance the capabilities of U.S. foreign allies.

During the Cold War, MAAGs had important authorities and had embedded in their structure CIA operatives who handled the political considerations of training. As a result of the fusion within MAAG of military trainers and CIA operatives, MAAG was used in covert operations. This usage was authorized by U.S. government directive NSC 10/2 in 1948. Importantly, the CIA integration with MAAG was a state secret and not known to the public or even to the general military forces. In reality, the MAAG program was a subset of the overall Military Assistance Program, or MAP, a vital component in the comprehensive European recovery project under the Marshall Plan. This was a highly classified project at the time. As we will see, CIA operations frequently cut across bureaucratic lines involving a political ecology of interdependency with other agencies involved in covert action.

The chief of MAAG in each country was usually a general officer, who was also the senior military adviser to the ambassador. The MAAG chief also worked closely with other senior U.S. officials who implemented non-military security programs, such as the Economic Cooperation Agency (ECA). Critical to understanding Skorzeny's relationship with the CIA is the vitally important fact that the ECA was a cover for CIA covert action. Much of the business dealings Skorzeny had with the U.S. and Spain as evidenced in the papers indicate they were carried out under the auspices of the ECA.

Established in 1948 by the United States, the ECA helped Europe recover from World War II but also served as a political counterweight to Soviet propaganda. The ECA was specifically tasked with strengthening U.S. allies in Europe and oversaw the development and administration of both military and economic assistance programs. It also served as a cover for clandestine programs of U.S. intelligence. The specific contracts in the Skorzeny papers, such as his dealings in railroad equipment were ECA projects where he could carry out clandestine programs at the behest of the CIA. The ECA underwent another name change to the Mutual Security Agency and then in 1955 became the International Cooperation Administration or ICA. It also expanded its support to the CIA which was masked within ICA structure. Tasked by the National Security Council, the CIA mission within the ICA was to deal with communist inspired insurgencies and oversee the Overseas Internal Security Program to assist foreign countries in resisting communism. According to Robert Amory, Jr. the CIA had thirty-three employees integrated into ICA, who were a "highly trained nucleus of counter-subversive specialists." The ICA was replaced by the U.S. Agency for International Development, or USAID in 1961.

The ambassador, the ICA chief, and the MAAG chief functioned as a country team for the purpose of implementing all defense plans and economic recovery programs. The embassy staff handled the "nuts and bolts" of operations and was assigned to handle the details of the diverse economic, political, and administrative projects. The Skorzeny papers confirm he dealt directly with Arthur B. Emmons, the ICA representative on the embassy staff for many years. Emmons began his career as a foreign service officer and was in Spain when Skorzeny arrived there in 1950. It is not known if Emmons was also a CIA officer.

Depending on the various political or military considerations, the U.S. government weighed the different aid options in the implementation of MAAG programs. Colonel L. Fletcher Prouty, who worked the programs in the 1950s, summed it up this way: "In some countries, encouragement and perhaps minor technical assistance to recipient governments may suffice; in others, direct military assistance may be most appropriate, while, elsewhere, the answer may lie in ICA programs under MAAG supervision."

In April 1953, the Eisenhower administration sent Ambassador James Dunn to Spain "with orders to speed things up." Negotiations then proceeded at a more rapid pace. A military effort was dispatched, headed by USAF Major General August W. Kissner, commanding the Joint United States Military Advisery Group (JUSMAG) in Spain. The man who oversaw the day-to-day running of MAAG was Army Brigadier General Earl C. Bergquist, an experienced World War II combat staff officer, who also served as General Kissner's deputy commander.

Under the agreements signed with Spain, the Department of the Air Force was the lead agency for a massive base construction program. The Spanish Air ministry provided offices for JUSMAG. The Air Force constructed bases near Madrid, Seville, and Zaragoza. Other air bases were established in Spanish Morocco. Eventually, the 16th United States Air Force would be stationed in the country. The 16th Air Force was part of the legendary Strategic Air Command, or SAC. Squadrons of nuclear B-47 bombers were maintained at the new bases and placed on rotational alert, a status maintained until April 1965. Other undertakings included a major U.S. Navy port and naval airfield in Rota, while the U.S Army dispatched advisers to work directly with the Spanish Army to upgrade weapons and tactics.

The start of the program was covered in American newspapers, informing the public of the base construction and modernization of the Spanish military. For example, an article in the *Kansas City Times* on June 22, 1954, referred to Spain as a "bastion" and stated that the Spanish military was to receive intensive training from U.S. experts. However, the public was not informed of the more sensitive aspects of MAAG, including its relationship with U.S. intelligence.

As part of the classified portions of the MAAG program, secret training sites were also established. These were maintained with the permission of the

Spanish military and intelligence services. At these sites, clandestine training was carried out by CIA officers embedded directly into MAAG, many being "sheep dipped," or serving under cover as military officers. Some of these clandestine training camps were actually legacy sites from World War II intelligence operations. Over the coming years, the MAAG camps would be attended by a variety of units, including U.S. Special Forces, foreign paramilitary groups recruited by the CIA, and government secret agents.

In addition to the involvement of the U.S. military and the CIA, the primary government entity for military assistance programs was the Office of International Security Affairs, or ISA. This three-letter agency deserves more than a casual mention. In the passages above, we discussed the military assistance programs associated with MAAG. The ISA implemented the Mutual Defense Assistance Program (MDAP), which controlled military advisery assistance to "friendly" nations (i.e. MAAG groups). Putting this in the simplest terms—the ISA, working in close coordination with the Pentagon (MAAG) and the CIA managed the U.S. covert military assistance programs.

Although the average American has never heard of the ISA, its importance relative to covert activity is paramount. Actually, the ISA has "played a critical role in shaping the national security policy of the United States since 1949." The office traces its historical roots, as does the Department of Defense itself, to the early Cold War period. After World War II, military power "assumed a central position in U.S. foreign policy, as tensions between the United States and the Soviet Union began to reshape the postwar geopolitical systems." The overall effect of this tension gave rise, in 1947, to President Truman's containment policy and major expansion of covert operations. That same year, the landmark National Security Act was passed, which created the position of Secretary of Defense (SECDEF). The SECDEF was "to provide unified direction, authority, and control" over the vast military complex of U.S. national defense.

The forerunner to the ISA was the Office of Foreign Military Affairs and Military Assistance, formed in 1948. That office handled the initial stages of assistance issues connected with NATO, including the creation of the MAAG groups. With the outbreak of the Korean conflict in 1950, greater demands and responsibilities came upon the office. Due to the rapidly expanding military assistance programs, in 1951 Secretary of Defense George C. Marshall "ordered an increase in staff and resources for the office, including the creation of a new section (separate and distinct from the Foreign Military Affairs section)" to manage NATO. Marshall also changed the name to the Office of International Security Affairs. By the end of 1952, "ISA boasted a staff of nearly 200 and was fast becoming a full-fledged clearinghouse for politico-military affairs with the Department of Defense." The first head of the ISA was Frank C. Nash. He had directed the organization under its old title and, in 1952, the position was elevated from Assistant to the Secretary of Defense to Assistant Secretary of Defense. Thus, the ISA was, and continues to be, one of the Pentagon's highest offices. The head of the ISA is the senior representative of the Secretary of Defense.

In 1954, Secretary of Defense Charles Wilson "assigned ISA 'general supervision' of all DoD activities in the field of National Security Council affairs." Furthermore, a special assistant was placed within ISA to serve as his representative to the National Security Council's planning board. Together with the reforms that raised the office to an assistant secretary of defense, the ISA was given full authority over all military assistance programs.

ENTER H. STRUVE HENSEL

In 1954, H. Struve Hensel was nominated by President Eisenhower to succeed Assistant Secretary Nash as head of ISA. The timing of Hensel's appointment as ISA chief was during a period of MAAG expansion in Vietnam and the difficult days following the French defeat in Indochina. Hensel's background reveals evidence that he may have known about Otto Skorzeny's CIA association prior to becoming the head of ISA.

Hensel was born in Hoboken, New Jersey, in 1901. He attended Columbia University, graduating in 1925 with a degree in law. During World War II, he worked in the legal division of the Navy's procurement department, alongside another individual who will be central to our research, E. Perkins McGuire.

Before the end of the war, Hensel served as General Counsel and then as Assistant Secretary of the Navy before returning to his law practice in 1946.

There, he worked for the law firm of Carter Ledyard. Also at the firm was Frank Wisner, the future head of the CIA Office of Policy Coordination, who had recently gotten out of the OSS. Wisner was recruited in 1947 by George Kennan to lead the OPC and, as the reader discovered earlier, subsequently utilized Otto Skorzeny for covert operations.

It was from Carter Ledyard that Hensel was also recruited by Frank Wisner for OPC operations. In 1949, Hensel headed radio arrangements in Europe for the CIA cover organization the National Committee for a Free Europe. This cover group was created by Allen Dulles on March 17, 1949, in New York as an anti-Communist organization. It was headed by "political warfare" specialist C. D. Jackson, who began his career as right-hand man to Henry Luce, the magazines *Time, Life*, and *Fortune*. During World War II, Jackson headed the United States Psychological Warfare Division. Radio Free Europe was considered the most important operation of the NCFE. Through it, the National Committee for a Free Europe directed CIA funds to the Assembly of Captive European Nations (ACEN), a cover organization for the recruitment of covert assets. A curious activity connected to C. D. Jackson and of importance to the subject of this book was Jackson's spontaneous acquisition of the famous Zapruder film for *Time-Life*, taken on November 22, 1963, by Abraham Zapruder's home movie camera, recording the assassination of President Kennedy. Jackson held on to the film. The film was reviewed by the Warren Commission, but there were frames missing. Subsequently, in early 1967, *Life* released a statement that four frames (208–211) had been accidentally destroyed, and adjacent frames damaged, by a lab technician on November 23, 1963.

In 1952, Hensel would go on to serve as General Counsel for the Department of Defense, and then later as head of the ISA. Hensel would leave government service in July 1955, returning to private legal practice. He would also become a major lobbyist for the German steel industry, representing the firm of Otto Wolff, of which Skorzeny was also a representative. Hensel is found in the Skorzeny papers in reference to Otto Wolff business transactions, confirming he was dealing with Skorzeny.

ENTER E. PERKINS MCGUIRE

It is no coincidence that the most historically significant persons found in the Skorzeny papers are associated with the ISA. In addition to H. Struve Hensel, we also have the man who served as Hensel's deputy, Edward Perkins McGuire, or simply E. Perkins McGuire, as he is commonly known to history. McGuire is the senior-level U.S. government contact in the Skorzeny papers, a highly provocative finding. A review of his life gives a clear indication that his association with Otto Skorzeny is, by all historical standards, extremely important. McGuire, a lifelong friend of President Richard Nixon, a contract CIA officer, and former Assistant Secretary of Defense, is a major character in Skorzeny's covert history.

E. Perkins McGuire was born in Boston, Massachusetts, on October 22, 1904, to a Catholic family. He was the son of a successful Boston merchant and businessman. As a young man, he acquired the nickname "Perk" from his closest friends. He attended Worcester Academy and, later, Lowell Textile Institute (Lowell Institute of Technology) in Lowell, Massachusetts, from which he graduated with a degree in textile engineering. His school annual noted he was "a polished man" and had "no peer in matters sartorial." It was also said of him that he "could talk the devil into mending his ways." Overall, Perkins McGuire was perceived as a shrewd businessman who could "come out on top of any business deal."

After college, he was a very successful textile merchant, with various firms in Boston, New York, and Cleveland. At the outbreak of World War II, his extensive business background landed him an assignment to negotiate contracts for the Bureau of Ordnance. He would rise to the rank of commander and eventually head the Procurement Division, Office of Naval Material. He was awarded the Legion of Merit for his outstanding performance in his field. When the war ended, he left the service and resumed his career in business.

In 1955, McGuire was approached to re-enter government service as a civilian executive being named Deputy Assistant Secretary of Defense for the Office of International Security Affairs. Here, we find a major nexus in our research. As the Deputy Assistant Secretary of Defense for Mutual Defense Assistance

Programs, McGuire, would have been the government official who authorized the involvement of Otto Skorzeny with MAAG. This included Skorzeny use as an unofficial paramilitary adviser for clandestine training camps and covert arms sales. The ISA black arms sales projects connected to Skorzeny would have been managed by the International Logistics Negotiations Section located at the Pentagon. This office was run by the legendary chief of arms sales, Henry John Kuss, Jr., who is reported to have sold billions of dollars in arms to foreign governments for the U.S. arm sales documents in the Skorzeny papers are linked to this office and worthy of an independent study—here, we have but a brief mention to let the reader know about its extremely important connection to this history.

In 1956, McGuire would be named Assistant Secretary of Defense for Supply and Logistics. This position put Secretary McGuire at the center of all covert planning at the Department of Defense, including those carried out by the CIA. During his tenure as Assistant Secretary of Defense, McGuire worked very closely with his good friend, Deputy Under Secretary of State Robert Murphy, who was also keenly aware of Otto Skorzeny.

After the defeat of Richard Nixon by John F. Kennedy in the 1960 presidential election, McGuire would leave government service. In August 1960, McGuire, along with Percival Brundage, the former Director of the Bureau of Budget, would purchase a commercial airline, Southern Air Transport (SAT). This was a secret purchase for the CIA and a major acquisition of a proprietary airline for covert operations.

From 1961 on, McGuire became an investment consultant that he used as a cover for his continued covert work for the government. Evidence of this clandestine service as a CIA contract officer is recorded in a letter dated, February 26, 1974, from CIA Director William E. Colby. In the letter Colby expresses gratitude for McGuire's long service, thanking him for his "advice and counsel . . . over many years" and his "efforts in support of the mission" of the Agency.

SKORZENY'S PRIVATE COMMANDO

In 1950, Skorzeny began developing contingency war plans that proposed the formation of a cadre of German commandos in Spain to train special forces in the event of a war between NATO and the Soviets. According to the plan, the size and scope of the program could be regulated, depending on the global situation. At the same time, specialists could be formed into *Nachrichteneinheiten,* or intelligence and communications units. Incorporated into his plan was the creation of special sniper units. Skorzeny submitted this plan to the Pentagon through a military attaché, Major Bob Bieck, at the American Embassy in 1951. CIA officer Arnold Silver later claimed Pentagon planners rejected the concept. However, it is clear from the research and interviews conducted for this book that subcomponents of Skorzeny's plan were deemed of value and integrated into U.S. covert planning.

It will be recalled that upon his initial arrival at Camp King in 1947, Skorzeny was assigned to Captain Theodore C. Mataxis of the U.S. Army historical detachment. The historical work was the cover for the clandestine discussion between Skorzeny and the intelligence staff for his future role in covert operations. After leaving Camp King, Mataxis continued to advance in the Army with various assignments, including a tour as an infantry tactics instructor at Fort Benning and attendance at the Army War College. In 1958, he received orders for the 8th Infantry Division in Mainz, Germany. He rose through various staff positions, eventually becoming commander of the 1st Airborne Battle Group, 505th Infantry. He had also advanced in rank to colonel.

In his capacity as commander of the 505th, Colonel Mataxis was keenly aware of the various combat training centers in Europe, including special training schools set up with NATO countries and MAAG. He was also aware of the secret training being conducted in Spain by Otto Skorzeny. This was confirmed by an officer serving in Mataxis command.

In early 1960, First Lieutenant Anthony Herbert, a highly decorated U.S. Army combat officer, reported for duty with the 505th. Lieutenant Herbert was aware that his assignment to the 505th put him in honored company. After just two weeks in the unit, he was selected as E company executive officer. Herbert was an innovative thinker and favored special warfare operations. During his spare time, he developed a concept for a new ranger unit to be formed within the 505th. He took the idea to Colonel Mataxis, who liked it and gave Herbert his approval to form the group. In just a few weeks, Herbert was the commander of the Provisional Ranger Platoon of the 1st Battalion. Lt. Herbert had 180 men under him, making the rangers a powerful combat arm for Mataxis' battle group.

Herbert's first task was to train the unit to the best standards of the day for special forces. Herbert got permission from Mataxis to canvass Europe for training courses to hone the skills of his men. In the fall of 1960, the unit set off for France, to cross-train with tough French Foreign Legionnaires and elite French Air Force commandos. The French training area was located just outside the city of Pau, not far from the border with Spain.

Many years later, Herbert recorded his memories of Pau, including an unusual conversation with French commandos in which the subject of Skorzeny came up. Herbert was shocked to discover that the French were actually training with Skorzeny. After Herbert returned to Germany, he approached Colonel Mataxis on the subject, who commented that perhaps it could be arranged.

Colonel Mataxis was fully aware of the sensitivity of MAAG's association with Skorzeny's paramilitary group and, for security reasons, proceeded carefully. Herbert confirmed the sensitive relationship in his book, stating that Skorzeny "was still being very careful," and that the training was "conducted by a small group of German soldiers" who "had formed a corporation whose service was arming and training groups of guerrillas."

Arrangements were made for a trip to France as a cover for an initial meeting between the Herbert and Skorzeny. The actual meeting took place "in the mountains of the Basque section of Spain, in the mountains of the North." Like many who met the towering commando for the first time, Herbert was impressed with Skorzeny's height. Herbert's activities and experiences with Otto Skorzeny are recounted in a book he wrote, titled *Soldier*. In 1960, he noted that, although in his fifties, Skorzeny had a "lean, rangy physique," adding, "There was nothing pudgy about him." Also, Skorzeny spoke English, "although he did not do a great deal of talking."

With everything set, Herbert assembled his men and reported for duty at Skorzeny's "School of Commando Tactics," as he called it. Over the next few months Herbert's rangers met with Skorzeny's men in the "Basque country" some ten or eleven times. Herbert also indicated that there were other camps run by Skorzeny, and that he was not always present for training. One of Skorzeny's aides told Herbert, "You must understand . . . he has other students."

In regard to the training, Herbert revealed, "If you wanted to know how to blow up a bridge without blowing up yourself, Skorzeny could teach you. Whatever you thought you needed to know about an underground war, Otto was your man—for a price." Herbert adding "for a price" confirms one of the major findings in the research for this book—that Skorzeny's instruction was on a contract basis with the U.S. government. Herbert's rangers being officially sent to receive instruction from Skorzeny and his men further confirms that U.S. Army funding was used for the training.

Writing years later about Skorzeny's training, Herbert had mixed reviews, noting, "I was quite disappointed . . . his methods were good, but they were dated . . . everything his men mentioned I had already learned as an American Ranger." But he did compliment Skorzeny in two areas; one was the "fine art of arson" and the other was demolitions. Importantly, Herbert's overall description of Skorzeny's commando school confirms other evidence regarding Skorzeny's association with MAAG and the formation of a private paramilitary group.

Lt. Herbert had mentioned he was trained by Skorzeny's "men," a "small group of German soldiers." Who were these men? For clear evidence we can turn to the Skorzeny papers indicating Skorzeny was still in contact with some of the best and most experience soldiers of his old wartime commando. This included his trusted adjutant Karl Radl, Major Otto Begus, and others including members of the assassination unit SS *Sonderkommando*-Denmark, or the Peter Group. In particular, there is Horst Issel, the group's commander. The Peter Group had operated in Denmark in concert with Danish collaborators where it conducted "clearing murders," pinpointing specific Danes for assassination, to wipe out the Danish resistance.

First mentioned in this book in the background chapter on Skorzeny, the Peter Group was formed in December 1943. The first commander was *Obersturmfüehrer* Otto Schwerdt, one of Skorzeny's top officers, who had been on the Mussolini rescue mission. He is also in the Skorzeny papers. Schwerdt used the alias Peter Schafer, from which the unit got its name. Schwerdt directed Peter Group operations until November 1944, when he was recalled by Skorzeny. After Schwedt's departure, leadership of the group transferred to Horst Issel.

Issel had served in the RSHA (Reich Main Security Office). This was Skorzeny's higher headquarters, under Ernst Kaltenbrunner. He would remain at the head of the Peter Group until the end of the war. After the capitulation, the members of the group dispersed and went underground. They were among the most hunted men in Europe. Issel, in particular, was a focal point of capture.

An allied report on Issel issued at the end of the war, a copy of which is found in the Skorzeny papers, stated, "He is an extremely dangerous person, who would not shy from any means to attain his objective, and it is of paramount importance that really effective action is taken to trace him . . . He has a poison, hidden in a tie pin, and is in possession of two fountain pens; one with toxic gas, and the other is a pistol."

The Danish members of the Peter Group were not as fortunate as their German counterparts. Seven of the worst were executed; three were given life imprisonment. Some of the German members were captured, but none were executed. Despite being wanted all over Europe, Issel was mysteriously brought into U.S. intelligence operations immediately after the war. The details about how this happened are sketchy but, after escaping from Denmark, Issel first managed to evade capture. Then, around 1948, by unknown circumstances, he was recruited into the U.S. backed Gehlen Organization. His activities were evidently highly secret, for the British arrested him in Berlin, in early 1949, not realizing his undercover status with Gehlen.

Issel told the British he was working for the Americans, but, when the British went to U.S. Army counterintelligence, they said they denied his agent status. The British subsequently turned Issel over to the Danish authorities, where he joined several of his comrades who were also awaiting trial. By 1953, the CIA worked behind the scenes and got Horst Issel and others of the group released. By 1954, they were all once again in contact with Skorzeny. Other Peter Group members in contact with Skorzeny *after* he became an independent para-military adviser to U.S. and French intelligence in the early 1950s are SS *Obersturmführer* Otto Schwerdt, SS *Obersturmführer* Otto Wagner, and SS *Untersturmführer* Hans Kramer. The presence of these men in the Skorzeny papers indicates the experience level and lethality of Skorzeny's paramilitary network.

SS Captain Otto Skorzeny on Gran Sasso moments after the rescue of Benito Mussolini. (Ganis Collection)

Adolf Hitler personally congratulates SS Commando leader Otto Skorzeny on his rescue of the Italian dictator Benito Mussolini. For his bravery and success Skorzeny received the Knight's Cross to the Iron Cross. (Ganis Collection)

The original Knight's Cross award
document presented to Skorzeny.
(Ganis Collection)

Allied wanted poster for Skorzeny.
(Ganis Collection)

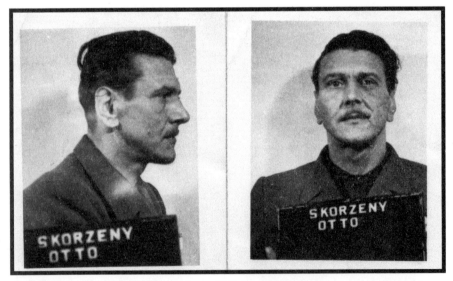

Skorzeny mug shot after his surrender to U.S. forces in Bavaria. (Ganis Collection)

Identity card for Otto Skorzeny under the alias, Rolf Steiner-Hardt identifying him as a "journalist" from the period just after his escape from Camp King. The identity card would have been provided by U.S. intelligence. (Ganis Collection)

Skorzeny identity card under the alias, Rolf Steinbauer. (Ganis Collection)

Early post World War II picture of Skorzeny (at back of table, head hidden by unidentified female) and Ilse (holding up paper) at Horcher's restaurant in Madrid with many former Nazi associates. (Ganis Collection)

Otto Skorzeny and Ilse at a wine shop in Madrid, Spain 1951. Note American flag near Skorzeny's shoulder. They were deeply involved with U.S. intelligence at this point. (Ganis Collection)

Skorzeny's seaside residence in Majorca, Spain. (Ganis Collection)

Skorzeny's 175-acre estate in Ireland acquired in 1959 only days after meeting with British SAS legend David Sterling. It was likely used as a clandestine training base and operations center for his covert missions. (Ganis Collection)

A very enigmatic photo that appears to show Otto Skorzeny on a Learjet with CIA officers Cord Meyer (seated) and David Atlee Phillips. Some historians have claimed that Phillips was Lee Harvey Oswald's case officer under the alias 'Maurice Bishop.' Meyer was the divorced husband of Mary Meyer who was found murdered in 1964. Mary Meyer was having a clandestine affair with President Kennedy, and it is claimed she had information on the network that killed him. (Ganis Collection)

Skorzeny's Third Reich decorations on display at his funeral–July 1975. (Ganis Collection)

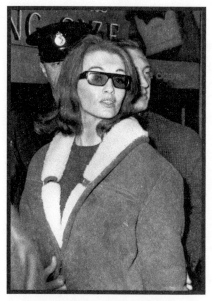

Portrait of alleged former prostitute
Christine Keeler in Great Britain,
March 28, 1963. (AP Photo)

Captain Jean Rene Souetre, French Air
Commando, OAS assassin and Skorzeny
mercenary. He was in Dallas November 22,
1963 and "deported" 48 hours later on an
aircraft that was likely a CIA proprietary.

Portrait of Ellen "Elly" Rometsch, 27,
taken in spring 1963 in Washington,
D.C. (AP Photo)

Lee Harvey Oswald being shot by Jack Ruby as Oswald is being transferred by police to the Dallas County jail, November 24, 1963.

CHAPTER FIFTEEN

FRENCH INDOCHINA

"Vietnam is important to all of us."

OTTO SKORZENY

F or nearly a decade after World War II, the French government attempted to hold on to the jewel of her empire—French Indochina. In 1940, Japan invaded French Indochina, declaring "Asia for Asians." Although the Vichy French government (an ally of Germany, and hence Japan) was allowed to remain in place, the Japanese changed their position in the last months of the war and moved to oust the French from power. On March 9, 1945, the Japanese arrested virtually all of the French government administrators and military authorities. As the conflict was coming to an end, the Japanese further complicated the political scenario in the region by granting Vietnam independence. However, the United States, Russia, and Great Britain agreed that Vietnam belonged to France. The British were dispatched into Vietnam from the south, releasing French soldiers from captivity and placing the French colonial government back in power.

Into this turmoil, the nationalist leader and Communist, Ho Chi Minh, moved to secure political power. Minh had provided intelligence on the Japanese to the American OSS during the war and was, at this point, perhaps more nationalist than Communist. On August 16, 1945, Minh declared himself president of a "free Vietnam," and on September 2, he proclaimed the independence of the Democratic Republic of Vietnam (DRV). He also carried out elections in North Vietnam (that were neither free nor democratic), in which he was certainly the winner. Minh realized, however, that he would have to contend with the French. To that end, he worked out an agreement with them recognizing the DRV as a free and independent state within the French Union. The French government made political concessions as well, allowing more freedom while retaining ultimate authority.

France then began a military buildup in the area to reassert its power in the southern part of Vietnam, in Cambodia, and in Laos. The French in Hanoi cheered the troops upon their arrival and viewed their return as the establishment of legitimate authority. Then, in direct violation of the treaty signed with Minh, the French declared the south separate from the north. Political turmoil over these issues within the French government between the right and left factions created a disastrous backlash in Vietnam. The Vietnamese insisted the south was part of their country, but the French remained resolute on the issue. Minh tried to achieve compromise, but to no avail.

Relations continued to deteriorate and hostilities erupted. In response, the French began military operations against the mounting rebellion. The French army believed that only force would stop the Vietminh (Minh's nationalist Vietnamese army) and initiated violent punitive operations. By late 1946, Minh's rebels were forced out of the cities into the countryside.

The French were confident they could defeat Minh's forces, and steadily the bloodshed increased. Also, a shift to the right in French politics closed any window for a negotiated peace. The Vietminh had the backing of the peasant population in the countryside, who swelled the ranks of Minh's rebel army. These rural people also established networks that provided valuable intelligence to Minh on French dispositions and activities. The Vietminh soldiers were led by General Vo Nguyen Giap, whose army continued to grow and to gain more territory.

In an attempt to delegitimize Minh's movement, the French created a rival government. The United States had only limited involvement in the war at this point, but CIA officers did urge the French to form counterguerrilla groups to engage the Vietminh.

The French forces were organized into three main military organizations—the Metropolitan Infantry (French volunteers), the Colonial Infantry (which comprised the bulk of the army, largely French and French-Africa volunteers assigned to static posts), and the French Foreign Legion. In addition to the standard military forces, private paramilitary groups and spy outfits were organized. Also, in a move to add more agile battle forces in-country, two battalions of Foreign Legion paratroopers were created in 1948. These two battalions, which were designated the 1st Foreign Parachute Battalion (1 BEP) and the 2nd Foreign Parachute Battalion (2 BEP), were formed in North Africa and deployed to Vietnam by the fall of 1948. Many of the officers and NCO's had been brought over from Metropolitan and Colonial paratrooper units of the 25th Airborne Division.

The Foreign Legion units were engaged in hard battles across Vietnam and were considered excellent soldiers. Overall, French airborne forces were "committed to an exhausting pace of operations . . . in every kind of offensive and defensive operation."

Starting in 1947, the French began organizing new units of a more specialized nature. A small detachment of French commandos and native soldiers was placed under the command of Lt. Colonel Edmond Grall to train indigenous soldiers in sabotage, communications, and intelligence gathering. This unit received training from former French SAS commandos and had regular contact with U.S. MAAG advisers (CIA), who supervised the distribution of U.S. military equipment and assisted French officers with training.

Although taking place far from France, these French commando operations in Vietnam actually impacted Otto Skorzeny. The reader will recall that Skorzeny and Ilse were relocated from their seclusion in Germany to secret locations near Paris. This was part of a joint Anglo–American–French covert project arranged with French intelligence chiefs Pierre Bateaux, Director of the *Sûreté Nationale* (National Police), and Roger Wybot, head of the DST (French counterintelligence service).

The joint French–U.S. MAAG operations established secret weapons and ammunition caches and provided training to covert forces. General Pierre de Bénouville and Captain Michel de Camaret were active in these covert operations. Both men were also part of the secret de Gaulle Intelligence Service

(*Service d'Ordre du RPF*). One of the units that received training from Skorzeny starting in 1949 and continuing for many years was the 11th Shock parachute regiment, a covert unit operating in concert with the Action Service of the French external intelligence agency, or SDECE. Officers and NCO's from the SDECE's 11th Shock Battalion were also ordered to Vietnam to carry out training with new, unconventional warfare units engaged in assassination. Soldiers from the 11th Shock attended Skorzeny's training sites in France and Spain. There, he and his men taught sabotage, demolitions, and other unconventional warfare skills. Skorzeny also became acquainted with many other French officers and NCOs from the French Foreign Legion who also trained at these camps. It was through the paramilitary training and intelligence work that Skorzeny provided to the French military that his close personal friendships with them would develop. At this point in history, a large percentage of the Foreign Legion was comprised of Germans. One estimate placed the number as high as 45–50 percent in 1954, and still over 30 percent by 1962. Quite a few within this group were former soldiers of the Third Reich, including some who had served with Otto Skorzeny.

In November 1950, General de Lattre de Tassigny, a popular and tough former World War II general, assumed command of all French forces in Indochina. His task was to bring vigor to the campaign, which had fallen into a stagnant battlefield situation. One suggestion came from Lt. Colonel Edmond Grall for the formation of new secret units focused on counterguerrilla operations and psychological warfare. In the spring of 1951, General de Tassigny authorized the formation of Grall's units under the cover name *Groupement de Commandos Mixtes Aéroportés*, or GCMA. One of Colonel Grall's first actions after taking command was to send for a hardened officer who could handle these assignments. That man was Major Roger Trinqiuer, a recognized leader in psychological operations, and one Grall had served with in previous commando units in Indochina. Trinqiuer arrived in December, this being his third Indochina tour. The core of the unit was built upon the earlier airborne commando units of the Colonial SAS, which included Captain Michel de Camaret, a principal French contact to Skorzeny.

The GCMA had expanded capabilities over the earlier commando groups. Specifically, the GCMA was tasked to train indigenous soldiers, called "Maquis," for highly dangerous infiltration operations into Vietminh-controlled areas. They would also carry out direct-action missions, such as sabotage, intelligence gathering, establishment of escape and evasion routes, and recruiting of agents. Since these sensitive missions were outside the operations of the regular French military, the GCMA was not part of the standard organizational structure but, rather, assigned to the Action Service of the SDECE. The status of the GCMA, outside of normal military channels, permitted it to be used for assassination missions, including the liquidation of Vietminh propaganda teams and cadres or suspected agents.

In early October 1951, Pierre Boursicot, the director of the French SDECE, informed the CIA that General de Tassigny had "agreed to accept a Senior CIA representative in Indochina," together with two officers from the Office of Special Operations (OSO) and two from the Office of Policy Coordination (OPC). Under the terms of the agreement, the CIA agreed to accept "two representatives of the French equivalent of OPC, in Korea."

By the end of October, the U.S. legation in Saigon requested State Department approval to establish a "covert relationship" with the Chief of French Intelligence, but the CIA opposed the move in favor of the "impending establishment of formal CIA-French Intelligence liaison in Indochina." By 1952, French liaison with the CIA continued to expand, with the closest coordination between CIA operators and their French counterparts in the GCMA.

Despite the development of these elite commando and special forces, battling the Vietminh continued to be a challenge for the French on a broader scale. The situation took an even more drastic turn when China and Russia began sending military supplies, via land, sea, and air routes, to supply the Vietminh. The most famous of the land routes was known as the "Ho Chi Minh Trail." Also, two other events occurred to move the struggle into a major East–West confrontation. The first was the outbreak of war on the Korean peninsula in 1950, and the second was the recognition of Minh's government by China and Russia. These new developments pushed the U.S. to recognize South Vietnam as the legitimate government.

Believing that a takeover of Vietnam by the Communists would lead to a "domino effect" in the region and perhaps act as a catalyst for other Communist expansions around the world, President Harry Truman authorized direct aid to the French in Vietnam beginning in May 1950, thus increasing the U.S. MAAG footprint in the region. By 1951, as the Vietminh began receiving direct military support from China, the battle in Vietnam changed from a guerrilla war to a conventional one. The French responded by forming a nationalist army in the south and built up this force, with massive U.S. material aid. The American advisers overseeing this U.S. military assistance program were assigned to MAAG-Indochina.

At this point, the Vietnam war was escalating into a major conflict, and by the end of 1953 the U.S. was paying for most of the French war effort in Vietnam. The French maintained control in the cities, but the Vietminh controlled the countryside. The war was extremely unpopular in France as it was for the American public only a few years later. Unable to institute a draft to prosecute the war, the French army relied on colonial troops and the French Foreign Legion. Many of the legionnaires were foreigners, including a sizable number of ex-German soldiers from Hitler's army and the armies of his allies. The basic tactics employed by these forces involved search and destroy missions into the rural areas. Although there were some successes, the overall situation was not militarily sustainable.

By 1953, the situation in Vietnam was not going well for the French. Despite the efforts of their top generals, they were unable to defeat Minh's army. The Vietminh had also taken over a large area of Laos, a French ally, permitting cross-border operations into Vietnam. The French defense had become static, focused on defending strong points and major cities, but there was no comprehensive plan to defeat the enemy. General Henri Navarre developed a strategy, designed to cut off the Vietminh from their supply bases in Laos by establishing a fortified airhead deep in a mountainous area of northwest Vietnam called Dien Bien Phu. The idea was to draw the Vietminh into open battle and destroy them by superior forces.

On November 20, 1953, "Operation Condor" began, as 1,800 battle-hardened French paratroopers descended into the valley of Dien Bien Phu. These tough sky warriors were among the best French combat troops, having fought in every major battle across the country. It was not the first time the French had been in Dien Bien Phu, since they had fought there a year before but were pushed out by the Communist guerrilla forces of Ho Chi Minh.

The battle lasted nearly two months. The human-wave tactics, and lack of medical care, had a negative effect on Vietminh morale, but fresh troops from Laos and a change in tactics to siege warfare eventually broke the French defense. Unable to be supplied adequately by air, and with massive casualties on the ground, the French finally capitulated after a final all-out attack by the Vietminh on May 7, 1954. Thousands of French soldiers went into a brutal captivity and were used as a bargaining chip in negotiations. A Geneva convention temporarily divided the country, with the Communists in the North and the French in the South.

Although there was no direct American military involvement in the battle, the U.S. did provide weapons, material aid, and maintenance crews for the French Air Force via contract CIA pilots. Additionally, the U.S. Navy supplied limited covert air support, and the United States Air Force provided 12 C-119 transport aircraft, flown by French aircrews.

The battle of Dien Bien Phu was a disastrous failure for the French army, although many units fought bravely and well. The decisive Vietminh victory at Dien Bien Phu would signal the end of French involvement in Indochina and marked the beginning of a withdrawal of French military forces that was completed in April 1956. On February 12, 1955, the United States and France agreed that the French military mission would be transferred to MAAG, which was renamed from MAAG-Indonesia to MAAG-Vietnam. On November 1, 1955, President Eisenhower deployed MAAG-Vietnam, marking the official beginning of the Vietnam War.

COLONEL EDWARD LANSDALE AND LUCIEN CONEIN

A little over a year earlier, on March 15, 1954, President Eisenhower signed National Security Council Order 5412 (NSC 5412), the National Security Directive of Covert Operations. This extremely important directive established the CIA as the lead for wide-ranging covert actions abroad. A partial list of responsibilities included propaganda, political action, economic warfare, preventative direct action (including sabotage), escape, evasion and evacuation, subversion, assistance to underground resistance, and support to guerrilla movements. Omitted were military deception operations, espionage, and counter-espionage. The NSC 5412 framework matches the scope of operations that would be levied upon Otto Skorzeny for his involvement in Cuba, the Congo, Algeria, and other places, not discussed in this book.

A highly secret group of senior government officials was tasked to coordinate covert actions implemented under the directive. This body was called the Special Group (or Special Team). In June 1954, a USAF officer named Edward Lansdale was sent under Top Secret orders to Vietnam to head up the Saigon Military Mission, a cover for CIA psychological operations. Lansdale was a former OSS officer, who had a great deal of experience in guerrilla warfare, gained during fighting the Japanese in the Philippines. Lansdale was noted for psychological operations to influence the enemy and gain support of indigenous forces. He arrived in Vietnam as a field grade officer but eventually rose to the rank of Major General. During the anti-Castro operations conducted between 1959 and 1962, he was deeply involved with the Deputy Assistant Secretary of Defense for Special Operations. Lansdale resigned from the service on November 1, 1963, twenty-one days before the assassination of President John F. Kennedy. He would later return to Vietnam in 1965 as a U.S. diplomatic officer, staying at that post until 1968.

Lt. Colonel Lansdale's cover in Saigon was as a U.S. Embassy air attaché. At that time, there was a second CIA mission, overseen by Emmett McCarthy. The two did not get along, which caused some problems in their working relationships. In July, another former OSS veteran, Major Lucien Conein, was dispatched to work with Lansdale. This was "Black Luigi," whose history with Skorzeny reached back to the Document Disposal Unit that had handled matters for the covert projects run out of Camp King in 1948. Conein had also worked with William K. Harvey in Germany between 1949 and 1953. Thus, Conein was very likely privy to the French Intelligence use of Skorzeny in France.

After his European assignment had ended, Conein was dispatched to Vietnam to assist Colonel Lansdale. His work primarily entailed mounting covert operations against the government of Ho Chi Minh in North Vietnam, a duty carried out in coordination with the U.S. MAAG. In 1955, two new officers joined the U.S. MAAG team in Vietnam: Brigadier General Earl C. Bergquist, the former deputy of MAAG-Spain, and Lt. Colonel Charles Askins. Both men had worked with Skorzeny in Madrid. General Bergquist's new assignment was as the deputy commanding officer for the Saigon Military Mission, who oversaw military training for South Vietnam. That year, the United States officially took over the military responsibilities for Vietnam from the French. General Bergquist, who had a high regard for Colonel Askins, asked to join him. Askins was assigned the duty of training Vietnamese soldiers in marksmanship and airborne operations. It surely cannot be coincidence that three senior U.S. miltiary officers, all assigned to MAAG-Vietnam in 1955, had worked with Otto Skorzeny just before arriving in Vietnam and with a French officer, Michel de Camaret who had also worked with him!

CHAPTER SIXTEEN

THE DIRTY WAR

"Assassination is part of the daily routine of the men in the Service Action of the SDECE. They dutifully carry out their orders and are proud of their skill, confident that it is equal to that of the Gestapo or the KGB."

PHILIPPE THYRAUD DE VOSJOLI,

FRENCH INTELLIGENCE OFFICER

Otto Skorzeny's role in the Algerian conflict was a carryover from his role as a paramilitary adviser to French intelligence in Indochina, that started in 1949. Although there are many important pathways contained in this book to the assassination of President Kennedy in Dallas, no historical period had greater importance to Skorzeny than the French war in Algeria. As was often the case in his well-eiled life, Otto Skorzeny's role in the Algerian conflict was cloaked in the shadows, but the evidence we have today enables us to view the outlines of a significant involvement. The central issue in the conflict was a division between the French people; those who favored keeping Algeria a French state, including a large segment of the French military, and the native Muslim separatists, that strove for independence. This political struggle developed into a long, tragic story, of which few are aware, but was a major factor in the progression of events detailed in this book. The French war in Algeria started in 1954, and continued until 1962, with the granting of independence to the country by President Charles de Gaulle. The conflict would dominate European news in a way similar to the Vietnam War ten years later in the United States.

Skorzeny had earlier been involved in supporting the French in Vietnam, an effort that also involved United States military advisers from MAAG-Vietnam who were secretly working with the French. The French defeat at Dien Bien Phu in 1954, and subsequent abandonment of Vietnam by the French government, served to inspire other independence movements in French territories, but most particularly in Algeria. Only six months after the battle in Dien Bien Phu, the French soldiers who fought in Vietnam found themselves locked in another bitter struggle to save their star French colony in North Africa. They had sworn never to be defeated again—a vow they intended to keep. For this reason, the French colony of Algeria would not exit the French colonial empire quietly.

THE FLN STRIKES

Beginning in 1952, an important nationalist movement began to take form in Algeria, the *Front de Libération Nationale* (FLN), or National Libération Front. It was organized to achieve political objectives by revolutionary means, and created a military wing, the *Armée de Libération Nationale*, or National Liberation Army (ALN). The formation of the FLN coincided with an evolving change in the attitude of the French people over Algeria with a rising call for France to grant the country independence.

By 1954, many French citizens had determined not to continue to hold on to Algeria, especially by force, seeing it as too costly, and an impediment to France's political and economic recovery. It was also seen as tarnishing France's international standing. The costly struggle in Vietnam, still fresh in memory, a decisively negative factor in the equation. This loss of will by the French people to hold Algeria, for all of these various reasons, was perceived by the FLN as an opening to be capitalized on. Plans were made to usher in a campaign of terror in order to push events over the threshold and achieve independence.

On November 1, 1954, All Saints Day, the FLN initiated nationwide attacks, including assassinations and bombings, in an attempt to break French resolve, once and for all, in holding the Muslim Algerian peoples in the French orbit. The attack caught the French totally by surprise, and they immediately dispatched reinforcements.

The FLN launched the war mainly in the rural areas, and in the mountains in particular. At the onset of the Algerian war, the FLN "drew chiefly on the Viet Minh as a model for organization," and from methods used by the French Resistance. The independence movement was moving out of the population centers into the rural zones, and was transitioning from a political party to a guerrilla movement. The goal was full independence, but, unlike the Viet Minh, holding terrain was not a priority. In military terms, the initial FLN actions initially had not accomplished much, and did not stir public opinion, but this would change as they instituted greater terror.

A strategic error was made early on by the French approaching the FLN as a Communist movement, when in reality it was nationalist. This early misinterpretation greatly affected the intelligence aspects of the conflict. In essence, the French were fighting the wrong enemy.

"GUERRE SALE" (DIRTY WAR)

The violence caused by the FLN was countered by the French Army with equal or greater force. A number of highly trained French officers in guerrilla warfare operations, who fought in Vietnam, were now fighting in Algeria. The effort in Algeria also involved Roger Wybot, the chief of the French external security service or DST. As head of the DST, Wybot had the primary responsibility of surveillance and intelligence gathering on subversive or rebellious movements in French overseas territories and protectorates. One of the most important was Algeria.

The Algerian War found Wybot once again working with his old wartime boss, Jacques Soustelle. Both men had helped organized the Free French wartime intelligence—Soustelle was overall head of the BCRA of which Wybot ran the counterintelligence section. Like Soustelle, Wybot backed the maintenance of Algeria as a province of France, and was a close confidant of the French locals or *colons*. Just after the initiation of FLN terrorism against the *colons*, Wybot undertook highly classified covert operations against the FLN bases of support. Wybot's secret war was focused mainly against international arms dealers supplying the FLN with small arms, ammunition and explosives. He ruthlessly carried out his FLN campaign by using a combination of official and unofficial intelligence organizations. Wybot's DST worked very closely with the *Service de Documentation Extérieure de Contre-Espionnage* (SDECE).

Within the SDECE, a special unit had been created to conduct covert warfare, "Service 29," later called Action Service. The Action Service was, in essence, a "dirty tricks" department. Colonel Jacques Morlane was the head of the Action Service. In the beginning of 1947, Morlane arranged for soldiers of the 11th Shock parachute regiment, specialists in unconventional warfare, to be assigned directly to Action Service. The 11th Shock had originally been formed in September 1946 from a nucleus of former French SAS commandos and other special forces soldiers. Initially only a battalion size unit, it would later be expanded to a regiment.

Only the most qualified candidates were selected with commanders carefully reviewing the dossiers of every former French special forces soldier or covert operator who applied. Its ranks also contained a number of reserve officers, including Jacques Foccart of the *Service d'Ordre du RPF*. The first commander of the 11th Shock was Captain Edgar Mautaint. He assumed command of the unit at Mont-Louis, a border town in the Pyrenees Mountain region between France and Spain also the location of Otto Skorzeny's paramilitary training camps. During World War II, Mautaint had served with the Jedburgh, special commando teams composed from the British Special Operations Executive (SOE), the American Office of Strategic Services (OSS), and the French *Bureau Central de Renseignements et d'Action* (BCRA).

As the organization of the 11th Shock continued to develop, a new officer, Captain Paul Aussaresses, was given command of the unit in July 1947. Like Mautaint, Aussaresses had an extensive Jedburgh background working behind enemy lines in World War II. He commanded the 11th Shock from 1947–1948. He later wrote about the 11th Shock, stating the unit's mission was to "perform what was then called 'psychological warfare,'" and that his men trained for clandestine operations "that could range from building demolition to sabotage or elimination of enemies." Here, Aussaresses means assassination. The unit's second commander, Yves Godard, was a former French parachute commander who fought in World War II. Godard was in Austria at the end of the war when French intelligence was setting up covert intelligence networks using former SS men, including Skorzeny's SS commandos.

THE RED HAND

Although the dates are not precisely clear, shortly before the initial revolt in Algeria by FLN rebels in 1954, and perhaps as early as 1952, a mysterious organization appeared in North Africa, called *La Main Rouge,* or the Red Hand. Author Joachim Joesten, a professional editor and freelance writer from the period, followed the trail of the Red Hand in the late 1950s and into the early 1960s. His discoveries were assembled in a small history, *The Red Hand* first published in 1962.

Joesten squarely places the Red Hand as a creation, or perhaps invention, of Roger Wybot's DST. Evidence gathered by Joesten indicated that the Red Hand grew out of the legitimate self-defense organizations of the *colons* during the earliest days of the FLN terror campaign. These were the groups close to Wybot that included former French soldiers and intelligence personnel, who had banded together in small comando outfits and vigilance groups for the protection of *colon* communities and estates. The groups began to grow, and eventually developed into a country wide self-defense network bent on revenge and reprisal.

It was from ranks of the French population in Algeria or *colons,* who had established paramilitary networks, that Wybot would create the counter FLN terror group, Red Hand. In fact, Joesten noted Wybot's link stating the Red Hand was the "offspring of the Secret Service," emphasizing that the DST and the Red Hand are as "inseparable as Siamese twins." Joesten also points out, most astutely, that despite the close relationship of the Red Hand with various French Secret Services, that relationship did not necessarily imply that the French government had knowledge of, or approved, its actions.

For the Red Hand, Wybot would call upon counterterror experts, such as Otto Skorzeny, to enhance the networks capability and distance the DST from Red Hand operations. As Joesten discovered, the origins of the Red Hand are difficult to pin down but appears to have started in Tunisia, although it eventually spread throughout the region. Its members were mostly French settler-types, but included Italian and Corsican operatives. The Red Hand ensured plausible deniability for Wybot's his cloak-and-dagger operations. To the press, the Red Hand was a terrorist organization, plain and simple; illusive, deadly and criminal. But, in reality, the organization operated in the manner of the paramilitary groups that sprang up in Germany after the First World War of which Skorzeny participated. It was also very similar to the old *Cagoule*, the "hooded ones," discussed in detail throughout this book.

Former French intelligence officers that fought in Algeria tended to remain mute about activities linked to the Red Hand. There is, however, enough documented evidence to accurately place Otto Skorzeny as a major player, coordinating the more sensitive enterprises of the Red Hand network, using his independent operators, free lancers, or French secret service operatives.

It is known, for example, that 11th Shock members were detailed, through "Bureau 24" of the SDECE, to thwart international arms dealers supplying the FLN. These secret soldiers had access "to almost every weapon in the '007' inventory to" liquidate their targets. Historian Alistair Horne wrote of Bureau 24 operations in his comprehensive history of the conflict, *A Savage War of Peace: Algeria 1954–1962*, that a man, known to history only as "the Killer," was personally responsible for many of these assassinations. This man, Horne noted, once worked for the Gehlen organization in West Germany, and for the French SDECE. Although there could be many candidates for "the Killer," one logical source would be Skorzeny's stable of assassins.

As a consequence of his clandestine support to Algerian operations, Skorzeny's group worked directly with the handpicked men of the 11th Shock in the SDECE Action Service. Paul Aussaresses, the first commander of the 11th Shock, admitted later that he had received orders to "liquidate the FLN as quickly as possible." Adding to this sobering commentary about the unit, author David Talbot wrote, "the 11th Choc [Shock] had grown into a dangerously unhinged killing unit, targeting representatives of the Algerian independence movement and their European supporters, even on the streets of France."

There can be no doubt DST chief Roger Wybot was an aggressive intelligence director, who did not shy from using assassination as a means to achieve an end. Wybot's attitude on the subject was captured clearly in an exchange that occurred in 1977 between him and William Colby, a former director of the CIA.

An article written in an issue of *New Scientist* magazine, dated June 16, 1977, repeated a French radio broadcast of an enlightening conversation between Colby, who had headed the CIA 1973–1976 and retired DST chief Wybot. It read, "The talk got around to murder (in the national interest, of course). Colby insisted that apart, from the attempts on Castro and Lumumba, which came to nothing, the CIA had never killed anyone. The 20,000 dead in Operation Phoenix, against subversives in South Vietnam, should really be put down to military action." Concerning the assassination of Admiral Darlan, Wybot, commented, "If I had been there, I should have taken part without any remorse." Colby disagreed with the premise of assassination, saying it might have been effective in the days of monarchies, but "not in the modern world." To Colby, this would be "playing God." Wybot maintained his position on the matter, noting he could not see any difference, considering Eastern Europe. Also of note is the fact that Colby's illusion to the attempts on Castro and Lumumba are interesting since it was Skorzeny under the highly classified QJ/WIN program, who carried out these operations. Certainly, the unreported part of their conversation was a discussion of Skorzeny.

THE WAR ENTERS A NEW PHASE—THE BATTLE OF ALGIERS

In 1956–1957, the FLN initiated a new plan of attack, moving their operations into Algiers. It was hoped that the French Army would not be as effective in the narrow confines of the city. This resulted in the main urban battle of the war, known as the Battle of Algiers.

The French forces were successful in eliminating rebel sanctuaries and establishing control, mainly by the use of very effective, but inhuman, interrogation. The FLN also suffered reverses due to infighting among various internal factions, and conducted terror against other Muslims to maintain its political supremacy. The Battle for Algiers would eventually be won by the French Army. By September 1957, the FLN leadership was broken up.

Within months of the Battle of Algiers, the government of the Fourth Republic would collapse. The French Army had secured a military victory, but, in political terms, the war was already lost.

On May 13, 1958 a large strike and mob of angry *colons*, frustrated over the government's weak positions and feeling their cause would be sacrificed, stormed the offices of the governor general. Then General Massu, along with senior *colon* leaders and three army colonels, formed a Committee of Public Safety. The committee urged Paris to call on General de Gaulle to return to the service of the Republic, in order to safeguard French Algeria. Behind all of the political maneuvering and public demonstrations were the secret activities of the Army and intelligence services, in support of the putsch.

De Gaulle entered the office, with full emergency powers for six months, to rule by decree, and, by ascending to office by vote, de Gaulle was not beholden to the army, despite the fact the junta had brought events to this ending. A writing of a new constitution followed, which was approved in September, creating the Fifth Republic. The new constitution gave de Gaulle strong executive authorities, and a seven-year term as president.

In the beginning of de Gaulle's rule, he actually escalated the war from in an attempt to finally crush the remnant of the FLN still operating in the countryside. But he, also, simultaneously opened up direct negotiations with FLN leaders, a move that met with displeasure by the *colons*.

De Gaulle also began removing ranking and mid-level officers. The military purges combined with the new direction in dealing with the FLN infuriated the military that had supported de Gaulle's return to power. They felt utterly betrayed.

De Gaulle's return also marked the end of Roger Wybot's reign as DST chief. Wybot believed, as did his secret confidants in the military and intelligence services, that de Gaulle's liberation policies were a disaster. He was also infuriated at being treated by de Gaulle "like a common criminal."

Prior to Roger Wybot's dismissal Otto Skorzeny was an integral part of DST covert operations involving the Red Hand and its interdiction of arms and material flowing into Algeria for the FLN. These operations had centered on assassination and intimidation. But the question arises, since Wybot was providing operational cover to the Red Hand through the DST, who picked up control and support of the terror group after Wybot's dismissal?

The answer can be found in the list of CIA personnel assigned to France at the time of Wybot's departure. Beginning in 1959, the CIA Chief of Station (COS) in Paris was Al Ulmer. This is the same CIA officer who initiated and directed clandestine contact with Skorzeny in Madrid from 1950–1951. Ulmer was also the former station chief of Austria in 1948, and thus also aware of the original release plan for Skorzeny from Camp King. Importantly, like Roger Wybot, Ulmer was secretly in league with the ultras and the French secret units supporting covert operations. Given Al Ulmer's pro-*colon* sympathies, it seems likely the CIA picked up cover for Red Hand operations or at a minimum used Skorzeny as a surrogate contact with the terror group. It is also likely Roger Wybot maintained contact with Skorzeny and continued to support Red Hand operations from the shadows of his retirement.

REVOLT IN ALGERIA

In January 1960, General Jacques Massu, commander of the 10th Parachute Division in Algeria, declared "he would not in all circumstances obey" President de Gaulle. The comment appeared in Paris papers and Massu was promptly recalled by a "furious de Gaulle." The recall of Massu, who was extremely popular with the ultras, was used as a pretext by ultra leaders to stir up political action in the streets of Algiers. This move was secretly supported by CIA Paris station chief Al Ulmer and it was at this point that Skorzeny suddenly emerged as the intermediary between the ultras and the CIA.

In January 1960, at the request of ultra leaders, Skorzeny approached his CIA contacts in Madrid and made a pitch for support to plans they were developing in Algeria. The CIA station chief at the time was Archibald Roosevelt, Jr. who was likely working closely with Al Ulmer in Paris. Skorzeny's request was forwarded to Washington, where CIA counterintelligence chief, James Angleton prepared a report indicating that Skorzeny "willingly or unwillingly" was a channel for black propaganda (false information relied as truth) to weaken de Gaulle and to encourage American mistrust of French government.

Angleton, like Al Ulmer and Roosevelt, had sympathies for the pro-ultra faction and saw an opportunity to use Skorzeny's network to their advantage. The green light was given for Madrid and Paris to engage Skorzeny's network to assist the ultras. The ultras initiated the revolt on January 24, 1960. The senior ultra leader at the head of the strike was Joseph Ortiz, the owner of *Bar du Forum*, a popular restaurant in Algiers. Ortiz headed the ultra group *L'Action* and was in league with several other ultra counterterrorist groups, including one established by Rene Kovacs. Other ultra leaders, including Jean-Claude Perez and Jean-Jacques Susini, joined ranks with Ortiz and Kovacs in forming a consolidated organization, known as the *Front National Française* (FNF). Author Anthony Clayton noted, "The style of the FNF was neo-fascist, with a Celtic-cross armband." The chief organizer of the FNF was Perez, a doctor "with a record of counter-terrorism vigilante activity, including bombing." Another ultra leader, Jacques Susini, was a popular political leader and head of a student association active in Algerian politics. All of the FNF leadership had worked closely with covert elements of French intelligence and the French military.

Joseph Ortiz and Rene Kovacs were identified as being affiliated with Skorzeny's network. Confirmation of this collusion came just over a year later by American journalist, Waverley Root, a writer for the *Washington Post* in February 1961. Root worked in Paris for the *Post* and cited his information from four defendants who had participated in the January uprising under the ultra leaders. The article dated Sunday, February 26, 1961, was titled, "Headed by Skorzeny? Neo-Nazis Linked to Algeria French" and stated that the ultras were actually part of Skorzeny's "ring." The article also stated that General Raoul Salan "was also a member of the Skorzeny network."

AMERICAN COMMITTEE FOR FRANCE AND ALGERIA

Occurring simultaneously with Skorzeny's operational involvement with the ultras was another CIA initiative to support the ultras with propaganda. To avoid the implications of the CIAs direct involvement, a private committee, or "pressure group," was formed outside CIA channels that would be used as a propaganda organ to promote support the ultra cause from the American side. Designed to employ white propaganda or information with aims and intentions identified, the committee would solicit help for the ultras. This would include moral, financial, and logistical support. A stand out clue that Skorzeny's intelligence impacted CIA operations is the selection of attorney Clifford Forster, Skorzeny's American business partner as the lead for the pressure group.

In February 1960, Forster, along with James Burnham, a contract CIA officer, founded The American Committee for France and Algeria. Forster was chairman of the committee. It will be recalled, Forster had first appeared in this history when Otto and Ilse Skorzeny first arrived in France in 1949 to work with French intelligence chiefs, Roger Wybot and Pierre Bertaux. At that time, the ubiquitous Forster was associated with the American Friends of *Paix et Liberté*, a CIA front for stay-behind operations in Paris. Later, Forster would also be involved with "The Committee for Aid to Katanga Freedom Fighters" another CIA-associated pressure group for the Congo. This group included CIA station chief Archibald Roosevelt, Jr. and and Colonel Jack Critchton of Dallas, among others linked to this story.

The existence of three separate CIA-associated "committees," all associated directly with Clifford Forster, a principle business associate and intimate friend of Otto Skorzeny, is inescapably compelling. *Paix et Liberté*, formed in 1949, The American Committee for France and Algeria, formed in 1960, and The Committee for Aid to Katanga Freedom Fighters, formed in 1961, all represent the exact geographical areas, at precisely the right time, for Skorzeny's covert operations in these areas.

The American Committee for France and Algeria's first publication, called "Integration (Bulletin of the American Committee for France and Algeria)," did not appear until September 1960. The organization's mission statement read, "The American Committee for France and Algeria has been organized to explain to the American people the reasons why we, a group of American citizens, believe that, in the interest of humanity and Western civilization, American policy is, as that of our allies will, be best served by an Algeria integrated with France."

The second issue clearly indicated the direction of support taken by Forster, "We, of the American Committee, consider Algeria the most important strategic area being contested in the struggle between East and West. It would be wrong for us to think of the Algerian rebellion in the simple terms of a colony fighting for its freedom. This is exactly what the Soviet bloc wants us to think." This is, exactly, the reasoning behind those U.S. intelligence officials supporting the French military and the ultras.

Oddly, the last issue of US/France Report appears to be Number 11, December 1963. That issue carried the headline title, "The Assassination." The article, perhaps evidence of black propaganda, lays blame for the Kennedy assassination on "the Conspiracy" which it explains is a vast communist network within the United States, aligned with the left. According to the article, the reason the assassination took place, was to lay blame on the far right, and this would have happened if not for the capture of Lee Harvey Oswald before his intended escape. It should be pointed out here that CIA counterintelligence chief James Angleton was the CIA liaison to the Warren Commission.

At every turn, we find Otto Skorzeny's role as a covert asset in a masked link to the CIA. Clifford Forster was in the shadows, confirming his role as a clandestine conduit between the CIA and Skorzeny. Again, we harken back to the NSC Directive 10/2 to confirm Skorzeny's covert role. The author reminds the reader here of the objective: Clandestine Assistance or as originally articulated by George Kennan "assistance to anti-Communist factions in countries outside Soviet orbit where local communist might gain power through democratic process"—here again the evidence is overwhelming:

- American Committee for *Paix et Liberté* (CIA front France)
- Katanga Freedom Fighters (CIA Congo)
- Committee for France and Algeria (CIA–OAS)

SKORZENY AND THE RISE OF THE SECRET ARMY ORGANIZATION (OAS)

By the end of 1960, the last holdouts of the French military command would turn to more desperate measures in a last attempt to keep Algeria French and to keep their promise to never be defeated again. In addition to CIA propaganda efforts to support the ultras, the CIA appears to have provided much more lethal forms of support. This would also involve Otto Skorzeny. It will be remembered that with the dismissal of French DST chief Roger Wybot, the secret counterterror group, Red Hand, had lost its official cover, at least from the French side. It is the contention of the author that the CIA, or at a minimum the pro-ultra factions within it, continued utilizing the Red Hand.

Historians credit the Red Hand with the October 16, 1960, assassination attempt on Dr. Wilhelm Beisner, a former SS officer who became involved in supplying arms to the FLN. One of the companies that Dr. Beisner was associated with was a Spanish arms company, Alpha, which had been infiltrated by Bureau 24, of French Intelligence service, SDECE. However, by late 1960, de Gaulle had conducted a number of purges within the army and intelligence services, so it is not determinable who controlled the assassination operation. In the attack, Red Hand operatives placed "a shrapnel-laden bomb" in Beisner's car, that "blew him through the roof" of the vehicle. His wife was also badly injured.

The attack shows that ultra operatives and the Red Hand were still interdicting FLN arms. A key component to this story, never before revealed, is the fact that Otto Skorzeny also worked for the arms company, Alpha, and was associated with Beisner in other business ventures. The attack has all the hallmarks of a Skorzeny design working through Red Hand networks.

Only two months later Skorzeny was again at the center of developing events concerning the ultras. In December 1960, General Raoul Salan, the former commander-in-chief of French forces in Algeria, clandestinely moved out of France and took refuge in Spain. His intention was to begin a process of consolidating the various ultra factions and organize a formal, secret military structure. He set up his headquarters at the Hotel Princesa in Madrid. According to historian Alistair Horne, the hotel was "a veritable colony for exiled right-wingers; Belgian Rexists, Argentinian Peronists, French 'Petainists,'" and former Nazi collaborators. Salan had come to Spain to *organize the forces* necessary to stop the fall of Algeria, *by whatever means he could.* Horne notes, "one of Salan's first contacts had been Otto Skorzeny."

Historical accounts of this meeting report that Skorzeny "did not hold out very high hopes for Salan's enterprise," but in reality, Salan's meeting with Skorzeny marked the beginning of the formation of the Secret Army Organization, or OAS.

Skorzeny also met with other OAS leaders, such as Jacques Susini. After the meetings by OAS leadership with Skorzeny the general concept for a secret army, one based on military lines was well underway. General Salan's clandestine move out of France appears to mark the formal beginning of this transformation.

Skorzeny's connections within the OAS are astounding. For example, General Salan's civilian aide, Jacques Achard, was a very close friend to Skorzeny's business partner since 1953, Clifford Forster. Achard would later be described as the most dangerous OAS leader. In the early days of the OAS formation, Achard was General Salan's "eyes and ears," making numerous trips into Algeria to coordinate with ultra networks in the country. As a resident of Algiers, Achard "had no trouble entering and leaving Spain." The close personal relationship between Forster and Achard places Skorzeny's network into the very heart of the OAS.

Greatly assisting General Salan with efforts to establish the OAS was Spanish General Serranno Suñer. Suñer was Francisco Franco's brother-in-law and former Foreign Minister. He was highly sympathetic to the OAS cause and very close to Otto Skorzeny. It was Suñer who first gave Skorzeny entry into Spain, in 1950, at the behest of French intelligence and it was Suñer who authorized Skorzeny's covert MAAG training sites across the country.

Ultimately, Spain would prove to be a major bastion for the OAS training and a base for launching its operations. General Salan and the other leaders of the OAS would depend on Skorzeny to train, organize, and equip, OAS forces. The men attending these camps were former officers and NCO's who had served in Vietnam and Algeria. Many of these had interacted with Skorzeny directly on covert operations connected to the Red Hand.

In addition to military training and physical conditioning, the camps also had political indoctrination. Historian Kurt Tauber, in *Beyond the Eagle and Swastika: German Nationalism Since 1945, Vol II,* noted, "[the] OAS contained a large contingent of French collaborators and former SS volunteers. This state of affairs led political wits to refer to the OAS as the 'OA SS'!"

As it happened, the core of the OAS leadership also contained members from the old guard of a prewar anti-Communist movement; specifically, the legacy terror group known as the *Cagoule* ("Hooded Ones"). The *Cagoule* was the brotherhood that bonded Skorzeny to the French right.

THE FRENCH GENERALS' PUTSCH

By 1961, the de Gaulle government determined that Algeria could not be maintained as part of France without continued rebellion. De Gaulle's referendum on an Algerian pathway to Independence proved to be the last straw for the ultras and French military commanders, who had labored for so many years for victory over the FLN.

The die was cast. Now, the OAS commanders in Algeria decided to take action. Working secretly with active officers of the French military, particularly the sympathetic corps of supporters within the ranks of the French Foreign Legion paratrooper units, a putsch was organized to seize control of the country. The effort was backed by U.S. military officers and intelligence officials linked to Skorzeny's clandestine network.

Suddenly, in a very hastily drawn plan, four French generals linked to the OAS, moved to take action in Algeria in a last-ditch effort to stop de Gaulle's policies. This was the Generals' putsch of April 1961, which included Generals Salan; Jouhaud; Zeller; and Challe. General Challe and Zeller had secretly entered the country, just before the event. General Salan arrived later from his base in Spain.

All of these men had all held high military posts in the Algerian War and were highly respected by the French population.

Initial operations began on the afternoon of April 21, 1961. The next morning, the radios announced that the army had seized control of Algeria. The generals were joined by the ultras and secret cells of the OAS. They were also heavily supported by units of the French Foreign Legion, primarily, the 1st REP. Other military units also joined the coups, including elements within the 11th Shock and French Air Commandos. The plan called for seizing the key cities of Algeria, and it necessary take key locations in Paris, but these were never acted on.

From the start the putsch did not garner the support from the population as needed and some key units remained loyal to the government. For these reasons, the putsch began to stall. De Gaulle moved quickly to quell the revolt. Dressed in his old uniform from the war he went on national television, delivering an impassioned speech. On April 26, the putsch collapsed.

De Gaulle then ordered the disbandment of units involved in the coup. On April 30, 1961, with heads held high, the legionaries, true to their beliefs, and defiantly singing their unit song—"*je ne Regrette Rien*," ("I regret nothing,") left garrison for the last time. On May 31, 1961, the Air Commando met the same fate, as did the illustrious 10th and 25th Parachute Divisions.

After the coups, stories of American involvement began to swirl. The *New York Times* reported that, on the day of the generals' putsch, rumors were afoot, generated by minor American officials in France, "that the general's plot was backed by strongly anti-Communist elements within the United States Government and military services."

Author William Blum, in *Killing Hope: U.S. Military and C.I.A. Interventions Since World War II*, also points out that the Americans were angry over de Gaulle's polices, "paralyzing NATO and rendering the defense of Europe impossible." Blum added, CIA men, "assured the generals that if they and their followers succeeded, Washington would recognize the new Algerian Government within 48 hours.

On April 28, the French paper, *Le Monde*, printed, "the behavior of the United States during the recent crisis was not particularly skillful. It seems established that American agents, more or less, encouraged [General] Challe." Curiously, the paper also reported that President Kennedy "did not know of this contact." If true, the CIA planners likely kept the use of Skorzeny hidden from the president who had already canceled Operation Tropical.

Due to press stories over potential U.S. involvement in the generals' putsch, the Kennedy administration went into damage control. Administration officials denied that the United States was involved in the plot or had contact with the French generals. But, the U.S. Secretary of State, Dean Rusk, contradicted this claim, telling the *New York Times* in an interview, "that an emissary of the rebellious French generals had visited the U.S. Consulate in Algiers to request aid, but had been summarily rebuffed." In fact, just prior to the coup, and prior to his resigning from the French military, General Maurice Challe as NATO Commander-in-Chief, Allied Forces, Central Europe, had daily interaction with senior U.S. Military commanders.

Concerning American military collusion with the French generals, an investigative reporter named Claude Krief reported in *L'Express,* a widely-read French liberal weekly," that "Both in Paris and Washington, the facts are known. In private, the highest French personalities make no secret of it. What they say is this: "The CIA played a direct part in the Algier's coup, and certainly weighed heavily on the decision taken by ex-general Challe to start his putsch." Krief went on to note that General Challe "had several meetings with CIA officers," who told him that "to get rid of de Gaulle would render the Free World a great service."

In a more significant claim, at least for the history here, Krief also reported on an important clandestine meeting supposedly took place in Madrid, on April 12, 1961, between "various foreign agents, including members of the CIA, and the Algiers conspirators, who disclosed their plans to the CIA men." Unknown to Krief, his comments contain a veiled reference to Otto Skorzeny's involvement in the ultras' attempt to seize Algeria.

CHAPTER SEVENTEEN

THE OAS FIGHTS ON

"Beware of the anger of the Legions!"

ROMAN CENTURION MARCUS FLAVINIUS,
AUGUSTUS' SECOND LEGION

U pon the collapse of the French generals' putsch in 1961, the OAS swore to fight on. At this point in time, the main goal of the organization was to prevent Algerian independence by whatever means necessary, including the targeting of President Charles de Gaulle. This decision would usher in an extremely violent era of history. As part of their strategy, the OAS turned to a terror campaign directed at the Muslim populations in order to provoke a response in kind, hoping to force the French army to reestablish authority.

For the OAS, the first order of business after the putsch was reorganization. Officers and enlisted men from the now-disbanded ranks of French Army units joined the OAS ranks. A new command and control structure was established, as well as zones of responsibility. Colonel Yves Godard, the former commander of the 11th Shock Regiment, now underground from the military for his participation in the putsch, took an active lead in the formation of this new structure. Using an FLN network model, which Godard had studied carefully, he created OAS terror cells across Algeria. Other senior colonels joined the organization, men with extensive intelligence, psychological warfare, and counterinsurgency warfare experience, including Antoine Argoud and Jean Gardes.

The senior OAS commander was General Raoul Salan. Acting as his deputy commander was General Edmond Jouhaud. The chief-of-staff was General Paul Gardy, the former inspector-general of the Foreign Legion. Colonel Godard was the operations officer. Three main divisions were created: a staff section, under Colonel Gardes; psychological warfare and propaganda, under Jacques Susini; and intelligence and operations, under Dr. Jean-Claude Perez.

OAS—DELTA COMMANDO

The intelligence and operations section was subdivided into action squads, known as commandos, each under a captain. The commandos carried out bombings and assassinations. One of the most notorious action groups of the OAS was the Delta commando, under Lieutenant Roger Degueldre, a former Foreign Legionnaire officer, who had deserted from the French Army. Degueldre was a tough, thirty-six-year-old combat veteran of both the Vietnam and Algerian Wars. Born in France, but in a town on the border with Belgium, he was rumored to have served in the *Waffen* SS, but, in reality, had seen action as a seventeen-year-old member of an anti-Communist French maquis. After the war, Degueldre joined the French Foreign Legion. He was very active in supporting the ultra-paramilitaries while serving in Algeria, and was a key participant in a failed coup attempt on de Gaulle, in 1961. After the putsch, Degueldre became an assistant to Dr. Perez, then later took command of the Delta commandos. Many of the men in Delta commando were former soldiers from the disbanded Foreign Legion 1st REP. The Delta commando would eventually number around 300. By the latter part of 1961, over 3,000 attacks per month were attributed to the Deltas. Degueldre was eventually captured, in April 1962, and subsequently executed by firing squad in July.

OAS—ALPHA COMMANDO

The Alpha commando was led by Jacques Achard, the close friend Clifford Forster, Otto Skorzeny's business partner. Forster, as mentioned in the previous chapter, was chairman of the CIA-backed American Committee for France and Algeria. The committee was pro-OAS with several issues lending its pages as a mouthpiece for the outlawed organization.

Jacques Achard directed OAS activity in the Orléans-Marine district of Algiers. Noted as an extremely dangerous man, Achard was by characterized by police as, "the most dangerous man of all and perfectly capable of carrying out an attempt on de Gaulle's life single-handed . . ."

Another OAS officer with Skorzeny links was Captain Pierre Sergent, a former Foreign Legionnaire. Sergent had commanded a company from the French Foreign Legion 1st REP, a unit disbanded by de Gaulle. Sergent was a seasoned soldier having fought in the Resistance during World War II. After the war, he fought in Indo-china, where he was both wounded and decorated for bravery. Later, he was to serve in Algeria where he was deeply devoted to the cause of keeping Algeria French. In April 1961, he became heavily involved in the plotting for the generals' putsch. Hospitalized in France, just prior to the putsch, he secretly returned to Algeria and led the Foreign Legion paratroopers in support of the rebellious generals. Once the putsch had failed, and his unit disbanded, Sergent went underground, joining the OAS. Later he would rise to be the leader of the OAS in France.

Captains Sergent and Achard, along with other OAS commando commanders, used safe houses in Algiers to discuss operations. One of the most secret was a house owned by the Contessa Dagmar Álvarez de Toledo Lausanne. The confirmation of her residence as an OAS base comes from a letter written by the countess to Otto Skorzeny in 1964. In the letter, she also recounted her days harboring OAS operatives in Algeria. She referred to her dwelling as "the OASis for [Captain] Sergent." She noted in the letter the great respect Captain Sergent and the others had for Skorzeny, stating, "EVERYONE spoke of you with admiration."

Interestingly, she had also harbored SS soldiers at the end of World War II. Describing the event to Skorzeny, she proudly wrote that the SS *Leibstandarte* "quartered in my castle." Expressing her own personal admiration for Skorzeny, she wrote, "you and your comrades are the LAST Knights, in the last of the crusades."

SKORZENY AND THE OAS MURDER SQUADS

Reorganized after the failed Generals' putsch the OAS leadership continued to look for outside assistance including approaches to Portugal, Spain, Israel and South Africa, all countries, it should be noted, dealing directly with Skorzeny in covert matters. But, the primary patron would continue to be the American CIA who did not give up on the OAS as a vehicle to undermine de Gaulle.

Historian Alexander Harrison evidenced contact between General Salan and a "Colonel Brown" of the CIA, in France. The author was unable to identify "Colonel Brown," but Harrison claims Brown offered the OAS commander "enough weapons to equip an army." Colonel Brown also set down the conditions for U.S. support, telling the rogue French general that, if the OAS were successful in gaining control of Algeria, the U.S. would be allowed to establish military bases in the region.

General Salan would later reflect on his belief he was dealing directly with the CIA, stating, "I was sure they were serious, because they knew all the right people, and their credentials were perfect." General Salan's confidence in his CIA contacts is also reflected in the fact that, in December 1961, he wrote a confidential letter to President Kennedy explaining the OAS position and appealing to support their cause. Salan alluded in the letter to Colonel Brown's offer of assistance on the condition of allowing U.S. bases in Algeria, telling the president, France would "play its part in defense necessitating the integration of all Atlantic forces." Then he added, "Within this defensive system, American bases on French soil, particularly in Algeria, will clearly constitute the weapon of deterrence which Europe and Africa so sorely need." Salan's letter was sent to Washington "by a special USAF aircraft," dispatched, under orders, from Al Ulmer, CIA chief-of-station in Paris.

After consultation with his staff, President Kennedy decided not authorize assistance to General Salan and forbid CIA operations supporting the OAS. In the light of subsequent events, it appears support did continue, however, albeit through surrogates such as Skorzeny. Additionally, given what we do know about Skorzeny's close contact with U.S. MAAG groups, and his extensive paramilitary training camps, CIA support could have easily been facilitated without formal authority. Under this cover, Skorzeny could direct unconventional warfare support to the OAS for the CIA.

Oddly, it is Skorzeny's Congo connections that reveal further evidence of his direct involvement in OAS affairs. Skorzeny's episode in the Congo as QJ/WIN was covered earlier. In a bizarre twist, the Congo crisis and the Algerian War were very closely linked in the history of Otto Skorzeny. The relation derives from French soldiers who fought first in Algeria then later as mercenaries in the Congo, merging the two histories. Skorzeny, in 1961, had offered the CIA-backed break-away country of Katanga training for the Katanga army at his commando schools in Spain. This offer was accepted and in mid-March 1961, thirty Katanga soldiers arrived in Spain for the special training. Journalist Waverley Root, who had exposed Skorzeny's links to ultra leaders Joseph Ortiz and Rene Kovacs, also described the complex intrigues between the French ultras of Algeria, the sympathetic Belgian Rightists, and former French soldiers fighting in the Belgian Congo for the newly-declared country, Katanga. Again, Root's information zeroed in on Skorzeny's network.

The Algerian–Katanga connection was also revealed in a March 21, 1962, article posted in the *Dallas Morning News*. This article detailed the violence of the OAS and, citing *New York Times* writer C. L. Sulzberger, relayed, "The OAS relies on two Katanga mercenary veterans to organize its murder squads." The article also mentioned the French government's response and reported the existence of a special "security detachment" called "Yatagan Commando," composed of French veterans of the Indochina War, and Vietnamese, tasked to hunt down the OAS organization. As multiple documents corrolate, precisely, there can be little doubt that Sulzberger's reference to an OAS "murder squad," utilizing "two Katanga mercenary veterans," is none other than Skorzeny's commando group.

THE MYSTERIOUS "JONSON COMMANDO"

There are also indications that Skorzeny's OAS commando involvement was an extension of, or in some way connected to, CIA covert operations in Algeria. This CIA link comes from the mention of an enigmatic OAS group written about in the book, *Target de Gaulle,* by authors Pierre Démaret and Christian Plume. In their book, they noted the existence of an organization called, "the Jonson commando." They stated that the group had actually appeared on the scene prior to the April 1961 Generals' putsch. The "Jonson commando" also has tangible, yet mysterious, links to Otto Skorzeny.

According to Démaret and Plume, the "Jonson commando" consisted "of Americans and Canadians in direct touch with the CIA," and was attempting "to contact student circles." Here, we must take note, the similarity in name between the "Jonson commando" and the name of the previously mentioned U.S. foreign service officer serving in Algeria at the time, Richard G. Johnson. Could the "Jonson commando" be connected to the U.S. foreign service officer, Johnson?

The evidence for an affirmative answer is compelling. Johnson claimed that, while at his post in Algiers, he was an impartial observer in this affair. This may be true, but Johnson had an interesting link to Otto Skorzeny. Perhaps a matter of coincidence, but likely not, one of Johnson's closest friends was a CIA officer named Steve Tanner who apparently developed a friendship with Skorzeny after the Second World War when Tanner worked for the CIA. Johnson and Tanner had served in the same military intelligence unit during the war. In the latter days of the conflict, they were serving in Italy where they were assigned to interrogate captured members of Skorzeny's *Jagdverband* operating in that country. It was at this time that Tanner coordinated some of the first clandestine use of the SS by the U.S. Army CIC.

Future research is needed to determine if Tanner was involved with CIA covert operations in Algeria, but Tanner did maintain a postwar relationship with Skorzeny, whom he referred to in postwar correspondence as "my old friend Tanner." Since Skorzeny was also involved with early CIA covert operations directed by Tanner in Germany, an argument could be made that Tanner continued to be a key CIA conduit to Skorzeny throughout his clandestine service to the Agency, such as the case with Arnold Silver, Miles Copeland and Al Ulmer.

Finally, Johnson met with the generals during the putsch, as revealed by a later interview. He also revealed in the same interview, when speaking about the

OAS, that there existed "a kind of funny supporting group of the OAS," that he said contained "students." Johnson's comment that the OAS had a group that supported students seems to align with the description given by Démaret and Plume of the "Jonson Commando" seeking "student circles." In fact, OAS commander Jacques Susini, who later admitted to meeting with Skorzeny in Madrid, was the leader of the General Association of Students, a cover organization for ultra-paramilitaries.

It would seem by all of the above evidence that the CIA had a conduit to the OAS through Skorzeny, who was advising or even directing various OAS commandos. Author Démaret and Plume wrote that the internal OAS communications indicated that the "Jonson Commando" was offering weapons and, potentially, financial assistance in the recruitment of its members. Clearly, the CIA would be in a position to do precisely these things, particularly through Skorzeny, acting as a cut-out between the two organizations. In the end, it is an internal OAS communication, warning its own members about the "Jonson commando," that may be the most telling—it reads, "This commando is extremely dangerous." Coming from the OAS, an organization known for its extreme violence, this comment speaks volumes about the Skorzeny network.

On March 18, 1962, the French government signed the Évian Accords, initiating a formal cease-fire with FLN. As part of the agreement, France was to keep control of industrial interests in the country, and control of the Sahara oil reserves. *Pieds-noirs* (French Algerians) and Jews were given religious freedom and property rights. A plan for the withdrawal of French forces was also included over a two-year period, with the exception of a garrison at Mers El Kébir. Naturally, the OAS opposed the Évian Accords. They had lost their battle to keep Algeria French, and they were outlawed. After the Évian Accords, the OAS fought on only for revenge—for honor alone. The elimination of de Gaulle would become their primary goal.

Between 1961 and 1962, the OAS would conduct thousands of attacks. They targeted FLN networks, general Muslim populations, French officials, officers loyal to de Gaulle, and disloyal *pieds-noir*. The attacks were carried out in Algeria and in metropolitan France. But, despite the OAS attacks, de Gaulle pushed forward with Algerian independence. He also created new intelligence organizations, to hunt down the OAS.

BACKGROUND OF AN ASSASSIN—CAPTAIN JEAN RENÉ SOUÈTRE

Now that the reader has the history of Otto Skorzeny's involvement in the French Algerian conflict and key individuals associated with it, we turn our attention to Captain Jean René Souètre, an important OAS officer who would join the ranks of Otto Skorzeny's private paramilitary.

Jean René Marie Souètre was born October 15, 1930 at La Breda, in the Girande Department of France. As an OAS operative, Souetre had as many as eleven aliases, including Michel Mertz, Michel Roux, Eugene Constant, Grammont, and Mangin. Physically, Souètre was nearly six feet tall, with a thin, but muscular, build. In addition to his native French, he spoke almost perfect English, Spanish, and German. He married three times. His first wife divorced him shortly after his entry into OAS activity.

Souètre's family had a military tradition, so, in 1950, he enlisted in the French Air Force. By 1954, he had received a commission as a junior officer, and succeeded in becoming an airborne soldier. He also volunteered for a new commando unit that was being formed by the air force, called the *Commandos Parachutistes de l'Air*.

This command put him under Colonel François Coulet, a remarkable officer, who had been given permission to create the air commandos for fighting in Algeria. Colonel Coulet had seen combat in the Second World War as a parachute captain and, after the war, served as a French diplomat, but remained in the reserves. Later, he reentered the service, to establish the air commandos.

The air commandos were a very small unit, with fewer than 200 men. As such, the unit was broken down into small detachments that were attached to Foreign Legion Parachute regiments and other airborne units. Souetre's air commando detachment, designated CPA 10, was attached to the Foreign Legion 1st REP. Souetre excelled in the commandos, serving in Algeria from 1955–1959, and was involved in intense combat operations. The air commando unit would later be disbanded by de Gaulle for its leading role in the April 1961 Generals' putsch.

Like many of the paratroopers and commandos in Algeria, Souetre would become a rabid supporter of the ultras and for keeping Algeria French.

In April of 1960, Souetre was assigned to command the French air commando training battalion, significant for the unit's connections to Otto Skorzeny's training school. The date of Souetre's assignment to the training battalion is the same period that American rangers from the 505th Airborne Infantry, out of Germany, under Lieutenant Anthony Herbert, arrived at Pau to conduct training with the French commandos. A full account of Lieutenant Herbert's rangers' time at Pau was described in Chapter Fourteen.

As the French commander of the training area, Captain Souetre would have worked with Lieutenant Herbert and the American rangers, who were tasked with learning unconventional warfare tactics. It will be recalled that while conversing with the French paratroopers, Lieutenant Herbert had learned about Otto Skorzeny's school for commandos being used by the French. From this contact, Herbert's men would eventually find themselves at these very camps in the Pyrenean Mountains of Spain, just across the border from France. The arrangements that were made for Lieutenant Herbert to meet with Skorzeny confirm Captain Souetre's commandos were fully aware of Otto Skorzeny's training sites.

By late 1960, Captain Souetre was in trouble with French authorities, who had taken notice of his intense political views toward Algeria. Upon receiving orders for a garrison assignment in France, he failed to report for duty. Instead he deserted, taking with him a group of his loyal soldiers.

Souetre next surfaces in Algiers, where he organized a maquis in a rural area near Mostaganem, a port city in northwest Algeria. The formation of his group was announced in leaflets throughout the city. A second leaflet targeted the French military, as an enticement to support the OAS cause. On February 22, 1961, Souetre and another Maquis leader, three sergeants, and five civilians, were arrested on the premises of a Muslim religious brotherhood sanctuary.

After his arrest, Souetre was transferred, first to France, then back to Algeria, to a prison at de Maison Career. While awaiting trial, the group was transferred yet again, for security reasons; this was before the April putsch. On July 21, 1961, it was decided to place Souetre before a special military tribunal, formed

after the Generals' putsch. Then, on December 17, 1961, the members of Souetre's "First Algerian Maquis," as his organization was called, were put on trial.

Four days later, Souetre was sentenced to a three-year sentence, then the sentence was suspended, but, instead of release, they were transferred to Saint-
Maurice-l'Ardoise, in Algeria. The conditions under which Souetre was placed
were a type of administrative detention, with some generous liberties in the
camp; so much so, that in January 1962, he was allowed to marry Josette
Marcaihou, of Aymeric. The camp commander, General Claude Clement,
assisted in the ceremony. Within days, however, Souetre and seventeen others
made an escape from the camp. Ten of the party were recaptured, but Souetre
managed to escape.

In March, Souetre was in Spain, and then traveled to Portugal. There, he was
joined by his new bride, who had been furnished false identity papers. Soon, perhaps because of his OAS activity, his wife left him, and returned to France, where
she started divorce proceedings. However, this did not go well, due to her false
documents. She was arrested, paid a fine, and then disappeared from history.

Souetre, in the meantime, made his way back to Algeria where he worked
with Jacques Achard and Pierre Sergent. Achard, of course the very close friend
of Skorzeny's business partner, Clifford Forster. This seals tight this OAS circle
around Skorzeny. The association with Pierre Sergent would also place Souetre
at the safe-house (OASis), run by the Contessa Dagmar Álvarez de Toledo
Lausanne, previously mentioned.

As the war between de Gaulle and the OAS ramped up, de Gaulle's political
agenda continued to move forward in Algeria. In May 1961, the French government had started negotiations with the FLN. These did not have immediate
success, so over the course of the next year a tremendous amount of violence
continued. Finally, in March 1962, a cease-fire was obtained, setting the stage
for the Évian negotiations, that would eventually lead to independence.

The OAS, in this final phase before Algerian independence, was in a desperate state; terror attacks escalated, and the organization took to robbing banks to
generate funds for operations. De Gaulle had ordered his intelligence organizations to hunt down the OAS. However, this proved difficult.

The traditional French intelligence services, such as the SDECE and the DST, were mainly targeting the Muslim FLN, and there existed a substantial body of OAS sympathizers in the ranks of these services. The man appointed by de Gaulle to take the lead in targeting the OAS, Jacques Foccart, went so far as to call the DST (French external intelligence service), "an OAS rabble." To solve this internal situation, Foccart reorganized the old de Gaulle intelligence service, and purged disloyal members. This organization, the *Service d'Action Civique,* or SAC, executed ruthless counterterror operations against the OAS. Recruited into the ranks of the SAC were the *barbouzes,* or "bearded ones," including criminal elements and "Vietnamese experts in torture." This description appears to match the French news reporting on the "Yatagan Commando," composed of French veterans and Vietnamese targeting the OAS. Yet, despite these counterterrorist operations by French intelligence, the OAS soldiered on.

Then, on April 20, 1962, the commander of the OAS, General Salan, was arrested in Algiers. This development, combined with increasing isolation of the organization, had dramatic effect. Still, in May, the OAS killed 230 Muslims in a single week in Algeria, and escalated attacks in France. The French government continued its pressure, as the OAS grasped to hold on to Algeria.

A new internal reorganization took place, under Georges Bidault and Jacques Soustelle, who together set up a National Resistance Council (NCR). Other OAS groups also began to break ranks, as the group began to splinter into separate factions. It was also in May 1962 that the organization began to take flight, out of Algeria, for other points in Europe.

By June, General Gardy, who had replaced Salan as OAS leader, departed Algeria, establishing a new headquarters in Spain. Spanish intelligence, sympathetic to the OAS, provided much assistance. Pursuit of the OAS organization continued by the French Secret Services, and the French government also began to lean on the Spanish government to arrest its support for the outlawed group.

In Spain, the OAS established several areas as centers for consolidating its forces. One of the more prominent was Palma de Mallorca. Historians have identified this area as a major safe haven and operational zone for the OAS during the year 1962. In fact, the OAS leadership were at this time investing in real estate in Palma de Mallorca area. This included Joseph Ortiz, Dr. Rene Kovac, Jacques Achard, and Jean René Souètre. Not coincidentally, Skorzeny was heavily involved in hotel construction in Palma de Mallorca in April 1962.

During this period, Souetre was said to have used the alias "Commander Constant," and, in addition to his business dealings in Palma de Mallorca, he also controlled a Madrid "extermination and fumigation company," with the on-the-nose name "Will Kill." The company "hired veteran survivors of Delta commando," and included a man named Lajos Marton, and two Hungarians, Laszlo Varga, and Gyula Sari, a former Foreign Legionnaire.

On July 3, 1962, Algeria finally gained its independence. President de Gaulle declared, "The Algerian War is finished. There remains the terrorism." Meanwhile, high-level planning continued, within the OAS, for de Gaulle's elimination, and alerted its networks in France to action. Here, Souetre reenters the picture. Working with secret OAS cells in Spain, Souetre, as part of a planning group, selected a suburb of Paris to ambush President de Gaulle's motorcade. This occurred on August 22, 1962.

The attack, the most infamous of all the OAS attempts on the French president's life, was a classic ambush by automatic gunfire. The dramatic event only lasted minutes, but in that short time the President's vehicle was raked by fire. The attempt nearly succeeded, and barely missed de Gaulle, by inches. Incredibly, no one was injured.

The assault team was led by an ex-French Air Force officer, Lt. Colonel Jean Bastien-Thiry. After the attack, Bastien-Thiry and several others in the party were arrested and later put on trial. From his court examination, Bastien-Thiry revealed some of the details involved in the action, which he claimed was meant to be a kidnapping. He stated that, within the OAS structure, above his level, was a "Study Group," that formulated a plan based on information supplied by OAS intelligence. Orders were then passed, via clandestine means, to Lt. Colonel Bastien-Thiry, instructing him to form "an assault detachment."

Although Bastien-Thiry did not name the members of the Study Group, the French police identified the following OAS personnel: Captains Pierre Sargent, Jean Curutchet, and Jean Rene Souetre. The police believed Souetre "played a leading part in planning the attack at Petit-Clamart." Evidence that this is true is revealed by the arrest afterward of Marton, Sari, and Varga—all of Souetre's "Will Kill" exterminators, out of Madrid. A few days after the attack, French newspapers quoted Souetre as saying de Gaulle needs to be "struck down like a mad dog."

After the assault, nearly all of the OAS Assault Detachment was arrested, later to receive various sentences. Bastien-Thiry was eventually captured. His trial ran from January to March 1963. Found guilty of attempted murder and crimes against the state, he was executed on March 11, 1963. Two others received similar sentences. The only man to escape capture was Georges Watin, also known as "the limp," who had been a member of the ultra-paramilitaries in Algeria. Perhaps most telling of all was the dismissal from France of CIA station chief Al Ulmer by French President Charles who suspected CIA complacency in his assassination attempts.

THE END OF THE OAS

Beginning in January 1963, the French Senate proposed the creation of a powerful new court to deal with internal enemies of the state. The bill was passed on January 5, empowering the court to try "traitors, rebels, mutineers, and terrorists," including many members of the OAS. Still, the violence continued. Papers reported a wave of "gangsterism spurred by ex-Secret Army terrorists," including armed robbery with machine guns. Interior Minister Roger Frey blamed the violence on "transplanted French Algerians," citing the fact that the OAS was running out of money. The fear was, with a need to replenish their war chest, the OAS would launch an offensive on French banks. On January 28, the French Interior Minister conferred with Spanish Foreign Minister, in what was described as a cordial meeting, on possible control of former members of the OAS living in Spain.

After the assassination attempt, Souetre's name appeared in various French press reports, identifying him as a major OAS leader. In January 1963, Paris papers reported he was in Spain. Then, on January 15, 1963, a US Spanish newspaper, *Iberica,* citing French newspapers, *Le Figaro* and *Combat,* reported on the arrest by French police of eleven members of the OAS, who had been training in Spain at a sabotage camp near Valladolid. This was, in fact, one of Skorzeny's sites. That area had been used by the French, dating to a period just after the Second World War, when former French members of the *Waffen* SS retreated to Spain. In Valladolid, a very mysterious group formed in 1947, calling itself "DOS 88." It was a "secret German organization," consisting of a group of former French collaborationist militia, Gestapo, SS, and Spanish collaborators. Most were former *Cagoule*, and in the group, was Henri Antoine-Marcel Deloncle, whose brother founded the *Cagoule* organization.

One of those arrested told French police, as reported by *Iberica*, that the training at Valladolid had been done under the supervision of ex-General Gardi and ex-Captain Souetre. It also stated, "They had been entrusted with a special mission, to assassinate French Depute M. Alexandre Sanguinette." The article went on to say that the group belonged to an OAS commando group, "Monjo," named after Rene-Jean Monjo. Monjo was a French reserve officer, who was killed by a Muslim terrorist on February 15, 1962, in Algeria. The Monjo group had been given a course in sabotage at a specialized training camp set up on the French border. This was a clear reference to Skorzeny's paramilitary camps. One of those arrested, Michel Martineau, stated that another commando team, from a region near Poitiers, had also been trained in Spain.

During this time, to provide a means of existence and cover for the OAS members, a construction company was established at Salou, on the outskirts of Tarragona. Interestingly, the formation of this OAS-front company coincides with a construction proposal submitted by Otto Skorzeny to the Spanish government, for a chain of hotels between Madrid and Tarragona. However, safe haven in Spain for the OAS was about to take a turn.

In February 1963, French intelligence revealed an active plot against the president, at the same time as the trial of Bastien-Thiery and twenty-one others arrested in the Petit-Clamart plot. The new operation was organized by Colonel Antoine Argoud and involved army officers and the wife of one of the officers who was arrested. In the attempt, de Gaulle was to be shot with a sniper rifle from a rooftop while he was visiting the war college. A key operative in this new attempt was Georges Watin, "the man with the limp," who had managed to escape during the August 1962 attempt. The French security services also revealed that this plot was planned in Spain, which created a diplomatic stir, and forced the Spanish authorities to crack down on the OAS operations in their country.

Soon thereafter, several senior OAS leaders were arrested, and Spanish officials arranged for the captives to be moved to the Canary Islands, in the Atlantic. Other OAS leaders fled to safe areas in Europe. One group went to Italy, including Jacques Soustelle. Tellingly, Otto Skorzeny would make several trips to the Canary Islands between February and April, ostensibly for business meetings but in reality, to coordinate with OAS leadership. With the Spanish OAS Redoubt collapsing, the OAS was at a critical point. The CIA station chief in Madrid at this time was James A. Noel, who had replaced Archibald Roosevelt, Jr.

In May 1963, a die-hard OAS group made a last-ditch effort to maintain CIA support. On orders from Major Pierre Sergent, who had assumed OAS leadership, Captain Souetre made an attempt to contact American representatives in Lisbon, Portugal. Information concerning the incident is actually found in a declassified CIA report from the period. That report indicates Souetre's request came to the CIA from a "competent American observer," who was notified by a "Western-European Journalist in close contact with Captain Souetre" that Souetre desired to meet with the Americans. Souetre never specifically stated he wanted to meet with the CIA; however, a meeting was arranged with an Agency representative. Since the requested meeting was in Portugal, it must be assumed Madrid would have been too risky, given the Spanish government's recent crackdown on the OAS.

At the meeting, Souetre was in company with another OAS officer named Captain Yves Guillou, operating under the alias Guérin-Sérac. Like Souetre, Captain Guillou was a decorated Algerian War veteran. He had also served in Indochina and the Korean War. During the Algerian War, Guillou deserted the 11th Shock Parachute Regiment, of which much has been written in this book. At that point, Captain Guillou assumed the alias Yves Guérin-Sérac. While in the OAS he served with Pierre Lagaillarde, one of the leading founders of the organization.

Souetre identified himself to the CIA as "coordinator of external affairs" for the OAS organization, serving under Major Pierre Sergent. He explained the overall need for U.S. assistance in getting other governments to stop suppressing OAS activities in their countries and inquired on the possibility of obtaining logistical and monetary aid for the organization. Souetre also said he intended to provide information about the activities of the OAS that would be of interest to the U.S.

The CIA representative, who was not identified, asked Souetre about his status in Portugal, to which he replied he traveled on various passports, including one from the U.S. He also claimed to be a naturalized citizen of Martinique and to have U.S. contacts who could arrange for documentation.

The declassified CIA document states that when the meeting concluded, the CIA representative told Captain Souetre and Captain Guérin-Sérac that the United States had no intentions of working with anyone or group against a duly-constituted government such as France.

The movements of Skorzeny during this period point to his being in attendance at the Lisbon meeting between Souetre and the CIA. In fact, Skorzeny made several trips to Portugal between March and July 1963 concerning his businesses. With the OAS cause now unsustainable, it appears Souetre left the meeting with a new option for employment, signing on with Skorzeny. Captain Jean Rene Souetre was now a soldier of fortune working for Otto Skorzeny in one of the most guarded secret organizations in the history of American intelligence.

CHAPTER EIGHTEEN

ILSE

"She was a little firecracker . . . very sharp on the business side."

LT. COLONEL "TAD" SKLADZIEN,

INTERVIEW WITH AUTHOR, AUGUST 2012

Throughout the 1950s, Skorzeny continued to expand his network of companies out of his office in Madrid. Skorzeny had a seemingly endless list of business ventures that he was directly or indirectly involved with. An incomplete list includes steel, scrap metal, cement, oil, electronics, arms and ammunition, aircraft and aircraft parts, financial lending, land ventures, real estate, construction, import/export, energy development, automotive companies, meat products, and even snake skins. It has been pointed out at several junctures in this book the critical importance of the steel industry to Skorzeny's clandestine network.

In the conduct of his company operations, Skorzeny's greatest asset was his wife Ilse, who, by all accounts, was herself a brilliant businesswoman. She was constantly engaged in developing contacts and attending meetings at locations outside of Spain and then reporting back to Otto. Ilse had a sister named Gertrude living in New York. Gertrude had met a Jewish American Army captain named Sydney P. Barnett at the end of World War II, and returned to the United States as Captain Barnett's wife in 1946. The author could not find out details on Sydney Barnett despite significant attempts to do so. We do know that after returning to the States, he left the service, settled in New York City and went into the fine fur business. His father, Barnard Barnett, had been a clothing merchant and tailor from England who immigrated to the United States in 1901. Captain Barnett war service also remains an unknown. Despite the lack of information on the family of Sydney Barnett, in an ironic twist of fate, the marriage between Ilse and Otto in 1954 effectively gave Skorzeny a Jewish brother-in-law. Beginning in the late 1950s Ilse would travel to the United States and was often with Gertrude and her husband Sydney in New York. She would continue to visit them when they later moved to Florida.

In March 1957, a significant expansion of Skorzeny's activity occurred when Ilse arrived in New York to establish a headquarters, of sorts, for their overt and covert operations. Her arrival was noted by Jane Roman, of James Angleton's CI staff at the CIA, in a secret interagency message to the State Department and the FBI. Roman, one of Angleton's executive secretaries, informed State that Ilse Skorzeny was "in the United States for the purpose of assisting her husband in promoting some business deals." The State Department responded that they were "fully aware of Mrs. Skorzeny's presence" in the U.S.

The business that Ilse Skorzeny then became associated with in New York was Previews, Inc., a luxury real estate company. Exactly who arranged her position with the company is not known. Previews was run by John C. Tysen, a powerful real estate tycoon born in Paris, France, of American parents. Tysen grew up in England and attended schools there, including Trinity College in Cambridge. In 1936, he came to New York and was hired as a salesman for Previews, in their NY office. By 1940 he was sales manager and at some later point became president. A 1960 article on the company said it was an international clearinghouse that handled everything from farms to feudal estates.

The Skorzeny papers reveal that Ilse Skorzeny's employment at Previews was clearly related to intelligence operations and suspiciously major criminal syndicates in the Bahamas. The man she worked directly under at Previews was a Reserve USAF colonel named Herschel V. Williams. Colonel Williams was from New Orleans, Louisiana, and graduated from Yale in 1931. Just prior to World War II, he was an advertising executive in New York. During the war, he served in the United States Army Air Forces in North Africa as an intelligence officer under Colonel Robert G. Storey, a military officer and Dallas native with many appearances in the pages of this book. Colonel Williams briefly left military service after the war but was recalled for special duty at the Pentagon in 1948 for unspecified reasons. By 1957, he was executive vice president for Previews, Inc.

Ilse Skorzeny's arrival in New York was the beginning of extensive travel by her—not only within the United States, but to Cuba, the Caribbean, and other countries around the world. Skorzeny was in constant contact with her by phone, telegram, and post. At least some of this correspondence was written in code, confirmed by the existence of a code sheet relating to arms sales in the Middle East and intelligence-related matters to be discussed in detail later. Unfortunately, there is only one cipher sheet in the papers, but it does confirm the couple were writing in code. The rest is a task for future sleuths to crack.

While Ilse was operating from New York, Otto traveled from Madrid to Ireland to develop that country as another base for their operations. In June 1957, Skorzeny attended a "high-class" party at Portmarnock Country Club in County Dublin. The purpose of the visit is not known, and he returned to Madrid shortly thereafter.

ENTER TEX MCCRARY

Another extremely important connection to Skorzeny was John Reagan "Tex" McCrary, a remarkable man with the highest connections in the United States government. He was also a power player in organized crime, with strong ties to Meyer Lansky. Incredibly, McCrary was also a senior-level government adviser at the presidential level, and a CIA conduit to foreign governments. Much of McCrary's intimate connections originated from the fame he obtained as a radio and TV personality and his highly classified work with the OSS during the Second World War.

Tex McCrary was born in Calvert, Texas, in 1910, but spent a considerable amount of time in New York City, where he had family. He attended Yale, graduating in 1932, and, in later years, was considered the wise sage of the Skull and

Bones fraternity. A number of important future CIA officers who passed through the halls of Yale were his closest friends, and he was also close to Ilse Previews, Inc. boss, Colonel Hershel Williams.

McCrary served in World War II as a public relations officer in the United States Army Air Forces. He would rise to the rank of lieutenant colonel and was part of a special group that saw considerable frontline action. An extremely brave man, McCrary flew bomber missions with the Eighth Air Force out of England. Later, he attended parachute jump training with the OSS and accompanied a Jedburgh team into occupied France. At the end of the war, he was one of the very first correspondents to enter Hiroshima after the city was leveled by the first atomic bomb.

In June 1945, McCrary married the famous movie actress and fashion model Eugenia Lincoln "Jinx" Falkenburg. Born to American parents in Barcelona, Spain, Jinx Falkenburg would rise to become one of the most popular and highest paid cover-girl models in America.

By the early 1950s, Tex McCrary was considered one of the most important political insiders within the Republican Party. Jinx McCrary was equally admired for her abilities as an interviewer and intellectual. Tex became an active campaigner for men he felt should be in power. He is considered the key figure behind Dwight D. Eisenhower's presidential run in 1952. McCrary's counsel was highly sought after in Washington circles. His clandestine connection to Otto Skorzeny, unknown until the writing of this book, is a major discovery.

An interesting fact about McCrary is that his number-two man was William Safire, the future White House speech writer for President Richard Nixon. Safire was with McCrary's firm from 1954–1961. It is not known if McCrary disclosed his close friendship with Otto and Ilse Skorzeny to Safire, but it is difficult to imagine he did not know. Both McCrary and Safire were close informal advisers to Richard Nixon and accompanied him to Russia from June to August of 1959 when he was Vice President.

By the late 1950s, McCrary already had extensive links to organized crime through his Hollywood connections, but in 1959 they expanded even further. At that time, he entered into a close partnership with a 300-pound Canadian financier named Lou Chesler, nicknamed "Moose." As the public relations adviser for Chesler's General Development Corporation, McCrary promoted a number of enterprises, including real estate, movie companies, casinos, and horse track racing. Chesler was also a point man for Meyer Lansky, a major organized crime figure.

By the early 1960s, Lou Chesler would also be in business with Wallace Groves and Sir Stafford Sands, two prominent figures in the Bahamas who ran the Lansky enterprise there. This occurred after the mob was pushed out of Cuba by Castro. Another Chesler partner was mob boss Dino Cellini, who ran a number of casinos for Lansky.

Through Tex McCrary, Otto and Ilse Skorzeny became connected to broad criminal enterprises and, in particular, the Bahamas Mafia intrigues of Sir Stafford Sands around 1962. Supporting Skorzeny's deep connections to organized crime are direct references in Skorzeny's papers to meetings during this period with Fulgencio Batista and references to mob bosses Jake Lansky (brother of Meyer) and Dino Cellini. The entire Tex McCrary Mafia connection involving Skorzeny is likely a CIA-directed intelligence operation involving criminal networks. Importantly, all of this occurred under the watchful eyes of James Angleton, who controlled the Caribbean desk and headed the Counterintelligence Staff at the CIA. While Ilse was in Cuba, Tex McCrary was wheeling and dealing with Mafia bosses like Dino Cellini and Meyer Lansky. This overlap ideally positioned Ilse as an intelligence operative working alongside Tex McCrary who was a secret back channel to the Mafia, effectively placing separation between the Agency and the underworld crime bosses.

CHAPTER NINETEEN

THE MYSTERIOUS QJ/WIN

*"Today the 'Skorzeny' theory of the conduct of war by kidnapping and even
assassination, and after all the murder of one man is more acceptable than
that of hundreds of millions as would be the case in all out nuclear war,
offers a viable and perhaps more humane alternative . . . "*

CHARLES WHITING, *SKORZENY: BALLANTINE
ILLUSTRATED HISTORY,* 1972

*"No, I do not. Knowing the system, and so forth, normally it would have
something to do with Spain. It does not ring any bells with me. That is all I
can give you, a sort of Pavlovian response. You flash QJ/WIN on the screen,
I am telling you now I do not know, but it probably has something to do
with Spain."*

THEODORE SHACKLEY, CIA OFFICER,
WASHINGTON, D.C., AUGUST 19, 1975

In 1958, William K. Harvey, the hard drinking, flamboyant Chief of the Berlin
Operations Base, got notification of a new assignment. He was to lead a new
arm within the CIA called Staff D. The special unit had responsibility for
handling highly classified intercept communications provided to the CIA by the
National Security Agency. The unit also had its own "in-house" intercept capa-
bility. But the unit had an even more sensitive mission assigned to him by the
Deputy Director of Plans, Richard Bissell, on direct orders from Director Allen
Dulles. This was to establish a high-level government assassination program

exceeding all previous security programs, such as those used for enemy agent liquidations. The intended purpose was to give the United States a deniable strategic capability that could be used against foreign leaders. Very importantly, Staff D had special liaison with James Angleton and a few select members of the Counterintelligence Staff (CIS) who also knew details of its operations.

It is very possible, that CIA operations associated with the code word QJ/WIN was initiated because of Harvey's preexisting covert relationship with Otto Skorzeny. The Skorzeny papers confirm Skorzeny had contact with men with extensive assassination experience from his old command, including Horst Issel, easily the leading assassin of the Third Reich.

The cryptonym QJ/WIN first appeared publicly in 1975, when it was revealed during a U.S. Senate Select Committee hearing investigating the CIA and its various assassination programs. QJ/WIN was said to be the Agency's "Executive Action" program, as it was euphemistically termed. As the committee pieced together various aspects of the program, there was great interest in the identity and history of the foreign agent said to have been selected by Harvey to be the foreign "deniable" head of the project. This resulted in the cryptonym QJ/WIN being associated with that individual.

Despite the challenges of analyzing the QJ/WIN program, the basic organizational structures of the program did surface, such as the operation being housed in Staff D. Also, uncovered were two historical milestones of the program, an associated project known as ZR/RIFLE and the dispatch of QJ/WIN's foreign lead to the Congo in 1960. Other basic facts confirm that the QJ/WIN program contained operators with past involvement with the OSS, U.S. Army Counterintelligence Corps, foreign intelligence services and various criminal outfits.

The Committee was never given the name of the QJ/WIN program lead, but they were given background data on him, or what appears to a fragmented arrangement of sometimes undeterminable documents. Reliance on testimony from CIA officers grilled in the investigation on QJ/WIN should be weighed with the knowledge they were under oaths of secrecy. Harvey himself suggested records concerning the QJ/WIN program be backdated, altered or deleted to mystify and mislead those attempting to decipher the program.

These difficulties aside, a few prominent points about QJ/WIN align with the personal history of Otto Skorzeny. It was revealed for example that QJ/WIN had a reputation "as a cold-blooded killer" while in the service of French intelligence. This matches precisely with Skorzeny's involvement with Roger Wybot's DST and other French elements described earlier. Harvey's handwritten notes on the QJ/WIN program also recommended using veterans from the French Resistance. Here again, a match to evidence in the Skorzeny papers showing a close relationship to harden covert operators like General Pierre de Bénouville and Captain Michael de Camaret amongst others.

QJ/WIN according to Harvey suggested the use of a Middle Eastern gambling syndicate that had a "pool of assassins." Within the Skorzeny papers is direct evidence for such an outfit, including numerous Middle Eastern contacts. Also present is repeated mention Otto Begus, a former SS officer who served under Skorzeny with extensive experience in organizing gambling and assassination operations in Greece and later Italy during World War II. In fact, a clandestine meeting took place May 16, 1958, between Skorzeny and CIA officer David E. Wright from the Madrid Embassy concerning the Agencies use of Begus. Skorzeny mentions the contact to Ilse stating the exchange with Wright "will result in work opportunity for Begus." Another quill in Skorzeny's covert directors' hat. Also, the Skorzeny's notification to Ilse of potential CIA work for Begus brings us to another QJ/WIN point of identification. QJ/WIN's wife was described as "extremely discreet" and totally aware of QJ/WIN's activities. This dramatically aligns with Ilse.

Another dramatic and perhaps decisive point of comparison between QJ/WIN and Skorzeny comes from information stating QJ/WIN was supposed to go on trial in Europe 1962 over a nickel smuggling charge dating back to 1954. In fact, Skorzeny was involved in nickel smuggling in 1954 as confirmed by a declassified CIA document from Skorzeny (201 File) personnel file. This document, dated 15 July 1954, states:

According to overt information H. S. LUCHT COMPANY maintains business connections with a firm which is "known to engage in illegal trade with the Soviet Zone."

The Madrid representative of LUCHT COMPANY is Otto Skorzeny, *who appears to be involved in the smuggling of nickel out of Spain for eventual Bloc destination.* The unidentified firm reported as engaging in illegal trade may be one of the links in this traffic. (emphasis added)

In a letter to Ilse dated April 14, 1962, Skorzeny says he is expecting the arrival that day of "Encio" who is arriving from Luxemburg and is curious as to "what news he brings" adding, "Nothing good." Encio was not further identified by Skorzeny in his papers but may have been Fulgencio Batista, the former dictator of Cuba who was living in Portugal at the time. Twelve days later, on April 26, 1962, a message from the CIA Station Chief in Luxemburg was sent to Director Allen Dulles concerning QJWIN and a nickel smuggling case from 1954. This QJ/WIN nickel case appears to be the same case as the one described for Skorzeny. Other details in the 1962 message to the director suggest QJ/WIN was being utilized in CIA Congo operations and as we shall see, Skorzeny was indeed dealing with Congolese officials during this timeframe.

The mysterious business H. S. Lucht mentioned above is far too complex to advance upon in this book, but the company was created in the 1950s involving Werner Naumann, the former Nazi State Secretary to Propaganda Minister Joseph Goebbels. Naumann survived the war but was arrested in February 1953 by the British secret service as a suspected leader of a neo-Nazi group. This was called the Naumann Affair and involved the company H. S. Lucht to which both Otto Skorzeny and Victor Oswald were also tied. The British penetration of the Lucht company was in reality a deep intelligence operation centered on the acquisition of nuclear material—the subject of a future study.

SKORZENY AS QJ/WIN

The foreign head of the QJ/WIN program was considered a highly trained and talented intelligence operative with impeccable skills in the arts of deception, disguise, evasion, and overall counterintelligence work—skill sets well known to Otto Skorzeny. The Committee report points out that QJ/WIN (the foreign head of the program) was hired not to be an assassin, but instead, to "spot," "identify," "recruit," and perhaps direct assassins. In other words, he was a sort of "commander of assassins," thus the term "assassin's assassin." As one particularly revealing 1962 CIA financial document distilled his role, in part: "QJ/WIN is under written contract as a principal agent with the primary task of spotting candidates." The placement of the assassination program within Staff D, the most secure office within the Agency was intentional. One retired CIA officer who wrote a biography on William Harvey stated, "Staff D was simply off-limits and rarely mentioned—not even in the sardonic jokes that rippled along the temps' fusty corridors."

Since Staff D was the recipient of classified intercepts obtained by the NSA, the reports provided an excellent control mechanism for Harvey as he could monitor foreign government entities, intelligence networks, and even the underworld. If any information came to light exposing QJ/WIN program operations, both Angleton, as CI chief, and Harvey, as head of Staff D, could then initiate countermeasures. This would include modifications of plans, changes in ongoing operations, or outright cancellation.

In the initial phases of the QJ/WIN assignment, Harvey reportedly started looking for a foreign asset to lead even before leaving his job at the Berlin Operations Base. This was sometime in early 1958. Staff D which would be activated the following year. An excellent organizer of operations, Harvey discreetly queried top CIA station chiefs for a suitable person who had the trustworthiness, the background, and, most importantly, the connections to be approached for the position. He then began to travel around Europe to gather data for the project. Harvey returned briefly to the United States in September 1959 only to turn around and take an "extended tour of Europe and the Middle East" with his wife, who also worked for the CIA. No one seems to know the details on this mysterious trip and some even denied it happened such as veteran CIA officer Jim Critchfield who returned from Germany at the same time as Harvey. Critchfield stated that he had "no recollections of Harvey making a trip to any part of the Middle East at the time." But according to an officer that worked with Harvey, the trip did occur.

When Harvey returned he was awarded the CIA Distinguished Intelligence Medal from Allen Dulles for his rather illustrious if not controversial service as head of the Berlin Operations Base. He then promptly set about his new duties—the QJ/WIN program was officially open for business.

The code letters "QJ" indicates Spain, where, of course, Otto Skorzeny lived. This fact is derived from the testimony of Theodore Shackley, Associate Deputy Director for clandestine operations, testifying under the alias "Mr. Halley" before the Senate Select Committee to Study Governmental Operations with Respect to Intelligence Activities, U.S. Senate Select Committee on Intelligence, in Washington, D.C., on August 19, 1975. Twice, Shackley directly linked Spain to the QJ/WIN program after he was asked: "Do you recall a CIA asset who went by the cryptonym QJ/WIN?"

Shackley answered: "No, I do not. Knowing the system, and so forth, normally it would have something to do with Spain. It does not ring any bells with me. That is all I can give you, a sort of Pavlovian response. You flash QJ/WIN on the screen, I am telling you now I do not know, but it probably has something to do with Spain."

During the information gathering phase of the QJ/WIN program, Harvey would have reviewed all available data on Skorzeny. This included a report sent to CIA headquarters by Archie Roosevelt, chief of the Madrid CIA station, in March 1958. Ostensibly, the report was a visa request; however, in reality, it was a sanitized summary of CIA contact and events related to covert operations conducted by Skorzeny. The report covered the background of Skorzeny from his war service through his years in France and Spain but purposely left out specifics on his operational support to the Agency. This was because not everyone who would see the document was privy to the clandestine relationship. However, Roosevelt ended the report with a clear operational recommendation for Skorzeny: "In the opinion of the Embassy officials who know him and *in view of his proven activities*, it strains the imagination the Subject has designs which are prejudicial to the United States," (emphasis added).

Roosevelt's report was written at nearly the same time as a separate dispatch sent in April by Arnold Silver, then Chief of Station, Luxembourg to William Harvey. This document was a recommendation for QJWIN. Silver was, of course, the man who had facilitated Skorzeny's "escape" from Camp King in July 1948. It is documented that Silver had been working with the mysterious QJ/WIN for over a year on an important joint CIA–FBN drug case. Given their past clandestine relationship, Silver's recommendation to Harvey for QJ/WIN could have actually been Skorzeny.

From the 1975 Senate Committee's findings, we also know that QJ/WIN performed work for the Federal Narcotics Bureau and other federal agencies, and that QJ/WIN himself was "of criminal background." One astute writer and researcher, Steve Rivele, had pointed out that this is a curious phrase, "of criminal background": QJ/WIN is not said to be "criminal" himself, but that his "background" is one of a criminal nature. When former DCI Richard Helms was asked about QJ/WIN, he replied: "[If] you needed somebody to carry out murder, I guess you had a man who might be prepared to carry it out."

Arnold Silver contracted QJ/WIN in the autumn of 1958 and continued operational activities with him for eighteen months. Silver was impressed with QJ/WIN's ability, just as he had been impressed with Skorzeny back at Camp King. Silver's connection to the drug interdiction operation could be understood as having utilized Skorzeny's global business networks for covert drug operations. Skorzeny did have extensive import–export businesses in agricultural commodities with African nations that were trading with China, a perfect cover for such operations. Tellingly, Arnold Silver transferred from his position as COS, Luxembourg to Staff D. This effectively made Arnold Silver a potential focal point officer for handling Otto Skorzeny within Staff D. Hence, Silver's selection to Staff D placed one Otto Skorzeny's closest American confidants at the heart of assassination operations.

By 1960, William Harvey's Staff D was fully operational. Harvey's deputy was a senior case officer named Justin O'Donnell. The Staff D office worked closely with the Office of Security, headed at that time by Colonel Sheffield Edwards. Edward's office focused on CIA internal security, while Angleton's

CIS handled foreign threats. Colonel Edwards' security officer, James "Big Jim" O'Connell, was the CIA liaison officer to Staff D.

SKORZENY'S SECRET MEETING WITH COLONEL DAVID STIRLING

Peter Wright, a senior intelligence officer for MI5, the British counterintelligence agency, confirmed in his book *Spycatcher*, published in 1987 that William K. Harvey and James Angleton made a visit to London sometime in 1959 during the run-up phase to the establishment of an American assassination program. The two CIA officers were wanting to know about British capabilities in covert planning and operations. They questioned Wright on the details of recent British operations in Africa and other places. Then as Wright explains it, Harvey announced, "We are developing a new capability in the Company [CIA] to handle these kinds of problems and we're in the market for requisite expertise." Harvey seemed particularly interested in the Special Air Service or SAS commandos, the highly successful special operations unit originally set up in World War II. The SAS were considered the best trained special forces unit in the world. Wright then explained to Harvey that the elite SAS did not "freelance" but, "You could try to pick them up retired," also putting in a word of caution that any contact with the ex-SAS would need to be cleared by MI6.

Right on cue, June 10, 1959, Otto Skorzeny arrived at the London airport from Spain to meet personally with an equally legendary British SAS commando from World War II, Colonel David Stirling. The meeting between Stirling and Skorzeny supposedly took place at the London airport. Often reported as a casual greeting between old foes, this was actually far from the case. Unknown to anyone at the time, Skorzeny was taken into London, to an undisclosed location, for confidential discussion of an extremely important nature. It is likely, William Harvey was present with Skorzeny at his meeting with Colonel Sterling, having taken up Peter Wright's advice on contacting former SAS operatives. CIA officer Bayard Stockton, who knew Harvey well and published an account of Harvey's CIA career wrote, "Harvey would have especially wanted to meet QJWIN out of sheer curiosity, bordering on magnetic attraction. . . ."

To understand the backstory to Skorzeny's visit to London and why it has implications for Harvey's Staff D project, we turn to the pages of *Commando Extraordinary,* written by the enigmatic British author Charles Foley who detailed Skorzeny's life. First published in 1954, Foley gives a foreshadowing of Harvey's Staff D activities in 1960 and hints of the QJ/WIN program. In a section of the book dedicated solely to an exposé on the use of special forces in future war, Colonel David Stirling speaks to the very formation of professional private commando groups. Stirling states, "In my view, there should be set up a directorship of strategic assault personnel. The terms of reference of this new directorship would enable it to straddle the watershed between the para-military operations carried out by troops in uniform and the political warfare which is conducted by civilian agents." This description accurately describes the mission areas assigned to Skorzeny's paramilitary by the CIA.

Stirling continued, "It would be the primary task of the director to plan operations within the widest scope of the highly diversified force at his disposal," making "full use of all current military and political intelligence for the selection of his targets and the assessment of their priority." Again, these are key points that are found in the Skorzeny model.

Stirling then added that the force would retain "a high state of readiness, day to day, for specific tasks," and that the director should have "vision and boldness" and be "backed by the Chiefs of Staffs," with full authorities from the government.

By 1960, Colonel Stirling was documented to have formed just such an organization, by recruiting former members of the elite SAS, for work with Middle Eastern and African countries. The same month David Stirling met with Skorzeny, he formed a company called Television International Enterprise, or TIE. TIE was later a cover for Watchguard, a clandestine mercenary unit operating out of the same offices as TIE. British intelligence, like the CIA, was also involved in major covert operations at the time, in many areas of the world. One area of particular interest was Yemen, where the British were supporting the Royalist government fighting the Egyptian regime. The British did not want an official military force, either conventional or special forces, to be involved;

instead, Prime Minister Harold Macmillan agreed to the formation of a mercenary unit—"The British Mercenary Organization." Stirling's BMO was capable of staging its own covert operations, independent of London, and was used extensively in Yemen and other areas of the Middle East and Africa.

Only seventeen days after his meeting with Stirling, Otto Skorzeny purchased a 165-acre farm in County Kildare, Ireland. The land was sold to Skorzeny by Dan Stephenson, of James North & Co. The author was unable to determine if Dan Stephenson was related to Sir William Stephenson cited many times throughout this book. If he was the land purchase by Skorzeny would take on even more significance.

The sale was reported by the press, but the meetings with Colonel Stirling just prior to the purchase were not known to the public. It would appear that the Skorzeny–Stirling meeting indicates high-level approval from both the British and American governments for developing private paramilitary capabilities. This approval also involved collaboration between the CIA and British intelligence as Harvey was instructed by Peter Wright to clear his contact with former SAS with MI6. In effect, it is highly possible the British had turned to Stirling for use in the Middle East, while the Americans gained Skorzeny for Staff D. Wright also mentioned that during his 1959 meeting with William Harvey and James Angleton that, "It was apparent the CIA was preparing for covert action against Cuba."

THE CUBA CONNECTION

In the 1950s, Cuba was a money-spinning environment due to the criminal relationship between the Mafia and Dictator Fulgencio Batista. Having originally served as an elected president of Cuba from 1940–1944, Batista seized power by military coup in 1952. The island had become a Mafia stronghold after the arrival of mobster Lucky Luciano after World War II.

Once in Cuba, the Mafia quickly expanded operations with large-scale gambling operations, beginning in 1955. Other big names in the Mafia were welcomed by Batista, including the notorious Meyer Lansky and Santo Traffi-cante, Jr. The island exploded with gambling houses, exotic hotels, and large-scale prostitution, all of this attracting the rich and famous. The island had also been visited during these years by powerful U.S. politicians, including Vice President Richard Nixon and Senator John F. Kennedy.

Both Nixon and Kennedy had a passion for Cuba and its captivating entice-ments. Nixon had visited the island just after getting married in 1940. He returned as U.S. Vice President in 1955 and, despite pleas from a group of con-cerned exiled Cuban businessmen to take notice of Batista's despotic rule, he turned a blind eye. However, Nixon soon developed important Mafia ties, including significant ones through a friend and close confidant named Charles "Bebe" Rebozo. These Mafia links would be developed by Nixon over the years into major clandestine assets he used once in office as vice president.

The exploitation by Batista and his Mafia friends was devastating the nation's population, giving rise to unimaginable poverty. Resisting the corrupt govern-ment was a band of guerrilla leaders led by Fidel Castro and a former Argentine doctor named Che Guevara.

As the situation continued to spiral out of control, Batista increased his police state terror with torture and assassination. These outrages caused the American intelligence officials to back clandestine efforts to help the rebels. Although known later as fervent Communists, at this point Castro and Guevara were not considered as fully committed to that doctrine and had support within U.S. government circles. Some Americans were actually moved by Castro's revolu-tion and went to the island to assist as fighters. Among them were men with connections to the CIA, who helped facilitate the transfer of funds and weapons to the rebels. Two of the more famous of these adventurers were former Ameri-can Marines William Morgan and Frank Sturgis. Sturgis would be remembered later for his infamous role as a Watergate burglar.

These men had organized a rebel army called the 26th of July Movement, or MR-26-7. The name memorialized the date of one of their attacks on Batista's forces. MR-26-7 operated in both rural areas and in the cities. It was romanti-cally attached to stories of Castro's band, operating with impunity from secret bases in the Sierra Maestra mountains. The movement and its leaders were the hope of the Cuban people.

It is also known that Otto Skorzeny was approached to help Castro, a fact he himself admitted in an interview with Canadian television in October 1960. The interviewer was Pierre Berton, a noted Canadian author. During the interview, Berton asked Skorzeny if he had been contacted by Cuban rebels to assist the country with paramilitary activity. Skorzeny answered "yes" but the contact was "unofficial," and he would not say who approached him, nor would he specify exactly what they wanted him to do. Skorzeny's reference to an "unofficial" approach may be a veiled reference a business partner of his named Jorge Antonio who had met with the rebel leader Che Guevara around this same time. Berton's interview is also very important for another reason, which will be revealed later in this narrative.

Although the United States government was not exactly clear on a strategy to replace Batista, it was believed that a leader would be found if the revolution was successful. All of the support for Castro by the CIA and its surrogates was an attempt to transfer power to a government with interests aligned with United States foreign policy.

Then on January 1, 1959, Castro's forces initiated a full-scale attack on the island at multiple points. Che Guevara seized Santa Clara, while other rebel forces took control of Havana. Castro, meanwhile, seized the nation's second largest city, Santiago de Cuba. These rebel forces were heavily supported by sympathizers in the cities, and soundly defeated Batista's forces. The Cuban people rushed to the streets to celebrate their long-awaited liberation, and Batista beat a hasty retreat for the Dominican Republic, flying out with some of his key staff in planes loaded with millions of U.S. dollars. Seven days later, Castro entered Havana, making his headquarters in the Hilton Hotel.

On February 13, 1959, the Cuban Prime Minister, José Miró Cardona, resigned his post at the insistence of the United States government and, in his place, Fidel Castro took over. Cardona was soon destined to play a role in one of Skorzeny's most secret endeavors. On March 10, 1959, the U.S. National Security Council (NSC) held a classified meeting concerning options on installing a new government in Cuba.

A decision was then made in Washington with the intent of opening a channel of communications with Castro to divine his intentions. This incredibly historic mission was passed to Tex McCrary, who was, at the time, staying at the Hilton Havana. It was hoped that this clandestine diplomacy might bear fruit in swaying the new leader to remain in the U.S. camp and not drift toward the Soviet Union. On April 11, 1959, McCrary managed to carry out the mission and met secretly with Castro and his cabinet at a location outside Havana. Also present was a top aide of McCrary, Barry Farber, later a noted radio celebrity. Farber admitted he was on an espionage mission at the "midnight meeting with Castro's cabinet." Castro agreed at the meeting to go to New York and meet with Nixon. The meeting between the two was subsequently announced in the press, on April 12, 1959.

Castro was flown out of Cuba on an aircraft piloted by former USAF colonel-turned-CIA-contract-pilot Charles S. "Chuck" Hayes. Earlier that year, Hayes had flown dangerous clandestine airdrops of arms and ammo to Castro and his men during the CIA support phase to Castro. It was reputed by J. Orlin Grabbe that these CIA arms drops were financed by oilman George H. W. Bush.

Castro arrived in New York to enthusiastic crowds, who wanted to get a glimpse of Cuba's revolutionary chief. The American papers had been following his exploits and succeeded in making him into a celebrity. The Castro trip was couched as an invitation for him to speak at a convention of the American Society of Newspaper Editors. He would not meet with President Eisenhower, who conveniently was away during his visit. Instead, Vice President Nixon was assigned the task, an appropriate duty for the man spearheading the Cuba effort within the U.S. Government.

Nixon had invited Castro to his residence, but the Cuban leader refused the invitation. Instead, they met in Nixon's Washington office. The meeting, held only between the two men, lasted for three hours, after which both left disappointed with the other. Nixon filed a report afterwards indicating he did not trust Castro and felt he was going to be a danger to America. Castro, too, was unimpressed with the U.S. Vice President and was disgusted that his starving country was not offered aid, complaining, "That son of a bitch, Nixon . . . he treated me bad."

Mysteriously, Castro also met for three hours with Gerry Droller, a CIA officer leading a secret effort to raise a "Caribbean Legion" to retake the island. What this side meeting was about is anyone's guess, but it was likely a complete ruse to allow Droller to secure information that could be gleaned from Castro for intelligence purposes.

In January 1960, CIA Director Allen Dulles had taken a Cuban covert-action plan before the 5412 Committee, or Special Group (or Special Team), a handful of senior government officials from the CIA and National Security Council who advised the president on highly classified projects. After hearing Dulles' plans, the Special Group granted conditional authorization. The Special Group included Assistant Secretary of Defense for Logistics Perkins McGuire, who established the original MAAG program connected to Skorzeny.

A Cuba Project team was formed to handle the operational planning. This effort was led by CIA officer Tracy Barnes. Other important government officials involved with the task force were Admiral Arleigh Burke, Livingston Merchant, National Security Adviser Gordon Gray (a close friend of Perkins McGuire), and Allen Dulles. At the operations level, the team included E. Howard Hunt, a later senior-level CIA officer who was linked to the Watergate affair; Alfonso Rodriguez, the original CIA chief of station in Madrid when Skorzeny arrived in 1951; Gerry Droller (known under the alias "Frank Bender"); and, finally, two top CIA officers, Jake Esterline and David A. Phillips.

Official approval for the Cuba Project came on March 17, 1960, directly from President Eisenhower. The committee was directed to create a Cuban government-in-exile, initiate a propaganda campaign, create an operational intelligence capability inside Cuba, and form a paramilitary force for future operations. It is known that Vice President Richard Nixon was the "action officer" for the group. Author Gus Russo presented evidence in his book, *Live by the Sword: The Secret War Against Castro and the Death of JFK*, in which he cites interviews from government sources strongly suggesting "that Nixon, along with his Military Aide, General Robert Cushman, secretly undertook an anti-Castro operation that operated outside of Presidential and Security Council controls."

As part of the program to create a Cuban government-in-exile, Nixon turned to Mario G. Kohly, a prominent Cuban investment banker. Kohly had lost power once Castro took over and moved to the U.S. in early 1959, where he immediately began to organize former members of the Cuban military into an organized body called the "Cuban Liberators." In May 1959, Kohly had met a very prominent D.C. attorney named Marshall Diggs, a former Deputy Comptroller of the U.S. Treasury. Diggs was heavily involved with international corporate financing and banking. Diggs was born in Tennessee but for many years before World War II he called Dallas, Texas home and served in the city government. He had many old acquaintances in Dallas and he was also a close personal confidant of Vice President Nixon.

With authorization to proceed at full speed against Castro, things now moved in a very serious direction. Eisenhower's chief National Security adviser, Gordon Gray, later recalled that the president's original order for covert action in Cuba contained what he termed "drastic" measures, a clear reference to assassination.

SKORZENY (QJ/WIN), ZR/RIFLE, AND "OPERATION TROPICAL"

One such drastic measure was reportedly conceived by Castro's Ambassador to Britain, Sergio Rojas Santamarina, who resigned his post in late June of 1960 and returned to Cuba. Information on this assassination attempt on Castro comes from a copy of an unidentified newspaper retained by Skorzeny that he had secured within his papers. Before proceeding with the description of events from the article we briefly pause to highlight a memo written by William Harvey, exposed during the Senate Investigations on Assassinations in 1975. The memo stated that the asset QJ/WIN had been "developed for the *original* ZR/RIFLE project," (emphasis added). ZR was "a digraph for Division D"; and the RIFLE designation, a secret code reference for an operation to assassinate Fidel Castro. Harvey's memo suggests that there were two different versions of this project—the *original* ZR/RIFLE, and a subsequent one. Much has been written about the subsequent ZR/RIFLE missions involving Harvey and the Mafia boss Johnny Roselli after 1961. This has been analyzed by the author and determined as evidence Skorzeny was involved in the original ZR/RIFLE project, the one referenced in the article retained by Skorzeny in his papers.

We also note, that Santamarina was in London at the time of Skorzeny's timely meeting with Colonel Stirling in June 1959, in which it is believed by the author that William Harvey was also present. Santamarina had in fact stated to the press that his resignation was in response to Cuba's shift toward Communism. His first act was to seek refuge in the Argentine Embassy in Havana, and his second was a mission to remove Castro.

The article begins with details of a meeting at the Argentine Embassy where Santamarina began to collaborate with Dr. José Miró Cardona. Cardona had accepted the role as Cuban Ambassador to the U.S. after Castro's takeover but later resigned around the same time as Santamarina. The two men were aware that plotting already existed in exile circles to remove Castro and decided to initiate their own plan for assassination. It was through discussions, as reported in the article, the idea was hatched to approach Otto Skorzeny to lead the mission.

However, on the surface, the man they selected to approach Skorzeny is a seemingly odd choice. This was a well-known Hollywood press agent and public relations man named Guido Orlando. Orlando was born in Barisciano, Italy, and immigrated to the United States in 1917. It is not clear why Orlando was selected for such a secret matter, perhaps to not draw attention.

Orlando was an interesting character in his own right, having influenced the careers of the famous movie stars Greta Garbo, Rudolph Valentino, and Ingrid Bergman. But, he also had a mysterious side, having served in the United States Army Air Forces during the Second World War, and had some confidential relationship with Howard Hughes involving secret government aircraft projects. A final hint is Orlando's claim he participated directly in the Italian elections in 1948 to defeat the Communists. This makes it possible he was connected to the OSS or early CIA, as were so many others in the public relations and entertainment fields. Regardless, as the article maintains, once Skorzeny heard about Santamarina and Cardona's plan, he decided to back the venture. The information for the plan was then passed to CIA planners who gave the plan the name Operation Tropical. The approximate date for these events would have been between mid-July to early August of 1960.

The article states that in August 1960, planning for Operation Tropical began. That month, the CIA purchased, through Assistant Secretary of Defense Perkins McGuire, the civilian airline Southern Air Transport, or SAT. The airline had been operating out of Miami, Florida, since 1947 and was previously owned by former USAF pilots. The purchase of the airline was explained by Fred C. Moor III, whose father was an original owner. Moor's small book on the company, *Then Came the CIA: The Early Years of Southern Air Transport,* gives the details of its acquisition by the Agency. Moor cites a CIA document he acquired in 2010 under the Freedom of Information Act that states that SAT was being acquired as a CIA proprietary due to "operational missions levied on the Agency." It went on to say that SAT "possessed certain air rights in the Caribbean which were also of interest to the Agency for contingency operational use." This was a clear inference to Operation Tropical and other covert missions for the Cuba project. Importantly, SAT was given the CIA code word ZR/CLIFF, establishing a hard link to William Harvey's Staff D.

In addition to Perkins McGuire the purchase of SAT included Percival Brundage, former Director of the Bureau of Budget. Brundage had left his post at Bureau of Budget in 1958 but remained for two years afterward as a key "consultant." As a senior officer of the Bureau of Budget, Brundage was heavily involved with "black budgets," dealing with covert operations of the CIA and military. Brundage, a Unitarian, was, curiously, a founder of the American Friends of Albert Schweitzer College, the mysterious university in Switzerland that Lee Harvey Oswald applied to but never attended. The timing and purchase of Southern Air Transport by McGuire and Brundage placed a major CIA air proprietary at the disposal of Otto Skorzeny.

According to the article, training began in September 1960 at secret locations. The final plan involved a classic Skorzeny-style airborne commando operation, with the objective not only to assassinate Fidel Castro, but Raúl Castro and Che Guevara as well. It is likely that Southern Air Transport was tapped to supply the aviation assets for the paratrooper commandos.

On the suggested timeline for the operation, intelligence would have been provided by the CIA Chief of Station James A. Noel, who was in contact with secret assets throughout the country. Later, in November 1963, Noel would be assigned as the chief of station in Madrid. One of Noel's chief contacts in Cuba was Bernard Barker, a former member of Batista's secret police who had worked with the FBI. At this point, it may come as no surprise to the reader that Barker was also a future Watergate burglar.

The ambush site selected for Operation Tropical was a remote area near a Cuban military training base. Intelligence had been received that Castro would be returning to Havana from a visit to the base. Intelligence also reported Castro had a bodyguard contingent of thirty well-armed men. The force for Operation Tropical consisted of forty-seven paratroopers, including twenty Cubans, twenty Germans, and seven headquarters personnel. According to the plan, Skorzeny was to personally lead the raid. The Commando unit trained for seven months, and millions of dollars were spent in its preparation. The commando group was reported to have trained at secret locations in the Florida Keys. As a note of curiosity, the CIA had a secret training base on the coast of North Carolina, known as "Isolation Tropic," at the same time.

Coinciding with the suggested start date of Operation Tropical was the initiation of what appears to be a simultaneous propaganda campaign, a task set out under the original Cuba committee orders. Right on cue, both Santamarina and Skorzeny became involved in the psychological warfare effort by making public statements directed at Cuban leadership. Skorzeny's quip came first, when he took an opportunity during the same Canadian television interview mentioned above involving Pierre Berton. This aired on September 15, 1960, for the Canadian Broadcast Company TV show *Close-Up*. Berton began by asking Skorzeny if he had been approached since the war to conduct operations like the type he did during the war. Skorzeny answered yes, that many countries had approached him, including the United States. When asked to elaborate what he did, Skorzeny simply said with a smile, "Oh . . . some special work." When Berton continued to press, Skorzeny added, "I wouldn't say it, you don't talk about such things."

Berton then asked if Skorzeny had been approached by Cuba. Skorzeny answered honestly but with little detail, replying, "I was not officially approached but, unofficially, I was approached also." Berton quickly returned, "Was that by Castro?" Skorzeny mused, "It was first by Castro and *now* by the enemies of Castro," (emphasis added). Here, Skorzeny appears to be making a point. Given the orders for psychological warfare, Skorzeny's reference in the present tense, "and now by the enemies of Castro," appears to be for effect. This is supported by the fact that, at that very moment, the initial training phase of Operation Tropical was underway. These "mind games" are precisely in line with Skorzeny's warfighting principles as recorded in Charles Foley's book, *Commando Extraordinary*—In Skorzeny's words, "That is the psychology of panic. Broadcast that you will hit a certain [target]—and hit it."

Santamarina joined in on October 24, 1960, with headlines in U.S. newspapers announcing a coming struggle to regain Cuba—"Fidel Revolt Aim of Ex-Envoy." It said Santamarina had managed to escape Cuba and get back to Britain, and now was preparing to fly to Florida to join in the formation of a counterrevolutionary army of 150,000 Cuban émigrés. He warned, "It will be a civil war—another Korea," and colorfully added, "Castro is a mad dog. He must be wiped out." He stated that he had been "having important talks with people all over Europe" for three weeks, and "This is not just another Latin-American Revolution," but "a battle against Communism in the Caribbean." Shortly after the newspaper interview given by Santamarina, he flew from London to the U.S. His exaggerated statements for the paper intentionally inflated the Cuban exiles' capabilities and served to deflect from the actual planning being conducted for Skorzeny's "surgical" strike.

The two "Psyop" efforts described above were part of an overall plan that had many other examples, including a CIA leaflet drop on Havana by an ex-Cuban air force officer named Pedro Luis Díaz and Frank Sturgis, the future Watergate burglar mentioned earlier.

Two important events occurred in the late fall of 1960 that would have directly impacted Operation Tropical. First, was an exploding crisis in the Congo that started earlier that summer and the second was the presidential election. The Congo crisis temporarily diverted Skorzeny from Operation Tropical and sent him on an emergency reconnaissance to assess the situation in the Africa nation for the CIA. This mission will be covered in the next section. The disruption in the Operation Tropical timeline had other implications since Vice President Nixon wanted to remove Castro before the U.S. elections, thus helping his bid for the presidency. The final assault date for Operation Tropical was set for April 18, 1961. This date coincides with the eventual Bay of Pigs operation that occurred on the next day.

According to the article on Operation Tropical, although millions of dollars were spent and thousands of hours conducted in training, the mission would not go down. In November, Nixon lost his bid for the presidency to Senator John F. Kennedy. In January, within twenty-four hours of leaving office, Nixon arrived at Perkins McGuire's island resort home in the Bahamas. It should be pointed out here that after the election of John F. Kennedy, McGuire left his position as the Assistant Secretary of Defense and became an executive-level CIA contract officer.

Also present was Lindsay Hopkins of Zenith Technical Enterprises, a cover company for the CIA deeply involved in covert operations against Cuba. Some plan of action relative to Operation Tropical must have been discussed, including briefing the new president. At this point, things were evidently still proceeding, as former Cuban Ambassador Santamarina was reported as the leader of anti-Castro forces.

The Operation Tropical article intimates that President Kennedy was briefed on the full details of the assault, including the use of Otto Skorzeny. The article also stated those in attendance included CIA Director Allen Dulles, Secretary of Defense Robert McNamara, Secretary of State Dean Rusk, and Senator J. William Fulbright (the man Kennedy wanted as Secretary of State), and Attorney General Robert Kennedy. Fulbright was reported as shocked at the revelation concerning the use of Skorzeny. Rusk, McNamara, and Dulles were in favor of the action, but Robert Kennedy and Senator Fulbright worried that if the mission failed, the political fallout of using Skorzeny would be disastrous. Kennedy concurred with Senator Fulbright and canceled the mission.

The validity of the Operation Tropical article seems highly probable. More analysis is needed but preliminary findings appear to confirm the accuracy of events. Interestingly, President Kennedy abolished the Operations Control Board, the government's covert action approval body at the point of the timeline he would have received the Operation Tropical briefing. Irony is also not lost on the fact that President Eisenhower had kept a picture of Skorzeny on his desk in the oval office!

Kennedy went on to approve other Cuba operations but ones not involving Otto Skorzeny, including an invasion by Cuban paramilitary forces. This revised plan became the Bay of Pigs operation, which failed on the beaches for lack of U.S. support. Retired U.S. Army Colonel Anthony Herbert, who, as a captain, had been slated to lead an army pathfinder team in the invasion, noted the anger and frustration over the cancellation of the mission: "When the invasion was called off, I began to hear generals and colonels cursing President Kennedy as a weak-kneed, candy-assed, chicken-livered coward." The colonel went on to point out that their anger over missing "their chance for glory" was misguided, as "There were international complications and considerations, and that the civilian commander-in-chief had given an order." Ironically, Captain Herbert had earlier attended Skorzeny's School of Commando Tactics.

The fact that historians have never mentioned Operation Tropical is interesting since there were references to it in the newspapers. Perhaps this was because the basic storyline seems sensational, or the lack of evidence at the time confirming Otto Skorzeny as a covert asset of the United States. This book presents just such evidence throughout it pages thus changing the view of Operation Tropical. In determining the validity of Skorzeny's involvement the author did make one dramatic discovery that has high significance not only for Operation Tropical but more importantly for the final conclusion of this book. The stunning revelation was made by a former CIA contract officer named Robert Morrow who worked on Cuban covert operations for the Agency.

Morrow authored several books in which he claimed the CIA covert operations he was involved with were somehow connected to a covert network that was linked to the assassination of President Kennedy. His specific participation in covert operations was directed at Cuba and involved gun running and counterfeiting operations. Morrow admits he did not have direct knowledge of the events in Dallas but established the links in retrospect. He also claimed that Jack Ruby was involved in the gun running network. Thus, in hindsight, Morrow attempted to piece together the assassination story using his own personal experiences combined with various hypothesizes he felt fit.

In his book *First Hand Knowledge,* Morrow firmly established that his CIA boss, while working as a CIA contract officer was the afore-mentioned Washington attorney Marshall Diggs. Morrow claimed that Diggs had requested an urgent meeting with him prior to the death of Mary Meyer, the wife of CIA officer Cord Meyer, Jr., and shortly after the Warren Commission report was released in the fall of 1964. Morrow said Diggs was worried about a potential compromise in the CIA operations they had been working on and explained, "There is a prominent lady here in Washington who knows too much about the Company [CIA], its Cuban operations, and specifically about the President's assassination." Diggs would go on to tell Morrow that Myers' loose lips were a threat to their still classified CIA's operations.

Morrow was not sure of the significance of Diggs comment since his participation had been dealing with counterfeiting and covert arms. These operations had been shut down by Attorney General Bobby Kennedy some time before the assassination. As the conversation progressed however, Diggs made it clear that the woman in question was Mary Meyer and she knew the men behind the Cuba operations were also behind the assassination of Kennedy. This was correct, at least in the broader scheme of things. Diggs then told Morrow that Mario Kohly, the Cuban leader they had worked with, must be warned. He then instructed Morrow to go to New York and warn Kohly about Mary Meyers' potential for disclosure. According to Morrow, a few days later he did meet with Kohly, who responded, "Just tell Diggs I'll take care of the matter." One week later, Mary Meyer was murdered on the banks of the Chesapeake and Ohio Canal.

Here the author will inform the reader that Marshall Diggs office phone number is listed in the Skorzeny papers with an annotation on the side of it—"M. G. Kohly." This document confirms Skorzeny knew of these men. The document is dated 1967, sometime after the events described, but long before Morrow's story was ever revealed. It must be assumed therefore, that Morrow was totally unaware of Otto Skorzeny or how the network functioned. This is why Morrow could never come to a definitive answer on who was responsible for the murder of JFK. However, it is evident Mary Meyer had inside information on the overall network that was connected to Skorzeny and could compromise its security.

Morrow believed (or was led to believe) Mary's information centered on the Mafia and Cubans and that these groups were behind the president's assassination. In Morrow's mind, to stop this threat, the Cubans, and specifically, Mario Kohly, liquidated Mary Meyer. That may be true, but the Skorzeny papers also indicate Kolhy knew Skorzeny and it was Skorzeny who was at the head of an assassination capability. But Morrow, did not know about Skorzeny. Therefore, his analysis could only go so far. The Mafia and Cubans had nothing to do with the central assassination but were connected to the Skorzeny network and may have had uses in post assassination cleanup operations. Regardless, digging into these links (and for that matter Operation Tropical) would eventually expose the Skorzeny's paramilitary assassination group. A group that was fully active and in Dallas on November 22, 1963. Mary's voice is no longer silent.

TARGET LUMUMBA—THE UNITED STATES SECURES URANIUM

In the late summer of 1960, just as the CIA was gearing up for covert operations in Cuba, another international crisis was erupting in central Africa that reveals Otto Skorzeny association with Staff D's QJ/WIN program. The events that led to Skorzeny's rather unexpected Congo mission began on June 30, 1960. On that date, the Congo became engulfed in turmoil and strife when the Belgian government suddenly granted the country independence. The Congolese people were unprepared for the transition, which had been announced only months earlier. The chaos created by this rapid decolonization released a torrent of intense political rivalries, enflamed long-standing tribal conflicts, and propelled a native population into statehood that was totally unprepared for the challenges of government management. These circumstances left the region teetering on the verge of civil war.

The situation in the Congo was a serious international problem and potential flashpoint for Cold War confrontation far outweighing CIA operational planning for Cuba. Besides the significant geopolitical implications and humanitarian issues, there was also the issue of important mineral resources, including cobalt, tantalum, bauxite, iron, manganese, zinc, gold, and, most importantly, uranium. The uranium and other radioactive elements were critical to America's nuclear programs and linked to ultra-secret matters involving U.S. national security. These ore deposits had been the focus of U.S. intelligence since 1939, when then President Franklin Roosevelt established a Uranium Committee as an advisery body on this important issue.

The Uranium Committee secretly negotiated with Edgar Sengier, director of the Union Minière, a Belgian mineral company, to safeguard and transport uranium stockpiles from the Shinkolobwe mine in the province of Katanga to the United States. By the end of 1940, 1,200 tons of uranium were shipped from the mine to New York and delivered to the African Metals Corporation on Staten Island. Little known to many Americans is the fact that the uranium used in the atomic weapons dropped on Japan in 1945 originated in the Congo.

On October 9, 1941, Roosevelt authorized the establishment of the highly secret Manhattan Project. The project head, General Leslie Groves, moved to secure the Congo and all areas associated with the uranium ore project from the Nazis. This included communications, logistics, facilities, transportation, and personnel. It was a huge undertaking, and part of the most guarded project in history up to that time. The Shinkolobwe mine was the most important deposit of uranium in the world. Germany had access to only one mine, in

Czechoslovakia, but its deposits were just a fraction of Shinkolobwe's. General Groves knew the Nazis would target the Congo to acquire uranium through espionage, using existing smuggling routes out of the region. In 1943, OSS agents were dispatched to Africa to counter Nazi smuggling threats and other German intelligence activity on the continent.

The importance of Shinkolobwe did not end with the war, nor did the secrecy of U. S. intelligence operations in the Congo. The newly-created CIA would take over the OSS mission and turn its attention toward the new threats posed by Russia, China, and other nations striving to advance a weaponized nuclear program. In 1953, the U.S. was still getting its largest supply of uranium ore from the Congo. According to historian Susan Williams, author of *Spies in the Congo: America's Atomic Mission in World War II*, "The procurement of ore was a persistent and acute concern." Williams also noted, "The protection and defense of Shinkolobwe was expanded . . . a vast 100,000-acre NATO military base was built at Kamina in Katanga." Security was increased in the region, with "shoot on sight" orders issued to patrol guards and check points set up at Union Minière. With these strategic nuclear interests at stake, protection of the uranium ore was a prime strategic objective for the United States.

The Congo was immediately plunged into instability when, on the first day of independence, the newly elected Prime Minister Patrice Lumumba openly lambasted his former colonial rulers and insulting the Belgian King at a public ceremony. Just before these abrasive remarks, Belgian officials had announced the country's independence and praised their King and his benevolent rule. The situation was disastrous and dangerous. At the moment of Lumumba's declaration, the Belgium government, for all intents and purposes, was still intact and European officers still controlled the country's security forces.

As well-founded as Lumumba's words may have been, they were politically ill-advised. This tense atmosphere was further compounded by the lack of a plan for an organized transition of power. Only five days after independence riots broke out in the military, as black troops revolted against white officers—the country was poised for complete anarchy. The Belgians felt compelled to act to protect their citizens, businesses, and mining interests. Only ten days after their withdrawal, the Belgian military was redirected back into the country. This was the catalyst for even further violence and confrontation.

On July 11, 1960, Katanga, the mineral-bearing region of the country, declared its independence, a result of CIA back channel operations to secure Uranium. Belgian mining companies immediately moved to protect these valuable resources by backing Moïse Tshombe, a national political leader, as president of a new breakaway nation. This move was supported by the CIA, who had a long history of cooperation with the Belgian mining companies dating back to the Manhattan Project. Tshombe immediately appealed to the Belgian government, which was sympathetic to the succession, to send military advisers to train his army. At the time, Belgium had over 200 officers in the region, who were then attached to a 10,000-man Katanga Gendarmerie. Tshombe also made appeals to mercenary groups offering security services. The military intervention by Belgium and the influx of mercenaries into Katanga led to an international crisis, resulting in the dispatch of United Nations peacekeeping forces to provide internal security.

The events described above were the opening pages of what became known to history as the Congo Crisis. Skorzeny would have been closely following the Katanga developments from Madrid, due to his various business connections in Africa, and the effect of the crisis on his private intelligence network. Skorzeny's involvement in the Congo actually started during World War II immediately upon his assumption of command in July 1943. Prior to Skorzeny's arrival, planning was already underway for a long range special mission into the Congo. The planner was Arno Besekow, an expert in small unit special missions, who became one of Skorzeny's top men. The existence of the mission was uncovered during a postwar interrogation of Ludwig Nebel, who had taken over for Besekow, by U.S. Army counterintelligence. Nebel reported the mission was to carry out sabotage against oil wells by a ten-man team dropped off by U-Boat. But the Nazis were also aware of the Congo uranium. The team was to receive support from Flemish fascists, "a small group of missionary fathers and few disaffected Belgian colonist" Nebel also claimed the project was never implemented as planned but still indicates the Nazis established intelligence networks in the region.

SKORZENY IN THE CONGO

During the 1950s, Skorzeny initiated a number of significant businesses in countries neighboring the Congo, including Angola. There he established a lumber company and concrete supplier and from 1953 onward he was the official Otto Wolff steel company representative in the country. From the Skorzeny papers we can also confirm he traveled to the Congo in 1951 and again in 1954.

Skorzeny's mercenary contacts in the Congo, included his paramilitary trainers. Contract negotiations were underway by Skorzeny with Major Guy Weber, Tshombe's senior military adviser and new military chief of staff, to provide military support to the new nation. Just when this occurred is not exactly known, but a former Belgian wartime Nazi collaborator, Jean-François Thiriart, who had trained with Skorzeny's SS special forces during the war and afterward with Skorzeny's mercenaries, was documented to have met with a Tshombe representative on September 7, 1960, in Brussels.

Colonel Weber was a highly experienced soldier, having served as a Belgian colonial officer. Importantly, he had close ties with the mining companies and the CIA. Jean-François Thiriart was a successful businessman who operated a company called Opterion, a network of opticians. He was also the guiding force behind an organization called the *Comité d'Action et de Défense des Belges d'Afrique* (Action Committee for the Defense of Belgians in Africa, or CADBA). This committee was created shortly after Katanga's succession by hardline Belgian monarchists at Etterbeek's Café Tanganyika, a hangout for soldiers and mercenaries. Among the clientele were former French soldiers dismissed from service after the 1958 putsch in Algeria against French President Charles de Gaulle. These men saw their battle to keep Algeria French in the same light as the fight to keep the Belgian Congo. CADBA had proclaimed in leaflets, ALGIERS AND LÉOPOLDVILLE, TWO FRONTS, ONE WAR.

Tshombe's representative at the Brussels meeting with Thiriart was Hendrick Bas, a fanatical Katanga secessionist who directed the Elizabethville airport. Thiriart, along with Colonel Jean Cassart, a former Belgian SAS reserve colonel, explained to Bas that they could assemble 3,000 former French soldiers for a unit they dubbed the "Brigade Tshombe." However, it is believed Bas turned down this proposal because Thiriart and Cassart had included plans for the force to also participate in a coup d'état in Belgium to restore direct rule by the King. Whether that is true is not precisely clear.

Despite being turned down, Thiriart would remain involved in Congo intrigues. Shortly after his rejection by Bas, Thiriart transformed CADBA into the *Mouvement d'Action Civique* (Civic Action Movement), or MAC. This group would take up operations in Algeria, in support of the ultras. It is also highly significant in regard to Skorzeny that Colonel Cassart would remain in Katanga to support Tshombe. This assistance came in the form of arms, as well as "fronting a German company" that sold airplanes to Katanga for a hefty profit. Skorzeny at that moment was involved in the sale of surplus aircraft and aviation parts to African countries.

An examination of CIA covert aviation support to Tshombe's military reveals significant aviation connections linked to the companies that Skorzeny also dealt with. Our attention is thus directed to the CIA's use in the Congo of an incredibly short take-off and landing (STOL) aircraft known as the Helio-Courier. The Couriers were leased by the CIA through a joint marketing/leasing program entered into between Helio Aircraft Corp., of Norwood, Massachusetts, and the American Industrial Leasing Corp., of New York. The Helio Aircraft Corporation was owned by Dr. Lynn Bollinger, who stated many years later that "U.S. Governmental officials with substantial international responsibilities" urged him to give Africa his top priority. American Industrial Leasing, the acting CIA intermediary in the deal, was run by Daniel Cavanaugh, a principal business associate of Skorzeny.

In the weeks after the Congo's independence in June 1960, Prime Minister Lumumba departed for Washington soon after being elected to request economic aid but was not greeted by then-President Eisenhower. Lumumba did see Secretary of State Christian Herter and made a public appeal to the American people, expressing friendship. Despite some positive overtures, Lumumba was highly disappointed and did not consider the American response respectful of his position. The feeling was mutual, and the official U.S. position was not inclined to back the new leader, especially in light of strategic considerations.

Upon his return to the Congo, Lumumba moved to seek help for his fledgling nation by turning to the Soviet Union, a move that would ultimately seal his fate. The Soviets responded quickly, sending in a large airlift of supplies and technical support personnel and, of course, intelligence operatives of the KGB. The Western press response was swift to denounce Lumumba's action, branding him as a Communist. Lumumba responded in kind, stating he was not a Communist but a Congolese nationalist attempting to secure support for his new government. This was to no avail, as CIA officers on the ground began sending back to Washington dire assessments of the situation and its apparent consequences—a Communist takeover of the country.

CIA Deputy Director for Plans, Richard Bissell, later recalled the sense of urgency for the U.S. in helping to protect Katanga resources, noting, "The importance of the Congo's natural resources, combined with the most primitive (indeed, nearly nonexistent) political arrangements anywhere in the world, rendered central Africa the kind of political vacuum into which power flows. This set of conditions set the stage for an *immediate critical threat*," (emphasis added).

In a matter of days after the CIA cables were received from the Congo, Allen Dulles was meeting with President Eisenhower. At a meeting of the National Security Council on August 18, 1960, the president was reported to have expressed strong concerns about Lumumba which were interpreted by Allen Dulles as authorization to assassinate the African leader. It is said Eisenhower expressed a "necessity for very straightforward action" against Lumumba. At the meeting, members of the Special Group "agreed that planning for Congo *would not necessarily rule out consideration of any particular kind of activity which might contribute to getting rid of Lumumba*," (emphasis added).

On August 19, Dulles cabled the Congo station: "In high quarters it is the clear-cut conclusion that if [Lumumba] continues to hold high office, the inevitable result will at best be chaos and the worst pave way to Communist takeover of the Congo with disastrous consequences for the prestige of the UN and for the interest of the free world generally. *Consequently we conclude that his removal must be urgent and prime objective and that under the existing conditions this should be a high priority of our covert action*," (emphasis added). Evidence given before the Church Committee in 1975 stated it was clear "that the Director of Central Intelligence, Allen Dulles, authorized an assassination plot." By the end of September, the CIA had dispatched to the Congo a chemist named Sidney Gottlieb, an expert in poison, to consult with the chief of station, Larry Devlin, on assassination options. This was not the only plan under review; other plans included using a sniper, and a less lethal option involved a commando raid to carry out an abduction.

QJ/WIN ARRIVES IN THE CONGO

On April 16, 1952 an article penned by author Charles Foley for the *Daily Express* titled, "The Toughest Man Alive," Skorzeny is quoted as saying, "I have had a little practice at kidnapping. I have proved the possibilities and I know the lesson has been taken to heart by, among others, the Russians. Next time, no king or president will sleep securely, wherever he is put." In August 1960, American intelligence was contemplating just such an operation for Patrice Lumumba. But evidence suggest they were also plotting his assassination. This was to be one of the first tests for William Harvey's Staff D.

Otto Skorzeny was well aware of the geopolitical situation in the Congo as evidenced by the various businesses he had in the region and as previously mentioned had numerous mercenary contacts there as well. We also find evidence for Skorzeny's presence in the Congo, precisely at the time of CIA covert planning to remove Lumumba. This is found in an incident involving Lieutenant Colonel Mario de Silvestro who had been assigned as the CIA contact cover officer to Skorzeny after the departure of USAF Captain Thaddeus S. Skladzien in January 1960. The use of air attachés for contact with Skorzeny at the Madrid Embassy was covered in Chapter Three and was a key aspect of his relationship to the Agency.

In the first week of September 1960, Lt. Colonel Mario de Silvestro was expeditiously dispatched to the Congo on a classified operation. The mission was in some way related to the murder of Henry "Harry" Noble Taylor, son of Henry Taylor, Jr., U.S. Ambassador to Switzerland. Harry Taylor, a reporter for *Scripps-Howard*, had been sent to the Congo from Moscow, where he had been covering the trial of U-2 pilot Gary Powers. Although we cannot verify Skorzeny was with Colonel de Silvestro it does prove his CIA contact officer was on station in the region to facilitate his arrival if needed.

As these events were occurring, Lumumba was locked in a political power struggle with President Joseph Kasavubu and Joseph Mobutu, chief of the Congolese armed forces, over the country's destiny. Then, on September 14, Kasavubu dismissed Lumumba from government service causing the flight of Lumumba. He promptly sought the protection of United Nations forces in Léopoldville.

Testimony given to the Church Committee by Staff D's deputy Justin O'Donnell under the pseudonym Michael Mulroney, indicated that in October 1963, Richard Bissell, the Deputy Director for Plans directed O'Donnell to go the Congo and carry out the assassination of Lumumba. O'Donnell testified that he refused to carry out an assassination but told Bissell he would attempt to get Lumumba away from his UN protectors.

By mid-November the CIA station chief in Léopoldville, Larry Devlin had sent two cables urging CIA headquarters to send QJ/WIN with the following message:

"LOCAL OPERATIONAL CIRCUMSTANCES REQUIRE IMMEDIATE EXPEDITION OF QJ/WIN TRAVEL TO LEOPOLDVILLE."

The operational circumstances were not explained but the request for QJ/WIN may have indicated the situation was ripe for exploitation and an opening had presented itself for access to the target, Lumumba. CIA financial documents from the first week of November confirm QJ/WIN was "dispatched to the Congo to undertake a mission that 'that might involve a large element of personal risk.'"

Then Headquarters, CIA responded to Léopoldville station confirming the dispatch of QJ/WIN:

> In view of the extreme sensitivity of the objective for which we want [QJ/WIN] to perform his task, he was not told precisely what we want him to do ***. Instead, he was told *** that we would like to have him spot, access, and recommend some dependable, quick-witted persons for our use ***. It was thought best to withhold our true, pending the final decision to use [him].

The message was considered highly classified and the station was given clear instructions for destruction: "this dispatch should be reduced to cryptic necessary notes and destroyed after the first reading." Senate testimony suggests QJ/WIN arrived in Léopoldville on November, 21, 1960 and immediately met with Justin O'Donnell. O'Donnell had arrived earlier on November 3, 1960 and started making plans for "neutralizing" Lumumba, which according to O'Donnell was a reference to "drawing him away" from his UN guards.

It was at this time QJ/WIN came into contact with another CIA contract agent dispatched to the Congo with code name WI/ROGUE.

Testimony of CIA officers who were in contact with WI/ROGUE said he attempted to enlist QJ/WIN to join a separate assassination operation being planned for Lumumba but QJ/WIN turned him down. The deflection in testimony by CIA officers during the committee hearings makes it nearly impossible to get clarity behind the incident.

Subsequent CIA cable traffic after O'Donnell's arrival has the distinct aura of Skorzeny operational involvement. On November 29, the CIA station chief reported QJ/WIN "had begun implementing a plan to 'pierce both Congolese and U.N. guards' to enter Lumumba's residence and 'provide escort out of residence.'" Here, we have echoes of Operation *Panzerfaust* in October 1944 when Skorzeny pulled off his successful castle raid to snatch Hungary's Regent, Admiral Miklós Horthy. It is also identical to the operational planning being carried on by O'Donnell.

O'Donnell stated during the Senate hearings that as far as he knew "he was the only CIA officer with supervisory responsibility for QJ/WIN, and QJ/WIN did not report independently to anyone else. O'Donnell was then asked if it was possible QJ/WIN had a mission independent of O'Donnell's operation. O'Donnell responded, "Yes, that is possible—or it could have been that somebody contracted him after he got down there, that they wanted him to do something along the lines of assassination. I don't know." Here it should be reiterated that at the time of O'Donnell reference, Skorzeny was in fact carrying on independent mercenary contract with Major Guy Weber, Tshombe's senior military adviser.

On November 29, the CIA station chief sent a cable indication QJ/WIN had initiated a plan to "pierce both Congolese and U.N. guards" secure Lumumba and escort him out. Without warning, on December 1, Mobutu's troops managed to capture Lumumba as he was leaving his residence in an attempt to reach a friendly stronghold in Stanleyville.

Lumumba's sudden movement disrupted the CIA's penetration plan at the residence and a new cable was issued:

"View change in location target, QJ/WIN anxious go Stanleyville and expressed desire execute plan by himself without using apparat."

QJ/WIN's desire to execute the plan by himself sounds like Skorzeny's method of operations having a desire to maintain effective command and control in a now more unstable operational environment. It is also not clear if the plan had switched from abduction to assassination. A new cable went out expressing concerns over deniability:

"Concur QJ/WIN go Stanleyville *** We are prepared consider direct action by QJ/WIN but would like your reading on security factors. How close would this place [United States] to the action?"

On January, 11, 1961 a CIA cable from William K. Harvey to the Director-ate of Plans, Richard Helms, noted:

"QJ/WIN was sent on this trip for a specific, highly sensitive operational purpose which has been completed."

Only six days later, on January 17, 1961, Lumumba was transferred to Eliza-bethville, where he was tortured and then executed by Belgian mercenaries and Katanga soldiers. Kennedy's inauguration took place on January 20, 1961. The CIA Deputy Director for Plans, Richard Bissell, stated later, "The CIA pre-pared to deal with Lumumba, but, as events unfolded, the agency was relieved of having to implement any kind of executive action."

In the end, there was no clear evidence QJ/WIN was involved in any direct-action mission against Lumumba. However, based on newly released information, historians now believe Major Guy Weber, who had contact with Skorzeny in the fall of 1960, was heavily involved in the assassination.

Equally incriminating, shortly after Lumumba's murder Skorzeny had secre-tive contact with others now implicated in the assassination. On March 20, 1963, the Skorzeny papers confirm a meeting in Lisbon, Portugal between Skorzeny and high-level Katanga government ministers. Also in attendance was the Portuguese Minister of the Interior, the Minister of War, and the Chief of Staff of the Portuguese Legion. The purpose of the meeting was to secure a loan from Skorzeny's financial banking contacts for "special purposes." One of the ministers involved in this deal was Godefroid Munongo, the Interior Minister of Katanga and in charge of the country's security forces. Munongo had served as interim President of Katanga from April 26 to June 22, 1961. Historians have pointed to Munongo as having played an important role in the assassination of Lumumba, even claiming he carried out the killing himself. When faced with the accusation, Munongo replied, "I will speak frankly, if people accuse us of killing Lumumba, I will reply: Prove it."

THE COMMITTEE FOR AID TO KATANGA FREEDOM FIGHTERS

One last facet of the Congo saga that is a unique and important link connecting Otto Skorzeny to the CIA efforts in the country is a private psychological warfare group formed in the wake of Lumumba's death. This was a pressure group aligned with conservative elements within the United States government supporting an independent Katanga, called "The Committee for Aid to Katanga Freedom Fighters." The committee was a small, but powerful lobby directed at garnering U.S. public support for the breakaway province in the Congo. It appeared on the scene in the fall of 1961, months after Skorzeny's jaunt down to the Congo to conduct his Lumumba assassination assessment, but well within the CIA's continued period of covert action in the country. That interest actually never abated, and the Congo Crisis went on for years. Skorzeny is directly linked to The Committee for Aid to Katanga Freedom Fighters and, from all available evidence in the Skorzeny papers, was a hidden adviser to the group. His principal contact to the group was one of his main business partners, Clifford Forster, the well seasoned veteran of the psychological warfare and political operations such as those in France in 1949 involving *Paix et Liberté*. Forster will also support a similar pressure group for the French Algerian crisis. Significantly, a member of the Katanga committee was Dallas, Texas oil executive, and U.S. Army Reserve intelligence officer, Colonel Jack Crichton. Crichton also knew Skorzeny from the Delta oil drilling project in Spain beginning in 1953 and continuing through 1963. Critchton's involvement with the Congo pressure group brings him even deeper into the covert operations of the Skorzeny network.

To gain international attention, the committee took out a full-page ad in the *New York Times* in December 1961, explaining the mission and goals of the organization and declaring, "Katanga Is the Hungary of 1961." The stated purpose was "a wholehearted desire to keep alive the spirit of resistance of the Katangan people, who only wish to lead their lives in peace, without outside interference."

The committee operated in conjunction with a Belgian expatriate named Michel Struelens. He ran the Katanga Information Service (KIS), a Katangese government organization, from its headquarters on Manhattan's Fifth Avenue. The KIS engaged in a massive press campaign directed at the American public, including Washington politicians, business leaders, and academia from around the country. Assisting Struelens at the time was ubiquitous David Martin. The reader will recall that Martin, the former head of the International Relief Organization in 1949, had originally met with Otto Skorzeny during the epic all night meeting with Frank Wisner OPC staff, including Colonel Boris Pash.

In 1961, at the time of his involvement with the Katanga committee, David Martin was a senior aide for Senator Thomas Dodd, a staunch supporter of the Katanga president, Moïse Tshombe. Historians have speculated that Senator Dodd's motivations in supporting Katanga may have been rooted in his business links to the region. Other high-ranking U.S. government officials were also a part of the committee's efforts, including former Vice President Richard Nixon and Senator Barry Goldwater.

The executive committee of the Katanga pressure group deserves more than a casual mention, since it contains many names associated with Skorzeny and CIA covert programs. Of particular note is William J. Buckley, Jr., the conservative author who had served in the CIA in Mexico City in 1951 when E. Howard Hunt, the famous CIA officer was chief of station. The two men maintained a lifelong friendship.

Another member was Buckley's brother, Reid, who had moved to Spain in 1956, and later, in 1959, he was in Madrid. Reid, a staunch Catholic and fanatical Carlist, was well-connected in Madrid society and friends with Skorzeny. Still another Buckley family connection on the Katanga list was L. Brent Bozell, who moved to Madrid in 1960. Bozell was the brother-in-law of the Buckley brothers and, like Reid, was a neighbor to Skorzeny in Madrid. Lastly, there was CIA contract officer James Burnham of which much has been written in CIA histories.

While only a brief overview, the activities and people mentioned above strongly suggest that they are part of a calculated effort to sway public opinion for strategic outcomes aligned with CIA covert operations in the Congo.

THE HUNT FOR QJ/WIN

CIA documents reveal the operational cover for QJ/WIN leading into the year 1963 was that of an international art dealer. Not by coincidence, several letters in the Otto Skorzeny papers confirm Skorzeny was involved in the sale of fine art on an international scale for the year 1963 and 1964. Also, on the eve of the Kennedy assassination there was a leadership change at Staff D when William K. Harvey departed in to accept the position of Chief of Station in Rome. This was primarily due to friction between Harvey and members of the Kennedy administration, particularly Attorney General Robert Kennedy who was upset with Harvey over unauthorized covert operations in Cuba. Harvey's position at Staff D was taken over by Desmond FitzGerald, a veteran officer who had served with Frank Wisner's OPC and thus fully aware of the Agency's use of Skorzeny. FitzGerald came over from the Special Affairs Staff or SAS, a CIA group tasked with the overthrow of Castro by President Kennedy.

In later testimony before Congress on CIA assassinations, Harvey stated that QJ/WIN had been retained until February 14, 1964, except for a "lifeline." The exact meaning of this is not known, but likely meant the QJ/WIN program network had been shut down on that date with only a contingency capability remaining. In fact, the CIA did continue to carry on extensive covert operations with Skorzeny after February 1964, but these were focused heavily on paramilitary training, covert arms sales and associated air proprietary missions. Although there are no Skorzeny links to CIA Staff D after 1963 there was a major spike in Skorzeny's assistance to the U.S. military and CIA run assassination programs in Vietnam beginning in the fall of 1964. After 1963, Skorzeny would also continue working clandestinely for other countries. The records thus indicate that the QJ/WIN project had a program life from 1958–1963. In the end, the existence of Otto Skorzeny as a key CIA covert operator with a timeline and activities that quite literally match major elements of the QJ/WIN profile would appear to indicate they are one and the same, although it cannot be confirmed. It is also possible the elusive QJ/WIN was one of Skorzeny's operatives within his phantom network. Either way, William K. Harvey's Staff D had direct or indirect access to Skorzeny's assassination capabilities. All of this would have been monitored by James Angleton and his Counterintelligence Staff—a relevant fact when one considers that Angleton was later assigned as the official CIA liaison to the Warren Commission!

CHAPTER TWENTY

THE MOTIVE

"Only history can write the importance of this day: Were these dark days the harbingers of even blacker ones to come, or like the black before the dawn shall they lead to some still as yet indiscernible sunrise of understanding among men. . . ."

WALTER CRONKITE, MONDAY, NOVEMBER 25, 1963

"I wonder with the CIA plot to assassinate Castro, about the possibilities of setting up something of this kind for whatever international purpose. I'm not as happy as I once was with the Warren Commission Report."

WALTER CRONKITE, 1981, *COLUMBIA JOURNAL REVIEW*

"I can't honestly say that I have been completely relieved of the fact that there might have been international connections. . . ."

PRESIDENT LYNDON JOHNSON IN AN OFF-THE-RECORD
INTERVIEW WITH WALTER CRONKITE, SEPTEMBER 1969

Why was President John F. Kennedy killed? The motive and those behind the assassination are both cryptic and obscure with regard to what initiated and drove the event. Does the confirmation of an assassination network operated by Otto Skorzeny help answer the question of motive and who order the act? The author believes it does and the answer is found in something called command and control.

Although the facts behind the motive are very difficult to discern, for the first time, the revelation of the Skorzeny clandestine network presents an opening into the dark shadow of the assassination plot. The author submits to the reader that the act to assassinate President Kennedy was carried out for reasons that far exceeded concerns over U.S. national security. In particular, they arose out of a pending international crisis of such a grave nature that the very survival of the United States and its NATO partners was at risk. At the source of this threat was breaking scandals that unknown to the public involved President Kennedy. To those around the President there was also the impact these scandals had on the president's important duties such as control of the nuclear weapons and response to nuclear attack. It also appears the facts were about to be known. The two scandals at the heart of this high concern were the Profumo Affair and the Bobby Baker Scandal.

THE PROFUMO AFFAIR

On June 5, 1963, the British Secretary of War, John Profumo, resigned his post following news that he had deceived the House of Commons about a sexual affair with Christine Keeler, an alleged prostitute. Keeler was also involved with a Soviet naval attaché, Yevgeny "Eugene" Ivanov, who some suspected was a spy. Profumo assured the British government that he had not in any way compromised national security, but the scandal threatened to topple Prime Minister Harold Macmillan's government. President Kennedy was highly alarmed by the Profumo events and by all accounts was transfixed on following the outcome of events and the investigations concerning the players involved. This interest may have centered on his own brewing scandal that was remarkably similar—the Bobby Baker Scandal.

THE BOBBY BAKER SCANDAL

In 1962, Robert "Bobby" Baker, a close political adviser to Vice President Lyndon B. Johnson and organizer for the Democratic Party, became the Senate Secretary to the Majority Leader. Behind the scenes Baker handled private sexual affairs for politicians and lobbyists at various hotels and confidential apartments in Washington, D.C. President Kennedy was involved in this secret sexual network and had personally met with a party girl supplied by Baker.

This entire network risked exposure when another illegal activity being conducted by Baker was compromised. Earlier, Baker, along with an associate, established a company dealing in vending machines that worked on government contracts. In 1963, information that came to the Senate about possible criminal dealings led to an investigation into Baker's businesses and political activities. These investigations leaked over into Bakers other activities, including the private affairs he was arranging for politicians and the president. The investigation included allegations of bribery and facilitating sexual liaisons in exchange for Congressional votes and contracts.

The Senate investigation went deep into Baker's associations during the 1950s. This included LBJ and other high-ranking government officials. The entire affair sent shock waves through Washington, and there were rumors of very high-level exposures. Baker was finally forced to resign from his position in October 1963, but the investigation continued.

A highly damaging aspect of the Bobby Baker case involved the use of a beautiful "party girl" named Ellen Rometsch. Declassified U.S. government documents confirm Rometsch's links to East German government officials and perhaps the Soviets. Currently, historians are taking a hard look at this information, but preliminary findings indicate Rometsch was perhaps a Soviet agent. She had originally come to the United States with her husband a West German air force sergeant with orders to the United States. Her potential as a Soviet agent is explosive since Baker had arranged for multiple secret sexual liaisons between her and President Kennedy. This brings in the possibility Kennedy was having liaisons with a Soviet spy and thus an immediate and grave national security risk. An indication of the gravity of the situation is found in the expeditious departure of Rometsch and her husband to Germany in August 1963 at the bequest of the State Department.

Much is available on Kennedy's private life in regard to his indiscretions and sexual liaisons that will not be repeated here. Boiled down—the Bobby Baker investigation had the potential to expose devastating information that, if it became public, would have destroyed the Kennedy presidency and perhaps bring down the entire U.S. government. It may also have provided a pathway to link the scandal to the Profumo Affair creating an international crisis for the entire Western alliance.

Attorney General Robert "Bobby" Kennedy, in a desperate effort to save his brother and the office of the presidency (and embarrassment for the U.S. government), made a personal appeal to FBI director J. Edgar Hoover to help quell the press and others from the cascading Bobby Baker revelations. All of this occurred during a period when there was the belief in the halls of the FBI that President Kennedy was preparing to sack the legendary FBI chief. That Hoover had contentious relationship with both the president and the attorney general is a matter of history. Now, with the leverage of assisting Bobby Kennedy over the Bobby Baker Scandal, Hoover was able to secure his position for years into the future. But Hoover could not fully stop the news media and others who were still hot on the case. As President Kennedy was arriving in Dallas, Texas, on November 22, 1963, a very dark cloud of doom was poised over Washington, and the impending storm of information was hanging by a thread.

It is indeed telling that the first order issued by Lyndon Baines Johnson upon assuming the office of the presidency was to stop the Bobby Baker investigation. For his crimes, Baker eventually went to prison but was alleged to have received a high payoff to keep his mouth shut. With the assassination of President Kennedy, the entire Bobby Baker scandal faded into a distant memory—the storm vanished into thin air. It now appears that indeed a desperate act of national survival was implemented in November 1963, and the network used to carry it out was the one directed by Otto Skorzeny.

COMMAND AND CONTROL

Given the facts concerning the highly volatile nature of potential disastrous scandals that led directly to the White House and beyond, the murderous act in Dallas may have been the only viable way to save the Office of the Presidency and spare the public of the heartbreaking knowledge. It is also certain that the information, once made public, would have not only enraged the citizens of the country, but have been immediately seized upon by Soviet propagandist providing the Communist state with fertile ground for a moral victory.

The Profumo Affair and Bobby Baker scandals erupted at the most critical point in the Cold War. The damage to U.S. and NATO prestige would have been incalculable as the Soviet swung into action to proclaim the supremacy of their Communist ideology and morality. In an age before the term information warfare existed, but entirely in line with its purpose and design, a Soviet propaganda victory of this magnitude would have paralyzed the function of U.S. government and its Western partners. With these concerns over the office of the presidency, combined with a potentially horrific public disclosure, only weeks or perhaps days away, the most tragic order ever conceived in the history was issued. The question now emerges—who was at the source of the command authority for assassination?

Generally used in military terminology, "command and control" is defined as "the exercise of authority and direction by a properly designated commander" in the accomplishment of a mission. It lies at the very heart of this entire book and ironically is a term never before used in any study of the JFK assassination. The dramatic description of motive described above could only be initiated as a result of command and control methods. This effectively removes the possibility that the assassination in Dallas was the act of a lone gunman or originated with a petty personal vendetta. The assassination of President Kennedy was deeper and more serious, a mercy killing, a coup de grâce, conducted to counter a grave self-inflicted mortal wound.

With this book, for the first time in history a major new finding comes to bear on the JFK assassination, the existence of a covert assassination capability of the United States, one shared by its NATO allies. The clandestine network operated under formal command and control. With these facts in mind, our focus on motive must be directed on those who had intimate knowledge of Skorzeny and most importantly, those with authority to activate his network and assign its targets. Certainly, the national command structure of the United States government in 1963 was in such a position.

Given this in extremis case, in which, the President of the United States was the target, the Vice President becomes the most logical choice as the originator of the order. However, the existence of senior NATO officers with knowledge of the network, also elevates the potential that the decision originated not only from the United States. In fact, it may have been a joint NATO decision by strategic military decision makers of a clandestine group. Ironically, it was President Johnson who delivered the greatest evidence for this line of command and control. In an off-the-record interview conducted in September 1969, Johnson told the venerable reporter Walter Cronkite that an "international conspiracy" was at play in the Kennedy assassination. Johnson would later ask Cronkite to remove the comment "on grounds of national security." Cronkite himself was later to admit he was not satisfied with the Warren Commission findings and thought that there was an international element to the assassination.

Cronkite worked for CBS which had created a special documentary on the Kennedy assassination in 1975, called *The American Assassins*, which focused on Lee Harvey Oswald. In the film, which included correspondent Dan Rather, a detailed frame-by-frame analysis of the Zapruder film was conducted and evidence was examined that the CIA had a hand in the assassination. The film analysis showed Oswald was the only shooter and no conclusive evidence of outside influence by American intelligence was found. However, both findings are now in serious contention. What CBS did not know (or what they did not reveal) is the company that conducted the analysis on the Zapruder film was ITEK, a high-tech camera company that made spy equipment for the United States government and whose president, since at least February of 1962, was CIA officer Frank Lindsay. This was the same Frank Lindsay who originally brought Otto Skorzeny into CIA covert networks in 1949, and who directed Colonel Boris Pash's office, PB7, in the conduct of assassination operations. This was the legacy group—the long odyssey of the men who killed President John F. Kennedy is about to come to its dramatic conclusion.

CHAPTER TWENTY-ONE

THE "NETWORK"

"If you knew the facts, you would be amazed."

JACK RUBY, 1964

"Oswald leads us everywhere and nowhere."

JERRY KROTH, *CONSPIRACY IN CAMELOT*

"I said the only time that I felt that any assassination would be justified was if somebody could categorically state that if it is not done . . . and the safety of the United States was at stake on that particular action, in other words, if you don't do it, the United States is destroyed."

COLONEL BORIS T. PASH, FORMER CHIEF OF OPC BRANCH,
PB7, TO THE SENATE SELECT COMMITTEE ON
GOVERNMENT INTELLIGENCE ACTIVITIES, 1976

O n April 30, 1958, the *Greensboro Patriot* published an article by a well-known journalist of the period, Robert C. Ruark, covering a gathering in Spain of a small, eclectic group of socialites who met regularly to attend Spanish bullfights. Ruark mentioned three people in particular, Texas oil executive Jake Hamon and his wife, Nancy, and Skorzeny's business associate Ricardo Sicre of the World Commerce Corporation (WCC). Of course, Skorzeny was not named in Ruark's article, but he was at the specific bullfight mentioned by Ruark. We know this because Skorzeny himself mentioned in his papers he was in attendance. Ruark also did not mention the WCC or the fact that Ricardo Sicre was a former OSS officer. In fact, Ruark was also member of the WCC and a close friend of Sicre. This places Ruark in Skorzeny's business and social circles in Madrid, a very significant fact, as we shall see. Ruark noted that the group resembled, "a secret society of people who stride the world." In retrospect, Ruark's commentary of the Madrid social group is a very accurate description of Skorzeny's social circle. Of course, for some, but certainly not all members of the group, the biggest secret was the fact that World Commerce Corporation was an operational cover for clandestine paramilitaries originally created for Operation Compass Rose ten years earlier.

Obviously, Ruark's intention in writing the article was simply to describe for the reader the excitement of the bullfighting festival, the music, the dancing, and the camaraderie of this tight knit group. But underneath the veil of this human interest story was the inadvertent revelation of the actual group at the center of the Skorzeny–Dallas connections of 1963. What Ruark had cryptically referred to as "a secret society" consisted in fact of the individuals at the actual heart of Skorzeny's business and social network channel into Dallas, Texas.

Besides Ruark, Hamon, and Sicre, other members in this group, derived from subsequent articles and other sources, included: Frank Ryan, president of World Commerce Corporation; Victor Oswald, representative of Chase Manhattan Bank in Spain; Artie Shaw, famous jazz musician; actor William Holden; author Ernest Hemingway; and numerous other celebrities and international corporate executives. Several Dallasites were also active members of the group, including Skorzeny's principal Dallas business partner Algur Meadows; Jake H. Lutzer and his wife, Dorothy; public relations executive Elizabeth Forsling; Mr. and Mrs. Royal Miller; and Elizabeth Bacon Hopkins. And, we can add to this list the famous Hollywood actress, Ava Gardner. As it turns out, Ricardo Sicre and his wife, former OSS agent Betty Lussier, were very close friends with Gardner. Incredibly, Gardner lived in a luxury apartment in downtown Madrid on the floor directly above Otto and Ilse Skorzeny! Sicre was of course aware of Skorzeny's clandestine paramilitary role as were many other OSS men at World Commerce. As for the rest of this strange mix of writers, business executives and entertainers, they were either knowingly or unknowingly cavorting with the very man (Skorzeny) selected as an official point man for privately executed covert operations.

In 1958, Skorzeny was conducting business with Ricardo Sicre and Frank Ryan although the exact nature of the business could not be determined. Skorzeny references the San Isidro festival and bull fights attended by Sicre, Ruark, and Hamon in his correspondence for May 1958. Skorzeny also had a friendship with Ava Gardner. This was confirmed to one of the authors by Gene Murphy who met Skorzeny in Spain. This occurred in 1957 when Murphy, a young U.S. Army soldier stationed in Germany. Murphy was visiting a childhood friend in Madrid named Werner Voight, Jr. Voight's parents lived in the apartment directly below Skorzeny. Murphy related that while he was at the Voigts, Skorzeny came by to visit and Murphy got a chance to meet him. He also got a glimpse of Ava Gardner, but only for a moment when she arrived at the apartment.

Werner Voigt, Sr. was business partner of Skorzeny and is mentioned in Skorzeny's papers. This automatically places Voight in the World Commerce circle of business associates. Gene Murphy would later recall that the thing that struck him as unusual was when he was informed that Skorzeny was "working for the United States Air Force." That was in fact correct. The Skorzeny papers confirm that he had had received a formal USAF contract for base construction with the 3977th Support Group of the Sixteenth Air Force that year. Skorzeny was evidently providing pipes and metal rebar for the base projects. This again, was another example of a potential cover for operations. The reader may recall, that William Harvey had used the USAF contract office as a cover for the Berlin Operations Base only a few years earlier.

ANALYZING THE SKORZENY NETWORK IN DALLAS

Above, the author revealed the social network connected to Skorzeny and the corporate executives of World Commerce. The question arises as to who in this network knew Otto Skorzeny was a paramilitary adviser and director within the network? The answer is not easily discerned, and much more research will be needed to uncover the full story. However, there can be no doubt Skorzeny's network extended into Dallas, a fact never revealed by the Warren Commission that included Allen Dulles. Skorzeny's Dallas business and social circles were *the* critical piece for carrying out the assassination of President Kennedy. Importantly, their association with Skorzeny raises the level of suspicion for their involvement in the assassination.

Ruark's self described "secret society" has not received the attention of historians before this book, especially in regard to Skorzeny or the assassination of JFK. In addition to his newspaper writings, Ruark's personal papers, located at the University of North Carolina Wilson Library, reveal an amazing alignment to the Skorzeny papers. The Ruark papers are another unexploited document resource and potential treasure trove of new discoveries concerning the JFK assassination. A review of the Ruark papers by this author did confirm that Ruark's business network, specifically the World Commerce Corporation, overlapped with that of Otto Skorzeny. These will be looked at in detail below and in the pages ahead the author will isolate some critical activities of the Ruark social group placing them into the context of other activities linking them to both Otto Skorzeny and the Dallas affair.

The common bottom-up approach of focusing on the activities of Lee Harvey Oswald for attempting to unravel the mysteries of the JFK assassination has resulted in a lack of understanding concerning key aspects of what actually happened. This book takes a fundamentally different approach and addresses the problem from a strategic perspective, while focusing on Otto Skorzeny— and more specifically on what was revealed by the Skorzeny papers. By carefully analyzing Skorzeny's Dallas business network, we can see for the first time a coherent covert assassination operation.

On the day President John F. Kennedy was shot in Dallas, Texas, Otto Skorzeny was in Madrid, Spain, and his wife, Ilse, was in New York. The couple was outwardly tending to routine business concerns related to their business network of contacts in the United States. Actually, this was far from the case, and to an unknowing world, the events being played out in Dallas were actually intimately linked to Skorzeny's business network, which was operating as a private intelligence (and paramilitary) apparatus within the World Commerce

Corporation. This clandestine arrangement was known and monitored by the Central Intelligence Agency. The evidence shows that Skorzeny's network had access to and control of essential operational elements necessary for an assassination, the structure to deflect participation, and the ability synchronize the entire affair.

Here the author will use three descriptive groups for ease of understanding and apply them to the analysis of the Skorzeny papers and the networks found in them. The groups are: the action arm, those individuals responsible for the assassination; the deception group, those responsible for the cover story and setup of a scapegoat; and the support elements, those in charge of communications, transportation, logistics, security, safe houses, and other operational necessities.

The network also had to respond to an apparently unexpected situation when Lee Harvey Oswald, who was clearly alerted immediately after the assassination, suspected a set-up and altered his activities. To eliminate this threat of exposure to the entire group, another man also linked directly to the Skorzeny network, Jack Ruby, was sent in to liquidate Oswald.

ACTION ARM

It has been a matter of public record since 1977 from information in declassified government documents that former OAS captain Jean Rene Souetre was also present in Dallas, Texas, on November 22, 1963. We have previously established Captain Souetre's association with Otto Skorzeny. It is clear someone dispatched Souetre to Dallas and at the time he was part of Skorzeny's network. With his history as an OAS assassination expert and Algerian combat experience, Souetre had the nerves, the skill, and the reliability to be the chief agent in the Dallas assassination operation. As such, Souetre represents the action arm of the plan. What is not known is who may have accompanied Souetre. It would be logical to assume however, given his background, he was the handpicked leader of a small team of operators that carried out the actual shooting of JFK.

DECEPTION GROUP

In the realm of literature on the assassination, much has been written on Lee Harvey Oswald. The Warren Commission, after quickly gathering and examining evidence, determined that Oswald was a lone gunman. This conclusion is not compatible with the network analysis of the Skorzeny papers, which clearly points to Oswald as a fall guy for the operation. Simply put, Oswald was manipulated and used as a deception, designed to draw attention away from the Skorzeny network. The manipulators of Oswald, already the subject of suspicion by historians, were mostly members of the Russian émigré community. This included George de Mohrenschildt, Paul Raigorodsky, George Bouhe, and others. However, deeply hidden in the background facts on Oswald were clues to the Skorzeny network, but only if you know what to look for. Raigorodsky did give just such a clue in his testimony before the Warren Commission. He mentioned that an important group that assisted in Dallas was the Tolstoy Foundation, a Russian émigré support group. This comment was not given any particular weight by the Warren commission, but in reality, the Tolstoy Foundation was a major secret arm of the Skorzeny network. This will be discussed in more shorty.

It is a well documented fact of history, that George de Mohrenschildt, the fifty-one-year-old Russian émigré and petroleum geologist, had befriended Oswald in Dallas in the months preceding the assassination of President Kennedy. Some have also suspected de Mohrenschildt was acting as an agent of deception. The evidence presented in this chapter will weigh heavily in this direction. As we shall see, de Mohrenschildt was intimately associated with people within the Skorzeny business networks of Dallas. It is the opinion of the author that de Mohrenschildt was a secret agent within the Skorzeny network. Furthermore, he was specifically tasked to create smoke screens concerning Oswald, setting the stage for his use as a fall guy. Chief among these tasks was establishing Oswald as being mentally unbalanced.

Some evidence in this regard is found in the run up to the Kennedy assassination in an odd shooting incident reported carried out by Lee Harvey Oswald. The central character in this event was a retired U.S. Army major general named Edwin Walker. General Walker was a Texan and graduate of the United States

Military Academy at West Point. He had a very distinguished combat record during World War II leading a unit of the Canadian–American First Special Service Force. This unit saw heavy fighting in Italy. After the war, Walker advanced through the military ranks and in various positions. He was also highly vocal of his political views which leaned far right, leading him to be a somewhat controversial military leader. Despite this political cloud, in 1959, Walker was selected by President Eisenhower to lead the 24th Infantry Division in Germany.

While commanding the 24th Infantry, Walker instituted a program called "Pro-Blue" designed to inform soldiers about Democratic ideals. However, the press got wind of the program suggesting it was linked to the John Birch Society, a highly controversial anti-Communist group considered on the extreme fringe of the far right. At this point, John F. Kennedy had been elected president presenting a high profile political dilemma for the new chief executive.

The article led Secretary Robert McNamara to relieve General Walker of his command and directed a military inquiry to investigate the accusation. Ultimately, the investigation found no wrong doing on Walker's part, but he was none the less blocked from future command by President Kennedy. Walker then retired to public life returning to Texas and becoming a vocal advocate of anti-Communism causes. He also ran a campaign for governor of Texas, but he was never successful and garnered little support. His public actions also reflected his racist views, particularly for his strong stance in support of segregation.

In February 1963, Walker began an anti-Communist tour around the nation. He made a speech on March 5, were he called on the U.S. military to "liquidate the [Communist] scourge that has descended upon the island of Cuba." Seven days later, Lee Harvey Oswald ordered a Carcano rifle by mail order using the alias "A. Hidell." On April 10, 1963, General Walker was at his home sitting in his dining room when someone took a shot at the house. The bullet barely missed the general who was reported to have been hit by fragments.

The case went unsolved and Walker blamed the attack on his political enemies. Months later, during the post-assassination investigation conducted by the Warren Commission it was established through testimony of principle witnesses that Lee Harvey Oswald had planned and executed the assassination attempt by himself. The principle account came from Oswald's wife, Marina, who suggested Lee targeted Walker because he thought he was the head of the clandestine Fascist organization. George de Mohrenschildt corroborated Marina's story and added critical observations that eventually pegged Oswald as unbalanced. Mohrenschildt referred to Oswald as "a lunatic."

Before the Kennedy assassination, police investigators had not any suspects for the Walker shooting incident. However, within hours after Oswald's arrest for the murder of the president he was also declared a suspect in the Walker case. Some historians have suspected that the Walker affair was part of the back plan to establish Oswald as unstable and a lone gunman type.

More evidence will be presented below that point to George de Mohrenschildt as a member of the Skorzeny covert network. This finding would bring into question the entire sequence of events related to the Walker shooting and present a strong case it may have been a staged event.

Before moving on from the subject of General Walker we also find a curious connection to World Commerce Corporation prior to the shooting incident of April 1963. This was a newspaper commentary coming to the defense of General Walker after he was relieved of command in 1961. The article appeared in the New Orleans *Times-Picayune*, on June 15, 1961 and was written by WCC president Frank Ryan:

> The action taken regarding Major General Edwin Walker is amazing. Is it a crime nowadays to be a patriot? Is it a crime to teach Americanism to our troops? Must a general be "relieved of command" when he is giving his troops something to fight for? Who is relieving of command those in government who are responsible for the Communist foothold in this hemisphere? Who is being "relieved of command" for other Communist favoring actions in our state department?

At a minimum the article above shows that Frank Ryan was a supporter of General Walker, it may also mean Walker was part of the "network." More research is needed.

SUPPORT ELEMENTS

Now, we will identify the support elements within the Skorzeny network. Here again, we find businesses, civic organizations, and even underworld links in Dallas that were directly linked to Otto Skorzeny. It is also worth mentioning that the Dallas mayor in 1963 was Earle Cabell, the brother of General Charles Cabell, one of the first high-level U.S. intelligence officers aware of Skorzeny's covert use.

Overall, the Skorzeny papers confirm that Dallas, Texas, was an important business location for Otto Skorzeny. He also had other important business connections in Chicago, New York City, Miami, and the Bahamas, but none of these rises to the same level of importance as Dallas in terms of his businesses. In the Texas capitol, Skorzeny had direct access not only to businesses but also to individuals and organizations with deep CIA connections. This includes the Tolstoy Foundation, which acted as a major cover for U.S. intelligence operations vetting Russian émigrés for national security or for recruiting potential espionage agents.

Since Skorzeny was, in fact, overseeing a secret covert network that extended into Dallas, he may have personally selected the city for the operation. A question then arises—was President Kennedy orchestrated into Dallas for the specific purpose of assassination or did the amazing opportunity present itself? Can it be coincidence that everything that was needed was in place in Dallas and also contained in the Skorzeny covert network? The author believes not.

SYNCHRONICITY

The key to the entire Dallas operation was synchronicity. The action arm under Souetre had to be in position at the precise moment the deception group positioned Lee Harvey Oswald as the fall guy. Oswald had met George de Mohrenschildt, a man identified in this research as a member of the deception group, in early 1963. Since the motive indicated a sense of urgency sparked by the potential disclosure of information utterly disastrous to the U.S. government, Oswald's original contact may have had other purposes. Specifically, Oswald's odd friendship with de Mohrenschildt in early 1963 may have been coincidental or for some other clandestine reason, such as covert Cuba operations. Either way Oswald was conveniently available as a stooge. The use of Oswald also brings into the equation the Texas School Book Depository. This is the building where it is claimed Oswald took the shot that killed JFK. But the book depository is also in close proximity to the infamous grassy knoll, a suspected sniper's nest in the assassination story. As we shall soon see, the Skorzeny network had a support group which controlled the book depository and the immediate area surrounding it.

THE ORDER

The order to carry out the assassination of President Kennedy necessarily originated at the highest level of the United States government. Who exactly issued the order is not known, nor do we have details of the decision-making process that led to the order. However, if we view the Skorzeny network as a weapons system (which it essentially was as a foreign leader assassination program), it could only have been activated by direct orders from the highest quarters of the government. This is reasonable to deduce, since using it would have had major geopolitical implications. Thus, it is also logical to assume that any order to carry out a strategic assassination of this magnitude came to Skorzeny verbally via a trusted agent. We do not know who delivered the fateful order.

There are two very high-level U.S. Government officials found in the Skorzeny papers. The first is Dr. Lawrence Levy, introduced here for the first time since the author was unable to determine exactly when his relationship with Otto Skorzeny began. Dr. Levy is a very obscure figure, but a man who played a major role in U.S. government scientific research from the 1950s and decades afterward. He died in 2014. At age twenty-eight, while an instructor at Massachusetts Institute of Technology, he launched a company calledAllied Research Associates Inc. Over the years he established himself as a leading defense industry executive.

In 1961, President Kennedy appointed Dr. Levy as the senior civilian representative for Defense Secretary Robert McNamara. His area of responsibilities included Europe, North Africa, and the Middle East as well as defense adviser to Thomas Finletter, U.S. Ambassador to NATO. As the senior civilian NATO adviser, he also worked with the NATO commander General Lyman L. Lemnitzer. There is one, undated document of correspondence between Dr. Levy and Ilse Skorzeny, in the Skorzeny papers. It is written on Allied Research Letterhead and contains Dr. Levy's itinerary in Europe, so that Ilse could arrange a meeting with him. Specifics as to the agenda are not given, but the letter clearly indicates they know each other well, and the nature of their business is some government business of a clandestine nature. Based on analysis of the letterhead the author estimated the letter was written around 1964. It is a stunning revelation that Otto and Ilse had this high level of contact during this period. Dr. Levy was essentially at the Presidential level of government.

The other high-ranking U.S. government official in the Skorzeny papers is the former Assistant Secretary of Defense E. Perkins McGuire of which much has already been covered in this book. After the election of President Kennedy in 1960, McGuire left his office as part of the outgoing Eisenhower administration, but reentered service as an executive contract officer for the CIA. Given his rank with the government and his intimate knowledge of covert programs, Perkins McGuire is a logical choice to have been a messenger. However, I caution the reader, this remains unconfirmed.

There can be no doubt the covert network connected to Skorzeny carried out the Dallas assassination of JFK. However, there is no incontrovertible evidence he directed the operation. At the first level of analysis this a moot point since Skorzeny managed an assassination capability in the network, not to mention it was the Skorzeny papers that revealed the network. He would certainly have been aware of its use. These facts may also relate to the letter written by Frenchman Paul Gluc found in the opening pages of this book that spoke of Skorzeny having "guilt" in the matter of the assassination.

Certainly, this book has verified that there were a considerable number of U.S. military and CIA personnel who were fully aware of Otto Skorzeny's relationship with U.S intelligence, his school of commando tactics, and his private paramilitary group. Logically, only a fraction of those with any knowledge of his organization would have known of his involvement with highly sensitive assassination missions.

No known declassified government document evidences Otto Skorzeny's use as an assassination asset, although his profile and activities parallel to a great degree the CIA QJ/WIN assassination program. Destruction of evidence, falsification, use of ciphers, and deception can be expected both in the planning and the aftermath of such activity. Certainly, all government documents relating to this subject may have been destroyed. The existence of Skorzeny's personal papers, however, allows for the confirmation of a clandestine network capable of such operations. Even so, it can only be derived through careful analysis of the organizational and personal relationships contained within them. A very significant main point is the fact that senior American officials with clandestine links to Skorzeny are also individuals documented in history as the architects and controllers of U.S. covert operations, including assassination.

Any investigation of assassination programs must proceed with caution and suspicion. Incomplete or false information can facilitate unsubstantiated conclusions. Many of those closest to Skorzeny, whether friend, business associate, or even within the U.S. government, likely knew nothing of his network's capability for assassination work. The author was extremely vigilant in his analysis—guilt by association is not sufficient evidence for collusion in a study on assassination programs. It is also certain that any involvement of Skorzeny with assassination was compartmented and on a strict need-to-know basis. History has shown how mere association can be extraordinarily benign. For example, who would have believed that Vice President Harry Truman did not know of the atomic bomb before the death of President Roosevelt, had he not revealed it himself after the war? How much more closely associated to a government could a person be, and yet he was innocent of the atomic bomb development?

Skorzeny's experience and knowledge could not be easily duplicated, nor could his extensive network of former associates who served as his staff and operators. From these, he could tap those with the unique skills required for assassination work. This group included many different nationalities and backgrounds. Previously, we covered Skorzeny's early involvement in CIA covert operations and its associated missions. These projects utilized Ukrainians and other Eastern Europeans adept as secret agents. Skorzeny maintained Ukrainian and East European contacts throughout the Cold War period.

When analyzing Skorzeny's private assassination network, it is important to remember that the lines of demarcation between his covert network and U.S. intelligence were intentionally masked. Hence, the network was controlled solely by Skorzeny, thus allowing plausible deniability for the U.S. government. Here, we must also delineate between Skorzeny's role as a trainer for MAAG, in which assassination techniques were taught, and his role as a coordinator of U.S. government–sanctioned assassination missions. In the end, Skorzeny was in position to receive an order to carry out an executive action (i.e. high-level assassination).

THE DALLAS OPERATION IN DETAIL

A key component in Skorzeny's private network was the ability to leverage his business connections for covert operation. This means any CIA role was without signature. Skorzeny's business network could provide logistics, safe houses, communications, transportation and other important aspects needed for covert operations. He also had important underworld contacts in Dallas through his business associations that were linked to the Mafia, such as those that existed between the Mafia and the Bahama finance minister, Sir Stafford Sands. Hence, Skorzeny could also use the Mafia to his advantage either with or without the knowledge of those involved.

The specific Dallas businesses identified in the Skorzeny papers are: The General American Oil Company and its associated oil partners, such as Delta oil; Brown Raymond Walsh (BRW), a major construction outfit; and the Bahamas Development Corporation, a real estate venture headed by Sir Stafford Sands. A basic history of these connections was introduced in Chapter Eighteen.

These Skorzeny–Dallas business connections actually open up the entire Dallas universe of oil businesses, civic groups, professional organizations, state and federal government offices, law enforcement, and military. Some of these appear to be critical channels for operational exploitation.

These business connections are the ones Skorzeny could have used to facilitate all of the necessary support pieces to a covert operation in the city. Again, I remind the reader, this could have been done with or without the knowledge of people in the network, making it entirely possible that some were unwitting agents. Let's take a look.

GENERAL AMERICAN OIL COMPANY, ALGUR H. MEADOWS, AND OTHERS

As covered in Chapter Eleven, Skorzeny became involved in a major oil exploration venture in Spain headed by Algur Meadows and other Dallas oilmen, beginning in 1952. The Meadows oil venture in Spain was arranged by Hjalmar Schacht, the German banker, economist, and politician that Ilse called "uncle." In 1953, Schacht founded a banking house in Düsseldorf and became a chief financial adviser to Otto Skorzeny.

An additional company involved with the oil venture and other Spanish development projects was Brown Raymond Walsh (BRW), which was also selected as the contract representative for the USAF base in Morón. BRW, also known as Brown and Root, rose to prominence under Texas politician Lyndon Baines Johnson. As a senator Johnson was a lead promoter of the BRW contracts for building air bases in Spain, France, and Guam. This is now a curious fact, as Otto Skorzeny managed to secure, and in fact handled, a major portion of BRW contracts in Spain. Did LBJ have knowledge of the Skorzeny–BRW contracts? Much of the BRW business dealt with steel projects going through contracts that Skorzeny set up through ARMCO steel. The reader will recall that Skorzeny became an ARMCO representative around 1950, working with Colonel Robert A. Solborg. This was part of the cover setup for Donovan's "Special Paramilitary Group" (a term created by the author for this book).

Skorzeny stated in an interview with CIA officer Daniel E. Wright in 1958, that from 1954 through 1958 he handled 20 percent of all the subcontractors European purchases for the United States air bases in Spain. These contracts amounted to $2 million. In supplying sub-contractors with German steel and other materials for the bases, he handled further contracts totaling another

$1 million. At the time Skorzeny secured the BRW contracts for base construction, E. Perkins McGuire was Assistant Secretary of Defense for Logistics.

Another company that was involved in the Meadows's Spain oil venture was DeGolyer & MacNaughton. The vice president and director of DeGolyer & MacNaughton was Dallas oilman and U.S. Army intelligence officer Jack Crichton. Colonel Crichton is a man widely believed to be involved in clandestine aspects of the JFK assassination. As mentioned in an earlier chapter the colonel had served as an OSS officer in the European Theater during World War II. He also met with Skorzeny in 1952, as part of the oil group under Algur Meadows. Crichton remained in the U.S. Army Reserve after the war and by 1956 had organized a U.S. Army Intelligence unit in Dallas—the 488th Military Intelligence Detachment. The unit was tasked with strategic analysis. Colonel Crichton's ties to Skorzeny opens up the possibility it had a covert mission within the network as well. Certainly, Colonel Crichton had a secure channel to Skorzeny in Madrid via General American Oil Company.

General American Oil was located in the Meadows Building, one of the more modern high-rise offices in Dallas in the 1950s. The Dallas Club, an elite high society establishment, was located in the Meadows Building and was also a popular gambling operation. After the JFK assassination, the FBI looked into one "Albert Meadows"—a noted gambler and associate of Jack Ruby who was said to frequent the Dallas Club. These reports may have been a ruse to deflect attention *away* from Algur H. Meadows.

Meadows was a passionate collector of Spanish art, especially El Greco and Goya, and traveled often to Madrid in pursuit of art treasures. Obviously, Meadows would visit Skorzeny and Ilse on these trips. It will be remembered that in 1963, Otto Skorzeny was involved in international art dealing—the documented profession of the mysterious CIA asset QJ/WIN.

COLONEL (JUDGE) GORDON SIMPSON

Meadow's principal business partner was Colonel Gordon Simpson, of whom much has already been written about in this book. Both men stand out in the

Skorzeny papers and are significant contacts. It was Judge Simpson, in his position as a judge advocate officer, who examined the evidence in the Colonel Peiper case previously discussed. Simpson was also in communication with Skorzeny and visited him at least once in Madrid in 1958. In that year, Simpson was listed as president of General American Oil.

In December 1955, the Meadows Building was completed, with Algur Meadows as executive chairman and Gordon Simpson as president. Prior to this move, the offices of General American Oil were located in the Republic National Bank Building. Some historians have determined that the Republic National Bank was a location for CIA offices in Dallas. Like many oil executives in Dallas, Meadows and Simpson were members of the Dallas Council on World Affairs (DCWA). The February 1958 letterhead for the council lists Judge Gordon Simpson, as treasurer, and General American Oil owner Algur Meadows as a member of the board of directors. This places Otto Skorzeny's network directly into the heart of the DCWA organization, which included geologist George de Mohrenschildt among others of note connected to Lee Harvey Oswald.

COLONEL ROBERT G. STOREY

After the Kennedy assassination, Colonel Storey, a senior legal officer in Dallas mentioned at various points in this book was appointed as a special counsel to the attorney general of Texas. This was essentially a liaison to the Warren Commission. Colonel Storey was present in the Dallas jail cell when Chief Justice Earl Warren met with Jack Ruby. Evidence was previously presented confirming Colonel Storey's role in high-level CIA psychological warfare in Germany throughout the 1950s. These programs included Otto Skorzeny. Storey may have known Skorzeny then, or during his time as a military judge during the Nuremberg Trials immediately after the war. In any case, Colonel Storey served on a number of boards and committees with the above-named Algur H. Meadows and Judge Gordon Simpson, Skorzeny's principal Dallas oil business associates.

One of Colonel Storey's intimate friends was Leonidas (Leon) Jaworski, a Dallas attorney who was also a close friend of, and lawyer for, Lyndon B. Johnson. After the assassination of JFK, Jaworski and Colonel Storey launched an immediate and independent Texas-based investigation of the assassination under authority granted by the Texas attorney general.

Although Justice Warren ultimately did not authorize the independent Texas-based investigation or the inclusion of Texans on the Warren Commission for fear of public skepticism, he did allow Storey and Jaworski to handle the Texas end of the investigation for the commission under a compromise. Under the conditions of this agreement, the Texas attorneys were also allowed to have a member of their group present at every commission hearing. In this special capacity, they monitored closely the entire proceedings, including the testimony of George de Mohrenschildt, the closest contact to Lee Harvey Oswald.

SIR STAFFORD SANDS

Beginning in 1951, Sir Stafford Sands, finance minister of the Bahamas, came to Dallas, Texas to drum up business in Dallas for an organization called the Bahamas Development Board. His main business contacts were Algur Meadows and Leo Corrigan. The formation of the board was announced in the Dallas Morning News on April 15, 1951, by Sands. The board was to work with travel agents and transportation companies.

Sands's partner, Leo Corrigan, was a highly influential Dallas power player active in major construction projects. As part of his partnership with Sands, he built the Emerald Beach Hotel in the Bahamas. Algur Meadows and his wife would stay at Emerald Beach Hotel on their many jaunts to the Caribbean. The Emerald is also where President Kennedy and British Defense Minister Macmillan met in 1962. It will be recalled that Macmillan was brought down by the Profumo Affair.

Since Corrigan is connected to the Skorzeny network through Sir Stafford Sands and Algur Meadows, it will likely astonish the reader to see the list of Leo Corrigan's links to the Kennedy assassination. Perhaps leading the list is the fact that Leo Corrigan was Jack Ruby's landlord, holding the lease on Ruby's night clubs. In fact, Ruby called Corrigan "the Boss."

It was Leo Corrigan who built the Republic National Bank using the same architects who built the CIA building in Washington. In 1951, Gordon

Simpson was listed as chairman of the bank, with Algur H. Meadows as trustee. Also, Corrigan owned the Adolphus Hotel, where Marina Oswald stayed after the assassination. Marina's connection to this group continues to expand, as Gordon Simpson was affiliated with the law firm of Thompson & Knight, an outfit associated with the Great Southwestern Corp., which provided Marina Oswald with legal assistance after the assassination.

Details concerning Sands connections to the Mafia have already been discussed including his association with Meyer Lansky. The full extent of Skorzeny's involvement with the Mafia has not yet been fully determined. We do know Skorzeny was involved in real estate, gambling, and gambling machines in the Bahamas that overlap into Mafia-run operations. The author suspects that Otto and Ilse Skorzeny became associated with Sands through Algur Meadows, who was supporting Bahamas development projects at the same time he was conducting his oil operations in Spain. The reader may also recall that Tex McCrary, the famous radio host and entertainment specialist, was part of this same Bahamas business group. The CIA officer that handled the Caribbean desk was James Angleton.

THE DECEPTION GROUP

A central character in the history of the assassination of President John F. Kennedy is George de Mohrenschildt, the man who befriended Lee Harvey Oswald in early 1963. Although de Mohrenschildt is not found in the Skorzeny papers, he has several distinct associations and activities that lend convincing evidence he was part of the Skorzeny network. Mohrenschildt would later garner fame as a key witness in the Warren Commission investigation of the Kennedy assassination.

Described by the commission as a "highly individualistic person of varied interest," George de Mohrenschildt hailed from an Russian aristocratic family, having arrived in the United States in the years just prior to World War II. He held a master's degree in petroleum geology and was very well connected in Dallas executive oil business circles. In his Warren Commission testimony, he claimed to have worked for French intelligence prior to World War II, gathering information on pro-German activity in the states. He had also applied for a position during the war with General Donovan's Office of Strategic Services (OSS) but was rejected after an investigation that suggested he might be a Nazi agent. This may have been true, and if so, opens up a possibility he was known to Skorzeny even during the war. The SS office in the Third Reich that controlled Skorzeny's commando also controlled foreign agents in the United States. Also, De Mohrenschildt's own statement concerning his work with French intelligence brings in the possibility he was a former asset of some French intelligence officer in the Skorzeny network.

In fact, digging deeper, we find George de Mohrenschildt's associations with Skorzeny appear to have developed very early on in the historical timeline covered in this book. As a starting point, it should be noted that Mohrenschildt worked closely in the early 1940s with a man described as either his uncle or cousin, Baron Konstantine Maydell. Along with Merwin K. Hart, an American businessman from New York, the two embarked on the promotion of the pro-Franco film, *Spain in Arms*. Hart was a well-known anti-Semite and founder of an organization called the National Economic Council, or NEC. Established in 1931, the NEC opposed the economic policies of President Franklin D. Roosevelt and supported the fascist regime of Francisco Franco in Spain.

In the 1950s, Hart was also in league with several well-known Nazi sympathizers, including a New York advertising executive named Allen Zoll. In 1949, Zoll founded the American Intelligence Agency. Unfortunately, the author could not find further details on this mysterious organization. Zoll and Hart received backing from Dallas oilman H. L. Hunt, who in the 1950s promoted both men through his radio show *Facts Forum*.

The men involved in this fascist promotion ring were being monitored closely by U.S. law enforcement, and their activities finally received national attention in the press after authorities arrested key individuals associated with the promotion schemes. This included Baron Maydell, who was arrested and held under Federal detention during the war. Evidently, de Mohrenschildt had avoided notice by authorities and left New York before the bomb dropped on the others.

But the above activity of de Mohrenschildt takes on great importance after the war, when Skorzeny became a close business partner with Merwin K. Hart. In fact, Hart and his NEC were a major part of Skorzeny's international commercial network and are found throughout the Skorzeny papers. This effectively means that a principal postwar business partner of Otto Skorzeny was once himself in business with George de Mohrenschildt. Also, it is an established fact that the planning sessions for the pro-Franco film, *Spain in Arms*, which would have included de Mohrenschildt, were held in Merwin K. Hart's New York City office!

Two other associates of Hart who were postwar members of Skorzeny's business network were Freda Utley, an English scholar who was a former member of General Donovan's OSS and New York lawyer Clifford Forster, mentioned in several chapters of this book. Skorzeny's overt relationship with Hart, Utley, and Forster dealt with promoting European imports and exports and European capital investment schemes. These activities also gave Skorzeny access to a wide range of European business networks, which he could use for intelligence or operational purposes. The extent to which Hart and Utley had knowledge of Skorzeny's covert activity cannot be accurately determined, but evidence indicates Clifford Forster was an intelligence operative.

THE PIERRE AND JACQUES VILLERES—A PERMINDEX CONNECTION?

Previously, the author outlined Clifford Forster's connection to *Paix et Liberté* and several American support groups that align to CIA psychological operations. During the initial period of his contact with Skorzeny, Forster was working in the international office of Bauerlein, Inc. an advertising company out of New York. A high-ranking company official at Bauerlein was Pierre Villere, a native of New Orleans, Louisiana. Villere was also a Reserve Army intelligence officer. In 1948, Pierre Villere joined the advertising firm Bauerlein, Inc. as an account executive. By 1951 he was vice-president of the company, and from 1959–1967 he was executive vice-president. During World War II, Villere served as an intelligence liaison officer to the French who had set up a station in Venezuela. His contact there was a man who is mentioned frequently in this book, Jacques Soustelle, later with the OAS and Otto Skorzeny.

Pierre Villere's older brother of was Jacques Villere, a banker who lived in Dallas, Texas. Jacques Villere was an international financial officer at the Mercantile Bank in Dallas, Texas. He moved from New Orleans to Dallas in 1946. He was a member of First Unitarian Church and president of the church men's group that included Michael Paine, a friend of Lee Harvey Oswald.

Jacques Villere was also a cofounder of the Dallas Export-Import Club and a member of the foreign trade committee of the Dallas Chamber of Commerce. He knew many of the principle oil and businessmen of Dallas mentioned in this chapter. Both Pierre and Jacques Villere were acquainted with Clay Shaw, a controversial businessman from New Orleans who was brought to trial in 1967 by New Orleans District Attorney Jim Garrison, who believed Shaw was involved in a conspiracy to kill President Kennedy. However, Garrison focused solely on Shaw as the central character in the plot and therefore brought into question men who had nothing to do with the actual conspiracy. In simplest terms, the Garrison trial was focused on individuals who were not in the same network orbit as the Skorzeny group but were remotely linked to it. Thus, Shaw was ultimately found not guilty on all of the conspiracy charges.

Researchers have also revealed that Shaw was associated with an international company called Permindex. That company is also linked to Skorzeny, but the network analysis is highly complex. The research for this book indicates Clay Shaw was on the outer edge of the true conspiracy through his association with the Villeres. It is possible, that Jim Garrison might have found his way to the Skorzeny network, had he not been disrupted by external factors and had a means to develop link analysis. In the end, the Clay Shaw connection is interesting, but not critical for reaching any of the findings in this book or, most importantly, the conclusions concerning the Skorzeny network's role in Dallas.

LEE HARVEY OSWALD

The author has determined that Lee Harvey Oswald was a deception, set up by the Skorzeny network of operatives in Dallas. The deception group was the Dallas Russian community, including George de Mohrenschildt and others. They made contact with Oswald and began to "process" him for exploitation. *The initial purpose may not have been for assassination but some other use.* But, at some point, when the assassination was ordered, Oswald was placed as the fall guy.

He may not have been the only fall guy prepared by the network in Dallas. We must also bear in mind that Skorzeny's network existed in other cities, creating the possibility that there were similar operations being planned at other locations around the country.

The deception group monitored Oswald and maneuvered him into position at the Texas School Book Depository, setting him up as the patsy. The presence in Dallas of the Skorzeny network and its contact with Oswald destroys the lone gunman theory. Further study into the Skorzeny connections to Dallas may allow for the full exposure of Oswald's story. Time will tell.

Since Oswald's behavior immediately after the shooting of Kennedy is both frantic and filled with inexplicable events, it appears Oswald may have realized his vulnerable position and was attempting to take flight. Whatever the circumstances, his liquidation was necessary to prevent the exposure of the entire network. This will lead us to Jack Ruby.

THE RUSSIANS IN DALLAS—THE SKORZENY NETWORK'S BIG LINK TO LEE HARVEY OSWALD

Lee Harvey Oswald had arrived in Texas in June 1962. Less than a week later, he was in contact with a Russian exile named Peter Gregory in Fort Worth. Oswald wanted to get a letter verifying his proficiency in speaking Russian. Gregory was an oil engineer and active among the White Russian and East European émigrés in Dallas. Here we have a highly significant clue into the heart of Otto Skorzeny's network, and the deep beginnings of his involvement with the city of Dallas. Let's examine the Dallas Russian community in more detail . . . *This connection is paramount to understanding the Skorzeny network deception group that manipulated Lee Harvey Oswald.*

"MR. MARTIN"—AGAIN

On December 18, 1950, David Martin, Executive Director of the International Rescue Committee (IRC), and his special assistant, Dr. Richard Salzman, arrived in Dallas. This is the same David Martin who had secretly met with Otto Skorzeny and Ilse in January 1949, bringing them into the intelligence network assembled by the CIA that included the International Relief Organization (IRO) and World Commerce Corporation (WCC). By 1950, the IRO had changed its name to the International Rescue Committee (IRC). Martin had arrived in Dallas to promote support for displaced scholars and scientists being relocated to the city. The event took place at the Baker Hotel and was backed financially by the Dallas Council on World Affairs. This event and the subsequent establishment of the White Russian community in Dallas by Martin and the IRC confirm that it was an extension of the very same covert intelligence operations set up with Otto Skorzeny less than two years earlier. At the time of Martin's arrival in Dallas, Skorzeny had just arrived in Madrid and was being fully integrated into CIA commercial and business covers, including those leading to Dallas.

Martin informed the assembled Dallas businessmen of IRC's plans for bringing over 2,000 top men of science and letters from Europe to the United States and placing them in areas where they were needed. He stated in a newspaper interview, "These 2,000 plus displaced scholars and scientists are the cream of a crop of 25,000 exiled professionals abroad who have fled from Communist countries. These scholars and professionals include engineers, medical doctors, journalists, veterinarians, artists, dentists, geologists, chemists, political scholars, legal experts, architects and professors of the technical sciences, the humanities and the arts."

Dr. Salzman added, "They are people Russia would pay heavily to import. They are men who would not only enrich our American culture but could be of infinite value to our war and defense efforts." Each of the refugees was to have a guarantee of a sponsor, housing, and work. Then Martin revealed his hidden association with U.S. intelligence, stating, "Each person is screened by the United States Army Counter Intelligence Corps. We work very closely with the government and the military. Each person is also screened by the Displaced Person Commission. And perhaps the most important screening is that given by his fellow refugees." The Martin trip to Dallas in the winter of 1950 had effectively opened the city to a number of potential foreign intelligence assets working directly with or for Otto Skorzeny.

It should also be pointed out at this juncture that one of Otto Skorzeny's principal business partners, Colonel Robert Solborg, former OSS deputy and European representative of Armco Steel, was himself a White Russian émigré and very well connected in White Russian circles. It is also worth recalling, that David Martin, after leaving the IRO went to work as a senior aide to Senator Thomas Dodd, who sent Martin to the Congo at the same time Skorzeny's network was operating in the African country.

The above facts spotlight the deep backstory on how George de Mohrenschildt came to know Lee Harvey Oswald. Both de Mohrenschildt and his wife claimed to have met Oswald and Marina *by chance* in the fall of 1962 through introductions made by their friends in the Dallas Russian community.

There is also information concerning de Mohrenschildt's contact with the head of the CIA Domestic Contact Division in Dallas, J. Walton Moore and their discussions about Oswald. During the Warren Commission testimony, de Mohrenschildt stated he knew Moore as "a government man—either FBI or Central Intelligence," and that they saw each other "from time to time." De Mohrenschildt claimed he approached Moore because of Oswald's former defector status, and he wanted to make sure the contact with Oswald was not putting him (de Mohrenschildt) at risk of being involved with a foreign agent.

The details of what actually transpired between de Mohrenschildt and Moore will likely never be known. Given what we know about the Skorzeny covert network in Dallas and de Mohrenschildt's solid links to it, one might assume the Moore contact is significant, but I remind the reader that the Skorzeny network and its operations were highly compartmentalized. Even though Moore was a senior CIA officer in Dallas and should have been aware of Oswald (which he was), it does not mean he was part of a Skorzeny assassination network. In other words, he may not have been "in the know" or "cleared" for the operation.

In the end, the evidence for inclusion in the Skorzeny network is directly on de Mohrenschildt as an operative of Otto Skorzeny's network. The Russian community connection is an incredible historical fact when one considers that a dedicated, Skorzeny-lead covert network was in place in Dallas *years* before the decision and necessity to kill JFK emerged.

DE MOHRENSCHILDT AND JUDGE DUVALL

During the post-assassination investigations, it came to the attention of the FBI that George de Mohrenschildt had met with Judge Jesse C. Duvall of Fort Worth, Texas, and discussed helping Lee Harvey Oswald. This meeting is remarkable, since Judge Duvall had been the presiding judge during the trial of Otto Skorzeny in 1947. The details of the trial have already been rendered in Chapter Four, including the meeting directly after the trial when Skorzeny presented Duvall with a decorative knife as a gift. Now, fourteen years after Judge Duvall had met with Skorzeny, de Mohrenschildt was meeting directly with Judge Duvall over the topic of Lee Harvey Oswald!

Judge Duvall gave an overview of the meeting to the FBI and the circumstances that led to it, now found in a declassified FBI report. The report states that Duvall first met George de Mohrenschildt and his wife in January 1963. He stated that an article on de Mohrenschildt's interesting travels through Mexico had caught his attention and, in his role as director of the local chapter of the Good Neighbor Council, he thought de Mohrenschildt would be a great speaker for the group. This led to correspondence between the two and ultimately to de Mohrenschildt's public speaking engagement for the Good Neighbors at the Ridgelea Country Club that same month. After the program, the judge invited de Mohrenschildt and his wife to stay over at his house.

One month later, de Mohrenschildt reciprocated, inviting the judge and his wife to a dinner in Dallas. The invitation was by letter, which also indicated that the de Mohrenschildt's would be leaving for Haiti "in the near future." The judge accepted the dinner invitation, and it was during the dinner that de Mohrenschildt brought up the possibility of the judge assisting Lee Harvey Oswald with his dishonorable discharge. De Mohrenschildt gave all the details of Oswald's defection to Russia and subsequent return to the United States.

At some point during the conversation over dinner, the two attempted to call Oswald on the telephone but were unable to reach him. Judge Duvall ended his interview with the FBI by stating that after the failed attempt to reach Oswald "the matter was dropped" and there was no further discussion on the subject.

Judge Duvall also informed the FBI of an incident that occurred on Sunday, November 24, 1963, the day Lee Harvey Oswald was killed. This involved one Roy Pike, a man described in FBI reports as Jack Ruby's bookkeeper. Evidently, the judge knew Pike from a court case while Pike was serving in the USAF in 1943. At that time, Pike was charged in a rape case, which ultimately resulted in a friendship of sorts between Pike and Judge Duvall.

Fast forward—"two or three hours after Oswald had been shot," Pike showed up at Judge Duvall's front door in Fort Worth and told him that Oswald had been seen at Ruby's club on numerous occasions and "had been there just recently." Pike worked at the club under the alias Tommy Ryan. Pike told the judge that came to get his opinion "as to what punishment *Ruby* would get for the crime he just committed." Judge Duvall also told the FBI that Pike explained to him how he came to work for Ruby.

The Pike incident is odd. Based on Judge Duvall's information, the FBI subsequently interviewed Pike and his wife. Their residence was in Hollywood, California but due to a marital spat, Pike had moved back to Dallas in September when he began working at Ruby's nightclubs, the Carousel and Vegas, as a bartender. Then in the first part of October, Pike moved back to California. Pike said he first met Ruby in 1962 and worked for a time as his bookkeeper. About a week before the President was shot Pike asked Ruby for a loan, but Ruby did not give him money. Pike claimed he did not know Oswald. He also told the FBI he had known Judge Duvall for twenty-five years, ever since his acquittal.

Nothing ever became of the FBI investigation into Judge Duvall or Roy Pike and the story was lost in the mountain of evidence compiled for the Warren Commission investigation. Further research is likely in order.

PAUL RAIGORODSKY

Another White Russian émigré from the community in Dallas critical for understanding the Skorzeny network is Paul Raigorodsky. He was a friend and neighbor of George de Mohrenschildt. Raigorodsky lived at Leo Corrigan's Stoneleigh Hotel in Dallas where de Mohrenschildt had also lived. The two were members of several oil and civic associations as well.

Born in Russia in 1898, Raigorodsky had immigrated to the United States and lived in Texas "off and on" since 1921. As in expert in petroleum operations he was called upon during World War II to serve on the War Production Board. Raigorodsky testified before the Warren Commission because of his friendship with George de Mohrenschildt and his contact with Lee Harvey Oswald. He related to the commission that he arrived in Washington to organize the Department of Natural Gas and Natural Gasoline Industries for the United States, which he did under the oil company DeGolyer. After establishing several offices around the country, he resigned in 1943 for health reasons and returned to his personal oil business in Houston.

In 1950, Raigorodsky transferred to Dallas at the behest of a very close friend, oil executive Jake Hamon. Shortly after, in 1952, Raigorodsky was selected to serve in an organization in Europe called the Special Representatives to Europe (SRE). He was handpicked for the position by Fred L. Anderson, another Dallas native, who was also serving in Europe as deputy to the chief of the SRE. At the time of his appointment Raigorodsky was given a top-secret office in Paris, the headquarters at the time for NATO. In an interview concerning his position, Raigorodsky said, "We use the word defense—not war."

The timing of Raigorodsky's arrival in Paris for this important SRE assignment coincides precisely with the Spain oil initiative involving Otto Skorzeny and the Dallas executive oil group under Algur Meadows. This means Paul Raigorodsky would have been fully aware of, and perhaps one of the approving authorities for, the Dallas–Spain oil venture. The importance of this occurrence cannot be overstated.

RAIGORODSKY AND THE TOLSTOY FOUNDATION—THE SKORZENY NETWORK LINK

After examining his oil background, Raigorodsky, considered an expert in the Russian émigré community in Dallas, described the Russian community in Dallas. He also explained to the Commission the vetting procedures of the foundation and his personal relationship with George de Mohrenschildt and Lee Harvey Oswald.

Raigorodsky stated that the centerpiece behind the Russian community was the Tolstoy Foundation and proceeded to give a short history. He stated that it had been founded by Miss Alexandra Tolstoy, the daughter of novelist, Leo Tolstoy, after she had arrived in the United States.

He pointed out that the Tolstoy Foundation processed Russian refugees with the assistance of various organizations and churches across the country. Through this method the Tolstoy Foundation was, in Raigorodsky's words, "able to place many, many Russians in this country" and in other countries. He also indicated the process was very thorough, "anybody who comes to the Tolstoy Foundation, you know right off of the bat they have been checked, rechecked and double checked. There is no question about them. I mean, that's the No. 1 stamp."

Other information related by Raigorodsky clearly indicated he was an important officer in the foundations operations, and told the Commission, "I am on the Board of Directors of the Tolstoy Foundation–but also in European countries." Here we find a *decisive* link to the Skorzeny network.

In his capacity as member of the Tolstoy Foundation Board of Directors, Paul Raigorodsky would have worked directly with Colonel Herschel V. Williams, also a member of the board. Colonel Williams was the USAF intelligence officer and boss of Ilse Skorzeny's in the international division of Previews, Inc. in New York. He was in daily contact with Ilse and corresponded with Otto frequently. This is strong evidence that Colonel Williams was "in the know" concerning operations in Dallas. Also, Previews Inc. had an active office in Dallas at the time. The document that confirms beyond any doubt that Colonel Williams worked with Raigorodsky is found in the Appendix. Colonel Williams' name is second from the bottom on the list. The document is dated November 16, 1962.

SMOKING GUN

The Tolstoy link takes on even greater significance with the knowledge that the Tolstoy Foundation is a documented front organization for the CIA émigré program, supporting the recruitment of covert operators. There are several former OSS and intelligence personnel on the board who had experience in handling covert émigré operations. Overall the foundation served as a communications, logistics and operations network for clandestine activity. With this one document, the Skorzeny network is confirmed to be embedded in the Tolstoy Foundation, the Dallas Russian community, and CIA covert networks. Furthermore, Raigorodsky's testimony on the Tolstoy Foundation clearly indicates that Lee and Marina Oswald were known to and vetted by the organization. This confirms that Skorzeny and his network had direct access to all information concerning Oswald, thus permitting the planning necessary for his manipulation. The communications link to Raigorodsky by Skorzeny via Colonel Williams goes directly to George de Mohrenschildt and Lee Harvey Oswald.

(Here too we refer back to the important NSC 10/2 Directive: Overt assistance—using public organizations to mobilize interest and support for selected émigré factions in the Unites States and Europe. Evidence amply found in the Skorzeny papers by virtue of Colonel Williams involvement in the Tolstoy Foundation.)

In the brief review of the testimony before the Warren Commission by Raigorodsky, we found the name of his close friend and associate Dallas oil executive Jake Hamon. We will now turn our historical investigation directly on Hamon who plays prominently in the background of George de Mohrenschildt, Paul Raigorodsky and the Skorzeny network as a whole. Both de Mohrenschildt and Raigorodsky considered Hamon a close personal friend and confidant. In fact, according to Raigorodsky it was Jake Hamon who introduced Raigorodsky to de Mohrenschildt in the early 1950s. And it was Jake Hamon who recommended de Mohrenschildt for his position with the International Cooperation Administration (ICA) working in Yugoslavia in 1957. The ICA was already established in an earlier chapter as a cover organization for the CIA with imbedded Agency officers. Otto Skorzeny also worked with the ICA and is heavily documented in the Skorzeny papers for the period covering the 1950s.

JAKE HAMON

As the Skorzeny network links continue to explode onto these pages we find ourselves entering the hot center of the network with a look a Dallas oilman, Jake L. Hamon. This chapter opened with the depiction of a gathering of a social elite group from Dallas that included Otto Skorzeny attending a bull fight festival in Spain in 1958. It was the journalist Robert Ruark who accurately pointed out that one of the main personalities of this group was Jake Hamon. Who exactly was Jake Hamon and what is his significance in Skorzeny Dallas network revelation?

Jake Louis Hamon was a legendary independent Dallas oilman. He was known widely as a successful wildcatter and civic leader. He was born in Lawton, Oklahoma in 1902 and later attended the University of Chicago where he studied law. In 1920, he began his oil career in the oil fields in Eastland County, Texas. In 1923, he formed a partnership with Edwin B. Cox, which lasted over twenty years. Hamon moved the company to Dallas in 1932, where he became very active in civic and professional associations.

In 1934, he was elected Director of the American Petroleum Institute, also serving as its President. In 1961, he was asked to serve as a member of the National Petroleum Council. Importantly, Hamon was a close friend of Paul Raigorodsky and George de Mohrenschildt, men who knew Lee Harvey Oswald. Hamon also knew Algur H. Meadows and Judge Gordon Simpson. This effectively places Hamon in the center of the Skorzeny network in Dallas.

Also, outside of his mutual business interests with those mentioned above, Hamon enjoyed great camaraderie with all of them through his active participation in community arts organizations, particularly the Dallas Civic Opera. But it was Hamon's participation with the others on frequent trips from Dallas to Madrid, Spain to attend ritual overseas parties that exposes closer ties to Skorzeny.

It was in Spain where they would join the native North Carolinian, novelist, and syndicated columnist, Robert Ruark and others from the Dallas jet set "secret society," mentioned previously and including, Jake and Dorothy Lutzer, musician Artie Shaw, advertising specialist Elizabeth Forsling, Mr. and Mrs. Royal Miller, and Elizabeth Bacon Hopkins.

A closer examination of several of these individuals reveals some rather interesting facts. For example, Jake and Dorothy Lutzer were also close friends of George de Mohrenschildt, Lee Harvey Oswald's Dallas friend. Jake Lutzer, was a salesman in the motion picture and entertainment business. Their connection to de Mohrenschildt resulted in Dorothy Lutzer being called to testify before the Warren Commission. She explained to the Commission how she had been the long-time neighbor of de Mohrenschildt and shared common interests such as art. There was of course no mention of any trips to Spain. Ultimately, the Commission gave little attention to Dorothy Lutzer's testimony, considering it routine background material on de Mohrenschildt. This may be the case, but her association with de Mohrenschildt places him squarely in the Skorzeny network, a fact just as important as his association with Oswald.

Elizabeth Forsling also has some interesting facts in her background relative to the assassination of Kennedy. It is documented that Forsling assisted Jack Peuterbauch and the Bloom Advertising Agency in arranging the motorcade route of President Kennedy through Dealey Plaza. As she is part of the Skorzeny network this would appear to be significant. Add to this oddity, Forsling was not called to testify before the Warren Commission.

Then we have the former big band conductor and jazz musician, Artie Shaw. His band once rivaled the famous Glenn Miller Orchestra. During World War II, Shaw toured the combat zones to entertain troops. At one point, while in the Pacific Theater, his tent mate was a young Naval officer named E. Howard Hunt, later a famous CIA officer and central character in the Watergate scandal. However, it should be pointed out that it has not yet been determined if this brief tent mate incident is important to the Skorzeny story.

Another connection with potential importance is the fact that Shaw also knew Jack Ruby. It was Ruby who arranged for Shaw to play at Bob Wills's

Ranchhouse nightclub in Dallas in 1952 where Ruby was a manager and co-owner. But the intrigue of Artie Shaw is nearly irrepressible, as we also discover he had given up his impressive jazz career by early 1960s and switched to collecting guns. In 1962, Shaw purchased a home in Spain using the services of Ilse Skorzeny and the real estate company, Previews, Inc. Much has been written in this book concerning Previews, and Skorzeny mentions these dealings with Artie Shaw in the Skorzeny papers.

Incredibly, by 1963, Shaw was considered one of the greatest marksman in the world. Shaw even dominated the cover of *Guns* magazine in February 1964. This was only one month after the assassination of President Kennedy. Shockingly, we find a very close acquaintance of Otto Skorzeny in an unnerving pose suggestive of a sniper's nest. Add to this, the magazine also contained a plea on page 3 for funds to help the widow and three children of officer J. D. Tippit, the policeman reportedly gunned down by Lee Harvey Oswald.

Perhaps it is no coincidence that shooting seemed to be a focal point of passion among the majority of the Dallas social group connected to Skorzeny. Another favorite pastime of these men was big game hunting. The Africa hunts were actually coordinated by Robert Ruark from Spain, who, in addition to being a journalist, and World Commerce officer, was the lead agent for an African safari group called Safarilandia.

WHO WAS ROBERT RUARK?

This chapter opened with the depiction of an article by Robert Ruark giving clues to his involvement with Skorzeny's circle of friends in Madrid. Let's take a closer look at Ruark's background.

Robert Ruark was born December 29, 1915 in Wilmington, North Carolina. After graduating from New Hanover High School, he enrolled in the University of North Carolina at Chapel Hill at age fifteen. Although later widely known as a journalist he had very little education in journalism. In 1930, after being fired from an accounting job at the Works Progress Administration, he joined the United States Merchant Marine. Later, he worked for two small town newspapers in North Carolina.

In 1936, Ruark moved to Washington, D.C., and after a few months ended up as the paper's top sports reporter. During World War II, Ruark was commissioned an ensign in the United States Navy and served ten months as a gunnery officer in the Atlantic and Mediterranean. In the 1950s, he moved to Spain and went into business with two previously mentioned OSS men—Frank Ryan and Ricardo Sicre of the World Commerce Corporation. This corporation is also part and parcel with the Skorzeny network, and both Ryan and Sicre are found in the Skorzeny papers. The WCC was established immediately after World War II by OSS chief, General William Donovan, and Sir William Stephenson, head of the British Secret Service in America, as a private intelligence group operating out of Madrid.

Ruark's wife Virginia Ruth Webb Ruark, an interior decorator and designer, was also associated with WCC. The two were married in 1938 and divorced in 1963 but in the interim, they were part of the Madrid jet set that also included Ryan, Sicre, Skorzeny, Jake Hamon, Artie Shaw and others. Often in their company was actress Eva Gardner, who was from 1945–1946 the wife of Artie Shaw. Shaw was married eight times in his life.

Robert Ruark, became known for his colorful and witty articles, including the ones about his network of friends. His articles appeared in newspapers around the world. Some of these were stories about his experiences in exotic locations. In the spring and summer of 1959, Ruark found his way to the Congo. The reader will recall that Skorzeny was also in the Congo at the same time as the mysterious CIA asset QJ/WIN.

Africa, it seemed, was one of Ruark's favorite areas to vacation, and where he became an avid big game hunter. At some point, apparently in the late 1950s, Ruark became the representative for a big game outfit in Portuguese East Africa known as Safarilandia. Ruark represented the company in Spain and arranged big game hunts for his American friends, including the members of the WCC and various oil executives from Dallas, Texas.

COLONEL BYRD'S ALIBI

The Safarilandia connection leads us to our next important revelation concerning another Dallas business executive, Colonel D. Harold Byrd, owner of the Texas School Book Depository. Byrd was also part of the elite jet set of Dallas associated with Skorzeny's network.

On November 22, 1963, the very day President John F. Kennedy was assassinated, D. Harold Byrd had the perfect alibi—he was out of the country on a hunting trip in East Africa. The hunt was conducted by Safarilandia! Exactly who arranged the trip is not known, the evidence would be weighted toward Robert Ruark. Regardless, the hunt *was* directed by Werner von Alvensleben.

Before looking closer a Safarilandia, let's examine some interesting facts about Colonel D. Harold Byrd. David Harold Byrd was born in Red River County, Texas in 1900. His first jobs in the oil business were as a workman, but he rose through the ranks to become a wealthy oil executive. In 1931, Byrd and another man named Jack Frost founded Byrd–Frost, an oil company with hundreds of wells in East Texas. The operation was highly successful. During World War II, Byrd was a founding member of the Civil Air Patrol (CAP), a citizen's flying corps that helped protect America's coast patrolling for German U-Boats and provided air security for U.S. industrial infrastructure. CAP later became the official auxiliary of the United States Air Force and would later include in its roles a young cadet named Lee Harvey Oswald. Byrd rose to the rank of colonel within the organization, which he remained active in his entire life.

Byrd also owned the Texas School Book Depository building. For our purpose in this history we have pointed out his odd hunting trip to East Africa as the events in the assassination of President Kennedy were playing out in Dallas. We shall continue with this examination in a moment, but must also point out a curious and likely important business connection of Byrd.

In 1958, Byrd became chairman of the board for a company called Space Corporation, headquartered near Garland, Texas. The company made Titan missile guidance control components for the United States government. The Titan missile was the premier underground nuclear delivery system for the USAF. Selected as head of security for Space Corporation was the former chief

FBI agent in Dallas, Jack Mumford. During World War II, Mumford worked highly sensitive internal security projects for the FBI throughout the United States, protecting the country from Nazi agents. In an incredible irony, Mumford was actually involved in the apprehension in the Eastern United States of two enemy agents dispatched to gather intelligence by Otto Skorzeny and the Reich Main Security Office.

Mumford was well acquainted with the law enforcement community in Dallas at every level and has major implications given the fact that he is associated with Colonel Byrd and others linked to the Skorzeny network. More research is needed on this highly provocative connection.

We return now to the adventures of Colonel Byrd and his African hunting alibi.

Safarilandia was run by Werner von Alvensleben one of the most famous African hunters of all time. His background was eerily similar to Otto Skorzeny, as was his looks. To start Alvensleben was a former member of the Austrian SS just like Skorzeny. Also, like Skorzeny he was reticent about his days in the SS. The author conducted a detailed review of the SS records of both men and determined it is likely Alvensleben knew and operated with Skorzeny in the SS before the war.

According to declassified OSS documents, Alvensleben was tasked by Heinrich Himmler, head of the SS, to participate in sabotage operations in the Tyrol border region of Austria. While in this region, von Alvensleben is reported to have received an assassination mission directed at a Dr. Stetiel. This occurred sometime around 1932 at a time when the Nazi party was outlawed in Austria. Von Alvensleben was subsequently arrested and found guilty of being an accessory before the fact to the assassination and for attempts to destroy government property.

Alvensleben was sentenced to three years in a political prison but was released after three months in a prisoner exchange. He was then turned over to the Bavarian police and released a few days later. Austrian newspapers also connected him to an attempted assassination of Major Fey, an Austrian Minister of Police who was responsible for banning the Nazi party in 1932. Von Alvensleben claimed he was never questioned about the case.

In 1934, von Alvensleben attended a military training academy in Munich and was commissioned as a Bavarian police officer in June 1934. He was then reported to have been arrested, along with his father, on June 30, 1934, a date infamously known to history as the "Night of the Long Knives," when Hitler purged the rival SA under Ernst Röhm. At this point, von Alvensleben was taken to Berlin and, after a bizarre period of being released, then rearrested, he was finally ordered to leave Germany.

In April 1935, he took passage from Bremen arriving in Cape Town, South Africa, the following month. Over the next few years, he worked a number of jobs in South Africa and Rhodesia for various mining companies. At the outbreak of the war he was placed into an enemy alien internment camp but escaped to Portuguese East Africa. At some point not made clear by records, von Alvensleben began working for the OSS, reporting to Huntington Harris, who may have recruited him to infiltrate Nazi smuggling rings. Harris later became a CIA officer.

After the war von Alvensleben opened a huge hunting preserve in Portuguese East Africa. Several of his hunting patrons are mentioned in the Skorzeny papers including a man named Jackie Maeder. Maeder was a shipping expert and moved freight for Skorzeny, he also shipped the animals killed in the African hunts for von Alvensleben. Another patron of Safarilandia was Hassan Sayed Kamil, an important Middle Eastern business man, also found in the Skorzeny papers. Kamil was connected to the arms company Oerlikon through a man named Wilhelm Mallet, also a business associate of Skorzeny. Despite all of this hunting activity swirling around Skorzeny, the author could find no evidence Skorzeny ever went to Africa on a big game hunt.

Given the above facts concerning the timing of Colonel Byrd's trip to Africa it is doubly fascinating to find out that in the immediate wake of Kennedy's assassination, Baron von Alvensleben and his wife arrived in Dallas, Texas, at the invitation of Byrd. The event was actually covered in the January 9, 1964, edition of the *Dallas Morning News* which featured a lengthy society article on the Baron and Baroness who were guests of Byrd. The article stated Byrd had "returned to Dallas three weeks ago from a hunt on the huge concession 1,000 kilometers north of the seaport city of Lourenco Marques."

The same paper carried a follow-on article titled, "Baron Takes Look at Texas Hunters" on January 19, 1964, describing Alvensleben as "tall enough to have been a basketball player, he had a scar on the left side of his face that ran from his mouth to his ear about which he volunteered nothing. . . ." Amazingly, the description of Baron Alvensleben could literally be used for Otto Skorzeny.

In a final shocking piece of evidence linking the above facts tightly to Skorzeny is the mention of Harold Byrd in a letter found in the Skorzeny papers. The undated letter, determined to be from early 1964 because of its placement with other papers in the Skorzeny archive, the Contessa Dagmar Álvarez de Toledo Lausanne writes to Skorzeny stating, "Yes I met Harold in Arusha and it was his great wish that we two would meet." (Arusha is in the East African country of Tanzania, the hunting grounds of Alvensleben's Safarilandia.) She ends the letter "I am a big game hunter and shoot darn well. . . ." It seems expert marksmanship was a common trait among those who knew Otto Skorzeny.

NOVEMBER 1963—THE RUN UP

On January 9, 1963, Dallas papers announced the formation of a new petro-chemical company called Premier Petrochemical. The company was to deal in synthetic fertilizers. An important fact for this book is the chairman for the new company was Algur H. Meadows and that one of the companies' stockholders was Colonel D. Harold Byrd. Others included Lewis W. McNaughton and Joe Zeppa of Delta Drilling, overseen by Colonel Jack Critchton. It should also be pointed out here that the Skorzeny papers also confirm he too was involved in synthetic fertilizer. The importance of the company formation is its potential use by Skorzeny in manipulating the support pieces to the Dallas operation.

In fact, on October 12, 1963, the Dallas papers carried an article on Mead-ows, stating he was to receive a medal from the Spanish government for his oil work in their country. The article mentioned he was to go to Spain "with his close personal friends" to accept the award. The author of this book was unable to confirm who these "close personal friends" were but likely many of those previously mentioned. The ceremony took place on October 18, 1963. As an importantly point of reference, it should be pointed out that Bobby Baker, the political adviser to Lyndon Johnson and focus of an investigation connected to the motive, had formally resigned on October 7.

At the ceremony, Meadows received the Great Cross of the Order of Civil Merit on order from Francisco Franco, but personally presented to him by José Sirvent of the Institute of National Industry. José Sirvent had been the lead Spanish official during World War II for liaison with SOFINDUS, written about earlier as the company transferred to the Allies after the war through the efforts of Skorzeny's principle Madrid business partner Victor Oswald.

The presence of Algur Meadows and other Dallas oilmen of the Skorzeny network in Madrid only forty days before the assassination is astounding. This occurrence would have allowed for clandestine meetings, planning, and perhaps rehearsals using Samuel Bronston's stage sets. There is yet much to be investigated in these connections. But clearly the Skorzeny Dallas business network was active in Madrid just prior to the assassination.

THE DALLAS OPERATION IN DETAIL—ACTION ARM

At the top of the list of Skorzeny Dallas connections, at least from an operational perspective, is information concerning the French OAS captain, Jean Rene Souetre and his presence in Dallas on the very day of the assassination. The author has isolated this man as the leader of the action arm for the assassination. The genius of this operation is the nearly total separation of the action arm from both the support group and the deception group. Indeed, the only real link is Otto Skorzeny—the coordinator of CIA assassination.

We last left Captain Souetre signing on with Otto Skorzeny since the OAS had, for all intents and purposes, dissolved in the later part of 1962. When one considers the that Souetre and the OAS had an established relationship with the covert paramilitary network run by Otto Skorzeny, the information presented below, derived from a document released in 1977 by the CIA, is truly dramatic. The document, which is dated April 1, 1964, and concerns the French defector and OAS Captain, Jean Rene Souetre, was one page out of 14 that has still not been publicly released.

The document, NOT REVIEWED BY THE WARREN COMMISSION, verifies Souetre was flown out of the United States shortly after the Kennedy assassination!

Here is the text of CIA document # 632-796:

8. Jean SOUETRE aka Michel ROUX aka Michel MERTZ—

On 5 March [1964], [Mr. Papich] of the FBI advised that the French had [hit] the Legal Attaché in Paris and also [the SDECE man] had queried the Bureau in New York City concerning subject stating that he had been expelled from the U.S. at Fort Worth or Dallas 48 hours after the assassination. He was in Fort Worth on the morning of 22 November and in Dallas in the afternoon. The French believe that he was expelled to either Mexico or Canada. In January he received mail from a dentist named Alderson living at 5803 Birmingham, Houston, Texas. Subject is believed to be identical with a Captain who is a deserter from the French Army and an activist in the OAS. The French are concerned because of de Gaulle's planned visit to Mexico. They would like to know the reason for his expulsion from the U.S. and his destination. Bureau files are negative and they are checking in Texas and with INS. They would like a check of our files with indications of what may be passed to the French. [The FBI's Mr. Papich] was given a copy of CSCI-3/776, 742 previously furnished the Bureau and CSD3-3/655, 207 together with a photograph of Captain SOUETRE.

This amazing document confirms that the French security services were still actively pursuing the renegade Captain Souetre. The French were also rightfully concerned about his presence in the United States, just across the border from Mexico where their President was due to visit in January. But the French inquiry into the Souetre matter inadvertently exposed the entire Skorzeny covert network in Texas at the precise time of the Kennedy assassination.

In the document, the FBI claimed not to have information on Souetre. The FBI officer mentioned in the document is Sam Papich. Papich was assigned as a lead FBI agent in the investigation of the assassination of President Kennedy. His main responsibility was coordinating CIA information for the Bureau agents assigned to investigate Lee Harvey Oswald. It is not clear if Papich knew about the Skorzeny network. He subsequently told a news journalist that he had serious doubts about the accuracy of the Warren Report. He said he found it difficult to believe Oswald was a lone gunman stating, "This would have been very fancy shooting even for the best marksmen in the FBI. But everything we had on Oswald indicated that he was a crappy shot."

The other person mentioned in the Souetre document was Dr. Lawrence Alderson. Dr. Lawrence "Larry" Mason Alderson was born on February 1, 1930. He grew up in Houston, Texas and graduated from the University of Houston, with a degree in Psychology, in 1952. He joined the U.S. Army in the early 1950s and was eventually stationed overseas at a French air base. There, he apparently met and befriended Jean Rene Souetre, who was serving as a young officer in the French Air Commandos. The two remained in contact over the years exchanging correspondence. The author was unable confirm that Dr. Alderson was anything more than a friend to Souetre. This would have been highly convenient during the planning of Souetre's operation in Dallas and he may have used this benign friendship as a cover for his movements in Texas. However, the possibility still remains that Alderson had some hidden support role in the Skorzeny network, although it appears doubtful.

JACK RUBY—THE SKORZENY CONNECTION

Jack Leon Ruby (Jacob Leon Rubenstein) was born March 25, 1911. He was a Dallas, Texas nightclub owner who murdered Lee Harvey Oswald on November 24, 1963, while Oswald was in police custody after being charged with assassinating President John F. Kennedy. Oswald was also suspected of shooting and killing Dallas policeman J. D. Tippit two days earlier.

Ruby was eventually found guilty of murdering Oswald. He claimed he did the act to avenge the president's murder and spare Jackie Kennedy the trauma associated with the trial. A Dallas court found Ruby guilty and he was sentenced to death. Later under an appeal he was granted a new trial. However, on January 3, 1967, just before his court date was to be set Ruby became deathly ill in his prison cell and died from lung cancer. In 1964 the Warren Commission concluded that Ruby acted alone in killing Oswald.

Although volumes have been written on Ruby, many exposing his underworld ties, this book zeros in on one critical point. Shortly after his arrest, Ruby asked Dallas attorney Tom Howard to represent him. Howard accepted, and during an initial interview with Ruby, asked if there was anyone who might damage his defense. Ruby told Howard of a man named "Davis," a man who Ruby had been involved with as a gunrunner supporting anti-Castro efforts. The reader may recall that CIA contract officer Robert Morrow, mentioned in an earlier chapter, had discovered that Ruby was involved in the Cuban gunrunning operations directed by Attorney Marshall Diggs. (The reader will also recall that Diggs's office phone number is in the Skorzeny papers.) Who then was this mysterious Davis that Ruby was so concerned about? Subsequent research by this author and others have confirmed that Davis was Thomas Eli Davis III.

ENTER THOMAS ELI DAVIS III

Thomas Eli Davis, III, a tall blond Texan, was born August 27, 1936 in McKinney, Collin Country, Texas. The mystery of his connection to Ruby and to the assassination story of President Kennedy ends with this book.

After high school, Davis joined the United States Army. His service is not believed to be remarkable, but his record has never been released by military authorities. After leaving the service under honorable conditions, Davis ran into trouble when he attempted to rob a branch of the National Bank of Detroit on June, 18, 1958. However, during the robbery, Davis lost heart and surrender to authorities. Later, he received a suspended sentence as a result of the judge's sympathy for his change of conscience.

His life after this is complex. Stories of involvement with mercenary groups and perhaps the underworld have been examined. A full history would likely make an excellent read, but the real importance of Davis, at least for our story, occurred on December 9, 1963. On that date the U.S. State Department at the consulate in Tangier, Morocco sent a "Priority" cable to Secretary of State Dean Rusk, indicating Davis had been arrested in that country for attempting to sell "two Walter pistols" on December 8. The charge against Davis was a minor infraction, but what caused the Moroccan security officers so much concern was a letter on Davis that he intended to mail. Stated in the body was, "I've seen Oswald" and also "This is the first Sunday AK [After Kennedy]." The letter was addressed to a lawyer, Thomas G. Proctor, living in New York and the legal agent for Morocco's World Fair exhibit in New York.

The letter received high-level attention in Washington, and the U.S. government swung into action to investigate the possibility that Davis was linked to the assassination of President Kennedy. Then, after only a few days, the matter seemed to be reconciled.

On December 30, 1963, a State Department telegram from the U.S. embassy in Madrid, Spain, to Washington presented information that seemingly explained away the Davis letter. The Madrid office had been asked to look into the matter since Davis claimed he stopped in Madrid before going on to Morocco. In Madrid, it was discovered that the "Oswald" in question was not Lee Harvey Oswald, but Madrid business man Victor Oswald. As related in this book, Victor Oswald was an original member of the SOE/OSS group that established the British–American–Canadian-Corporation (BACC) and the World Commerce Corporation (WCC). He was also in Otto Skorzeny's inner business circle.

A subsequent cable concerning Tom Davis' contact with Victor Oswald was sent directly to Secretary of State Dean Rusk stating:

Victor Oswald, a business man of Madrid, contacted this date, stated that Davis had came to Madrid approximately six weeks ago with a letter of business introductions to Oswald from a friend of Oswald's, a New York lawyer named Thomas Proctor. Oswald said that he only talked with Davis 5–10 minutes since Davis was only interested in cattle and was heading for Morocco. Oswald stated that this was the extent of his contact with Davis.

Although the cable sent describing Tom Davis' meeting with Victor Oswald cleared up the matter at the time, it certainly would not stand up if the facts in this research are known. Also, not revealed then, was that Thomas Proctor was also a business associate of Victor Oswald. But more significantly, that business was part of a U.S. psychological warfare initiative. This was a film project overseen by Charles Douglas "C. D." Jackson, the Special Assistant to the President on psychological warfare during the Eisenhower administration. The project also included a famous film director, Samuel Bronston. It was Bronston, who brought these men together for a film, titled *John Paul Jones*. The film was produced by Bronston's film company in Spain and released by Warner Brothers in 1959. Victor Oswald, as the senior Chase Manhattan bank official in Spain, was the key financial backer of the film. Chase was owned by the Rockefeller family who were also involved in the film's production. Thomas G. Proctor served as the entertainment lawyer for the production.

C. D. Jackson was born in 1902 in New York City. He graduated from Princeton University, class of 1924, and then went into the media industry. In 1931, he began working with Henry Luce at *Time* magazine. During World War II he was part of the OSS, and after 1943 was appointed Deputy Chief at the Psychological Warfare Division at Supreme Headquarters Allied Expeditionary Force (SHAEF).

After the war, Jackson became a director at *Time Life* International, however, his personal papers at the Dwight D. Eisenhower Library confirm he was a CIA officer. Jackson worked with OPC chief Frank Wisner in Operation Mockingbird, a program to influence the domestic American media. Jackson was also active in the various committee set up to counter Soviet propaganda. In February 1953, he was appointed as Special Assistant to the President. Throughout the 1950s C. D. Jackson was at the forefront of psychological warfare and considered a leading expert in the field.

Perhaps the author does not need to remind the reader that C. D. Jackson was the man who secured the Zapruder film after the assassination of Kennedy. This was previously covered in Chapter Fourteen along with Jackson's other amazing links to the Skorzeny network, both people and organizations.

Jackson's immediate response in securing the Zapruder film has always been seen as a rather suspicious action. With all of Jackson's connections to the Skorzeny network and with the revelation that he was in association with Skorzeny's inner circle, his Zapruder film acquisition approaches criminality.

So here, revealed for the first time is the fact that Jack Ruby's partner in gun running, Thomas Eli Davis, had personally met with an Otto Skorzeny confidant, Victor Oswald, thus linking to the broader U.S. intelligence network and command and control elements of the U.S. government only weeks before the assassination of President Kennedy! Let me repeat this in another way—Jack Ruby was associated with the Skorzeny network *before* the assassination of President Kennedy!

In the end, the assassination network that killed JFK was the unfortunate legacy of General Donovan's original Secret Paramilitary Group that included as a key adviser from its early conception—Otto Skorzeny. Furthermore, the evidence would seem to indicate Skorzeny organized, planned and carried out the Dallas assassination, however, we may never know what his exact role was. Notwithstanding the lack of proof Skorzeny orchestrated the Dallas assassination of JFK, there can be no doubt that the network he was connected to carried it out. Since the investigation into the assassination was conducted by government officials with knowledge of Skorzeny's network and its capabilities the conclusion can only be *conspiracy*. This includes Warren Commission member Allen W. Dulles, and others mentioned in this book. Lee Harvey Oswald was neither alone, nor a nut. He said he was a "patsy," which now appears to be true. All history books that have focused on Lee Harvey Oswald, are essentially books about the deception part of the Dallas operation.

In conclusion, the author returns to the point where this book began and refers again to the letter written by Frenchman Paul Gluc to the director of the FBI, making the plea, "Mr. Director, only you can clear Otto Skorzeny of the guilt of being [an] agent in the Dallas operation with [the] passive complicity of Allen W. Dulles."

While FBI connections to the Skorzeny network was not explored for this research, Paul Gluc's letter leaves open the possibility that J. Edgar Hoover may also have been aware of Skorzeny's secret network hidden within the World Commerce Corporation. Gluc concluded his letter, "I end here . . . with the hope of seeing the Dallas enigma solved."—a pathway provided by this author using Skorzeny's very papers.

Glossary

Abwehr, German intelligence service during World War II.

Algerian Conflict, a tragic and violent war fought over Algerian independence that lasted from 1954–1962. The Algerian War had a major impact on Otto Skorzeny who played a significant role in the shadows of the conflict working for French intelligence and supporting the renegade OAS.

ARMCO (American Rolling Mill Company), a U.S. steel company. The European representative of ARMCO before and after World War II was Colonel Robert Solborg, a high ranking American and British intelligence officer. Colonel Solborg was a business associate of Otto Skorzeny after World War II, but the relationship was a cover for covert paramilitary operations under operations linked to Operation Compass Rose.

BACC (British–American–Canadian-Corporation, S.A.), a highly enigmatic private corporation formed in May 1945 by Sir William Stephenson and other senior-level British intelligence officers including Charles Hambro and Colonel Rex L. Benson (among others). The New York based company had a Panamanian registry. Its corporate officers and almost all of its rank and file were former intelligence officers. The creation of BACC was tied to Operation SAFE-HAVEN. The BACC would later morph into the World Commerce Corporation, which served as a corporate business cover for a private clandestine paramilitary force created by General William Donovan in 1948 and operated in Europe against Communism during the early stages of the Cold War. (See also "**SPG**" and **WCC**).

BOB (Berlin Operations Base), a CIA base in Berlin after World War II run by William K. Harvey. BOB was in contact with and utilized Otto Skorzeny for certain overt operations directed against the Soviets.

Bloodstone, a major U.S. clandestine intelligence program involving the use of foreign émigrés from Eastern European nations for anti-Communist operations in Europe. Otto Skorzeny was brought into the Bloodstone program in 1948 as an adviser and recruiter.

BCRA (French *Bureau Central de Renseignements et d'Action*), Free French intelligence service during World War II. The BCRA counterintelligence section was created by Roger Wybot, who after the war headed the DST, an intelligence and security service connected to Otto Skorzeny.

Camp King, located in Oberursel, Germany the site was the location of the 7707th European Command Intelligence Center an intelligence command set up at the end of World War II to exploit and process German VIP prisoners of war.

CIA (Central Intelligence Agency), created in September 1947, the CIA was originally divided into two major components the OSO (Office of Special Operations) and the OPC (Office of Policy Coordination). The OSO and OPC were officially combined in 1952 into the Directorate of Plans.

CI (Counterintelligence), an intelligence function or branch designed to protect against espionage and enemy or hostile covert activity.

CIC (U.S. Army Counterintelligence Corps), an important branch of military intelligence during and after World War II. The CIC was initially responsible for the handling of ex-Nazis in the wake of World War II but was eventually relieved of that duty by other government intelligence agencies.

CIG (Central Intelligence Group), a post World War II intelligence organization formed out of the Strategic Services Unit (SSU) a direct predecessor to the CIA.

Clandestine, an action carried out in extreme secrecy for purposes of conceal-ment or deception.

Clandestine Planning Committee (CPC), a clandestine group that handled highly classified covert paramilitary operations and stay-behinds in Europe. The CPC was placed under the U.S. Military Assistance Advisery Groups, or MAAGs for operational cover.

COI (Coordinator of Information), title given to General William A. Dono-van in the early stages of World War II before the official formation of the Office of Strategic Services (OSS).

Compass Rose (*Rose des Vents*), a secret operation set up in France in 1947 by U.S., British, and French intelligence to counter internal communist threats to that country. Compass Rose was preceded by Plan Bleu, a short-lived operation that was compromised. Otto Skorzeny was directly involved in Compass Rose activity working for French intelligence and a private paramilitary group set up by General William Donovan using former OSS and SOE personnel.

Cover, false identity of a secret agent or the use of a business (commercial) enterprise or government entity to hide an intelligence or operational activity. Cover can be considered the cutout between an official agency and an unoffi-cial one in order to allow plausible deniability. The Skorzeny papers evidence the businesses that acted as the *cover* or *cut out* for his covert activity that he carried out at the bequest of the United States or other Western countries.

Covert, an intelligence or operational activity carried out under extreme secrecy.

Counterintelligence Staff (CIS), the main office of counterintelligence at the CIA headed for many years by James Jesus Angleton.

DDU (Document Disposal Unit), a sub-unit or cover designation of the War Department Detachment (WDD) set up by Allen Dulles near the very end of World War II. The DDU was a focal point for managing the disposition and control of intelligence networks involving former SS, SD, and Gestapo. Also, the DDU apparently emerged from or had a relationship with the Document Research Unit (DRU).

Deception, programs to mislead the enemy during warfare or hostile intelligence forces in peacetime. This is accomplished through psychological operations, information manipulation, visual deception and other methods. Lee Harvey Oswald was a deception (fall guy) in the assassination of President John F. Kennedy.

DIA (Defense Intelligence Agency), an intelligence service of the United States government founded in 1961 by President John F. Kennedy that supports the Department of Defense.

DST (*Directoire de Surveillance Territore*), a French intelligence and security service in France founded in 1944 responsible for counterespionage and counterterrorism. The first director Roger Wybot utilized the services of Otto Skorzeny during the 1950s for many of the DST's covert programs.

ECA (Economic Cooperation Administration), a U.S. government agency created to assist European countries with economic aid programs after World War II. It was embedded with CIA officers and was utilized by the CIA as a cover for clandestine operations. Otto Skorzeny's postwar businesses were part of the ECA program cover.

ENIGMA, code word for encryption machine used by Germans in World War II.

ECIC (7707th European Command Intelligence Center), an intelligence command set up at the end of World War II. Set up to exploit and process German VIP prisoners of war, the ECIC was located at Camp King (Oberursel, Germany). Otto Skorzeny was moved to Camp King in the fall of 1947 after his acquittal during the Nuremberg Trials and processed for use during the Cold War.

11th Shock Regiment, a French special forces unit utilized by French intelligence services to carry out assassination, particularly during the Algerian War.

Otto Skorzeny was associated with members of the 11th Shock and trained its personnel at his paramilitary training sites in Spain.

French Indochina War (1945–1954), a violent regional conflict after World War II between France and Communist forces in Vietnam. After the French defeat at Dien Bien Phu and subsequent withdrawal from the region, the United States took over control to maintain regional security ultimately resulting in the Vietnam War. Otto Skorzeny was a supporting player of these events from Europe acting as an unofficial military adviser and trainer for covert operations carried out by, first, secret French military intelligence units and later U.S. MAAG.

IRO (International Relief Organization), an agency set up to assist in the massive refugee situation in the wake of World War II. The émigré refugee networks of the IRO were exploited by U.S. intelligence and served as a recruiting field for secret agents and others deemed of value to the West. The IRO networks also served as cover for intelligence operations including the establishment of escape routes for former Nazi designated for use or protection by the West to prevent Soviet exploitation or targeting.

ISA (International Security Agency), an important United States government agency that handled covert programs during the Cold War concerning military and paramilitary assistance.

Jagdverband **(Hunting Group)**, Skorzeny's wartime SS commando unit.

Jagdverein **(Hunting Society)**, a suspected post World War II clandestine paramilitary formation set up by Otto Skorzeny.

KgU (*Kampfgruppe gegen Unmenschlichkeit* or Fighting League against Inhumanity), a West German political action group founded in 1948 and funded secretly by the CIA. The CIA code words associated with KgU are EARTHWARE, GRAVEYARD, and DTLINEN. The group conducted covert paramilitary operations behind the Iron Curtain. Otto Skorzeny was a paramilitary adviser to the KgU in 1951 through BOB, the nickname for the CIA's Berlin Operations Base.

La Cagoule **(Hooded Ones)** (*Comite de Secret Action Révolutionnaire,* or **Secret Committee of Revolutionary Action**), a dangerous secret organization that existed within the French political system prior to World War II. Basically, a secret Catholic brotherhood that was vehemently anti-Communist and had as a goal the return of the French monarchy. The *Cagoule* directed violent action against Communists and operated from 1935–1937. It conducted ruthless assassinations and bombings to achieve its objectives. Eventually infiltrated by the French government, the organization was never fully rooted out. An element existed within the French military after World War II that was associated with Otto Skorzeny.

MAAG (Military Assistance and Advisery Groups), a military organization formed after World War II to assist foreign militaries with training on weapons and equipment provided by the U.S. government, but a host of classified missions were also carried out, including unconventional warfare and stay-behind operations. MAAG worked closely with other government agencies including the International Security Agency (ISA) and the Central Intelligence Agency (CIA). Otto Skorzeny worked closely with MAAG as both a trainer and adviser.

MI5 (Security Service), domestic intelligence service of the United Kingdom.

MI6 (Secret Intelligence Service), external intelligence service of the United Kingdom.

NATO (North Atlantic Treaty Organization), post–World War II military alliance of Western nations to present a united front against the Soviet Union and East Bloc countries.

NSC (National Security Council), a very important senior-level United States government advisery and decision-making body to the President of the United States.

NSC Directive 10/2, a landmark directive that laid the foundations of the modern U.S. national security state. It vastly increased secret operations and issued specific guidance for all types of clandestine activity, including, white and black propaganda, economic warfare, preventive direct action, including sabotage, assistance to underground resistance movements, guerrilla formations, and use of refugee groups, just to name a few. It also authorized violation of international law and deception in the interest of national security. It served as the baseline document for plausible and deniable planning and execution of covert operations. NSC 10/2 served as the initial authorizing document for the inclusion of Otto Skorzeny (as well as many others) as a covert asset of the United States during the Cold War.

OAS (Secret Army Organization), a secret paramilitary organization set by dissident French officers and soldiers during the French Algerian Conflict (1954–1962). Otto Skorzeny was heavily involved in the inner workings of the OAS and served as an unofficial liaison between the renegade group and the CIA. After the OAS dissolved Skorzeny hired former OAS members for his private paramilitary group.

Operation Jedburgh, specialized resistance groups of the OSS and SOE inserted into occupied Europe during World War II to carry out irregular warfare with the French Resistance.

Operation Tropical, an elusive United States covert military operation to assassinate or abduct Cuban leader Fidel Castro in 1960. Operation Tropical reportedly was to be carried out by an elite clandestine paramilitary commando group led by Otto Skorzeny. The operation was briefed to President Kennedy who determined the use of Skorzeny was too great a risk if the mission failed. Operation Tropical was likely part of the CIA ZR/RIFLE project.

OPC (Office of Policy Coordination), an early major branch of the CIA (actually under the Department of State) formed in 1948 that planned and conducted extensive covert operations during the Cold War. The first director of the OPC was Frank Wisner who brought in Otto Skorzeny as a covered and protected clandestine asset. Skorzeny had no direct ties to the OPC but operated under commercial (and other) cover.

OSO (Office of Special Operations), an early branch of the CIA that handle espionage and secret intelligence collection. An early director of the OSO was Richard Helms.

OSS (Office of Strategic Services), an American intelligence and special operations organization headed by General William Donovan during World War II (1941–1945). Disbanded by President Harry Truman in late 1945 but considered a legacy organization of the CIA and United States Special Operations Command.

Paix et Liberté, a private group organized in France in 1949 to combat Communism through the use of art and literature. In reality it was a highly classified covert operation of the CIA and other Western intelligence organizations.

PB7, Planning Branch 7 of the Office of Policy Coordination (OPC) a division of the CIA. PB7 handled covert operations that included planning support for assassination operations. The office was headed in 1949 by Colonel Boris Pash who met with Otto Skorzeny in that year.

Peter Group (SS *Sonderkommando* Denmark), a notorious World War II assassination unit headed by Otto Skorzeny's commandos that carried out liquidations of the Danish resistance movement. Members of the Peter Group that survived the war ended up working for U.S. intelligence and Skorzeny's private covert paramilitary group (see also **Skorzeny's School of Commando Tactics**).

Plan Bleu, a secret operation to counter internal Communist threats in France 1946–1947. The operation was compromised and replaced by Compass Rose.

Previews, Inc, an international real estate company linked to Otto Skorzeny and connected to U.S. intelligence operations.

QJ/WIN, the CIA cryptonym for executive action or foreign leader assassination. Used to describe both a program and an individual. Otto Skorzeny's biographical profile and timeline revealed in this book aligns to an amazing degree with the known facts concerning the mysterious QJ/WIN.

Red Hand (*La Main Rouge*), a terror group bent on the disruption of Algerian independence from France during the French Algerian War 1954–1962. The group was initially created or exploited by Roger Wybot of the French intelligence service DST. Director Wybot utilized the services of Otto Skorzeny as an adviser and controller of cells within the group.

RSHA (Reich Main Security Office), the top Nazi organization for state security. Otto Skorzeny's wartime commandos were under RSHA Section VI-S (Sabotage).

SAFEHAVEN, formed late in World War II a secret project utilizing U.S. and British intelligence units to track down and block German assets in neutral and non-belligerent countries throughout Europe and the Americas. The SAFE-HAVEN program was overseen by the British Ministry of Economic Warfare that created special committees to identify SAFEHAVEN objectives. These groups were composed of both SOE and OSS personnel. A major target of SAFEHAVEN was a vast German corporate entity known as *Sociedad Financiera Industrial*, or SOFINDUS.

SDECE (*Service de Documentation Extérieure de Contre-Espionnage*), French post World War II intelligence service.

Service d'Ordre du RPF (SO du RPF), an *unofficial* French secret service created by General de Gaulle in the early part of 1947. It was hidden within an organization de Gaulle had formed called the *Rassemblement du Peuple Français* (Rally of the French People). Several of its members were close clandestine associates of Otto Skorzeny.

SCI (Special Counterintelligence), highly classified OSS program that utilized ULTRA material.

SD (*Sicherheitsdienst des Reichsführers-SS* or Security Service of the *Reichsführer-SS*), the intelligence service of the Nazi SS during World War II.

SAS (Special Air Service), British special forces unit formed in World War II and still in service.

Safarilandia, a big game hunting outfit in Portuguese East Africa run by a former SS officer and OSS asset Werner von Alvensleben. Dallas businessman and owner of the Texas School Book Depository, Colonel D. Harold Byrd was on a Safarilandia African hunt at the time of the JFK assassination. Safarilandia is linked to Otto Skorzeny and to the overall World Commerce Corporation (WCC) network.

SI (Secret Intelligence), an intelligence branch of the OSS.

Skorzeny's School of Commando Tactics, a clandestine network of paramilitary training sites set up in Spain after World War II and run by Otto Skorzeny and former members of his old SS commando group. The sites were utilized by special forces of the U.S. military, MAAG, foreign military units and private security groups (mercenaries) throughout the 1950s into the 1960s.

SO (Special Operations), a branch of the OSS that carried out direct action behind enemy lines such as sabotage and assassination.

SOE (Special Operations Executive), British covert warfare office in World War II that carried out direct action behind enemy lines including sabotage and assassination.

SOFINDUS (*Sociedad Financiera Industrial*), German corporate entity in Spain during World War II that served as cover for an intricate Nazi intelligence network that extended into South America. After the war the SOFINDUS business network was "absorbed" by the British and Americans and its associated Nazi networks revamped for use by the West in the new (Cold War) conflict with the Soviets. The former SOFINDUS network was incorporated into the World Commerce Corporation (WCC) which served as a cover for Western anti-Communist operations and other clandestine activity throughout the Cold War. The WCC network included Otto Skorzeny who established a covert paramilitary capability within the WCC structure. Orders came to the WCC network from the highest quarters of the United States government via cover agents and organizations. The WCC network extended into Dallas and links to Skorzeny from that network can be established to the assassination of President John F. Kennedy.

"SPG" or **"Special Paramilitary Group,"** an *unofficial* term created exclusively for this book to identify an otherwise unnamed post–World War II covert paramilitary organization formed by General William Donovan and Sir William Stephenson using former members of the American OSS and British SOE (and other intelligence personnel) to carry out clandestine warfare against Communism in Europe. The SPG utilized various government and non-government cover including businesses connected to Otto Skorzeny.

SS *Schutzstaffel*, a major paramilitary organization under Adolf Hitler and the Nazi Party (NSDAP). The SS was divided into two main branches the *Allgemeine* or General SS and the *Waffen or* Armed SS. The General SS handled state security and the enforcement of racial policy, including oversight of concentration and extermination camps. The *Waffen* SS or Armed SS was a combat force that fought alongside the German army. Otto Skorzeny and his commando group were *Waffen* SS.

Stay-Behind (Stay-Behind Forces), a term to describe covert paramilitary units that will activate and become operational after an enemy invades a territory or country.

SSU (Strategic Services Unit), post–World War II intelligence organization created October 1, 1945 from the disbanded offices of the OSS.

***Sûreté Nationale* (national police of France, equivalent to the American FBI)**, in 1949 the *Sûreté Nationale* was headed by Pierre Bertaux, who, along with Roger Wybot of the French DST utilized the services of Otto Skorzeny to fight internal Communist threats to France.

Tolstoy Foundation, an important private Russian émigré support group that received clandestine CIA funding. Both Lee Harvey Oswald and Otto Skorzeny are directly connected to the Tolstoy Foundation through mutual links.

ULTRA, Code word for the World War II Allied operation that deciphered the German ENIGMA.

Warren Commission, an official United States government investigative body set up on the presidential order of Lyndon B. Johnson after the Kennedy assassination. Its members included Chief Justice Earl Warren, Senator Richard Russell, Jr., Senator John S. Cooper, Representative Hale Boggs, Representative Gerald Ford, (later 38th President of the United States), Allen W. Dulles, former Director of Central Intelligence and head of the Central Intelligence Agency, and John J. McCloy, a high ranking government official. The Warren Commission released its findings in a massive report in September, 1964 that determined Lee Harvey Oswald was a lone assassin of President John F. Kennedy. The Warren Commission findings are inconsistent with the evidence found in the Skorzeny papers, and Allen Dulles, as well as John J. McCloy, were aware of the United States government's clandestine use of Otto Skorzeny during the Cold War.

WCC (World Commerce Corporation), a private corporation formed August 13, 1945 and tied to Operation SAFEHAVEN. The WCC was run by former OSS personnel. The president of WCC was Frank Ryan, a former OSS officer who had been Chief of Special Intelligence for Spain and Portugal during World War II. Ryan was assisted by another former OSS officer Ricardo Sicre. Both men are in the Skorzeny Papers and in business with Skorzeny providing key evidence that WCC was a corporate cover for Skorzeny's clandestine paramilitary activity including the assassination of President JFK.

WUCC (Western Union Clandestine Committee), formed in Paris, on March 14, 1948, the WUCC was a control group for covert stay-behind forces in Europe.

WDD (War Department Detachment), an intelligence organization created after World War II to handle the removal or retention of secret networks and agents. Cover name for Strategic Services Unit (SSU).

ZR/RIFLE, a CIA secret code reference for an operation to assassinate Fidel Castro. Otto Skorzeny was involved in certain aspects of the ZR/RIFLE program.

Appendix A

MACV-SOG, AND THE PHOENIX PROJECT

In 1957, a highly decorated soldier of World War II unconventional warfare arrived at MAAG-Vietnam. This was Donald C. Blackburn, a veteran of the Philippine campaign in the Pacific Theater. As an Army lieutenant, Blackburn had evaded Japanese capture at Bataan in 1942, escaping with a close friend, Captain Russell W. Volckmann. Both men were considered founders of American Special Forces and would later rise to become general officers. Following their evasion of the Japanese, Blackburn established a 5000-man guerrilla army that operated behind enemy lines in concert with conventional U.S. Army forces.

After World War II, Blackburn served in a number of important command and staff assignments, including a tour with NATO. He arrived in Vietnam in 1957 and served as the senior adviser to the 5th Military Region that covered the Mekong Delta. In 1958, he became the commanding officer of the 77th Special Forces Group (currently 7th Group), where he directed covert operations. Blackburn continued to impact special forces development from 1961–1964 during which time he served as a director for special warfare at the Office of the Chief of Research and Development. Also, during this period, he directed Operation Hotfoot and its follow-on, Operation White Star, a covert military training program for Laos.

In 1964, now Colonel, Blackburn became Deputy Chief of Staff for Operations, as Director of Special Warfare. In Vietnam, Lt. General William Westmoreland was appointed deputy commander of the United States Military Assistance Command Vietnam (MACV) on the first of January. On January 24, 1964, the U.S. activated a highly-classified joint unit for service in Vietnam called the Military Assistance Command Vietnam-Studies and Observations

Group (MACV-SOG), or simply "SOG." The unit's mission was to conduct covert unconventional warfare, including direct action, psychological warfare, strategic surveillance, and interdiction. Part of the psychological warfare mission was assassination. Although SOG was administratively part of the MACV, it answered "directly to the Joint Chiefs of Staff in the Pentagon, via a special liaison, the special assistant for counter-insurgency and special activities (SACSA)." Overall, SOG was the "largest clandestine organization since World War II."

Coinciding with the formation of MACV-SOG was the posting of Peer de Silva, the new CIA chief of station in Saigon. De Silva had served in the security department of the Manhattan Project with Colonel Boris Pash during the Second World War. Afterward, de Silva had a number of other important intelligence posts, including the vetting of European refugees with shadowy backgrounds for CIA work and duty in Austria. In these latter capacities, he may have been part of the intelligence operation connected to Otto Skorzeny's release plan. Regardless, de Silva had some level of contact or inside knowledge of Skorzeny at some later point, as we shall see shortly.

Colonel Blackburn would eventually be assigned as the head of SOG, in May 1965. However, the first commander was Colonel Clyde Russell, a veteran U.S. Army paratrooper with little unconventional warfare experience, although he had commanded the 77th Special Forces group at Fort Bragg, North Carolina. Colonel Russell encountered several difficulties in setting up MACV-SOG, including mission challenges, organizational problems, and internal politics. Perhaps most challenging, however, was SOG's lacking the detailed intelligence required for its missions. Initially, SOG did not have dedicated CIA support, but Colonel Russell worked hard "to obtain the cooperation SOG needed from the CIA."

Despite the challenges, Colonel Russell began operations into the coastal regions of North Vietnam soon after taking command. Then, on August 2, 1964, North Vietnamese patrol boats attacked the U.S. destroyer *Maddox* in the Gulf of Tonkin. This incident initiated a series of events that escalated the Vietnam conflict and resulted in the U.S. Congress passing the Tonkin Gulf Resolution of August 7, 1964, giving the president authorization to use conventional military power in Southeast Asia without a formal declaration of war. The mounting clandestine attacks by SOG against North Vietnam clearly provoked the North. In the final analysis, the decisions made by President Johnson concerning the Gulf of Tonkin incident and subsequent authorities granted him under the Tonkin Gulf Resolution escalated Vietnam into a major war and had the effect, whether intentional or not, of diverting public attention from the assassination of President John F. Kennedy.

Although seemingly unrelated to Otto Skorzeny, the events described above were the impetus for a new American involvement with Skorzeny, leveraging his expertise in unconventional warfare strategies involving assassination operations. In early October 1964, Skorzeny was visited at his residence by an unidentified U.S. military officer with the rank of colonel. The meeting was recorded by Skorzeny in a letter to Ilse dated October 9. Skorzeny's letter only rendered a few lines, but they are enough to place events into context. Skorzeny was excited about the information the colonel delivered, "Now for something very successful. I was visited by an American colonel from Washington who was active during the war and, afterward, all over the world. He came on behalf of a group of friends, and apparently certain changes are about to take place in America."

It is no coincidence that at the time Skorzeny describes the meeting with the "American colonel from Washington," Colonel Blackburn was Deputy Chief of Staff for Operations as Director of Special Warfare at the Pentagon. Most importantly, he had received notification that he was to assume command of SOG Vietnam, from Colonel Russell. Upon notification of his new assignment, Colonel Blackburn selected a close friend, Colonel Arthur D. "Bull" Simons, to lead his advance element to Vietnam. It is likely, the colonel who met with Skorzeny in Madrid was either Blackburn or Simons, and forthcoming information will strongly support these options.

Skorzeny had also mentioned that "changes are about to take place in America." This accurately coincides with a new direction in unconventional warfare strategies, as part of a joint project involving the CIA and MACV-SOG.

Early in 1964, the CIA had established formal relations with MACV in Vietnam under the direction of Peer de Silva, the newly-appointed CIA Chief of

Station in Saigon. De Silva was preparing to initiate new counterterrorism strategies in that country that went hand-in-hand with MACV-SOG strategic interdiction missions. On October 1, additional units arrived in-country, with the deployment of the 5th Special Forces. Now, under a new program instituted by de Silva, joint commando teams of Americans and South Vietnamese, called Provisional Reconnaissance Units, or PRU's, were to carry out punitive missions against the North.

The overall plan, as de Silva described in his autobiography, *Sub Rosa*, was

to bring danger and death to the Vietcong functionaries themselves, especially in the areas where they felt secure. We had obtained descriptions and photographs of known cadres who were functioning as committee chiefs, recruiters, province representatives, and heads of raiding parties. Based on these photographs and their known areas of operation, we had recruited really tough groups of individuals, organized teams of three or four, who were willing and able, by virtue of prior residence, to go into the areas in which we knew the Vietcong senior cadres were active, and to see what could be done to eliminate them.

It was noted by the historian Douglas Valentine in his outstanding book, *The Phoenix Program*, that in the above passage, de Silva was "describing Phoenix," a neutralization program carried out by the CIA, U.S. Army Special Forces, and SOG, with South Vietnam Special Forces. The CIA described the target of the program as the political structure of the Vietcong.

Adding to the mounting intrigue of the Colonel Blackburn–SOG connection to Otto Skorzeny, the author must inject yet another tantalizing piece into this mix. On Colonel Blackburn's personal command team was a remarkable soldier named Captain Larry Thorne. Thorne had been personally drafted into SOG by Colonel "Bull" Simons. The rightful subject of several books, Thorne was not only a true American hero but also, incredibly, the hero of two other countries, Finland and Nazi Germany!

It is not likely known by many Americans that a large number of former German soldiers, including *Waffen* SS, entered American military service after World War and served with distinction and honor in the Korean War and Vietnam. Larry Thorne was one of these soldiers.

Larry Thorne was born Lauri Allan Törni on May 28, 1919, in Viipuri, Finland. He entered the Finnish Army in 1938 and saw action against the invading Russians in 1939. For excellence as a soldier and bravery, he was promoted to 2nd Lieutenant in the Reserves and sent to Austria in 1941. Törni was then assigned to the *Waffen SS Freiwilligen Bataillon Nordost* (Waffen SS Volunteer Battalion Northeast) to train. He returned to Finland and led a special detachment deep behind Russian lines. He was decorated with the Mannerheim Cross, equivalent to the American Medal of Honor, on July 9, 1944, for gallantry in combat. In January 1945, Törni joined a pro-German resistance group that was preparing stay-behind units in the event of a Russian invasion, and was sent to Neustrelitz, Germany, for special training at a sabotage school run by Skorzeny's commandos.

At the close of the war, Törni made his way through evasion channels to South America and then to the United States, with the assistance of a Finnish Veterans' Group. Picked up by the FBI in 1951 for being in the United States illegally, his case drew the attention of former OSS chief William Donovan, who had returned to his law practice and, as we have seen in this book, organized a private intelligence group within the World Commerce Corporation (WCC). Donovan reviewed Törni's file, becoming aware of his combat experience and commando and special operations skills. Perhaps through the interview process, Donovan found out Törni had trained at Skorzeny's commando school during the war. Donovan's law firm swung into action, and on February 3, 1953, a Congressional bill was submitted by New York Congressman W. Sterling Cole that would grant Törni immigrant status. The bill was signed by President Eisenhower on August 12, 1953.

Törni's new status cleared the way for his induction into the U.S. Army and a name change to Larry Thorne. Soon after, he enlisted in the United States Army and, quickly thereafter, volunteered for U.S. Special Forces (SF). By 1954,

Thorne was at Fort Bragg for Special Forces training and, upon completion, assigned to the 77th SF Group as an instructor at the Special Warfare School. In 1957, Thorne was appointed a Signal Corps officer, and, after a Pentagon interview, received a direct appointment to first lieutenant. Also in 1957, Thorne was assigned to the 10th Special Forces Group in Bad Tölz, Germany, a unit organized by the legendary Colonel Aaron Bank. While in Germany, it is highly likely that Thorne took his men to attend Skorzeny's "School of Commandos," examined in detail in Chapter Fourteen.

Thorne continued to build upon his incredible history as a soldier. By 1964, he had been promoted to Captain and became one of the very first soldiers to be recruited by MACV-SOG. On October 18, 1965, Thorne led the first MACV-SOG cross-border mission into Laos. During the return from Laos to Vietnam, his helicopter crashed. Thorne's assignment to SOG creates a nexus between him and the subsequent meeting between Otto Skorzeny and the "colonel" [Blackburn or Simmons] in Madrid, when Skorzeny was approached to assist MACV-SOG.

It is clear from the above evidence that Otto Skorzeny had some vital role assisting U.S. Special Forces with conduct of MACV-SOG operations. This likely involved training of personnel in sabotage and assassination, two specialty areas of Skorzeny. This was an extension of his earlier assistance to French special forces in Indochina and likely the reason the Americans came to him.

An interesting postscript to this history occurred on November 21, 1970. On that date, the U.S. mounted a raid into North Vietnam to release American prisoners held at a North Vietnamese prison camp in Son Tay. The special forces unit sent on the mission had been organized by Colonel Blackburn, then a brigadier general and, at that time, special assistant for counterinsurgency and special activities (SACSA). The actual mission was led by Colonel "Bull" Simons. Unfortunately, the POW's had been removed prior to the raid, thus resulting in a military intelligence failure. However, despite the failure, the raid is considered a brilliantly led and executed operation. Furthermore, its successes had many similarities to Otto Skorzeny's Mussolini rescue mission in 1943. Coincidence?—Perhaps, but in a published 1992 interview conducted by Greg

Walker with then-retired Major General John Singlaub, who replaced Colonel Blackburn in Vietnam as SOG chief, the general stated that SOG began studying the possibility of a Son Tay raid "nearly a year and a half before" the actual mission was launched. General Singlaub, like so many others described in this book, was a World War II veteran of units and missions directly linked to OSS operations and to postwar covert activity in Indochina. He was also part of the same covert military network associated with Otto Skorzeny prior to 1966. Information acquired during the research for this book included confirmation from a reliable, confidential military source that Singlaub had worked in some covert capacity with Skorzeny.

Finally, as a major point of association, General Singlaub later received notoriety for his role in the Iran–Contra affair. That covert operation, coordinated by Lt. Colonel Oliver North, involved Southern Air Transport, the CIA proprietary airline connected to Perkins McGuire. This is an interesting connection, as McGuire was the previously-mentioned former assistant secretary of defense revealed in this book as a close confidant and business associate of Otto Skorzeny. In the final analysis, there can be no doubt from the evidence presented above that Skorzeny was in an advisory role to Vietnamese covert operations, starting with the French in 1949 and later with the Americans until the late 1960s.

In 1967, an article appeared in the San Diego Union with the headline, "German Army Colonel Set Green Beret Pattern." In the lengthy article written by a reporter named Ray McHugh, Skorzeny is credited as the model upon which U.S. Special Forces (commonly known as Green Berets) were formed. The article gave the highlights of Skorzeny's military accomplishment, but it's the revelation at the end of the article that draws our attention here. Skorzeny stated that his highest compliment came from a U.S. military attaché in Europe who had served in Vietnam—"This man told me that the biggest successes of the American Army in Vietnam were based on the training and tactics evolved by my special forces . . . I hope I made some contribution. Vietnam is important to all of us."

Appendix B

Cable Address: TOLFUND, New York

TOLSTOY FOUNDATION, INC.

989 Eighth Avenue, New York 19, N. Y.

Telephone Circle-7-2922

THE HONORABLE HERBERT HOOVER
Honorary Chairman

ALEXANDRA TOLSTOY
President

November 16, 1962

The Honorable
J. Edgar Hoover
Director
Federal Bureau of Investigation
Washington 25, D. C.

Dear Mr. Hoover:

The Russian language Daily "Novoye Russkoye
Slovo" published in New York (Sunday, November
11th) writes:

"Last week the deputy of the Exarch of the
Patriarch (Soviet controlled) Church, Bishop
Dosithey of New York, arrived in San Francisco.

"The Bishop reported that due to this efforts
last August the Exarch bought a large property -
250 acres of land and woods - two hours distance
from New York.

"It is planned to organize a home for the priest -
hood of the Patriarch jurisdiction, a church, an
old people's home, a seminary and an eastern Orthodox
cemetery on the property. The cost of the property
is $45,000 in cash of which $24,000 is already paid
from money partly given by the Exarch, partly collected by the parish of St. Nicholas Church."

Perhaps this fact was already reported to you.
We, the Executives of the Tolstoy Foundation, after
having started an appeal for the creation of a nursing
home at the Tolstoy Foundation Center, expected such
a move on the part of the Communists and we consider

SP8Moufude 531-94 (JEK)

4/3/85   SP6BJA/SC

TOLSTOY FARM • VALLEY COTTAGE, N. Y. • CONGERS 8-6140

Notes

At the onset of research for this book, the author formed a small collaborative group to assist with background research and document exploitation. The group included, a genealogist, a translator, a military intelligence analyst, and a geologist. The group's effort was informally known as Project Stone Tree, named after the boyhood home of the author in North Carolina. This name was applied to all reports and dossiers produced by the group. Nearly all the background data on several principal characters found in the Skorzeny papers had to be generated as no previously comprehensive biographies on them had ever been created. Likewise, all foreign language documents in the Skorzeny papers had to be translated before being analyzed. The data for most of the research dossiers and background papers created for this book was compiled from publicly available research websites or physical archives, both governmental and private. General historical events are covered by the bibliography, by subject. Specific citations and quotes were attributed directly to the source.

THE LETTER
Paul Gluc letter: Mary Ferrell Foundation research website, advance query.

Albarelli, H. P., Jr., *A Terrible Mistake: The Murder of Frank Olsen and the CIA's Secret Cold War Experiments*, Trine Day, LLC, 2009.

PROLOGUE
Macdonald, Bill, *The True "Intrepid": Sir William Stephenson and the Unknown Agents*, Timberholme Books Ltd., Surrey, British Columbia, Canada, 1998.

Foot, M. R. D., *SOE: The Special Operations Executive 1940–46*, Pimlico edition, London, 1999.

Smith, Richard Harris, *OSS: The Secret History Of America's First Central Intelligence Agency*, The Lyons Press, Guilford, Connecticut, 2005.

CHAPTER ONE

Churchill, Winston, *The Hinge of Fate: The Second World War*, Volume 4.

Brown, Anthony Cave, *The Last Hero: Wild Bill Donovan*, Times Books, 1982.

Waller, Douglas, *Wild Bill Donovan: The Spymaster Who Created The OSS And Modern American Espionage*, Free Press, New York, 2011.

Skorzeny Papers / Genealogical Report on Robert Solborg prepared by Research assistant, exclusively for Project Stone Tree; derived from publicly available online genealogical services and newspaper search queries.

Stafford, David, *Camp X: OSS, "Intrepid," and the Allies' North American Training Camp for Secret Agents, 1941–1945*, Dodd, Mead & Company, New York, 1987.

Murphy, Robert, *Diplomat Among Warriors*, Doubleday & Company, Inc., Garden City, New York, 1964.

Brunelle, Gayle K., and Finley-Croswhite, Annette, *Murder In The Métro: Laetitia Toureaux and the Cagoule in 1930s France*, Louisiana State University Press, 2010.

Tompkins, Peter, *The Murder of Admiral Darlan: A Study In Conspiracy*, Simon and Schuster, New York, 1965.

CHAPTER TWO

Luther, Craig W.H., Ph.D., and Taylor, Hugh Page, *For Germany: The Otto Skorzeny Memoirs*, R. James Bender Publishing, San Jose, California, 2005.

Foot, M. R. D., *SOE: The Special Operations Executive 1940–46*, Pimlico edition, London, 1999.

Smith, Richard Harris, *OSS: The Secret History Of America's First Central Intelligence Agency*, The Lyons Press, Guilford, Connecticut, 2005.

Rigden, Denis, *Kill The Fuhrer: Section X and Operation Foxley*, Sutton Publishing Limited, Great Britain, 1999.

WCC: Some historians erroneously report the formation date of World Commerce Corporation as September 1947.

Riebling, Mark, *Wedge: From Pearl Harbor to 9/11, How the Secret War Between the FBI and CIA has Endangered National Security, A Touchstone Book*, Simon & Schuster, New York, London, Toronto, Sydney, Singapore, 1994.

Brown, Anthony Cave, *The Last Hero: Wild Bill Donovan*, Times Books, 1982.

Waller, Douglas, *Wild Bill Donovan: The Spymaster Who Created The OSS And Modern American Espionage*, Free Press, New York, 2011.

Skorzeny Papers / Genealogical Report on Frank Ryan prepared by research assistant exclusively for Project Stone Tree; derived from publicly available online genealogical services and newspaper search queries.

The Secrets War: The Office of Strategic Services in World War II, George C. Chalow, editor, National Archives Records Administration, Washington, D.C., an uncommon valor reprint edition, date not specified.

Skorzeny Papers / Genealogical Report on Ricardo Sicre prepared by research assistant exclusively for Project Stone Tree; derived from publicly available online genealogical services and newspaper search queries.

SAFEHAVEN, See CIA online archives reading room: Steury, Donald P., *The OSS and Project SAFEHAVEN: Tracking Nazi "Gold."*

Luther, Craig W.H., Ph.D., and Taylor, Hugh Page, *For Germany: The Otto Skorzeny Memoirs*, R. James Bender Publishing, San Jose, California, 2005.

History of the War Department Detachment (WDD) and Document Disposal Unit (DDU) derived from:

- Forging an Intelligence Partnership: CIA and the Origins of the BND, 1945–1949. CIA History Staff, Center for the Study of Intelligence, European Division, Directorate of Operations, 1999.

- See also, CIA online archives reading room: Salvage and Liquidation: *The Creation of the Central Intelligence Group,* Michael Warner. Also, CIA AND NAZI WAR CRIM. AND COL. CHAP. 1–10, DRAFT WORKING PAPER and CIA AND NAZI WAR CRIM. AND COL. CHAP. 11–21, DRAFT WORKING PAPER.

- Eagle and Swastika: CIA and Nazi War Criminals and Collaborators, Kevin Conley Ruffner, History Staff Central Intelligence Agency Washington, DC, April 2003.

- "Way of Pole's Escape Secret, Crossed Russian Zone By 'Underground,'" *Omaha World-Herald* (Omaha, Nebraska), Tuesday, November 4, 1947, page 5.

- Robert J. Burns assignment to Document Disposal Unit APO 757, *The Ithaca Journal,* Ithaca, New York, United States of America, December 31, 1951.

- Ann Whiting With Army In Germany, *Cumberland Evening Times,* Cumberland, Maryland, 29 January, 1952.

- Obituary for Charles G. Brophy, *The Santa Fe New Mexican,* Santa Fe, New Mexico, 14 August 1961. (evidence WDD also operated in New Guinea, Philippines and Japan).

- Author Interview: CIA Officer Tom Polgar, Florida, 2012.

British Security Coordination, *The Secret History of British Intelligence in the Americas, 1940–1945,* Fromm International, New York, 1999.

CHAPTER THREE

Skorzeny, Otto, *My Commando Operations: The Memoirs of Hitler's Most Daring Commando*, Schiffer Publishing, Atglen, Pennsylvania, 1995.

Luther, Craig W.H., Ph.D., and Taylor, Hugh Page, *For Germany: The Otto Skorzeny Memoirs*, R. James Bender Publishing, San Jose, California, 2005.

Foley, Charles, *Commando Extraordinary*, G. P. Putnam's Sons, New York, 1955.

Innfield, Glenn B., *Skorzeny Hitler's Commando*, Military Heritage Press, New York, 1981.

Forczyk, Robert, *Raid: Rescuing Mussolini; Gran Sasso 1943*, Osprey Publishing, Oxford, UK, 2010.

Annussek, Greg, *Hitler's Raid To Save Mussolini: The Most Infamous Commando Operation Of World War II*, Da Capo Press, Cambridge, Massachusetts, 2005.

McRaven, William H., *Spec Ops: Case Studies In Special Operations Warfare: Theory and Practice*, Presidio Press, Novato, California, 1995.

Yenne, Bill, *Operation Long Jump: Stalin, Roosevelt, Churchill, and the Greatest Assassination Plot in History*, Regnery History, Washington, DC, 2015.

Williamson, Gordon, *Elite 177: German Special Forces of World War II*, Osprey Publishing, Oxford, UK, 2009.

Stahl, P. W., *KG 200: The True Story*, Jane's Publishing Company Limited, London, 1981.

Thomas, Geoffrey J., and Ketley, Barry, *KG 200: The Luftwaffe's Most Secret Unit*, Hikoki Publications, East Sussex, UK, 2003.

Dupuy, Trevor N., Bongard, David L., and Anderson, Richard C., Jr., *Hitler's Last Gamble: The Battle of the Bulge, December 1944–January 1945*, HarperCollins Publishers, Inc., New York, 1994.

Murphy, Robert, *Diplomat Among Warriors*, Doubleday & Company, Inc., Garden City, New York, 1964.

Hamilton, A. Stephan, *The Oder Front 1945: Generaloberst Gotthard Heinrici, Heeresgruppe Weichsel and Germany's Final Defense in the East, 20 March– 3 May*, Helion & Company Ltd., West Midlands, England, 2011.

Peter Group: Information derived from documents on the group in the Skorzeny papers. Skorzeny was in contact with Peter Group members after the war.

Biddiscombe, Perry, *The SS Hunter Battalions: The Hidden History of the Nazi Resistance Movement 1944–5*, Tempus Publishing Limited, Gloucestershire, UK, 2006.

CHAPTER FOUR

Ganser, Daniele, *NATO's Secret Armies: Operation Gladio and Terrorism in Western Europe*, Frank Cass, New York, 2005.

Roger Wybot: *The French Secret Services*, Martyn Cornick & Peter Morris (compilers), Transaction Publishers, New Brunswick (U.S.A.) and London (U.K.), 1993 p. 77–79.

Moreau, Alain, *Dossier: Comme Drogue, Collection Dirigee Par Jean Picollec am editions*, Paris. Undated.

Howarth, Patrick, *Undercover: The Men and Women of the Special Operations Executive*, Routledge & Kegan Paul, London, Boston and Henley, 1980.

Skorzeny, Otto, *My Commando Operations: The Memoirs of Hitler's Most Daring Commando*, Schiffer Publishing, Atglen, Pennsylvania, 1995.

Luther, Craig W. H., PhD, and Taylor, Hugh Page, *For Germany: The Otto Skorzeny Memoirs*, R. James Bender Publishing, San Jose, California, 2005.

Greene, Joshua M., *Justice at Dachau : The Trials of an American Prosecutor*, Broadway Books, New York, 2003.

"J. C. Duvall Dies At 83: Unorthodox Tarrant Judge Gained Notoriety As Modern-Day Roy Bean," *Dallas Morning News*, Sunday, February 14, 1982, Page 1.

Judge Duval: Mary Ferrell Foundation research website, advance query.

Skorzeny Papers / Genealogical Report on Jesse C. Duvall prepared by research assistant exclusively for Project Stone Tree; derived from publicly available online genealogical services and newspaper search queries.

A. P., "Fananciers Unite," *San Diego Union,* Wednesday, September 24, 1947

San Diego, California, Page: 1.

CHAPTER FIVE

Luther, Craig W. H., Ph.D., and Taylor, Hugh Page, *For Germany: The Otto Skorzeny Memoirs,* R. James Bender Publishing, San Jose, California, 2005.

Information on Camp King (ECIC): U.S. Army in Germany (www .usarmygermany.com) Walter Elkins, Webmaster.

Information on Captain Mataxis: Author Interview with LTC Theodore C. Mataxis Jr. U.S. Retired.

Silver, Arnold M, "Questions, Questions, Questions: Memories of Oberursel," *Intelligence and National Security,* Vol. 8, No.2 (April 1993), pp. 199–213.

History of the War Department Detachment (WDD) and Document Disposal Unit (DDU) derived from:

- Forging an Intelligence Partnership: CIA and the Origins of the BND, 1945–49. CIA History Staff, Center for the Study of Intelligence, European Division, Directorate of Operations, 1999.

- See also, CIA online archives reading room: Salvage and Liquidation: *The Creation of the Central Intelligence Group,* Michael Warner. Also, CIA AND NAZI WAR CRIM. AND COL. CHAP. 1–10, DRAFT WORKING PAPER and CIA AND NAZI WAR CRIM. AND COL. CHAP. 11–21, DRAFT WORKING PAPER.

- Eagle and Swastika: CIA and Nazi War Criminals and Collaborators, Kevin Conley Ruffner, History Staff Central Intelligence Agency Washington, DC, April 2003.

- "Way of Pole's Escape Secret, Crossed Russian Zone By 'Underground,'" *Omaha World-Herald* (Omaha, Nebraska), Tuesday, November 4, 1947, page 5.

- Robert J. Burns assignment to Document Disposal Unit APO 757, *The Ithaca Journal*, Ithaca, New York, United States of America, December 31, 1951.

- Ann Whiting With Army In Germany, *Cumberland Evening Times*, Cumberland, Maryland, 29 January, 1952.

- Obituary for Charles G. Brophy, *The Santa Fe New Mexican*, Santa Fe, New Mexico, 14 August 1961. (evidence WDD also operated in New Guinea, Philippines and Japan).

- Author Interview: CIA Officer Tom Polgar, Florida, 2012.

- U.S. Justice Report on Klaus Barbie and His Links to U.S. Intelligence, and source documents, Director of the Office of Special Investigations, Allen A. Ryan, Jr., 1983.

Background on Lucien Conein; Albarelli, H. P., Jr., *A Terrible Mistake: The Murder of Frank Olsen and the CIA's Secret Cold War Experiments*, Trine Day, LLC, 2009.

Skorzeny, Otto, *My Commando Operations: The Memoirs of Hitler's Most Daring Commando*, Schiffer Publishing, Atglen, Pennsylvania, 1995.

Luther, Craig W.H., Ph.D., and Taylor, Hugh Page, *For Germany: The Otto Skorzeny Memoirs*, R. James Bender Publishing, San Jose, California, 2005.

Skorzeny Papers / Genealogical Report on Hjalmar Schacht prepared by Research assistant, exclusively for Project Stone Tree; derived from publicly available online genealogical services and newspaper search queries.

Pyke, Diana, *Confessions Of "The Old Wizard": The Autobiography Of Hjalmar Horace Greeley Schacht,* The Riverside Press, Cambridge, Massachusetts, 1956.

Weitz, John, *Hitler's Banker: Hjalmar Horace Greeley Schacht*, Little, Brown and Company, New York, 1997.

Silver, Arnold M, "Questions, Questions, Questions: Memories of Oberursel," *Intelligence and National Security*, Vol. 8, No.2 (April 1993), pp. 199–213.

CHAPTER SIX

Ganser, Daniele, *NATO's Secret Armies: Operation Gladio and Terrorism in Western Europe*, Frank Cass, New York, 2005.

Bissell, Richard M. Jr., *Reflections of a Cold Warrior: From Yalta to the Bay of Pigs*, Yale University Press, New Haven and London 1996.

Riebling, Mark, Wedge: *From Pearl Harbor to 9/11, How the Secret War Between the FBI and CIA has Endangered National Security*, A Touchstone Book, Simon & Schuster, New York, London, Toronto, Sydney, Singapore, 1994.

Simpson, Christopher, *Blowback: America's Recruitment of Nazis and Its Destructive Impact on Our Domestic Foreign Policy*, Weidenfeld & Nicholson, New York, 1988.

Office of the Historian, U.S. Government web site: https://history.state.gov /historicaldocuments/frus1945-50Intel/d292.

National Security Council Directive on Office of Special Projects

Washington, June 18, 1948.

NSC 10/2

1. The National Security Council, taking cognizance of the vicious covert activities of the USSR, its satellite countries and Communist groups to discredit and defeat the aims and activities of the United States and other Western powers, has determined that, in the interests of world peace and US national security, the overt foreign activities of the US Government must be supplemented by covert operations.

2. The Central Intelligence Agency is charged by the National Security Council with conducting espionage and counter-espionage operations abroad. It therefore seems desirable, for operational reasons, not to create a new agency for covert operations, but in time of peace to place the responsibility for them within the structure of the Central Intelligence Agency and correlate them with espionage and counter-espionage operations under the over-all control of the Director of Central Intelligence.

3. Therefore, under the authority of Section 102(d)(5) of the National Security Act of 1947, the National Security Council hereby directs that in time of peace:

a. A new Office of Special Projects shall be created within the Central Intelligence Agency to plan and conduct covert operations; and in coordination with the Joint Chiefs of Staff to plan and prepare for the conduct of such operations in wartime.

b. A highly qualified person, nominated by the Secretary of State, acceptable to the Director of Central Intelligence and approved by the National Security Council, shall be appointed as Chief of the Office of Special Projects.

c. The Chief of the Office of Special Projects shall report directly to the Director of Central Intelligence. For purposes of security and of flexibility of operations, and to the maximum degree consistent with efficiency, the Office of Special Projects shall operate independently of other components of Central Intelligence Agency.

d. The Director of Central Intelligence shall be responsible for:

(1) Ensuring, through designated representatives of the Secretary of State and of the Secretary of Defense, that covert operations are planned and conducted in a manner consistent with US foreign and military policies and with overt activities. In disagreements arising between the Director of Central Intelligence and the representative of the Secretary of State or the Secretary of Defense over such plans, the matter shall be referred to the National Security Council for decision.

(2) Ensuring that plans for wartime covert operations are also drawn up with the assistance of a representative of the Joint Chiefs of Staff and are accepted by the latter as being consistent with and complementary to approved plans for wartime military operations.

(3) Informing, through appropriate channels, agencies of the US Government, both at home and abroad (including diplomatic and military representatives in each area), of such operations as will affect them.

e. Covert operations pertaining to economic warfare will be conducted by the Office of Special Projects under the guidance of the departments and agencies responsible for the planning of economic warfare.

f. Supplemental funds for the conduct of the proposed operations for fiscal year 1949 shall be immediately requested. Thereafter operational funds for these purposes shall be included in normal Central Intelligence Agency Budget requests.

4. In time of war, or when the President directs, all plans for covert operations shall be coordinated with the Joint Chiefs of Staff. In active theaters of war where American forces are engaged, covert operations will be conducted under the direct command of the American Theater Commander and orders therefore will be transmitted through the Joint Chiefs of Staff unless otherwise directed by the President.

5. As used in this directive, "covert operations" are understood to be all activities (except as noted herein) which are conducted or sponsored by this Government against hostile foreign states or groups or in support of friendly foreign states or groups but which are so planned and executed that any US Government responsibility for them is not evident to unauthorized persons and that if uncovered the US Government can plausibly disclaim any responsibility for them. Specifically, such operations shall include any covert activities related to: propaganda, economic warfare; preventive direct action, including sabotage, anti-sabotage, demolition and evacuation measures; subversion against hostile states, including assistance to underground resistance movements, guerrillas and refugee

liberation groups, and support of indigenous anti-Communist elements in threatened countries of the free world. Such operations shall not include armed conflict by recognized military forces, espionage, counter-espionage, and cover and deception for military operations.

6. This Directive supersedes the directive contained in NSC 4–A, which is hereby cancelled.

Simpson, Christopher, *Blowback: America's Recruitment of Nazis and Its Destructive Impact on Our Domestic Foreign Policy*, Weidenfeld & Nicholson, New York, 1988.

Skorzeny Papers / Genealogical Report on Robert Bishop prepared by research assistant exclusively for Project Stone Tree; derived from publicly available online genealogical services and newspaper search queries.

Skorzeny, Otto, *My Commando Operations: The Memoirs of Hitler's Most Daring Commando*, Schiffer Publishing, Atglen, Pennsylvania, 1995.

Luther, Craig W. H., PhD, and Taylor, Hugh Page, *For Germany: The Otto Skorzeny Memoirs*, R. James Bender Publishing, San Jose, California, 2005.

Silver, Arnold M, "Questions, Questions, Questions: Memories of Oberursel," *Intelligence and National Security*, Vol. 8, No.2 (April 1993), pp. 199–213.

CHAPTER SEVEN

Foley, Charles, *Commando Extraordinary*, G. P. Putnam's Sons, New York, 1955.

The Marshall Plan in Austria, Editors: Gunter Bischof, Anton Pelinka, Dieter Stiefel., Vol 18., Transaction Pub., New Brunswick, USA, London, UK, 2000.

Critchfield, James H., *Partners at the Creation: The Men Behind Postwar Germany's Defense and Intelligence Establishments*, Naval Institute Press, Annapolis, Maryland, 2003.

Skorzeny identity booklet: Skorzeny Papers.

Information Control Division (ICD): See *The Graduate Paper for PhD*, Kruger, Linda L., *Logistics Matters: The Growth of Little Americas in Occupied Germany*. University of Kansas, 2013.

Lee, Martin A., *The Beast Reawakens: Fascism's Resurgence from Hitler's Spymasters to Today's Neo-Nazi Groups and Right-Wing Extremists*, Routledge, New York, 2000.

Walters, Guy, *Hunting Evil: The Nazi War Criminals Who Escaped & the Quest to Bring Them to Justice*, Broadway Books, New York, 2009.

Reese, Mary Ellen, *General Reinhard Gehlen: The CIA Connection*, George Mason University Press, Fairfax, Virginia, 1990.

Cookridge, E. H., *Gehlen: Spy Of The Century*, Random House, New York, 1971.

Höhne, Heinz, and Zolling, Hermann, *The General Was A Spy: the Truth About General Gehlen and His Spy Ring*, Coward, McCann & Geoghegan, Inc., New York, 1971.

Critchfield, James H., *Partners at the Creation: The Men Behind Postwar Germany's Defense And Intelligence Establishments*, Naval Institute Press, Annapolis, Maryland, 2003.

Morerison, John, "The antics of France's dirty tricks brigade," *The Sydney Morning Herald*, Sydney, New South Wales, Australia, Wednesday, August 21, 1985, page 8.

Morrison, John, "French agency has a tough reputation," *Chicago Tribune*, 27 August, 1985. [French participation in Skorzeny release confirmed by French Colonel Michel Garder.]

Roger Wybot: *The French Secret Services*, Martyn Cornick & Peter Morris (compilers), Transaction Publishers, New Brunswick (U.S.A.) and London (U.K.), 1993 p. 77–79.

Moreau, Alain, *Dossier: Comme Drogue, Collection Dirigee Par Jean Picollec am editions*, Paris. Undated.

French Intelligence Service INSCOM Dossier ZE000214W Agent Report Chief of the de Gaulle Intelligence Service in Germany RE: French Intelligence activity 23 August 1948 Iv-A-14.9 p. 121.

Agent Report French Intelligence Service, 1 October 1948 IV-889 p 109–111.

Records of the Office of Strategic Services 1940–1946 (RG 226), Records of the Office of Strategic Services (RG 226): Entry 213, French Intelligence Services.

Skorzeny papers.

U. S. Army CIC Report, 7970th CIC Region IV, dated 1947, highly illegible, RE: Project Happiness.

Author interview with Retired CIA officer Tom Polgar, 2012. Polgar said ODESSA *was not* a neo-Nazi movement but a clandestine network linked to relief organizations. "ODESSA," CIC dossier 41878; and "Organization, 'ODESSA,'" 970th CIC Detachment, U.S. Army, July 15, 1947. National Archive records group 319, box 64, file no. ZF015116, "Odessa Organization."

CHAPTER EIGHT

Simpson, Christopher, *Blowback: America's Recruitment of Nazis and Its Destructive Impact on Our Domestic Foreign Policy*, Weidenfeld & Nicholson, New York, 1988.

Weiner, Tim, *Legacy of Ashes: The History of the CIA,* Anchor Books, A Division of Random House, Inc., New York, 2008.

CIA online archives reading room: CIA Cold War Records: THE CIA UNDER HARRY TRUMAN, Edited by Michael Warner, CIA History Staff; Center for the Study of Intelligence, 1994.

Alleged Assassination Plots Involving Foreign Leaders, An Interim Report of the Select Committee to Study Governmental Operations With Respect to Intelligence Activities United States Senate, Together with Additional,

Supplemental, and Separate Views, November 20, 1975, U.S. Government Printing Office, Washington, D.C., 1975.

CIA declassified Skorzeny Files, CIA Chief of Station Report, Madrid, 1959.

Skorzeny Papers / File/ David Martin: Project Stone Tree; derived from publicly available online genealogical services and newspaper search queries.

Skorzeny Papers / Genealogical Report on Boris T. Pash prepared by research assistant exclusively for Project Stone Tree; derived from publicly available online genealogical services and newspaper search queries.

Pash, Colonel Boris T., *The Alsos Mission*, Charter Books, New York, 1969.

John M. Crewdson, "Hunt Says CIA Had Murder Unit," *Dallas Morning News*, citing *N.Y. Times*, Saturday, December 27, 1975, Page 12.

Thomas, Evan, *The Very Best Men: The Daring Early Years of the CIA*, Simon & Schuster Paperbacks, New York, 1995, 2006.

CHAPTER NINE

Binder, L. James, *Lemnitzer: A Soldier for His Time*, Brassey's, Dulles, Virginia, 1997.

CIA Skorzeny File Letter from 7712 European Command Intelligence School, [redacted] to [redacted], 2 February, 1949.

Skorzeny Papers, Miscellaneous File (Skorzeny to Pierre Bertaux, 4 September 1953).

New Scientist, (Weekly) June 16, 1977 Vol 74, No 1056.

Skorzeny Papers, Passports.

"ACUE: Diplomacy & Statecraft: OSS, CIA and European unity: The American committee on United Europe, 1948–60," Richard J. Aldrich University of Nottingham, Online Publication Date: 01 March 1997.

"ACUE: Giles Scott-Smith, The Politics of Apolitical Culture: The Congress for Cultural Freedom, the CIA and post-war American hegemony,"

Routledge/ PSA Political Studies Series, University of Manchester, London and New York, 2002.

Skorzeny Papers / Genealogical Report on Robert Solborg prepared by research assistant exclusively for Project Stone Tree; derived from publicly available online genealogical services and newspaper search queries.

Ganser, Daniele, *NATO's Secret Armies: Operation Gladio and Terrorism in Western Europe*, Frank Cass, New York, 2005.

Binder, L. James, *Lemnitzer: A Soldier for His Time*, Brassey's, Dulles, Virginia, 1997.

Roger Wybot: *The French Secret Services*, Martyn Cornick & Peter Morris (compilers), Transaction Publishers, New Brunswick (U.S.A.) and London (U.K.), 1993.

CIA Directors Log 1949, online, archives reading room.

Ganser, Daniele, *NATO's Secret Armies: Operation Gladio and Terrorism in Western Europe*, Frank Cass, New York, 2005.

Cook, Bernard A., *Europe Since 1945: An Encyclopedia; Volume II, K–Z*, Garland Publishing, Inc., New York & London, 2001 p. 969–970.

Skorzeny Papers / Genealogical Report on Clifford Forster prepared by research assistant exclusively for Project Stone Tree; derived from publicly available online genealogical services and newspaper search queries.

Janney, Peter, *Mary's Mosaic: The CIA Conspiracy to Murder John F. Kennedy, Mary Pinchot Meyer, and Their Vision for World Peace*, Skyhorse Publishing, New York, 2012.

"QKACTIVE: Research Aid: Cryptonyms and Terms in Declassified CIA files," Nazi War Crimes and Japanese Imperial Government Records Disclosure Acts.

CIA Directors Log 1949, online, archives reading room.

"SEMIC: Skorzeny papers. See: Moreau, Alain, *Dossier: Comme Drogue, Collection Dirigee Par Jean Picollec am editions*, Paris. Undated.

Kruger, Henrik, *The Great Heroin Coup: Drugs, Intelligence, & International Fascism*. South End Press, Boston, MA 1980.

Skorzeny Papers / Biographical Report on Michel de Camaret prepared by the author exclusively for Project Stone Tree; derived from publicly available online resources.

Skorzeny Papers / Biographical Report on Pierre de Bénouville prepared by the author exclusively for Project Stone Tree; derived from publicly available online resources.

Brunelle, Gayle K., and Finley-Croswhite, Annette, *Murder In The Métro: Laetitia Toureaux and the Cagoule in 1930s France*, Louisiana State University Press, 2010.

Information on 11th Shock for this section see: Talbot, David, *The Devil's Chessboard: Allen Dulles, the CIA, and the Rise of America's Secret Government*, HarperCollins, New York, 2015. Also; Ganser, Daniele, *NATO's Secret Armies: Operation Gladio and Terrorism in Western Europe*, Frank Cass, New York, 2005.

Morerison, John, "The antics of France's dirty tricks brigade," *The Sydney Morning Herald*, Sydney, New South Wales, Australia, Wednesday, August 21, 1985, page 8.

CHAPTER TEN

"Nazi Colonel Flees, Leaves Memoirs," *Omaha World Herald*, February 14, 1950, p.2.

"Skorzeny Seen in Paris," *Evening Star* (Washington, D.C.), February 14, 1950 p. 4

"Six Policeman Hurt in Paris Demonstrations," *Charleston News and Courier*, Charleston, S.C. p 1.

Wallenstein, Marcel, "Police of Europe Hunting Phantom Nazi Fugitive," *Milwaukee, Journal Sentinel*. (Milwaukee, Wisconsin), April 16, 1950.

Skorzeny Papers, (1950 file)

SOFINDUS:

- David Kahn, *Hitler's Spies: German Military Intelligence in World War II,* 1978 Macmillan Publishing Co. Inc., New York, NY.

- SOFINDUS: Declassified files: Mosig, Walter Eugen, The National Archives (United Kingdom) reference KV-2-3574.

- Lieberman, Sima, *Growth and Crisis in the Spanish Economy: 1940–1993.*

- *Routledge Studies in the European Economy,* London and New York, 1995.

- Fundacion Nacional Francisco Franco: online archive resource, Joaquin Planell Riera, Minister of Industry and President of the National Company Calvo Sotelo.

- Declassified files: Mosig, Walter Eugen, The National Archives (United Kingdom) reference KV-2-3574.

- The Factual List of Nazis Protected by Spain, compiled by Eliah Meyer (internet resource citing declassified U.S. intelligence documents).

- Goñi, Uki, *The Real Odessa: How Perón Brought the Nazi War Criminals to Argentina,* Granta Books, London, 2003.

Skorzeny Papers / Genealogical Report on Victor Oswald prepared by research assistant exclusively for Project Stone Tree; derived from publicly available online genealogical services and newspaper search queries.

Skorzeny Papers / Genealogical Report on Hjalmar Schacht prepared by research assistant exclusively for Project Stone Tree; derived from publicly available online genealogical services and newspaper search queries.

Pyke, Diana, *Confessions of "The Old Wizard": The Autobiography of Hjalmar Horace Greeley Schacht,* The Riverside Press, Cambridge, Massachusetts, 1956.

Weitz, John, Hitler's Banker: Hjalmar Horace Greeley Schacht, Little, Brown and Company, New York, 1997.

CHAPTER ELEVEN

Skorzeny Papers.

Parker, Danny S., *Hitler's Warrior: The Life and Wars of SS Colonel Jochen Peiper*, Da Capo Press, Boston, Massachusetts, 2014.

General Heinz Guderian: Skorzeny Papers.

Building L (William K. Harvey): Stockton, Bayard, F*lawed Patriot: The Rise and Fall of CIA Legend Bill Harvey*, Potomac Books, Washington, D.C., 2006.

CERC, Catholic Education Resource Center, Chauncey Devereux Stillman (1907–1989), by Rev. George Rutler, online resource.

Parker, Danny S., *Hitler's Warrior: The Life and Wars of SS Colonel Jochen Peiper*, Da Capo Press, Boston, Massachusetts, 2014.

Skorzeny Papers / Genealogical Report on Algur H. Meadows prepared by Research assistant, exclusively for Project Stone Tree; derived from publicly available online genealogical services and newspaper search queries.

Presley, James, *Never In Doubt: A History of Delta Drilling Company*, Gulf Publishing Company, Houston, 1981.

Skorzeny Papers / Genealogical Report on Colonel Jack Critchton prepared by Research assistant, exclusively for Project Stone Tree; derived from publicly available online genealogical services and newspaper search queries.

Secrets of War: Cold War: Inside the CIA, DVD documentary by Mill Creek Entertainment, LLC., narrated by Charlton Heston, 2013.

CHAPTER TWELVE

Sources for this chapter included extensive interviews conducted by the author with a number of individuals who knew Skorzeny in Spain from

1950–1962; also derived from correspondence in the Skorzeny papers, 1945–1975 in possession of author.

Greene, Jack, and Massignani, Alessandro, *The Black Prince and the Sea Devils; the Story of Valerio Borghese and the Elite Units of the Decima Mas*, Da Capo Press, Cambridge, Massachusetts, 2004.

Information on Horcher's Restaurant: Goñi, Uki, *The Real Odessa: How Perón Brought the Nazi War Criminals to Argentina*, Granta Books, London, 2003 p. 74.

Major Robert Bieck, unpublished diary, copy in author's possession. Also, author interview with Attorney Robert B. Bieck, Jr., 2012.

All information on Skorzeny from this section derived from interviews by the author with U.S. Embassy Spain military attache's: Capt. Thaddeus T. Skladzien, USAF, Lt. Thomas W. Trout, USN, and Lt. Lamar W. Tuzo (rank cited is at time of duty in Madrid, covering period the 1950–1962).

Information on Skorzeny involvement in Operation Paper Clip comes from documents in Skorzeny Papers; Major Robert Bieck unpublished diary. Information on Operation Paper Clip see: Lasby, Clarence G., Project Paperclip: German Scientists and the Cold War, Atheneum, New York, 1971; see also, Jacobsen, Annie, *Operation Paperclip: The Secret Intelligence Program That Brought Nazi Scientists To America*, Little, Brown and Company, New York, 2014.

CHAPTER THIRTEEN

Hersch, Burton, *The Old Boys: The American Elite and the Origins of the CIA*, Tree Farm Books, St. Petersburg, Florida, 1992, 2002.

Mangold, Tom, *Cold Warrior, James Jesus Angleton: The CIA's Master Spy Hunter*, Simon & Schuster, New York, 1991.

Stockton, Bayard, *Flawed Patriot: The Rise and Fall Of CIA Legend Bill Harvey*, Potomac Books, Washington, D.C., 2006.

Author interview with Retired CIA officer Tom Polgar, 2012.

Thomas, Evan, *The Very Best Men: The Daring Early Years of the CIA*, Simon & Schuster Paperbacks, New York, 1995, 2006.

DTLINEN: Research Aid: Cryptonyms and Terms in Declassified CIA files, Nazi War Crimes and Japanese Imperial Government Records Disclosure Acts.

KgU: Author interview with Retired CIA officer Tom Polgar, 2012.

Author interview with former CIA officer Peter Sichel, 2015.

Skorzeny Papers / Genealogical Report on Severin Wallach prepared by Research assistant, exclusively for Project Stone Tree; derived from publicly available online genealogical services and newspaper search queries.

Skorzeny Papers / Genealogical Report on Robert G. Storey prepared by Research assistant, exclusively for Project Stone Tree; derived from publicly available online genealogical services and newspaper search queries.

"4 'Admit' Spying On East Germany: Red News Agency ADN Reports 'Confressions' Tying Officials to U.S.," *Providence Journal*, Saturday, July 26, 1952, Page 3.

Callanan, James, *Covert Action in The Cold War: US Policy, Intelligence and CIA Operations*, I.B. Tauris, New York, 2010.

Adams, Jefferson, *Historical Dictionary of German Intelligence, No. 11*, The Scarecrow Press, Inc., Lanham, Maryland, 2009.

Sereny, Gitta W. W., *The Healing Wound: Experiences and Reflections on Germany, 1939–2001*, Norton & Company, New York, London, 2001, 2000.

Murphy, David E.; Kondrashev, Sergei A.; and Bailey, George, *Battleground Berlin: CIA Vs. KGB In the Cold War*, Yale University Press, New Haven, 1997.

Secret Intelligence in the Twentieth Century, Editors Heike Bungert, Jan G. Heitmann, Michael Wala, Foreword by Nigel West, FRANK CASS, London, Portland, OR, 2003.

BOB letter: Skorzeny Papers, correspondence 1953 file.

Copeland Miles, *The Game of Nations, The Amorality of Power Politics*, Simon and Schuster, New York, 1969.

Mangold, Tom, *Cold Warrior, James Jesus Angleton: The CIA's Master Spy Hunter*, Simon & Schuster, New York, 1991.

Weiner, Tim, *Legacy of Ashes: The History of the CIA*, Anchor Books, A Division of Random House, Inc., New York, 2008.

Bar-Zohar, Michael and Mishal, Nissim, *Mossad*, An Imprint of Harper-Collins Publishers, New York, 2012.

Confidential Interview with Author.

Howard, Roger, *Operation Damocles: Israel's Secret War Against Hitler's Scientists, 1951–1967*, Pegasus Books LLC, New York, 2013.

United States Department of Justice, FBI, Memorandum, 25 August, 1955, To: Director CIA, Attn: Deputy Director, Plans. From: John Edgar Hoover, Director FBI. Subject: Roe Kapelle, Espionage-R.

Skorzeny Papers, 1955 File.

CHAPTER FOURTEEN

Confidential Interview with Author.

Skorzeny's School of Commando Tactics: Herbert, Anthony B., *Soldier*, Cloverleaf Books, Englewood, Colorado, 1973; also, Author interviews with U.S. Embassy Spain Military Attaché's, Capt. Thaddeus T. Skladzien, USAF, Lt. Thomas W. Trout, USN, and Lt. Lamar W. Tuzo (rank cited is at time of Embassy duty).

CIA Directors Log, Declassified Top Secret, October 26, 1951, MAAG was suggested as the cover for the Clandestine Planning Committee. Subsequent analysis of MAAG and its relationship to stay-behind programs in Europe available from declassified documents and historical narratives on the subject indicate the suggestion was implemented. For detail on stay-behind networks see: Ganser, Daniele, *NATO's Secret Armies: Operation Gladio and Terrorism in Western Europe*, Frank Cass, New York, 2005.

Crozier, Brian, *Franco*, Little, Brown and Company, Boston / Toronto, 1976 p. 445.

Prouty, L. Fletcher, *The Secret Team: The CIA and Its Allies in Control of the United States and the World*, Skyhorse Publishing, New York, 2011.

The first Agreement in 1953 was renewed in 1963. "Joint United States Military Group Military Assistance Advisery Group-Spain: Security Assistance Programs and Activities." by Colonel Robert G. Chaudrue, USA Chief, Security Assistance Division and others associated with program, date UNK; also: Crozier, Brian, Franco, Little, Brown and Company, Boston / Toronto, 1976 p. 444–446

Skorzeny Papers / Genealogical Report on Struve Hensel prepared by Research assistant, exclusively for Project Stone Tree; derived from publicly available online genealogical services and newspaper search queries.

- Skorzeny was also a representative of Otto Wolff. Skorzeny mentions Hensel in his correspondence in regards to the steel business for this period. A key businessman linked to the Hensel–Skorzeny association includes one Leon Frenk. Frenk and Hensel were business partners in a number of companies (most likely U.S. intelligence cover organizations) including the U.S Electronics Corps, a subsidiary of American Aircraft Engineering Corporation, Mundial Trade Corp (Mondale Corporation associated with Permindex), World Recovery Corp., and Western Tube Division (linked to Ferac Nagy), and Technical Equipment Co. The Mondail Corporation has been found in JFK conspiracy studies. The author regards the Mondail corporation as one facet in the overall military intelligence industrial structure, a facilitating entity for covert operations, but not the operational heart of that covert structure.

Christianson, Joel C., ISA: Office of the Assistant Secretary of Defense for International Security Affairs, Historical Office, Office of the Secretary of Defense, Washington, D.C., 2014.

Skorzeny Papers / Genealogical Report on E. Perkins McGuire prepared by research assistant exclusively for Project Stone Tree; derived from publicly available online genealogical services and newspaper search queries.

Thayer, George, *The War Business: The International Trade in Armaments,* Simon and Schuster, New York, 1969.

Evica, George Michael, A *Certain Arrogance: U.S. Intelligence's Manipulation of Religious Groups and Individuals in Two World Wars and the Cold War— and the Sacrificing of Lee Harvey Oswald,* Xlibris Corporation, 2006.

Spain's Value to NATO Cited *Evening Star* (Washington, DC) March 4, 1957 p9.

Murphy Washington, D.C. *Evening Star* dated March 4, 1957 under the title "Spain Value to NATO Cited," Secretary McGuire and Deputy Under Secretary of State Robert Murphy attended the Annual Communion breakfast of Archdiocese of Washington Spanish ambassador to the US Jose Maria de Areiza spoke of the potential contributions of the Spanish military to NATO. Held at the Willard Hotel. Present were: Perkins McGuire, Robert Murphy, Homer Gruenther.

Herbert, Anthony B., *Soldier,* Cloverleaf Books, Englewood, Colorado, 1973.

Information on Captain Mataxis: Author Interview with LTC Theodore C. Mataxis Jr. U.S. Retired.

Veritas, Journal Of Army Special Operations History V11/N1, United States Army Special Operations Command, Fort Bragg, North Carolina.

Here is a list of the Peter Group operatives (assassins) who are in contact with Skorzeny:

- SS *Hauptsturmführer* Otto Alexander Friedrich Schwerdt. Born on 7 September, 1917, in Eisenberg, Germany. After the war, he was arrested in Germany and transferred for trial in Denmark, where he was sentenced to death by the Copenhagen City Court, on January 27, 1949. The sentence was reduced to twenty-four years imprisonment by the High Court, on January 19, 1950. He was released and deported by Denmark, on December 1, 1953.

- SS-*Hauptsturmführer* Horst Paul Issel. Born September 10, 1912, in Berlin. Sentenced to death by the Copenhagen City Court, on January 27, 1949. Sentenced to twenty years imprisonment by the High Court, on October 19, 1950. He was released and expelled from Denmark, in June 1953.

- SS *Oberscharführer* Otto Wagner. Born Oct. 27, 1920, in Germany. Sentenced to ten years in prison in Copenhagen City Court, on January 27, 1949. Sentenced to seven years imprisonment by the High Court. on January 19, 1950. He was released and deported by Denmark, on October 20, 1950.

- SS *Untersturmführer* Hans Kramer. Disappeared in Germany after the war. Is still officially wanted by Denmark.

CHAPTER FIFTEEN

Windrow, Martin, *The French Indochina War 1946–1954*, Osprey Publishing, Long Island, New York, 1998.

O'Leary, Brad, and Symour, L. E., *Triangle Of Death: The Shocking Truth About the Role of South Vietnam and the French Mafia in the Assassination of JFK*, WND Books, Nashville, Tennessee, 2003.

Prouty, L. Fletcher, *The Secret Team: The CIA and Its Allies in Control of the United States and the World*, Skyhorse Publishing, New York, 2011.

Albarelli, H. P., Jr., *A Terrible Mistake: The Murder of Frank Olsen and the CIA's Secret Cold War Experiments*, Trine Day, LLC, 2009.

Skorzeny Papers / Genealogical Report on Earl C. Bergquist prepared by research assistant exclusively for Project Stone Tree; derived from publicly available online genealogical services and newspaper search queries.

Askins, Charles, *Unrepentant Sinner: The Autorbiography of Col. Charles Askins*, Paladin Press, Boulder, CO, 1985.

CHAPTER SIXTEEN

Porch, Douglas, *The French Secret Services: From the Dreyfus Affair to the Gulf War*, Farrar, Straus and Giroux, New York, 1995.

Horne, Alistair, *A Savage War of Peace: Algeria 1954–1962*, New York Review Books, New York, 2006.

Joesten, Joachim, *The Red Hand: The Sinister Account of the Terrorist Arm of the French Right-Wing "Ultras"—in Algeria and on the Continent*, Abelard-Schuman, London, New York, Toronto, 1962.

The French Secret Services, Martyn Cornick & Peter Morris (compilers), Transaction Publishers, New Brunswick (U.S.A.) and London (U.K.), 1993.

Talbot, David, *The Devil's Chessboard: Allen Dulles, the CIA, and the Rise of America's Secret Government*, HarperCollins, New York, 2015.

New Scientist, (Weekly) June 16, 1977 Vol 74, No 1056.

Anderson, Malcolm. *In Thrall to Political Change: Police and Gendarmerie in France*. Oxford University Press, Oxford, England, 2011.

CIA Memorandum Chief of Operations, DD/P reference #9937 (IN 16562) document 25 January 1962.

American Committee for France & Algeria: Copies can be viewed online: blumenfeld.campconstitution.net

Skorzeny Papers / Genealogical Report on Clifford Forster prepared by research assistant exclusively for Project Stone Tree; derived from publicly available online genealogical services and newspaper search queries.

Skorzeny Papers / Genealogical Report on James Burnham prepared by research assistant exclusively for Project Stone Tree; derived from publicly available online genealogical services and newspaper search queries.

Clayton, Anthony, *The Wars of French Decolonization, Longman*, New York, 1994.

CIA Dispatch, EGOA 13328 To: Chief of Base, Bonn, Chief, Munich Liaison Base; Chief EE, From: Chief of Station, Germany, Subject: Operational Wilhelm Beisner, 27 January 1961.

Henissart, Paul, *Wolves in the City: The Death of French Algeria*, Simon and Schuster, New York, 1970.

January 25, 1961 CIA document date Jan 27 (no document #) Otto Skorzeny file. Source CIA case officer (assigned temporarily to the same type of program which has been ongoing in Switzerland since October 1960.)

Tauber, Kurt P. *Beyond the Eagle and Swastika: German Nationalism Since 1945 Vol II*, Wesleyan University Press, Middletown, Connecticut 1967 1095 endnote 57.

Porch, Douglas, *The French Foreign Legion: A Complete History Of The Legendary Fighting Force*, Skyhorse Publishing, 2010.

Blum, William, *Killing Hope: U.S. Military and C.I.A. Interventions Since World War II*, Common Courage Press, Monroe, Maine, 2004.

Joesten, Joachim, *de Gaulle And His Murderers: A factual account of a dramatic piece of contemporary history*, Times Press and Anthony Gibbs & Phillips, 1964.

CHAPTER SEVENTEEN

Evans, Martin, *Algeria: France's Undeclared War*, Oxford University Press, Oxford, UK, 2012.

Henissart, Paul, *Wolves in the City: The Death of French Algeria*, Simon and Schuster, New York, 1970.

Horne, Alistair, *A Savage War of Peace: Algeria 1954–1962*, New York Review Books, New York, 2006.

Démaret, Pierre, and Plume, Christian, *Target de Gaulle: The True Story of the 31 Attempts on the Life of the French President*, The Dial Press, New York, 1975.

Joesten, Joachim, *De Gaulle and His Murderers: A Factual Account of a Dramatic Piece of Contemporary History*, Times Press and Anthony Gibbs & Phillips, 1964.

Skorzeny Papers: Correspondence with Contessa Dagmar Álvarez de Toledo.

Blum, William, *Killing Hope: U.S. Military and C.I.A. Interventions Since World War II*, Common Courage Press, Monroe, Maine, 2004.

Yatagan Commando: "Algeria Situation Loaded with Irony," *Dallas Morning News*, March 21, 1962 Section 4, Page 5.

The Association for Diplomatic Studies and Training, Foreign Affairs Oral History Project, Richard G. Johnson, Interview by: Charles Stuart Kennedy, October 7, 2009.

Skorzeny Papers / Genealogical Report on Jean Rene Souetre prepared by Research assistant exclusively for Project Stone Tree; derived from publicly available online genealogical services and newspaper search queries.

The newspaper *Le Monde* in an account of Souetre's life published August, 1962 described the French captain as a soldier of fortune.

Porch, Douglas, *The French Foreign Legion: A Complete History of the Legendary Fighting Force*, Skyhorse Publishing, 2010.

Christie, Stuart, *Granny Made Me an Anarchist: General Franco, The Angry Brigade and Me*, AK Press, Oakland, California, 2007.

"OAS Pursued as Algeria Free of Terrorist," *Omaha World-Herald,* Kirk, Russell, February 9, 1963, page 4.

The presence of Ortiz, Kovac, and Archard in Palma de Mallorca is confirmed in research by Anne Dulphy, PhD, History.

Skorzeny papers.

Joesten, Joachim, *De Gaulle and His Murderers: A Factual Account of a Dramatic Piece of Contemporary History*, Times Press and Anthony Gibbs & Phillips, 1964.

"Debate France Court Bill," *Register-Republic* January 5, 1963 (Rockford, Illinois) page 2.

"Crime Wave is Ex-OAS," *Omaha World-Herald* (Omaha, Nebraska) January 20, 1963.

"French-Spanish Talks," *Jersey Journal* (Jersey City, NJ), January 29, 1963, page 2.

CIA document # 7124 Job 76-780R Box 306, "Organization Secreta Alemana."

"O.A.S. Commandos Trained in Spain," *Iberica*, New York, February 15, 1963.

"French Businessmen in Algeria Lock Up," *La Grande Observer* (La Grande, Oregon) 17 Feb. 1962, page 1.

Skorzeny papers.

"O.A.S. Commandos Trained in Spain," *Iberica*, New York, February 15, 1963.

"Plot to Kill de Gaulle Foiled," Daily *Illinois State Journal*, February 16, 1963, p. 1.

"Anti-Gaullist Group Gets New Commander" *San Diego Union*, San Diego Thursday May 2, 1963, p. 27.

The Fensterwald investigation: Letter dated 1/11/82 Gilbert Le Cavelier, to Bernard Fensterwald, Jr. Attorney–supplemental–Court Document filing 13/07/1982 Gary Shaw, Plaintiff, v. Department of State, ET AL., Defendents. Civil Action No. 80-1056 Bernard Fensterwald, Jr. Counsel to Gary.

CHAPTER EIGHTEEN

Skorzeny business networks: Skorzeny Papers.

U.S. Government Office Memorandum, To: Mr. A.H. Belmont, From: Mr. R.H. Roach Subject: Otto Skorzeny, Internal Security Dated March 29, 1957.

Skorzeny Papers / Genealogical Report on Sydney Barnett prepared by Research assistant, exclusively for Project Stone Tree; derived from publicly available online genealogical services and newspaper search queries.

Skorzeny Papers / Genealogical Report on John Tysen prepared by Research assistant, exclusively for Project Stone Tree; derived from publicly available online genealogical services and newspaper search queries.

Skorzeny Papers / 1957 File.

Skorzeny Papers / Genealogical Report on Colonel Hershel V. Williams prepared by Research assistant, exclusively for Project Stone Tree; derived from publicly available online genealogical services and newspaper search queries.

O'Reilly, Terence, *Hitler's Irishmen*, Mercier Press, Cork, 2008.

Kelly, Charles J., *Tex McCrary: Wars, Women, Politics—An Adventurous Life Across the American Century*, Hamilton Books, Lanham, Maryland, 2009.

Thompson, Douglas, *Shadowland: How The Mafia Bet Britain in a Global Gamble*, Mainstream Publishing, Edinburgh, 2011.

Block, Alan A., *Masters of Paradise: Organized Crime and the Internal Revenue Service in The Bahamas*, Transaction Publishers, New Brunswick, New Jersey, 1991 / Skorzeny Papers.

CHAPTER NINETEEN

Whiting, Charles, *Skorzeny, War Leader Book No. 11*, Ballantine Books, New York, 1972.

Alleged Assassination Plots Involving Foreign Leaders, An Interim Report of the Select Committee to Study Governmental Operations With Respect to Intelligence Activities United States Senate, Together with Additional,

Supplemental, and Separate Views, November 20, 1975, U.S. Government Printing Office, Washington, D.C., 1975.

Stockton, Bayard, *Flawed Patriot: The Rise and Fall of CIA Legend Bill Harvey*, Potomac Books, Washington, D.C., 2006.

Albarelli, H. P., Jr., *A Terrible Mistake: The Murder of Frank Olsen and the CIA's Secret Cold War Experiments*, Trine Day, LLC, 2009.

QJ/WIN: File and notes on QJ/WIN, National Security Archives, Washington, D.C., William K. Harvey handwritten notes on QJ/WIN, CIA documents requested under the Freedom of Information Act.

Alleged Assassination Plots Involving Foreign Leaders, An Interim Report of the Select Committee to Study Governmental Operations With Respect to Intelligence Activities United States Senate, Together with Additional, Supplemental, and Separate Views, November 20, 1975, U.S. Government Printing Office, Washington, D.C., 1975.

Skorzeny nickel smuggling case: Declassified Skorzeny CIA 201 File, Document Control No. 6004, 15 July 1954.

QJ/WIN nickel smuggling case: Declassified CIA memo., 26 April 1962, To: Director, From: Luxembourg, Action: C/FI/D 2, Info. S/C 2, RYBAT ZRRIFLE.

QJ/WIN connection to FBN drug operations see: Valentine, Douglas, *The Strength Of The Wolf: The Secret History Of America's War On Drugs*, Verso, New York, 2006.

Wright, Peter, *Spy Catcher: The Candid Autobiography of a Senior Intelligence Officer*, Viking, New York, 1987.

Skorzeny Trip to London to meet with Colonel Stirling: Skorzeny Papers.

Foley, Charles, *Commando Extraordinary*, G. P. Putnam's Sons, New York, 1955.

"The Wild Geese: David Stirling and the Secret Life of Television International Enterprises," Online Resource posted, November 16, 2013 by Doctor Who Worldwide.

Armstrong, Stephen, *War plc: The Rise of the New Corporate Mercenary*, Faber & Faber Limited, London, 2008.

Author phone interview with property owner of Skorzeny's County Kildare estate.

October, 1960 interview (clip) by Pierre Berton and Otto Skorzeny can be viewed online.

Kelly, Charles J., *Tex McCrary: Wars, Women, Politics—An Adventurous Life Across The American Century*, Hamilton Books, Lanham, Maryland, 2009.

Author telephone interview with Kevin McCrary, son of Tex McCrary, 2015.

Barry Faber interview conducted by North Carolina newspaper writer John Drescher, Greensboro, N.C., March 8, 2013, News Observer Internet site.

Information on USAF Colonel Charles S. "Chuck" Hayes: Author telephone interview with Kevin McCrary, son of Tex McCrary, 2015.

Russo, Gus, *Live by the Sword: The Secret War Against Castro and the Death Of JFK*, Bancroft Press, Baltimore, 1998.

Skorzeny Papers / Genealogical Report on Marshall Diggs prepared by Research assistant exclusively for Project Stone Tree; derived from publicly available online genealogical services and newspaper search queries.

Operation Tropical details derived entirely from a copy of a newspaper article on the operation in the Skorzeny papers with a hand written date in Skorzeny's hand on the document. "Otto Skozeny Proyecto el secuestro de Fidel Castro, Segun Un Diario Romano" Ya—page 4 (in Skorzeny's hand 11-1-73 Newspaper (unknown).

CIA memo: approved for release 2007/01/22, Heading: "Otto Skorzeny Planned to Kidnap Fidel Castro" note mentions "Project Tropical" found in La Cronica, Lima Peru, 7 August 1966.

Summers, Anthony, *The Arrogance of Power: The Secret World of Richard Nixon*, Viking, New York, 2000.

Evidence for Perkins McGuire as CIA executive officer:

A letter, dated 26 February 1974, with official CIA letterhead, was posted online for an EBay online auction (History Channel Auction House). Apparently, the document was sold on June 20, 2015. The location of the letter is not known to the author, nor how it came to public auction. Auction #A15 [http://www.worthpoint.com/worthopedia/William-colby-letter-signed-central-1732893889.]

Full text of letter sent to E. Perkins McGuire:

Dear Mr. McGuire,

Let me express my appreciation and that of a grateful Agency for the advice and counsel you have furnished us over many years. Your specialized knowledge relating to both government and industry practices that you have been willing to share with us on a consultant basis has been most beneficial. Now that this relationship is coming to a close, I wanted you to know that we will miss these contributions and the most pleasant association which we have enjoyed over the years.

Your services to the U.S. Government in many and varied positions should be a source of pride to you. Please accept our thanks and best wishes in the future and our gratitude for your efforts in support of the mission of this Agency.

Sincerely,

//Signed//

W. E. Colby

Director

Skorzeny picture on Eisenhower's desk: McGowan, David, Understanding the F-Word: American Fascism and the Politics of Illusion, Writers Club Press, Lincoln, Nebraska, 2001.

Herbert, Anthony B., *Soldier*, Cloverleaf Books, Englewood, Colorado, 1973.

Author interview with Dr. George Robert Ganis, PhD, Geologist, 2016.

Williams, Susan, *Spies in the Congo: America's Atomic Mission in World War II*, Public Affairs, New York, 2016.

It is interesting to note that Colonel Boris Pash, head of the Alsos Mission in World War II and later head of the CIA office PB7 had as a strategic target in the fall of 1944, the offices of Union Miniere in Antwerp, Belgium and a uranium processing plant in Olen. This mission yielded great quantities of uranium for the United States.

Biddiscombe, Perry, *The SS Hunter Battalions: The Hidden History of the Nazi Resistance Movement 1944–1945*, Tempus Publishing Limited, Gloucestershire, UK, 2006.

Skorzeny's businesses in Africa: Skorzeny Papers.

Skorzeny's activity in the Congo: Skorzeny Papers.

Othen, Christopher, Katanga 1960–1963: Mercenaries, Spies and the African Nation That Waged War on the World, The History Press, Gloucestershire, Great Britain, 2015.

Skorzeny Papers / Genealogical Report on Daniel Cavanaugh prepared by Research assistant exclusively for Project Stone Tree; derived from publicly available online genealogical services and newspaper search queries.

Allen Dulles authorization for assassination of Lumumba: Church Committee-Interim Report: Alleged Assassination Plots Involving Foreign Leaders, p. 263.

Bissell, Richard M. Jr., *Reflections of a Cold Warrior: From Yalta to the Bay of Pigs*, Yale University Press, New Haven and London 1996.

Author interview with Lt. Colonel Thaddeus S. Skladzien, 2012.

LTC Mario de Silvestro: "Congolese Harass U.S. Plane," *Tucson Daily Citizen*, Tucson, Arizona Tuesday, September 6, 1960.

Johnson, Loch K., "Strategic Intelligence 3; Covert Action: Behind the Veils of Secret Foreign Policy," Praeger Security International, Westport, Connecticut, 2007.

Devlin, Larry, *Chief of Station, CONGO: Fighting the Cold War in a Hot Zone*, Public Affairs, New York, 2007.

The Skorzeny papers have no documents for the years 1959 and 1960. This omission is likely intentional.

Nutter, John Jacob, *The CIA's Black Ops: Covert Action, Foreign Policy, and Democracy*, Prometheus Books, Amherst, New York, 2000.

"Probe into Lumumba Killing Planned," *Santa Cruz Sentinel,* 13 February 1961, p.1.

Skorzeny Papers.

"Lumumba Killed in Congo Village," *Tucson Daily Citizen*, Tucson, Arizona February 13, 1961, Page 1.

Skorzeny Papers / Genealogical Report on Clifford Forster prepared by Research assistant exclusively for Project Stone Tree; derived from publicly available online genealogical services and newspaper search queries.

"U.S. Group Seeks Aid For Tishombe," *Register-Republic* (Rockford, Illinois), Thursday, December 14, 1961, page, 1.

Skorzeny may have had contact with the Special Affairs Staff. Skorzeny's declassified records contain a Form 245, an entry at the bottom has a handwritten note dated 4 April 1962, stating "Per. [redacted] Subj: allegedly met with T. SAS for business reason according to SAS." SAS did have contact with Lee Harvey Oswald. See: Waldron, Lamar, with Hartmann, Thom, Ultimate Sacrifice: John and Robert Kennedy, the Plan for a Coup in Cuba, and the Murder of JFK, Counterpoint, Berkeley, California, 2005.

Villafana, Frank R., *Cold War in the Congo: The Confrontation of Cuban Military Forces, 1960–1967*, Transaction Publishers, New Brunswick, New Jersey, 2012.

Mahoney, Richard D., *JFK: Ordeal in Africa*, Oxford University Press, Incorporated, 1983.

CHAPTER TWENTY

Brinkley, Douglas, *Cronkite*, Harper Perennial, New York, 2013.

CHAPTER TWENTY-ONE

"Ruark in the Midst of Them: Foreigners Get Together For Bullfight In Seville," Greensboro Record, Wednesday, April 30, 1958, Page 6

Skorzeny Papers.

"Relieved of Command," *Times-Picayune* (New Orleans, Louisiana) Sunday, June 25, 1961 Page 28

Kroth, Jerry. Conspiracy in Camelot: The Complete History of the Assassination of John Fitzgerald Kennedy, Algora Publishing, New York, 2003

Caufield, Jeffrey H., General Walker and the Murder of President Kennedy: The Extensive New Evidence of a Radical-Right Conspiracy, Moreland Press, 2015

Weiford, Nancy Wertz, The Faux Baron: George de Mohrenschildt: An Aristocrat's Journey from the Russian Revolution to the Assassination of John F. Kennedy, Lumiere Publ., 2014

"Levy Appointed to Defense Post," *Boston Herald*, Saturday, April 22, 1961, Page 15

LAWRENCE LEVY Obituary, Framingham, Massachusetts, see: http://www .legacy.com/obituaries/name/lawrence-levy-obituary?pid=170959888 &view=guestbook

*As Assistant Secretary of Defense for Logistics, McGuire had authority over the Military Assistance Program (MAP) throughout his tenure in officer. As previously covered, MAP was a controlling agent for Military Assistance and Advisery Groups (MAAG) and the International Cooperation Agency (ICA) development programs, both utilizing the services of Otto Skorzeny. It is likely, that McGuire was in the initial group of government officials that secret decided to use Otto Skorzeny for covert work.

Skorzeny Papers / Genealogical Report on Algur H. Meadows prepared by Research assistant, exclusively for Project Stone Tree; derived from publicly available online genealogical services and newspaper search queries.

*In a book with many surprises, we can add the fact that Algur Meadows brother, Curtis Washington Meadows, had worked for many years as the chief accountant of Southern Cotton Oil Company in New Orleans when the lead sales manager for the company was Herschel V. Williams, Sr., the father of USAF intelligence officer Colonel Herschel V. Williams, Jr.

Presley, James, *Never In Doubt: A History of Delta Drilling Company*, Gulf Publishing Company, Houston, 1981.

Skorzeny Papers / Genealogical Report on Hjalmar Schacht prepared by research assistant, exclusively for Project Stone Tree; derived from publicly available online genealogical services and newspaper search queries.

*In an enigmatic event, of which the background is still a mystery, Schacht made an appearance on live television in Chicago, Illinois on March, 1964, as part of a six-panel group that included Marguerite Oswald, the mother of Lee Harvey Oswald.

Skorzeny Papers / Genealogical Report on Gordon Simpson prepared by research assistant exclusively for Project Stone Tree; derived from publicly available online genealogical services and newspaper search queries.

Skorzeny Papers / Genealogical Report on Robert G. Storey prepared by research assistant exclusively for Project Stone Tree; derived from publicly available online genealogical services and newspaper search queries.

*Other positions held by Colonel Storey, include President of the Republic National Bank, head of the American Bar Association, Director of the State Bar of Texas, and Chairman of the Board of the Southwestern Legal Foundation. Storey also served as Dean of the Southern Methodist University School of Law from 1949–1959.

Skorzeny Papers / Genealogical Report on Sir Stafford Sands prepared by research assistant exclusively for Project Stone Tree; derived from publicly available online genealogical services and newspaper search queries.

Mangold, Tom, *Cold Warrior, James Jesus Angleton: The CIA's Master Spy Hunter,* Simon & Schuster, New York, 1991.

The Official Warren Commission Report On The Assassination Of President John F. Kennedy, Doubleday & Company, Garden City, New York, 1964.

Mellen, Joan, *Our Man in Haiti: George de Mohrenschildt and the CIA in the Nightmare Republic*, Trine Day LLC, Walterville, Oregon, 2012.

Skorzeny Papers / Genealogical Report on Merwin K. Hart prepared by research assistant exclusively for Project Stone Tree; derived from publicly available online genealogical services and newspaper search queries.

*Freda Utley, born in London, England, in 1896, had actually once been a member of the Communist Party of Great Britain. In 1928, she married a Jewish Russian economist who worked on a Soviet trade mission in England. She later became totally disillusioned with Communism after her husband was arrested by Stalin's secret police and sent to a Russian prison in Siberia, where he reportedly died. Years later, the family learned he had been shot by firing squad. Utley eventually came to the United States in 1939. After the outbreak of the war she was hired by General William Donovan to do studies for the OSS on China, an area in which she had considerable experience.

After the war, Utley served in Europe as a correspondent covering the Nuremberg Trials. She may have first met Skorzeny during this period and was likely present when he was interviewed by the press after his capture. Utley remained a lifelong friend of Otto and Ilse Skorzeny. Beginning in the early 1950s, she was a major promoter of Skorzeny's business ventures, but few details of her involvement are known. She was also active in political circles and discussion groups with people closely associated with Skorzeny. Among these were New York lawyer Clifford Forster and USAF intelligence officer Colonel Herschel V. Williams, who it may be recalled was also associated with Skorzeny's real estate ventures at Previews, Inc.

Skorzeny Papers / Genealogical Report on Pierre Villere prepared by research assistant exclusively for Project Stone Tree; derived from publicly available online genealogical services and newspaper search queries.

Carpenter, Donald H., *Man of a Million Fragments: The True Story of Clay Shaw*, Donald H. Carpenter LLC, Nashville, Tennessee, 2014.

Skorzeny Papers / Genealogical Report on Jacques Villere prepared by research assistant exclusively for Project Stone Tree; derived from publicly available online genealogical services and newspaper search queries.

*Oddly, Pierre Villere died from a sudden onset of cancer in 1967 and his brother Jacques the following year from a wasp sting.

"Group Seeks Entry for Gifted Refugees," *Dallas Morning News*, Tuesday, December 19, 1950, Page 3.

Skorzeny Papers / Genealogical Report on Jesse Duvall prepared by research assistant exclusively for Project Stone Tree; derived from publicly available online genealogical services and newspaper search queries.

Skorzeny Papers / Genealogical Report on Paul Raigorodsky prepared by research assistant exclusively for Project Stone Tree; derived from publicly available online genealogical services and newspaper search queries.

Chester, Eric Thomas, Covert, Network: Progressives, the International Rescue Committee and the CIA, M E Sharpe Inc, 1995.

Skorzeny Papers / Genealogical Report on Jake Hamon prepared by research assistant exclusively for Project Stone Tree; derived from publicly available online genealogical services and newspaper search queries.

Skorzeny Papers / Genealogical Report on Artie Shaw prepared by research assistant exclusively for Project Stone Tree; derived from publicly available online genealogical services and newspaper search queries.

Skorzeny Papers / Genealogical Report on Harold Byrd prepared by research assistant exclusively for Project Stone Tree; derived from publicly available online genealogical services and newspaper search queries.

Skorzeny Papers / Genealogical Report on Werner von Alvensleben prepared by research assistant exclusively for Project Stone Tree; derived from publicly available online genealogical services and newspaper search queries.

Skorzeny Papers / Genealogical Report on Lawrence Mason Alderson prepared by research assistant exclusively for Project Stone Tree; derived from publicly available online genealogical services and newspaper search queries.

Skorzeny Papers / Genealogical Report on Thomas Eli Davis, III prepared by research assistant exclusively for Project Stone Tree; derived from publicly available online genealogical services and newspaper search queries.

Skorzeny Papers / Genealogical Report on Victor Oswald prepared by research assistant exclusively for Project Stone Tree; derived from publicly available online genealogical services and newspaper search queries.

Skorzeny Papers / Genealogical Report on Thomas G. Proctor prepared by research assistant exclusively for Project Stone Tree; derived from publicly available online genealogical services and newspaper search queries.

APPENDIX A

Guardia, Mike, *Shadow Commander: The Epic Story fo Donald D. Blackburn, Guerrilla Leader and Special Forces Hero*, Casemate, Philadelphia & Newbury, 2011.

Clark, Allen B., *Valor In Vietnam 1963—1977: Chronicles of Honor, Courage, and Sacrifice*, Casemate Publishers, Havertown, Pennsylvania, 2012.

Valentine, Douglas, *The Phoenix Program*, iUniverse.com, Inc., Lincoln, Nebraska, 1990, 2000.

Cleverley, Michael J., "Born a Soldier: The Times and Life of Larry Thorne," *Booksurge.com*, 2008.

H.S. Gill, III, *Soldier Under Three Flags: The Exploits of Special Forces Captain Larry A. Thorne*, Pathfinder Publishing, Ventura, California, 1998.

Author interview with CW4 Anastasios "Tasso" Christian, U.S. Army Retired, Army intelligence. Mr. Christian, as part of POW/MIA : Task Force Full Accounting, found the remains of Major Larry A. Thorne.

Bibliography

Abro, Ben, *Assassination! July 14*, University of Nebraska Press, Lincoln and London, 1963.

Adams, Jefferson, *Historical Dictionary of German Intelligence, No. 11*, The Scarecrow Press, Inc., Lanham, Maryland, 2009.

Agee, Philip, and Wolf, Louis, *Dirty Work: The CIA in Western Europe*, Dorset Press, New York, 1978.

Albarelli, H. P., Jr., *A Terrible Mistake: The Murder of Frank Olsen and the CIA's Secret Cold War Experiments*, 2009.

Ambrose, Stephen E., *Ike's Spies: Eisenhower and the Espionage Establishment*, Anchor Books, New York, 1981.

Annussek, Greg, *Hitler's Raid to Save Mussolini: The Most Infamous Commando Operation of World War II*, Da Capo Press, Cambridge, Massachusetts, 2005.

Arnold, Edward J., *The Development of the Radical Right in France: From Boulanger to Le Pen*, MacMillan Press Ltd., 2000.

Bar-Zohar, Michael and Mishal, Nissim, *Mossad*, An Imprint of HarperCollins Publishers, New York, 2012.

Beavan, Colin, *Operation Jedburgh: D-Day and America's First Shadow War*, Viking Penguin, New York, 2006.

Bellant, Russ, *Old Nazis, the New Right, and the Republican Party: Domestic Fascist Networks and Their Effect on U.S. Cold War Politics*, South End Press, Boston, Massachusetts, 1991.

Biddiscombe, Perry, *The SS Hunter Battalions: The Hidden History of the Nazi Resistance Movement 1944–1945*, Tempus Publishing Limited, Gloucestershire, UK, 2006.

Binder, L. James, *Lemnitzer: A Soldier for His Time*, Brassey's, Dulles, Virginia, 1997.

Bissel, Richard M., Jr., *Reflections of a Cold Warrior: From Yalta to the Bay of Pigs*, Yale University Press, New Haven and London, 1996.

Block, Alan A., *Masters of Paradise: Organized Crime and the Internal Revenue Service in The Bahamas*, Transaction Publishers, New Brunswick, New Jersey, 1991.

Blum, William, *Killing Hope: U.S. Military And C.I.A. Interventions Since World War II*, Common Courage Press, Monroe, Maine, 2004.

Bohning, Don, *The Castro Obsession: U.S. Covert Operations Against Cuba 1959–1965*, Potomac Books, Inc., Washington, D.C., 2006.

Breitman, Richard, and Goda, Norman J. W., *Hitler's Shadow: Nazi War Criminals, U.S. Intelligence, and the Cold War*, National Archives, 2011.

Breitman, Richard, Goda, Norman J.W., Naftali, Timothy, and Wolfe, Robert, *U.S. Intelligence and the Nazis*, Cambridge University Press, New York, 2005.

Bresler, Fenton, *Interpol: A History and Examination of 70 Years of Crime Solving*, Mandarin, London, 1992.

Brinkley, Douglas, *Cronkite*, Harper Perennial, New York, 2013.

British Security Coordination, *The Secret History of British Intelligence in the Americas, 1940–1945*, Fromm International, New York, 1999.

Brogan, Patrick, and Zarca, Albert, *Deadly Business: Sam Cummings, Interarms, and the Arms Trade*, W. W. Norton & Company, New York, 1983.

Brown, Anthony Cave, *The Last Hero: Wild Bill Donovan*, Times Books, 1982.

Brunelle, Gayle K., and Finley-Croswhite, Annette, *Murder in the Métro: Laetitia Toureaux and the Cagoule in 1930s France*, Louisiana State University Press, 2010.

Burchett, Wilfred, and Roebuck, Derek, *The Whores of War: Mercenaries Today*, Penguin Books, New York, 1977.

Callanan, James, *Covert Action in the Cold War: US Policy, Intelligence and CIA Operations*, I.B. Tauris, New York, 2010.

Carpenter, Donald H., *Man of a Million Fragments: The True Story of Clay Shaw*, Donald H. Carpenter LLC, Nashville, Tennessee, 2014.

Christie, Stuart, *Granny Made Me an Anarchist: General Franco, The Angry Brigade and Me*, AK Press, Oakland, California, 2007.

Clark, Allen B., *Valor In Vietnam 1963–1977: Chronicles of Honor, Courage, and Sacrifice*, Casemate Publishers, Havertown, Pennsylvania, 2012.

Clark, Evert, and Horrock, Nicholas, *The Corsican Contract*, Bantam Books, New York, 1974.

Clayton, Anthony, *The Wars of French Decolonization*, Longman, New York, 1994.

Colby, Gerard, and Dennett, Charlotte, *Thy Will Be Done; The Conquest of the Amazon: Nelson Rockefeller and Evangelism in the Age of Oil*, HarperCollins, New York, 1995.

Conant, Jennet, *The Irregulars: Roald Dahl and the British Spy Ring in Wartime Washington*, Simon & Schuster Paperbacks, New York, 2008.

Constantine, Alex, *The Essential Mae Brussel: Investigations Of Fascism In America*, Feral House, Port Townsend, Washington, 2014.

Cook, Bernard A., Europe Since 1945: An Encyclopedia; Volume I, A–J, Garland Publishing, Inc., New York & London, 2001

Cook, Bernard A., *Europe Since 1945: An Encyclopedia; Volume II, K–Z*, Garland Publishing, Inc., New York & London, 2001.

Cookridge, E. H., *Gehlen: Spy of the Century*, Random House, New York, 1971.

Corke, Sarah-Jane, *US Covert Operations and Cold War Strategy: Truman, Secret Warfare and the CIA, 1945–1953*, Routledge, New York, 2008.

Courtney, Nicholas, *Lord of the Isle: The Extravagant Life and Times of Colin Tennant*, Bene Factum Publishing, London, 2012.

Critchfield, James H., *Partners at the Creation: The Men Behind Postwar Germany's Defense and Intelligence Establishments*, Naval Institute Press, Annapolis, Maryland, 2003.

Crozier, Brian, *Franco*, Little, Brown and Company, Boston, Toronto, 1967.

Dank, Milton, *The French Against The French: Collaboration And Resistance*, J. B. Lippincott Company, Philadelphia and New York, 1974.

Dawidoff, Nicholas, *The Catcher Was a Spy: The Mysterious Life of Moe Berg*, Vintage Books, New York, 1995.

Day, Peter, *Franco's Friends: How British Intelligence Helped Bring Franco To Power In Spain*, Biteback Publishing, London, 2012.

Démaret, Pierre, and Plume, Christian, *Target de Gaulle: The True Story of the 31 Attempts on the Life of the French President*, The Dial Press, New York, 1975.

Devlin, Larry, *Chief of Station, CONGO: Fighting the Cold War in a Hot Zone*, Public Affairs, New York, 2007.

Didion, Joan, *We Tell Ourselves Stories in Order to Live*, Alfred E. Knopf, New York, 2006.

Diefendorf, Jeffry M.; Frohn, Axel; Rupieper, Hermann-Josef, *American Policy and the Reconstruction of West Germany, 1945–1955*, German Historical Institute, Washington, D.C., 1993.

Dorrel, Major Thomas W., Jr., *The Role of the Office of Strategic Service in Operation Torch*, U.S. Army Command and General Staff College, 2008.

Dupuy, Trevor N., Bongard, David L., and Anderson, Richard C., Jr., *Hitler's Last Gamble: The Battle of the Bulge, December 1944–January 1945*, HarperCollins Publishers, Inc., New York, 1994.

Duthel, Heinz, False Flag Operations: The Intelligence Community; The Coincidence Of Crisis, 2011.

Epstein, Edward Jay, *Deception: The Invisible War Between the KGB and the CIA*, EJE Publication, New York, 2014.

Epstein, Edward Jay, James Jesus Angleton: Was He Right?, FastTrack Press, New York, 2014

Escalante, Fabian, *The Cuba Project: CIA Covert Operations 1959–62*, Ocean Press, Melbourne & New York, 2004.

Evans, Martin, *Algeria: France's Undeclared War*, Oxford University Press, Oxford, UK, 2012.

Evica, George Michael, *A Certain Arrogance: U.S. Intelligence's Manipulation of Religious Groups and Individuals in Two World Wars and the Cold War—and the Sacrificing of Lee Harvey Oswald*, Xlibris Corporation, 2006.

"Executive Intelligence Review, Dope, Inc.: Britain's Opium War Against the World," *ProgressivePress.com*, Joshua Tree, California, 2010.

Feinstein, Andrew, *The Shadow World: Inside the Global Arms Trade*, Picador, New York, 2012.

Foley, Charles, *Commando Extraordinary*, G. P. Putnam's Sons, New York, 1955.

Forbes, Robert, *For Europe: The French Volunteers of the Waffen-SS*, Stackpole Books, Mechanicsburg, Pennsylvania, 2010.

Forczyk, Robert, *Raid: Rescuing Mussolini; Gran Sasso 1943*, Osprey Publishing, Oxford, UK, 2010.

Furiati, Claudia, *ZR Rifle: The Plot to Kill Kennedy and Castro*, Ocean, Melbourne, 1994.

Ganser, Daniele, *NATO's Secret Armies: Operation Gladio and Terrorism in Western Europe*, Frank Cass, New York, 2005.

Gibson, Donald, *The Kennedy Assassination Cover-Up*, Progressive Press, San Diego, California, 2014.

Goñi, Uki, *The Real Odessa: How Perón Brought the Nazi War Criminals to Argentina*, Granta Books, London, 2003.

Greene, Jack, and Massignani, Alessandro, *The Black Prince and the Sea Devils; The Story of Valerio Borghese and the Elite Units of the Decima Mas*, Da Capo Press, Cambridge, Massachusetts, 2004.

Greene, Joshua M., *Justice at Dachau: The Trials of an American Prosecutor*, Broadway Books, New York, 2003.

Grose, Peter, *Operation Rollback: America's Secret War Behind the Iron Curtain*, Houghton Mifflin Company, New York, 2000.

Hamilton, A. Stephan, *The Oder Front 1945: Generaloberst Gotthard Heinrici, Heeresgruppe Weichsel and Germany's Final Defense in the East, 20 March—3 May*, Helion & Company Ltd., West Midlands, England, 2011.

Hancock, Larry, *Nexus: The CIA and Political Assassination*, JFK Lancer Productions & Publications, 2012.

Harrington, Dale, *Mystery Man: William Rhodes Davis, Nazi Agent of Influence*, Brassey's, Dulles, Virginia, 1999.

Hastings, Max, *The Secret War: Spies, Ciphers, and Guerrillas 1939–1945*, HarperCollins Publishers, New York, 2016.

Henissart, Paul, *Wolves in the City: The Death of French Algeria*, Simon and Schuster, New York, 1970.

Herbert, Anthony B., *Soldier*, Cloverleaf Books, Englewood, Colorado, 1973.

Hersch, Burton, *The Old Boys: The American Elite and the Origins of the CIA*, Tree Farm Books, St. Petersburg, Florida, 1992, 2002.

Höhne, Heinz, and Zolling, Hermann, *The General Was a Spy: The Truth About General Gehlen and His Spy Ring*, Coward, McCann & Geoghegan, Inc., New York, 1971.

Holden, Robert H., *Armies Without Nations: Public Violence and State Formation in Central America 1821–1960*, Oxford University Press, New York, 2004.

Holt, Thaddeus, *The Deceivers: Allied Military Deception in the Second World War*, Scribner, New York, 2004.

Horne, Alistair, *A Savage War of Peace: Algeria 1954–1962*, New York Review Books, New York, 2006.

Hougan, Jim, *Spooks: The Haunting of America—The Private Use of Secret Agents*, William Morrow and Company, Inc., New York, 1978.

Howard, Roger, *Operation Damocles: Israel's Secret War Against Hitler's Scientists, 1951–1967*, Pegasus Books LLC, New York, 2013.

Hunt, Jim, and Risch, Bob, *Warrior: Frank Sturgis—The CIA's #1 Assassin-Spy, Who Nearly Killed Castro but Was Ambushed by Watergate*, Tom Doherty Associates, New York, 2011.

Innfield, Glenn B., *Skorzeny Hitler's Commando*, Military Heritage Press, New York, 1981.

Irving, David, *The Service: The Memories of General Reinhard Gehlen*, World Publishing, New York, 1972.

Jacobsen, Annie, *Operation Paperclip: The Secret Intelligence Program That Brought Nazi Scientists to America, Little*, Brown and Company, New York, 2014.

Jaubert, Alain, *Dosser D . . . Comme Drogue, le Milieu et la Politique, les Gros Bonnets*, les Financiers et les Filièresen France, am editions, Paris, 1973.

Joesten, Joachim, *De Gaulle and His Murderers: A Factual Account of a Dramatic Piece of Contemporary History*, Times Press and Anthony Gibbs & Phillips, 1964.

Joesten, Joachim, *The Red Hand: The Sinister Account of the Terrorist Arm of the French Right-Wing "Ultras"—in Algeria and on the Continent*, Abelard-Schuman, London, New York, Toronto, 1962.

Johnson, Loch K., *Strategic Intelligence 3; Covert Action: Behind the Veils of Secret Foreign Policy*, Praeger Security International, Westport, Connecticut, 2007.

Jordan, Robert S., *An Unsung Soldier: The Life of Gen. Andrew J. Goodpaster*, Naval Institute Press, Annapolis, Maryland, 2013.

Kelly, Charles J., *Tex McCrary: Wars, Women, Politics—An Adventurous Life Across The American Century*, Hamilton Books, Lanham, Maryland, 2009.

Kross, Peter, *JFK: The French Connection*, Adventures Unlimited Press, Kempton, Illinois, 2012.

Krüger, Henrik, *The Great Heroin Coup: Drugs, Intelligence, & International Fascism*, South End Press, Boston, Massachusetts, 1980.

Lasby, Clarence G., *Project Paperclip: German Scientists and the Cold War*, Atheneum, New York, 1971.

Lee, Martin A., *The Beast Reawakens: Fascism's Resurgence from Hitler's Spymasters to Today's Neo-Nazi Groups and Right-Wing Extremists*, Routledge, New York, 2000.

Liptak, Eugene, *Elite · 173: Office of Strategic Services 1942–1945; The World War II Origins of the CIA*, Osprey Publishing, Oxford, UK, 2009.

López, Óscar González, *Wars and Battles No. 1: Fallschirmjäger at the Gran Sasso; The Liberation of Mussolini by the German parachutist on the 12th September 1943*, AF Editions, Valladoid (Spain), 2006.

Lucas, James, Kommando: *German Special Forces of World War Two*, Castle Books, Edison, New Jersey, 2003.

Luther, Craig W. H., PhD, and Taylor, Hugh Page, *For Germany: The Otto Skorzeny Memoirs*, R. James Bender Publishing, San Jose, California, 2005.

Macdonald, Bill, *The True "Intrepid": Sir William Stephenson and the Unknown Agents*, Timberholme Books Ltd., Surrey, British Columbia, Canada, 1998.

Mangold, Tom, *Cold Warrior, James Jesus Angleton: The CIA's Master Spy Hunter*, Simon & Schuster, New York, 1991.

Marnham, Patrick, *Resistance and Betrayal: The Death and Life of the Greatest Hero of the French Resistance*, Random House, New York, 2000.

Mayer, Kenneth R., *With the Stroke of a Pen: Executive Orders and Presidential Power*, Princeton University Press, Princeton and Oxford, 2001.

McFarren, Peter, and Iglesias, Fadrique, *The Devil's Agent: Life, Times and Crimes of Nazi Klaus Barbie*, Xlibris Corporation, 2013.

McGowan, David, *Understanding the F-Word: American Fascism and the Politics of Illusion*, Writers Club Press, Lincoln, Nebraska, 2001.

McNab, Chris, *Hitler's Elite: The SS 1939–1945*, Osprey Publishing, Oxford, UK, 2013.

McRaven, William H., *Spec Ops: Case Studies in Special Operations Warfare: Theory and Practice*, Presidio Press, Novato, California, 1995.

Meldal-Johnsen, Trevor, and Young, Vaughn, *The Interpol Connection: An Inquiry into the International Criminal Police Organization*, The Dial Press, New York, 1979.

Mellen, Joan, *Our Man in Haiti: George de Mohrenschildt and the CIA in the Nightmare Republic*, Trine Day LLC, Walterville, Oregon, 2012.

Miller, David, *The JFK Conspiracy*, Writers Club Press, Lincoln, Nebraska, 2002.

Moor, Fred C. III, *Then Came the CIA: The Early Years of Southern Air Transport*, Fred C. Moor III, 2011.

Morrow, Robert D., *First Hand Knowledge: How I Participated in the CIA-Mafia Murder of President Kennedy*, SPI Books, New York, 1992.

Munoz, Antonio J., *Forgotten Legions: Obscure Combat Formations of the Waffen-SS*, Paladin Press, Boulder, Colorado, 1991.

Murphy, David E.; Kondrashev, Sergei A.; and Bailey, George, *Battleground Berlin: CIA vs. KGB in the Cold War*, Yale University Press, New Haven, 1997.

Murphy, Robert, *Diplomat Among Warriors*, Doubleday & Company, Inc., Garden City, New York, 1964.

Nichol, John, and Rennell, *Tony, The Last Escape: The Untold Story Of Allied Prisoners of War in Europe 1944–1945*, Viking Penguin, New York, 2002.

O'Leary, Brad, and Symour, L. E., *Triangle of Death: The Shocking Truth About the Role of South Vietnam and the French Mafia in the Assassination of JFK*, WND Books, Nashville, Tennessee, 2003.

O'Reilly, Terence, *Hitler's Irishmen*, Mercier Press, Cork, 2008.

O'Toole, G. J. A., *Honorable Treachery: A History of U.S. Intelligence, Espionage, and Covert Action from the American Revolution to the CIA*, The Atlantic Monthly Press, New York, 1991.

Othen, Christopher, *Katanga 1960–63: Mercenaries, Spies and the African Nation That Waged War on the World*, The History Press, Gloucestershire, Great Britain, 2015.

Paddock, Alfred H., Jr., *US Army Special Warfare: Its Origins; Psychological and Unconventional Warfare, 1941–1952*, University Press of the Pacific, Honolulu, Hawaii, 2002.

Pallud, Jean-Paul, *Ardennes Elite · II: 1944 Peiper & Skorzeny*, Osprey Publishing, Oxford, UK, 1987.

Parker, Danny S., *Hitler's Warrior: The Life and Wars of SS Colonel Jochen Peiper*, Da Capo Press, Boston, Massachusetts, 2014.

Pash, Colonel Boris T., *The Alsos Mission*, Charter Books, New York, 1969.

Pauw, Jacques, *In The Heart of the Whore: The Story of Apartheid's Death Squads*, Southern Book Publishers, 1991.

Picknett, Lynn, and Prince, Clive, *The Sion Revelation: The Truth About the Guardians of Christ's Sacred Bloodline*, Touchstone, New York, 2006.

Pisani, Sallie, *The CIA and the Marshall Plan*, University Press of Kansas, 1991.

Porch, Douglas, *The French Foreign Legion: A Complete History of the Legendary Fighting Force*, Skyhorse Publishing, 2010.

Porch, Douglas, *The French Secret Services: From the Dreyfus Affair to the Gulf War*, Farrar, Straus and Giroux, New York, 1995.

Powers, Thomas, *The Man Who Kept the Secrets: Richard Helms and the CIA*, Alfred A. Knopf, New York, 1979.

Prados, John, *Lost Crusader: The Secret Wars of CIA Director William Colby*, Oxford University Press, New York, 2003.

Presley, James, *Never in Doubt: A History of Delta Drilling Company*, Gulf Publishing Company, Houston, 1981.

Prouty, L. Fletcher, *The Secret Team: The CIA and Its Allies in Control of the United States and the World*, Skyhorse Publishing, New York, 2011.

Pyke, Diana, *Confessions of "The Old Wizard": The Autobiography of Hjalmar Horace Greeley Schacht*, The Riverside Press, Cambridge, Massachusetts, 1956.

Ray, Ellen; Schaap, William; Van Meter, Karl; and Wolf, Louis, *Dirty Work 2: The CIA in Africa*, Lyle Stuart Inc., Secaucus, New Jersey, 1979.

Reese, Mary Ellen, *General Reinhard Gehlen: The CIA Connection*, George Mason University Press, Fairfax, Virginia, 1990.

Robbins, Christopher, *The Invisible Air Force: The True Story of the CIA's Secret Airlines*, Macmillan London Ltd., London, 1979.

Roosevelt, Archie, *For Lust of Knowing: Memoirs of an Intelligence Officer*, Weidenfeld and Nicholson, London, 1988.

Russel, Dick, *The Man Who Knew Too Much*, Carroll & Graf Publishers, New York, 1992.

Russo, Gus, *Live by the Sword: The Secret War Against Castro and the Death of JFK*, Bancroft Press, Baltimore, 1998.

Sallah, Michael, and Weiss, Mitch, *The Yankee Comandante: The Untold Story of Courage, Passion, and One American's Fight to Liberate Cuba*, Lyons Press, Guildorf, Connecticut, 2015.

Salter, Michael, *Nazi War Crimes, US Intelligence and Selective Prosecution at Nuremberg: Controversies regarding the role of the Office of Strategic Services*, Routledge-Cavendish, New York, 2007.

Sanders, Fred R., Ralph and Brown, *National Security Management: Global Psychological Conflict*, International College Of The Armed Forces, Washington, D.C., 1961.

Saunders, Frances Stonor, *Who Paid The Piper? The CIA and the Cultural Cold War*, Granta Books, London, 1999.

Schoenbrun, David, *Soldiers of the Night: The Story of the French Resistance*, E. P. Dutton, New York, 1980.

Schraeder, Peter J., *United States Foreign Policy toward Africa: Incrementalism, Crisis and Change*, Cambridge University Press, New York, 1994.

Scott, Peter Dale, *American War Machine: Deep Politics, the CIA Global Drug Connection, and the Road to Afghanistan*, Rowman & Littlefield Publishers, Inc., Lanham, Maryland, 2010.

Scott, Peter Dale, *Deep Politics and the Death of JFK*, University of California Press, Berkeley and Los Angeles, California, 1993.

Scott-Smith, Giles, and Krabbendam, Hans, *The Cultural Cold War in Western Europe 1945–1960*, Routledge, New York, 2003.

Scott-Smith, Giles, *Western Anti-Communism and the Interdoc Network: Cold War Internationale*, Palgrave Macmillan, New York, 2012.

Shetterly, Aran, *The Americano: Fighting with Castro for Cuba's Freedom*, Algonquin Books of Chapel Hill, Chapel Hill, North Carolina, 2007.

Silverstein, Ken, *Private Warriors*, Verso, New York, 2000.

Simpson, Christopher, *Blowback: America's Recruitment of Nazis and Its Destructive Impact on Our Domestic Foreign Policy*, Weidenfeld & Nicholson, New York, 1988.

Skorzeny, Otto, *My Commando Operations: The Memoirs of Hitler's Most Daring Commando*, Schiffer Publishing, Atglen, Pennsylvania, 1995.

Skorzeny, Otto, *Skorzeny's Special Missions*, Northumberland Press Limited, Gateshead on Tyne, Great Britain, 1957.

Smith, Bradley F., *The Shadow Warriors: O.S.S. and the Origins of The C.I.A.*, Basic Books, Inc., New York. 1983.

Smith, Richard Harris, *OSS: The Secret History of America's First Central Intelligence Agency*, The Lyons Press, Guilford, Connecticut, 2005.

Stafford, David, *Camp X: OSS, "Intrepid," and the Allies' North American Training Camp for Secret Agents, 1941–1945*, Dodd, Mead & Company, New York, 1987.

Stahl, P. W., *KG 200: The True Story*, Jane's Publishing Company Limited, London, 1981.

Stein, George H., *The Waffen SS: Hitler's Elite Guard at War 1939–1945*, Cornell University Press, Ithaca, New York, 1967.

Steinacher, Gerald, *Nazis on the Run: How Hitler's Henchmen Fled Justice*, Oxford University Press, Oxford, UK, 2008.

Stern, John Allen, *C. D. Jackson: Cold War Propagandist for Democracy and Globalism*, University Press of America, Lanham, Maryland, 2012.

Stevenson, William, *Intrepid's Last Case*, Willard Books, New York, 1983.

Stockton, Bayard, *Flawed Patriot: The Rise and Fall of CIA Legend Bill Harvey*, Potomac Books, Washington, D.C., 2006.

Summers, Anthony, *The Arrogance Of Power: The Secret World Of Richard Nixon*, Viking, New York, 2000.

Talbot, David, *The Devil's Chessboard: Allen Dulles, the CIA, and the Rise of America's Secret Government*, HarperCollins, New York, 2015.

Tanner, Hans, *Counter-Revolutionary Agent–Cuba*, G. T. Foulis & Co. Ltd., London, UK, 1962.

Thayer, George, *The War Business: The International Trade in Armaments*, Simon and Schuster, New York, 1969.

The Official Warren Commission Report on the Assassination of President John F. Kennedy, Doubleday & Company, Garden City, New York, 1964.

Thomas, Evan, *The Very Best Men: The Daring Early Years of the CIA*, Simon & Schuster Paperbacks, New York, 1995, 2006.

Thomas, Geoffrey J., and Ketley, Barry, *KG 200: The Luftwaffe's Most Secret Unit*, Hikoki Publications, East Sussex, UK, 2003.

Thompson, Douglas, *Shadowland: How The Mafia Bet Britain in a Global Gamble*, Mainstream Publishing, Edinburgh, 2011.

Tompkins, Peter, *The Murder of Admiral Darlan: A Study in Conspiracy*, Simon and Schuster, New York, 1965.

Trachtenberg, Marc, *History & Strategy*, Princeton University Press, Princeton, New Jersey, 1991.

Tully, Andrew, *CIA: The Inside Story; The facts about our government's most secret organization—the Central Intelligence Agency*, William Morrow and Company, New York, 1962.

Valentine, Douglas, *The Phoenix Program*, iUniverse.com, Inc., Lincoln, Nebraska, 1990, 2000.

Valentine, Douglas, *The Strength of the Wolf: The Secret History of America's War on Drugs*, Verso, New York, 2006.

Van Der Waals, W.S., *Portugal's War In Angola 1961–1974*, Protea Book House, Pretoria, 2011.

Van Dongen, Luc; Roulin, Stéphanie, and Scott-Smith, Giles, *Transnational Anti-Communism and the Cold War: Agents, Activities, and Networks*, Palgrave Macmillan, New York, 2014.

Vaughan, Hal, *FDR's 12 Apostles: The Spies Who Paved the Way for the Invasion of North Africa*, The Lyons Press, Guilford, Connecticut, 2006.

Veritas, Journal Of Army Special Operations History V11/N1, United States Army Special Operations Command, Fort Bragg, North Carolina, 2007.

Villafana, Frank R., *Cold War in the Congo: The Confrontation of Cuban Military Forces, 1960–1967*, Transaction Publishers, New Brunswick, New Jersey, 2012.

Waldron, Lamar, with Hartmann, Thom, *Ultimate Sacrifice: John and Robert Kennedy, the Plan for a Coup in Cuba, and the Murder of JFK*, Counterpoint, Berkeley, California, 2005.

Wall, Irwin M., *The United States and the Making of Postwar France 1945–1954*, Cambridge University Press, New York, 1991.

Waller, Douglas, *Disciples: The World War II Missions of the CIA Directors Who Fought For Wild Bill Donovan*, Simon & Schuster, New York, 2015.

Waller, Douglas, *Wild Bill Donovan: The Spymaster Who Created the OSS And Modern American Espionage*, Free Press, New York, 2011.

Walters, Guy, *Hunting Evil: The Nazi War Criminals Who Escaped & the Quest to Bring Them to Justice*, Broadway Books, New York, 2009.

Weiner, Tim, *Legacy of Ashes: The History of the CIA,* Anchor Books, A Division of Random House, Inc., New York, 2008.

Weitz, John, *Hitler's Banker: Hjalmar Horace Greeley Schacht*, Little, Brown and Company, New York, 1997.

Wenger, Andreas; Nuenlist, Christian; and Locher, Anna, *Transforming NATO in the Cold War: Challenges Beyond Deterrence in the 1960s*, Routledge, New York, 2012.

Whiting, Charles, *Kommando: Hitler's Special Forces in the Second World War*, Pen & Sword Military, South Yorkshire, UK, 2010.

Whiting, Charles, *Skorzeny, War Leader Book No. 11*, Ballantine Books, New York, 1972.

Whiting, Charles, *Skorzeny: The Most Dangerous Man in Europe*, Pen & Sword Military, South Yorkshire, UK, 2010.

Williams, Susan, *Spies in the Congo: America's Atomic Mission in World War II*, Public Affairs, New York, 2016.

Williamson, Gordon, *Elite · 177: German Special Forces of World War II*, Osprey Publishing, Oxford, UK, 2009.

Windrow, Martin, and Braby, Wayne, *French Foreign Legion Paratroops*, Osprey Publishing, London, 1985.

Windrow, Martin, *The Algerian War 1954–1962*, Osprey Publishing, Long Island, New York, 1997.

Windrow, Martin, *The French Indochina War 1946–1954*, Osprey Publishing, Long Island, New York, 1998.

Winks, Robin W., *Cloak & Gown: Scholars in the Secret War, 1939–1961*, Quill William Morrow, New York, 1987.

Wright, Peter, *Spy Catcher: The Candid Autobiography of a Senior Intelligence Officer*, Viking, New York, 1987.

Yenne, Bill, *Operation Long Jump: Stalin, Roosevelt, Churchill, and the Greatest Assassination Plot in History*, Regnery History, Washington, DC, 2015.

Index